WATCHING
WILDLIFE

WATCHING
WILDLIFE

CYNTHIA CHRIS

University of Minnesota Press

Minneapolis

London

Published by the University of Minnesota Press
111 Third Avenue South, Suite 290
Minneapolis, MN 55401-2520
http://www.upress.umn.edu

Library of Congress Cataloging-in-Publication Data

Chris, Cynthia, 1961–
    Watching wildlife / Cynthia Chris.
        p.   cm.
    Includes bibliographical references and index.
    ISBN 13: 978-0-8166-4546-6 (hc) — ISBN 13: 978-0-8166-4547-3 (pb)
    ISBN 10: 0-8166-4546-9 (hc : alk. paper) — ISBN 10: 0-8166-4547-7
(pb : alk. paper)
    1. Wildlife films—History and criticism.   2. Wildlife television
programs—History and criticism.   I. Title.
    PN1995.9.A5C47   2006
    791.43'632—dc22   2005033456

Printed in the United States of America on acid-free paper

The University of Minnesota is an equal-opportunity educator and employer.

12   11   10   09   08   07   06   10   9   8   7   6   5   4   3   2   1

Contents

Acknowledgments

Many people contributed in large and small ways, directly and indirectly, to this project, and I hope to credit as many of them as possible here. I begin where this work began, by acknowledging the elegant guidance lent to my work by members of my dissertation committee at the University of California, San Diego: Paula Chakravartty, Zeinabu Davis, Page duBois, Jane Rhodes, and especially Susan G. Davis and Ellen Seiter. Subsequently, at Washington University in St. Louis, I benefited a great deal from the support of William Paul and Jeff Smith of the Program in Film and Media Studies during a Mellon Postdoctoral Fellowship that allowed me to begin work on this manuscript. Currently, I could not ask for more engaged colleagues, especially Jeanine Corbet, David Gerstner, Edward Miller, and Jason Simon in the Department of Media Culture at the City University of New York's College of Staten Island, where I completed this work. I have also learned a tremendous amount from the astute and generous readers, mentors, and colleagues who provided feedback and intellectual counsel, including Sarah Banet-Weiser, Akira Mizuta Lippit, Toby Miller, Lisa Jean Moore, Nigel Rothfels, Dan Schiller, Jennifer Terry, Ken Wissoker, and Yuezhi Zhao.

This work was inarguably and pleasurably bettered by the scrutiny of others, first at the Representing Animals conference organized by Nigel Rothfels and Andrew Isenberg at the Center for Twentieth-Century Studies at the University of Wisconsin–Milwaukee in 2000, and subsequently at conferences sponsored by Console-ing Passions, the International Communication Association, the Society for Cinema and Media Studies, and the Society for Literature and Science, where colleagues far too numerous to mention challenged and inspired.

I am equally grateful to Barbara E. Hensall at the Martin and Osa Johnson Safari Museum in Chanute, Kansas; the UCLA Film and Television Library; Janet Lorenz at the Academy of Motion Picture Arts and Science's National Film Information Service; Cathy Hunter of the Records Library at the National Geographic Society in Washington, D.C.; Margaret Adamic at Disney Publishing Worldwide; and librarians at all the institutions I have recently called home, who facilitated access to research material.

When this work was ready to become a book, the University of Minnesota Press became a much-appreciated collaborator. Many thanks to the staff, including Douglas Armato, Catherine Clements, Dan Leary, and Jason Weidemann, as well as copyeditor Therese Boyd, all of whom were terrifically helpful. Special thanks go to Andrea Kleinhuber, who took initial interest in the manuscript for the press, and whose mindful encouragement was a real gift.

At various stages, friends grappled with this work and with me on a happily informal basis, including Jean Carlomusto, Ronald Duculan, Michael Gorman, Lynn Hudson, Adriene Jenik, Susan Larsen, Patrick Patterson, Gary Phillips, Stephen Phillips, Nic Sammond, Suzie Silver, and Polly Thistlethwaite. Pauline Kennedy lent ardent support, giving inestimably to me and to my work. Andrea Geyer enlivened the final stage of this process with insight and gentle wit. Tony Freitas contributed invaluable commentary and confidence throughout. I am deeply appreciative of all.

Introduction

Respect the cock. And tame the cunt. Tame it.
Take it on head first with the skills I will teach
you at work. . . . You are emitting this thought:
I am the one who is in charge, I am the one
who says yes, no, now, here. And it's universal.
It is evolutional. It is anthropological, it is
biological, it is animal. We are men.
—Frank T. J. Mackey, *Magnolia*

In the film *Magnolia* (1994), the character Frank T. J. Mackey, a self-help sex guru played by Tom Cruise, announces that male dominance in human mate selection is "universal . . . evolutional . . . anthropological . . . biological . . . animal."[1] Cruise-as-Mackey ventriloquizes an understanding of "natural" human sex roles. The character establishes the authority of his view by referring to particular bodies of scientific knowledge. How does he know what he knows? More precisely, because Mackey is a fictional character, we might ask, from what bodies of knowledge did the writer of this monologue derive such a theory of human sexual behavior? What scientific, social, or media institutions circulate this knowledge? What counter-discourses might undermine its certainty?

One of the many arenas in which theories of human behavior circulate is wildlife film and television. Over the course of the genre's century-plus history, alongside other themes—ecological and conservationist interests, predation, and animal intelligence, to name but a few—is an almost-always present preoccupation with sexual behavior, reproduction, difference, and norms. This preoccupation has taken a variety of forms, first focusing most intensively on the exuberant masculinity and exemplary femininity of human protagonists in expedition travelogues in the early days of cinema. In post–World War II wildlife films, the genre turned its attention to animal sex roles and family life, in animal-populated allegories of proper parenting, such as some of the Walt Disney Company's True-Life Adventures. Eventually, made-for-TV wildlife nonfiction, produced by and for the National Geographic Society, the British Broadcasting Corporation

(BBC), the Public Broadcasting System (PBS), and Discovery Communications, among others, took less allegorical and more directly didactic approaches. Following scientific trends, the genre's preoccupation with the animal family has been significantly reoriented since the 1980s, toward mate selection and sexual behaviors, at times extending interpretations of animal behaviors to humans, as sociobiology and its disciplinary offshoots entered the discourse of wildlife filmmaking.[2] That is, the genre shifted from a framework in which the animal appears as *object* of human action (and in which the animal is targeted as *game*), to an *anthropomorphic* framework, in which human characteristics are mapped onto animal subjects, to a *zoomorphic* framework, in which knowledge about animals is used to explain the human.[3] Thus, representations of animals articulate and reinforce new understandings of not only animal life but also human behavior. We look not only at animals to learn about them, but we also look through animals for ourselves.

Of course, not all images of animals comprise stories about our sexual selves, and looking at animals does not begin with wildlife television or even film. These media demonstrate the persistence of cultural practices originated in previous centuries, before the invention of cinema and TV. As John Berger argues:

> Zoos, realistic animal toys and the widespread commercial diffusion of animal imagery, all began as animals started to be withdrawn from daily life. One could suppose that such innovations were compensatory. Yet in reality the innovations themselves belonged to the same remorseless movement as was dispersing the animals. The zoos, with their theatrical decor for display, were in fact demonstrations of how animals had been rendered absolutely marginal. The realistic toys increased the demand for the new animal puppet: the urban pet. The reproduction of animals in images—as their biological reproduction in birth becomes a rarer and rarer sight—was competitively forced to make animals ever more exotic and remote.[4]

Berger considers means by which animals, receding from daily contact with increasingly industrialized and urbanized societies in the late eighteenth through the nineteenth centuries, returned in new commodity forms. These new visual technologies and practices—public zoos, realistic animal toys, pet-keeping—were among many that emerged in this period, subject not only to the effects of industrialization and urbanization.[5] According to Fatimah Tobing Rony, they were also reshaped by new transport routes between the imperial powers and their colonies, and by "the obsessive consumption [by Europeans and North Americans] of images of a racialized Other known as the Primitive." As Rony asserts, zoos and other means of reproducing animals were among a wide range of image-producing technologies, practices, and institutions—postcards, stereographs, magazines such as *National Geographic,* anthropology, natural history museums, world's fairs, and tourism—that proliferated in the nineteenth century.[6] At the end of the nineteenth century, filmmaking emerged from this social, political, and economic matrix, in which the supposedly primitive Other was already being sought, displayed, and observed as entertainment. It became yet another means of what Berger referred to as "reproduc[-ing] animals in images," followed a half-century later by the equally racialized discourses of television.

The wildlife film and television genre comprises not only a body of knowledges but also an institution for their containment and display, similar to those institutions that Michel Foucault described as heterotopias, which through their collection of normally unrelated objects, life forms, or representations expose visitors to worlds beyond their own reach.[7] In contrast to utopias, which Foucault emphasizes are always idealized and "fundamentally unreal spaces," heterotopias are constituted by "real places— places that do exist and that are formed in the very founding of society... in which the real sites, all the other real sites that can be found within the culture, are simultaneously represented, contested, and inverted."[8]

Foucault allows for several types of heterotopias, including those "capable of juxtaposing in a single real place several spaces, several sites that are themselves incompatible." He offers as heterotopias of this type the classical botanical garden, the zoological garden, the theater, the cinema, each of which purports to hold "the totality of the world" within its walls. But of course, the contents of each of these heterotopic institutions does not simply reflect the whole world in condensed form. The knowledge contained within the heterotopia is, rather, selected, framed, edited, and interpreted, according to an array of social forces and cultural contests over meaning. In this way, as Foucault acknowledges, these kinds of institutions, regardless of how ostensibly complete or supposedly representative, are "absolutely different from all the sites that they reflect and speak about."[9] Similarly, television, if we can conceive of it as a "real place" or network of places, encompasses within its spectrum at any given moment a range of images heterotopic in scope, especially since the widespread availability of cable and satellite services providing access to hundreds of channels. On any given day, one might flit from views of sharks off the coast of southern Africa to polar bears in Manitoba, rattlesnakes in Florida, crocodiles in Queensland, and pandas, real and replicas, in Sichuan Province.[10] The images of animals and their habitats, natural or artificial, found through television, are representations of real places and the creatures that live there, but they are "absolutely different" from those real sites and their inhabitants, constructed as they are by conventions of representation (including preferences or presumed preferences for particular kinds of narratives about particular kinds of people and animals), the economics of the film and television industries, and geopolitical conditions concerning the state of the environment and the relative openness or inaccessibility of some ecological sites.

Like visits to some of those other heterotopic spaces, such as the library or the museum, watching wildlife film and television may afford the viewer a sense of making a good media choice, as one opts for educational programming (or in industry slang, "edutainment") when so many other genres are available. Historically, some wildlife programming has been marked by such a highbrow sheen, especially whenever it sports ties with reputable institutions and has been critically touted for authenticity and aesthetic achievements: some lauded travelogues of early cinema, affiliated with the American Museum of Natural History; *National Geographic Specials*; much of the work of Sir David Attenborough for the BBC; and many episodes of the *Nature* series aired by PBS. Much like other supposed quality TV choices (*The West Wing* over *Fear Factor; Meet the Press* instead of *The Jerry Springer Show*), these kinds of wildlife TV have occupied a "TV that's good and good for you" niche. Making and watching these shows, the networks and their viewers exercise a bit of what Pierre Bourdieu called "cultural capital," through which one acquires, demonstrates, and reinvests learned allegiances. According to Bourdieu, "taste classifies, and it classifies the classifier. Social subjects, classified by their classifications, distinguish themselves by the distinctions they make."[11] That is, such shows are opportunities for the demonstrable acquisition and deployment of high-value ("legitimate") knowledge. In this case, knowledge pertains to the biological sciences and the natural world.

Consider the following review (recounted here in its entirety) of a ten-minute film called *Carl Hagenbeck's Menagerie at Hamburg*, published in a 1908 issue of *Variety:*

The moving picture at the New York this week is evidence of enterprise on the part of someone. It is of Carl Hagenbeck's menagerie of wild animals at Hamburg, Germany. The camera takes in the entire animal farm. It seems more like witnessing the interior of a zoological garden. Nothing startling, sensational nor exciting is shown on the sheet, but the different views of the animals, from leaping does to an elephant pushing up tree trunks, is very interesting. The series is a departure from the irrational lot of melodramatic matter foisted upon the public in lieu of legitimate subjects of late.[12]

The reviewer applauds the film for two reasons: first, because it is "interesting" rather than "irrational," "legitimate" instead of "sensational," and more "enterpris[-ing]" than "exciting." That is, the film affords an opportunity to watch wildlife and thus to imagine oneself being *educated* by a natural history lesson, however vague. In the positivist tradition, to see, in this instance, is to learn. Second, the reviewer admires the efficiency of a tour taken by film rather than on foot ("the camera takes in the entire animal farm"), excising the tiresome bits of any real visit to a menagerie or zoo: animals that have hidden themselves out of view, sleeping or otherwise inactive animals, long walks between displays. Thus, animals on film are even better than animals in zoo enclosures, and surely better than animals in the wild: they are not only captive and visible at our whim, not their own, but they are at their very best. The film operates in a niche that is set apart from the rest of film, a very special genre, both a heterotopic display and a source of distinction.

In contrast, some wildlife films and nonfiction animal TV might appear to constitute lowbrow indulgences: from faked newsreels and staged animal stories of cinema's first few decades, to reality-based TV programs of the late twentieth century, such as *When Animals Attack* (1996–97, Fox), *Animal Cops* (2002–, Animal Planet), *Wildboyz* (2003–, MTV), and *Venom ER* (2004, Animal Planet), in their morbid fascination with injury and potential injury caused to or by animals; and *The Pet Psychic* (2002–, Animal Planet). Rather than the cultural capital accrued and exercised by those who value knowledge of science and nature, these kinds of shows incorporate elements of spectacle and melodrama ("Is there a future for the kitten rescued from the drain?" the narrator of *Animal Cops: Detroit* implores) that provide "more direct, immediate satisfactions."[13] Each is undeniably sensationalistic and just as undeniably *entertaining*—and, in tales of the ramifications of cruelty to animals *(Animal Cops)*, and the potential dangers to humans in close contact with abused or wild animals *(When Animals Attack, Venom ER)*, these shows also offer a set of lessons about human-animal relations. In reality, most wildlife film and television programming blends elements of its most educational and entertaining modes, a generic tension that will be revisited throughout this book.

The wildlife genre is, then, a prism through which we can examine investments in dominant ideologies of humanity and animality, nature and culture, sex, and race. It also provides a historical case, in its volatile genre cycles, around which this volume is organized, of some of the ways in which media economics, the structure of the industry, and even the demand for distinction, shape and reshape the media audiences receive. I chose to study this genre for these reasons, but it was my own television viewing habits that led me to it. In the fall of 1995 the Discovery Channel first consolidated its library of nature programming under the title *Wild Discovery*. The series' aesthetic, narrative, and nostalgic pleasures caught my attention; its penchant for tacking happy endings onto tales of ecological disaster and its representations of race and sex sometimes puzzled, sometimes disturbed me. Discovery's investment of resources and time slots in this series appeared to contradict prevailing television industry logic that nonfiction wildlife shows are insufficiently commercially viable, and that nature, if it is to be represented at all, must be confined to the noncommercial, educational realm of public television. Then Discovery Communications, partnering with the BBC, launched the "all animals, all the time" spinoff, Animal Planet, in 1996, and National Geographic, in partnership with leading media conglomerates, launched its own channel in 1997. Both were soon widely distributed throughout global television markets. It became clear to me that the meanings circulated by this venerable but rapidly changing genre, and its place in the complex of industry practices, institutions, and representations that Arjun Appadurai calls "mediascapes," deserved further consideration.[14]

I quickly learned that friends and colleagues were sharply divided on the subject. Some confessed that they loved wildlife films, delighting in new peeks at or bits of knowledge about the natural world, or recalling the genre fondly from childhood experiences with Disney's True-Life Adventures or *Mutual of Omaha's Wild Kingdom* (1963–71, NBC; 1971–88, syndicated). Others hated it, repulsed by the occasional gore of scenes depicting predation or disdaining its formulaic contrivances. But I wasn't the only one who was watching. I began to see casual references to the Discovery Channel and Animal Planet as the new primary loci for representations of nature and animals in widely dispersed cultural corners. Some were critical. In *Spin* magazine, rap artist Method Man proclaimed his dislike of animals: "I can't handle them motherfuckers. I won't even watch the Discovery Channel when they start showing the animal shit."[15] In the alumni magazine of the School of the Art Institute of Chicago, which I attended as an undergraduate, an international student commented on why he believed new acquaintances held such limited knowledge about his part of the world: "Every time I see something about Venezuela in the American media it's something on the Discovery channel about the jungle." The observation suggests that the media situates the so-called Third World more comfortably into narratives of the presumably primitive and of nature than into modernity.[16] Eventually, Animal Planet became the butt of jokes that ranked some sources of knowledge as more authoritative and some kinds of knowledge as less useful than others. In a *CSI: Crime Scene Investigation* episode called "Fight Night" (2002) investigator Nick Stokes (George Eads) throws some esoteric knowledge about migratory habits of puffins into a conversation with the crime lab's entomologist, Gil Grissom (William Peterson). Gil is momentarily puzzled, then brightens, wagging his finger as he chides, "Animal Planet!" dismissing both Nick and a likely source of the trivia. Gil walks off, and Nick calls after him, "How come when you talk about bugs, everyone says you're a genius, but when I talk about birds, everyone says I watch too much TV?"

Other pop-culture references to wildlife TV suggested some of its pleasures, as erotic resource, as growth industry, as shared cultural referent, and as virtual natural-world respite from the stresses of daily life. In 1999 a band called Bloodhound Gang released "The Bad Touch," a song that contained the lyrical refrain, "You and me baby ain't nothing but mammals/ So let's do it like they do on the Discovery Channel." The Geffen Records CD single's cover pictured copulating zebras. In the music video that aired on MTV, members of the group, costumed as monkeys and armed with blowdarts, chase mini-skirted women through the streets of Paris. Instead of quibbling over trademark infringement, Discovery's director of publicity, Karen Baratz, gloated: "It just goes to show how the Discovery Channel has disseminated into the popular culture."[17] On January 31, 2001, Patricia Hearst, the publishing heiress kidnapped in 1974 by the radical Symbionese Liberation Army and convicted of participating in a bank robbery with her abductors, told the host of CNN's *Larry King Live* how she learned she had been granted a pardon by President Clinton on the last day of his term in office: having tired of hearing about the incoming Bush administration, she was watching Animal Planet's *Crocodile Hunter* when the phone call came. Such diffused mentions of the wildlife genre, and such decisive responses to it, confirmed my suspicion that these films and television programs constituted a more significant cultural signpost than their typically modest ratings might suggest.

While wildlife film and TV had to date garnered relatively little critical attention, I was aware that animals, relationships between humans and nonhuman animals, likenesses and distinctions between these categories, and representations of animals have been subject to dynamic multidisciplinary discussions for over a quarter century. New kinds of attention to animals had been jumpstarted by trends in the sciences, philosophy, cultural history, and the arts. Growing bodies of research on the biological influences on behavior (animal and human) and on understanding social formation as outcomes of evolutionary processes coalesced as a then-new field with the publication of E. O. Wilson's *Sociobiology* in 1975.[18] Also in 1975 philosopher Peter Singer's *Animal Liberation,* an inquiry into ethics and animal life widely recognized as a text foundational to the modern animal rights movement, first appeared.[19] Berger's influential "Why Look at Animals?," versions of which were first published in 1977, was followed by a still-growing and wide-ranging array of works on symbolic uses of animals in popular culture and art, zoological displays of animals and animal performances, and the literal *place* of animals in contemporary life, which now constitute the emergent interdisciplinary field of animal studies.[20] Around the same time, animals, long a subject in the visual arts, began to appear in new ways, in works such as Josef Beuys' performance with live coyote titled *I Like America and America Likes Me* (1974).[21]

Despite the variety and vigor of studies of the animal following these innovations, most have contended minimally or not at all with film and television's representations of animals. Most general film histories emphasize the development of narrative filmmaking techniques and pay less attention to early nonfiction forms such as newsreels and travelogues in which hunting expeditions are common subjects. Some mention expedition films, such as those by Cherry Kearton and Martin and Osa Johnson.[22] A few give brief attention to the nonfiction Disney nature films issued under the series title True-Life Adventures, as instances of decayed documentary ethics.[23] The genre is almost entirely absent from television studies textbooks.

Even so, a small but rapidly growing number of scholars have recently turned their attention to representations of animals in mass media and

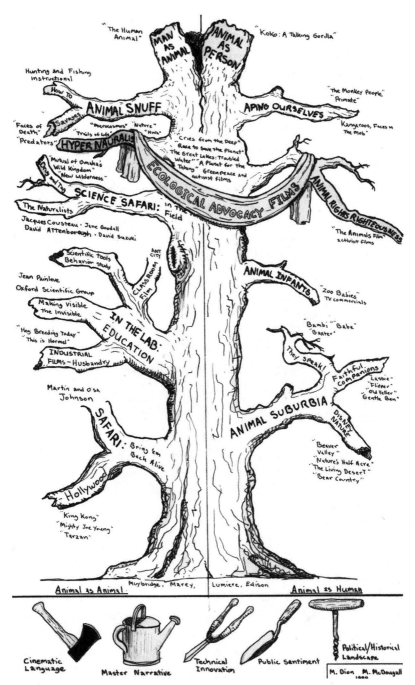

Mark Dion and Marina McDougall, *Schematic for the History of Nature Documentaries,* 1998. Pen and ink on illustration board, 14 x 8.5 inches. Courtesy of Tanya Bonakdar Gallery.

culture. Donna Haraway provides a spectacularly interdisciplinary model for subsequent inquiries into the meaningfulness of representations of nature and animals in her *Primate Visions* (1989), especially its important feminist consideration of National Geographic's documentary portraits of leading female primatologists.[24] Environmental historian Gregg Mitman's landmark *Reel Nature: America's Romance with Wildlife on Film* (1999) excavates the historical role of popular film in promoting conservationism.[25] Mitman examines trends in nonfiction animal films from the early 1900s through the postwar Disney True-Life Adventures, emphasizing textual description and analyses of films, broaching televisual versions of the genre only up to the 1970s, through Marlin Perkins's *Zoo Parade* and *Wild Kingdom.* Filmmaker and scholar Derek Bousé's *Wildlife Films* (2000) offers a history that ranges from the early cinema of the late nineteenth century to the new medium of high-definition television at the end of the twentieth century.[26] Bousé concentrates on the genre's narrative influences and forms, from the "nature writers" of the Victorian era— John Burroughs, Ernest Thompson Seton, Jack London, and others—to classic Hollywood film style, arguing that these conventions have distorted rather than explicated the realities of animal life, compressing them into mythic adventure, romance, and coming-of-age archetypes. Jonathan Burt's *Animals in Film* (2002) considers animals found in early cinematic actualities, in experimental film and video art such as Luis Buñuel and Salvador Dalí's *Un Chien Andalou* (1928) and Bill Viola's *I Do Not Know What It Is I Am Like* (1986), and dramatic film such as *Blade Runner* (1982, directed by Ridley Scott) and *The Horse Whisperer* (1998, Robert Redford).[27] Burt links these distinctive media practices through their capacity to represent a range of human-animal relationships, especially the powerful emotional responses engaged by images of animals, real or simulated, and the ethics and politics of the animal as contested within these kinds of representations. These volumes, and a handful of recent contributions to academic journals, constitute a still small but growing body of scholarship around a media genre that was previously almost unstudied.[28]

If most film and television historians have ignored wildlife film and television, members of the media industry have reinforced this oversight by framing the genre as especially nonideological, even trivial compared to other kinds of content. In the mid-1980s, the Corporation for Public Broadcasting (CPB) considered but rejected a programming exchange with the Soviet Union's television network. Richard Brookhiser, a CPB board member appointed by then–President Ronald Reagan, explained the decision:

"I mean, the Bolshoi is fine. You know, ballet is ballet. . . . Nature programs . . . little things grazing in the tundra. Fine . . . but if we are going to be opening the doors to wonderful Soviet ideas on their own history or something, this is just disastrous."[29] Brookhiser recognized only overtly political material as ideological, casting culture and nature together into an unthreatening neutral zone. But media scholars such as Todd Gitlin recognized just as long ago that "television entertainment amounts to politics conducted by other means," performing ideological work both intentionally and unintentionally.[30] The wildlife genre in particular, and the extra-media discourses that inform it, are sites of both purposeful ideological work and unconscious elaboration of beliefs so normalized as common sense—about nature, animals, race, gender, sexuality, economic and political formations—that they may not be recognized (by filmmakers, by television programmers, by scientists, by audiences) as ideological. Over two decades ago Bill Nichols suggested that recognizing the ideological positions taken by the media consists of "learning to see signs where there appears to be only natural and obvious meaning."[31] The wildlife genre, as much if not more so than other cinematic genres, presents itself as an objective record of "natural and obvious meaning" when it is in fact, like any other representational medium, a carefully chosen, framed, edited, and narrated set of signs.

I approach this set of signs with the tools of historical and textual analysis in order to unpack the meanings contained within a genre that is so lauded for its feats of visual spectacularity that its other features are all too readily underestimated, their stakes in scientific and ideological contests too often trivialized or assumed to be nonexistent. This is neither a production history nor a comparative study of the genre's foremost auteurs. Instead, as a cultural critic, writing from a feminist perspective and with interests in both representations and the institutional contests in which they are produced and circulated, I have sought to understand these depictions of animals through the artifacts that wildlife filmmakers and those working in related nonfiction modes leave behind: the films and television programs themselves, scrutinized in light of contemporaneous discourses of which they are expressions and to which they contribute.

My focus is the popular wildlife genre, films and television programs intended for general audiences and distributed theatrically or through broadcast, cable, or satellite television outlets, for both commercial networks and public broadcasting (rather than strictly educational films intended for scientific or classroom use). I concentrate primarily (but not exclusively) on the history of U.S. film and television; notably, in the contemporary global media order, many new productions in this genre are international coproductions and are distributed on channels available throughout global television markets. I concentrate on representations of *wildlife,* separating wildlife as a unit of analysis from the broader category *nature* (which may include botanical, geological, or meteorological topics), while acknowledging that the genre is flexible enough to hold, at times, working animals, companion animals, and *Homo sapiens* as well as wild animals within its gaze.[32] I use the common term *wildlife* despite historical conditions that contest the concepts *wild* and *wilderness.* There remain relatively few animal populations that are "truly wild," neither managed within the boundaries of conservation parks nor controlled by hunting regulations.[33]

The genre is also so flexible that its classic forms have been hybridized with (or jettisoned in favor of) other putatively nonfiction genres such as game shows, talk shows, sport, "unscripted" or "reality-based," instructional or "how-to" programming. And audiences have long looked at animals (and simulations of animals) in fictional as well as nonfiction media ranging from Merien C. Cooper and Ernest B. Schoedsack's *King Kong* (1933), to Disney's animated *The Jungle Book* (1967), to live-action television series such as *Lassie* (1954–74, CBS) and *Flipper* (1964–67, NBC), to the dramatic films *L'Ours (The Bear)* (1988) and *Two Brothers* (2004), both by the French director Jean-Jacques Annaud. These fictional projects use trained animals, animation, computer graphics, and mechanical animals. Wildlife filmmakers generally avoid these kinds of substitutions, except where the subject is extinct, as in *Walking with Dinosaurs* (1999, a coproduction of the BCC, the Discovery Channel, Asashi TV of Japan, Pro-Sieben of Germany, and France 3), or would cause harm, as in *Animal Face-Off,* a series featuring staged animal attacks using mechanical models and computer simulations, produced by Natural History New Zealand and airing on Animal Planet beginning in 2004. Wildlife filmmaker Stephen Mills writes that in the 1960s Oxford Scientific Films produced images of fish, insects, and flowers in their studios that were "so good that films shot exclusively in the wild could not easily compete," and that many wildlife filmmakers agree that staging does not in itself violate professional ethics: "any scene can be staged provided it depicts a scientifically observable fact."[34] For example, *Rats among Us* (1997, a coproduction of Great North Productions of Canada and Interspot Film of Austria for Discovery Communications, Discovery Channel Canada, and ZDF), about the behavior of rats and the history of their interactions with humans, contains few scenes gathered in "the wild." Instead, much of *Rats among Us,* including scenes set in the plague-stricken European Middle Ages using actors, is staged under controlled conditions. The program names a rat trainer and five rat wranglers in its credits. The boundaries of fiction and nonfiction, then, are blurred, and both found-in-nature and naturalistically staged footage are conventional to the genre. Nevertheless, my focus remains on wildlife nonfiction and hybrid forms, leaving pet-keeping practices and predominately dramatic representations of animals (the *Lassie*s and *Bear*s of film and TV history) off to the side but not entirely out of view.

The roots and early development of the wildlife genre, its allegiances to both science and showmanship, to education and entertainment, are found not only in motion studies credited as its precursor. Many of the earliest cinematic representations of wild animals were filmed records of hunting expeditions and photographic safaris in the same style. Elements of these traditions persisted in the 1920s, even as scientific and conservationist interests counteracted some of the persistent sensationalism in the genre. Around 1930, amid the rise of the studio system, the onset of the Great Depression, and the institution of the Production Code governing film content, the genre receded almost entirely into obscurity, save for scientific and experimental films, until the Walt Disney Company repopularized the wildlife film with its True-Life Adventure shorts and features, in theatrical release from 1948 to 1960.

While Disney kept nonfiction nature in theaters, the new medium of television quickly codified a number of its own options for representing animals. Early TV animal shows were largely confined to show-and-tell formats in studio and, later, zoo settings. By the 1960s, *Wild Kingdom* and film projects by Jacques-Yves Cousteau and the National Geographic Society shifted the location of these series from the studio or zoo to natural habitats—usually conservation parks—worldwide. Despite a surge in wildlife TV production in the 1970s when federal regulations gave a boost to the syndication market, commercial television all but abandoned the genre by the end of the decade, leaving virtually all documentary programming on any topic to public broadcasting. But in the 1980s, in a cable-television environment expanding dramatically both in terms of market penetration and channel capacity, many commercial networks turned to nonfiction as a means of relatively inexpensive production. Nonfiction representations of animals proliferated across the television spectrum, around the clock, and throughout much of the world, as Animal Planet and the National Geographic Channel engineered successful global launches prominently featuring wildlife content. Images of animals—and meanings old and new ascribed to them—exploded on television during the cable and satellite era from the 1980s to the early twenty-first century.

Throughout the history of the wildlife genre, from its precinematic roots to the global cable-era boom, filmmakers have in various ways revisited the process of mate selection and the act of mating. In recent years, the genre has also begun to address forcible copulation (animal "rape") and same-sex sexual behaviors. These preoccupations are material for viewers' voyeurism, means by which sociobiological theories of behavior have been circulated popularly and in which the findings of animal research have been extended both implicitly and explicitly to humans, sometimes incorporating the human-as-animal into a genre that is ostensibly not about people, and texts that articulate the boundaries of normative sex practices and roles. The imperatives of commercial and public television, international joint ventures, the interests of conservation groups and filmmaking companies, general attitudes about animals and official policies controlling them, assumptions about sex roles and reproductive processes, all play parts in determining what animals are documented and how they are represented. Cinematic and televised images of animals, as shown throughout this book, provide educational pleasures and entertaining lessons, even as their meanings are shaped by political-economic constraints, by social constructions of the categories animal and human, and by both dominant and disruptive possibilities vis-à-vis race, sex, nation, and nature.

1

The Wildlife Film Era

ROBSON: Out on the Serengeti, where those
niggers are from, you know how you send a
message to the leader of the pack? You kill
the youngest and the weakest of the herd.
UNNAMED INMATE: I seen that on those wildlife
shows.
ROBSON: Well. I think it's time we did a little big
game hunting.

—*Oz* (television show)

Moving pictures of animals—domesticated, captive, and wild—have
been a part of cinematic history from its earliest days. Some scholars,
looking for cinema's precedents in scientific motion-study photography
and persistence-of-vision mechanisms, claim that moving images of animals predate cinema itself. However, the images of animals that reached
early movie screens did not derive directly from motion studies but rather
from the conventions of precinematic visual technologies that had long
been used to describe and delineate the boundaries of racial difference,
sexual difference, and colonial power, as well as from the often conflictual,
occasionally overlapping efforts of scientists, naturalists, conservationists,
hunters, adventurers, and the film industry itself.

For many decades, capturing photographic images of animals, still or
moving, was no easy task. In the first few decades of the photographic era,
long exposure times excluded all moving subjects, and therefore most live,
free-roaming animals. The earliest photographic images of animals display
only carcasses and live specimens confined in close quarters. After about
1870, photographers could take advantage of increasingly mobile equipment, with increasingly quick shutters and sensitive emulsions, when seeking images of animal subjects in their natural habitats. Likewise, the motion-

1

study photographers, such as Eadweard Muybridge, produced images of animal movement in sumptuous still sequences, but always using captive animals in unnatural situations. By the turn of the century, naturalists and photographers were modifying cameras to maximize their portability and focal length, using flash capabilities for photographing nocturnal activity, reducing camera noise that might alarm animals within close range, and, likewise, innovating cinematographic equipment to facilitate documenting animals in the wild.[1]

But the characteristics of early wildlife film cannot be reduced to the technological conditions of their making. The most widely circulated wildlife films in the days of early cinema—some staged, some authentic—were produced by entrepreneurs in the film industry and hunting parties seeking trophy kills. But by the 1920s and '30s, interests that on the surface might seem incompatible struggled to reshape the genre. On one hand, many films of the era still took the form of travelogues documenting the expeditions of white, mostly American and British adventurers in colonized territories; wildlife footage might have been intermingled with sometimes amateur ethnographic accounts of encounters with indigenous peoples of equatorial Africa, the South Pacific, and other popular expedition destinations. Scientific institutions supported these films, intended for release as popular entertainment, to raise public interest and funds for research, conservation, and museum projects. On the other hand, profit-seeking producers and distributors welcomed the genre, not so much to popularize scientific knowledge as to appeal to mass audiences through the films' exoticism and action-adventure themes. As the genre tended toward greater sensationalism, conservation-minded institutions withdrew their support. Marginalized by controversy and by shifting conditions in both the film industry and the world at large, the genre retreated from mass distribution for almost two decades. In the late 1940s, the Walt Disney Company returned nonfiction wildlife filmmaking to the theatrical market with its True-Life Adventure shorts and features, exercising its considerable distribution clout and a new set of narrative imperatives that would show their mark on generations of wildlife film to come.

Throughout the first half of the twentieth century, and influencing generations of those engaged in the genres to come, ethnographic and wildlife filmmaking would often conflate, representationally and discursively, observations of animal behavior and assumptions about the behaviors of nonwhite people. In this model, as shown in the epigraph to this chapter, members of the Aryan Brotherhood on the HBO prison drama *Oz* (1997–

2003) would refer metaphorically to the murder of a black inmate as "big game hunting." In this episode ("Next Stop: Valhalla," first aired January 27, 2002), Robson (played by R. E. Rodgers) devises a plot to "send a message" to African American inmates based on recollections of animal behaviors seen on wildlife TV shows. Not only do the early twentieth-century motion pictures establish wildlife filmmaking as an arena in which the meaning of race is interrogated and racial ideologies articulated for popular consumption, but they also establish wildlife filmmaking as a largely masculine project, one that assigns particular tasks to women as helpmates, that includes women within its acquisitive and inquisitive gazes, and that sanctifies the feminine labors of childbearing and childrearing, both human and animal, in propagation of species and nation.

Precursors of the Wildlife Film

Most histories of the wildlife film link its origins to precinematic modes of representation.[2] Indeed, aspects of wildlife cinematography develop from the traditions of still photography by naturalists, by hunters, by the so-called camera hunters, and by those engaged in the study of motion. The impulse toward representation expressed by the "camera hunters," and later by the expedition filmmakers, derives from the same set of desires that sought visual satisfaction in other imperial representational practices of the eighteenth and nineteenth centuries, such as panoramas and dioramas, the museological collection of artifacts, public zoological parks, and ethnographic displays of colonial subjects. While heads of state have held private collections of animals since the ancient world, the zoological garden turned public as early as 1793, when revolutionary France opened the Jardin des Plantes, followed by major public zoos opening in London (1828), Amsterdam (1843), Berlin (1844), and New York's Central Park (1862), as sites in which recreation, education, scientific activity, and, possibly, the appreciation of the nation's wealth and power, represented by the extent of its collection, might take place.[3] Later, photographs and films of animals performed many of the same functions.

Likewise, the public and private exhibition of humans from explored or conquered lands became spectacles substantiating colonial power and scientific and pseudoscientific racism. Such spectacles were well known in Europe by at least the early 1800s. Perhaps most prominently, an entrepreneurial Boer farmer took his brother's servant, Saartjie Baartman, a member of the Khoi-San ethnic group from what is now South Africa, to Paris and London, exhibiting her in a cage. *The Times* of London reported in 1810 that the woman known as the "Hottentot Venus" was "more like a bear in a chain than a human being."[4] Refusing to recognize the range of anatomical differences among humans, and seeking evidence of incontrovertible racial hierarchies, scientists who examined her body after her death in 1815 decided that she bore resemblance to the orangutan, and interpreted the information drawn from her body as evidence that Africans constitute a separate race, inferior to whites.[5]

State-sanctioned events also displayed nonwhite colonial subjects. From the Exposition Universelle of 1889 in Paris to the British Empire Exhibition of 1924–25 at Wembley, early world fairs included realistic simulations of cities and villages of Egypt, Senegal, the Sudan, and elsewhere, complete with groups of people and working animals transported from their homelands to live, labor, and perform daily-life activities for the entertainment of onlookers. Thus, zoological and ethnographic displays provided nineteenth-century European capitals with not only "world exhibitions," that is, physical proximity and visual access to objects and performances derived from faraway lands and cultures, but also, as Timothy Mitchell has argued, access to the "world-as-exhibition," a taken-for-granted assumption that these representations and simulations provided reliable mirror-images of faraway and apparently primitive ways of life.[6] Those who peered through this looking glass saw what they expected to see: always-true, always-the-same, and always already-known subjects to be captured, contained, colonized, and commodified.

Emerging into this culture of spectacular live exhibition at the end of the nineteenth century, filmmaking also became a tool by which individuals and institutions produced and participated in discourses of race, gender, nationality, and colonialism. Instead of bringing people and pieces of the colony home, photographers and, later, filmmakers traveled abroad to accumulate visual data in the form of easily transported and endlessly reproducible pictures. Zoos and ethnographic exhibitions only simulated "natural" settings; photographers and filmmakers represented them using images that were widely assumed never to lie, but that have always been subject to selection, manipulation, and historically situated interpretation. As Ella Shohat and Robert Stam have written, photographers and filmmakers of the colonial period "did not simply document other territories; they also documented the cultural baggage they carried with them. Their subjective interpretations were deeply embedded in the discourses of their respective European empires"; their cameras recorded information that, through "display... dissection and montage" was constructed as evidence for military, economic, scientific, and cultural domination.[7] In the specific case of expedition filmmaking in sub-Saharan Africa, what has ended up on the screen has often been a display of landscape and animal life around which human activity and agency—at least for humans of African descent—are trivialized. As Nwachukwu Frank Ukadike argues, Western filmmakers have both justified colonial power in their representations of African people as uncivilized and diverted attention from indigenous populations through underrepresentation driven by their "fascination with African wildlife, more so than with its human inhabitants."[8]

If imperialistic and ethnographic displays are the geopolitical and representational roots of the wildlife film genre, its technological features emerge from another nineteenth-century development. While photography was invented in the late 1830s, photographs of living, free-roaming animals were not achieved until over three decades later. Early cameras and photosensitive plates required long exposure to light, thwarting efforts to photograph moving subjects. Whereas inanimate objects and human subjects could be relied upon to hold poses to be photographed by cameras with relatively slow shutters and sluggish photosensitive surfaces, a flock of birds or herd of antelopes might take to wing or hoof before even experienced photographers could set up their cumbersome equipment. If one did manage to expose some film, any motion on the part of the animal would render the image blurry. Most late nineteenth-century photographers found animal corpses and captive animals to be more cooperative subjects in less arduous settings than their wild counterparts. Mid-century, at least one British photographer, J. D. Llewellyn, specialized in images of taxidermy specimens—deer, birds—stuffed in lifelike positions and placed in naturalistic settings. Staging such scenes with dead animals must have seemed like the next best thing to actually photographing a live animal in the out-of-doors, and it demonstrated fine craftsmanship in several technologies at once.[9]

While early photographers were unable to capture images of living animals in their natural habitats, some set out to solve the problem under decidedly unnatural conditions and for different purposes. Eadweard Muybridge's studies of animals (and humans) in motion contributed significant innovations in shutter design and speed to the medium, and are invoked in many media histories as an origin story that Terry Ramsaye called in 1926 the "accepted first chapter of Genesis" for filmmaking in general.[10] But Muybridge's intention was something other than the birth of cinema. In

1874 Leland Stanford commissioned Muybridge to document the phases of a horse's gait, in order to discover whether or not, during the trot and gallop, a horse has all four hooves in the air at once. (It does.) Most sources indicate that Stanford was simply seeking to settle a $25,000 bet on the matter.[11] He hired an engineer named John D. Isaacs to help Muybridge set up a series of cameras with unusually quick shutter mechanisms, to be triggered electromagnetically one after another as the horse trotted or galloped down a track. By using stereoscopic (two-lensed) cameras, and displaying the images on a modified version of the zoetrope dubbed the "zoöpraxiscope," Muybridge simulated motion twenty years before the invention of cinema. After completing his work for Stanford in 1879, Muybridge continued the project at the University of Pennsylvania, attracting interest in both the scientific and artistic aspects of the images. Muybridge produced thousands of pictures of wildlife species such as the elephant, the ostrich, and the baboon, domesticated animals such as house cats and riding horses, and human subjects, including athletes and dancers.

Simple gaits, postures, and gestures were not Muybridge's only preoccupations. More elaborate actions and interactions, some violent, also appear in his work, as in photographs depicting a tiger allowed to attack a buffalo, courtesy of the Philadelphia Zoo, foreshadowing the wildlife genre's later attention to the chase and kill.[12] Other images are vaguely erotic. As Linda Williams points out, Muybridge's humans exemplify John Berger's incisively succinct observation about the distinct roles for male and female subjects in lived social relations and in representation: "*men act* and *women appear*" (emphasis in original). According to Williams, "Naked and semi-naked men, for example, walk, run, jump, throw, catch, box, wrestle, and perform simple trades such as carpentry." When women "perform the same activities as the men, these activities are often accompanied by some superfluous detail, such as the inexplicable raising of a hand to the mouth ... grasping her breast ... they blow kisses" and sometimes appear in elaborate sets rather than with plain backdrops. Instead of boxing or wrestling, "a woman pours a bucket of water over a woman seated in a basin ... [and] into the mouth of a second woman," or they lean against one another while smoking cigarettes.[13]

When a nude woman rides sidesaddle in *Tom with Rider*, she displays more of her body—both breasts, both legs—than the male rider's profile yields in *Smith with Rider (.063 second)* and *Smith with Rider (.082 second)*.[14] Each of these three panels is comprised of twelve sideviews and twelve alternate views of the same stride. In *Tom with Rider*'s alternate views, the horse takes a step toward the camera; the female rider's right breast is partially visible behind the horse's head. In both of the *Smith with Rider* series, the horse steps away from the camera, which provides a consistent view of the male rider's back. Muybridge's images arrest motion in order to provide visual access to the placement of feet taking a step, the bobbing of a head, the appearance (then disappearance) of a breast, beyond that which is typically available through unassisted vision. These pictures operate according to what Williams describes as the "principle of maximum visibility," a kind of privileged looking at the animal and human body in which Williams finds parallels in the close-up glare of "hard-core" pornographic films, as resources for knowledge and pleasure.[15]

In the 1880s, influenced by Muybridge but more directly innovating Pierre Jules Cesar Janssen's device for photographing astronomical phenomenon, Etienne Jules Marey developed a camera with gun-like mechanics to document phenomena such as birds in flight. Marey, a French physiologist interested in human and animal movement, exposed different sections of a glass plate in split-second intervals to produce motion-picture sequences lasting a few seconds. Perhaps Marey's most important innovation was his 1888 use of a strip of flexible paper instead of cumbersome glass plates, but paper negatives were largely replaced a year later when Kodak introduced the more durable celluloid.[16]

Marey trained French physician Felix-Louis Regnault to use the same technique, known as chronophotography, to document human postures and motions. Regnault, a comparative anthropologist, sought means of categorizing ethnic groups as either "Savage" or "Civilized." A staunch positivist, Regnault believed that he could prove racial difference through the use of visual technologies that would assist the tasks of measurement, comparison, and classification. In 1895 he photographed the movements of performers in ethnographic expositions that brought Africans from colonized French Sudan and Senegal to Paris to perform everyday tasks for onlookers.[17] Comparing these photographs, he set about ranking ethnic and national populations as primitive, modern, and degrees between, based on gaits, postures, carrying styles, and other characteristics. Regnault employed photography as a tool in his racial project, to produce scientific data that he interpreted as proving his theory of racial difference and white superiority even as some leading anthropologists, such as Regnault's compatriot Paul Broca and, in the United States, the German-American anthropologist Franz Boas, rejected the notion and put forth that race was a socially constructed system of categorization.[18]

Even as these projects contributed to—and took advantage of—innovations in photosensitivity and shutter speed, it may be only in retrospect that they appear to necessarily foreshadow the motion picture. Muybridge's work signaled a shift in the range of conceived uses of photography, toward creating images of moving as well as still subjects, but Muybridge sought most vigorously to stop, not simulate motion. Janssen, Muybridge, Marey, Regnault, and others working in the same vein sought to scrutinize phenomena that could not be perceived by the unassisted human eye. The motion photographers—save for a streak of showmanship in Muybridge's public exhibitions of his work using the zoöpraxiscope—held little interest in actually representing motion. The zoöpraxiscope and countless other mechanisms built to project a series of slides in rapid succession appeared in the final quarter of the nineteenth century, some of which contributed directly to the development of motion-picture technology. One of the innovations that most closely prefigured motion-picture cameras and projection apparatus came about in the 1890s when W. K. L. Dickson, an associate of Thomas Alva Edison, replaced the plate-glass slides used in these devices with celluloid film for the Kinetograph and Kinetoscope. Such inventions reasserted "the hegemony of vision" in representations that simulated, rather than deconstructed, visual perception, and anticipated cinema far more immediately than the motion studies of Janssen, Muybridge, Marey, or Regnault.[19]

The motion-study photographers represented captive animal subjects in controlled studio settings and volunteer or paid human subjects performing prescribed tasks for the camera. In contrast, wildlife photographers sought out animal subjects in their natural habitats and stepped into the film frame themselves. According to James R. Ryan, beginning in the late 1850s, professional hunters, wealthy sportsmen, and those engaged in the colonial administration of British East Africa often posed for photographs with the animals they killed, and photographed their stuffed trophies. If some of these pictures had scientific value, and others served primarily as souvenirs of great adventure, Ryan argues that they fulfilled other ideological goals:

> Such photographs of white men with dead animals or antlers, tusks and skins are a common, even clichéd, feature of the repertoire of Victorian and Edwardian colonial photography, and they testify further to the significance of hunting as a ritualistic display of power by white colonial elites over land, subject peoples, and nature. . . . Indeed, photographs and taxidermy shared the power to fabricate nature in new spaces, to capture

animals in their supposedly natural attitudes and display their form to audiences eager for glimpses of exotic wilderness and knowledge of natural history.[20]

More than simply reiterating in visual terms the relationship of the colonizer to colony and its resources, photographs (and stuffed carcasses and mounted trophy heads) could be shipped back to the home country and circulated in public and private displays that engaged the citizenry in the colonial project, if only as spectators.

Not content to document poseable kills, some Victorian sportsmen made "camera hunting" a primary goal of their expeditions. Possibly the first was British elephant hunter James Chapman, whose photographic efforts during an 1862 expedition along the Zambezi River to Victoria Falls were thwarted by bad weather, damaged equipment, spilled chemicals, and difficulties he faced setting up cumbersome equipment before his subjects moved out of range. Chapman produced a few images of animals killed by his expedition's hunters, but failed to record images of live wildlife. In the 1870s increasingly quick shutter speeds and increasingly sensitive photographic plates made capturing legible images of mobile and capricious subjects—including live, unconfined animals—possible. In fact, the earliest known and still extant image of a truly "wild" animal may be a picture of a stork taken in 1870 not in a colonial outpost but in Strassbourg by Charles A. Hewins of Boston.[21]

By the turn of the century, utilizing new photographic technologies, the camera hunters had become prolific image-makers. Part of the thrill of their new sport seems to have resided in the physical closeness of photographer and subject. Some claimed to be unarmed during these encounters, but the best known of these adventurers—Carl Schillings, Arthur Radclyffe Dugmore, Edward North Buxton, and Marius Maxwell—obtained their most dramatic images of big game such as rhinoceros and elephants by provoking the animals to charge, sometimes by wounding them in a manner that would not be apparent in the photograph. This strategy required that the "camera hunter" work with a marksman who would pull the trigger of his gun just after he heard the click of the camera's shutter, to kill the charging animal before it could reach and attack its provoker.[22]

Wildlife photographers found new outlets for their work after the development of the halftone screen process, first utilized in magazines in 1867.[23] Perhaps the first natural history book to abandon conventional hand-drawn illustrations in favor of photographs was Richard and Cherry

Kearton's *British Birds' Nests* in 1895.[24] A year later, in 1896, the eight-year-old *National Geographic* magazine published its first issue to include photographs. Subscriptions, acquired through membership in the Washington-based National Geographic Society, increased threefold within a year and photographs were firmly established "as the mainstay and distinguishing feature of the magazine."[25] Still, many publications continued to reproduce engravings (sometimes copied from photographs) even as they introduced photographs to their pages. Both drawn and photographed images appeared together in the British magazine *Animal Life and the World of Nature,* published from 1902 to 1904. A decade later, another British periodical *Wild Life,* published in 1913 and 1914, used only photographs. Cherry Kearton, Oliver Pike, and other nature photographers of the period experimented with motion-picture cameras and became accomplished wildlife filmmakers, but their work found few outlets in the early movie market, which embraced dramatic forms. As Gregg Mitman has noted, "Scientists, in utilizing film, could never escape its entertainment role. Hollywood had decisively defined the terms in which the medium would be used, seen and understood."[26]

Animals in Early Cinema

Despite extensive work in representing animals by motion-study photographers such as Muybridge, and by naturalist-photographers such as Kearton, the camera-hunters' work most closely predicts the interests of early moviemakers who developed a wildlife-film genre. When animals appeared in early popular cinema—even in the actualities of the turn of the century—it was frequently in circumstances that would produce unfortunate outcomes, at least for the animals. Representations of animals in Thomas Alva Edison's films tended to dwell on human-animal interaction, as in the placid *Feeding the Doves* (1896), or, more often, on human-animal conflict, as in *Runaway [Horse] in the Park* (1896), and *The Burning Stable* (1896).[27] For *Electrocuting an Elephant* (1903), Edison not only filmed the electrocution but was also the elephant's executioner. Topsy, one of several elephants at Coney Island's Luna Park, killed a handler who tried to make her eat a lit cigarette. Edison, then advocating to make direct current the standard for U.S. electrical systems, offered to electrocute Topsy with alternating current (his competitor George Westinghouse's preferred system, which eventually became standard) to demonstrate how dangerous it was. An audience of 1,500 watched the event live, and Edison's film has brought the scene—of Topsy being led to the contraption Edison had rigged, bearing the jolt of electricity, and falling to the ground, twitching—to thousands more.[28] Action, violent conflict, and sensationalistic spectacle also marked representations of animals in travelogues, newsreels, and eventually feature films of the 1910s and 1920s.

While the nickelodeon market developed in New York City and other urban centers, cinema also reached audiences in other forms. During the first decade of the twentieth century, traveling exhibitions of motion pictures (including films from Edison's studio, sometimes under revised titles), presented by charismatic showmen, took cinema into far-flung communities. One of the most successful of these entrepreneurs, Lyman H. Howe, regularly advertised animal titles including *The Perils of Whaling* (1906), *A Real Bullfight* (1906), *Polar Bear Hunt* (1906), *Boar Hunting in France* (1907), and *Hunting the Hippopotamus* (1907), in which the animal is shot, skinned, and butchered. Howe exhibited similar material throughout his career: a film called *Thrilling Capture of Huge Seal Elephants* (1919) was part of his final tour in 1919. During screenings, these films were often interspersed with travelogues and footage of military exercises, public appearances by royalty and other elites, parades, and industrial processes. According to Charles Musser and Carol Nelson, "The processes of hunting a wild animal or manufacturing industrial goods achieved a kind of equivalence in these programs. One showed how wealth was spent, the other how it was accumulated." The range of subject matter embraced by the nickelodeon industry and the traveling exhibitors thus contributed to the codification of celebrity, the exertion of power, and the exotic as spectacles that would comprise cinematic entertainment for mass audiences.[29]

Many of these short films screened at nickelodeons and traveling exhibitions were, then, nonfiction precedents for what became the classic newsreel. Others, such as *Hunting Big Game in Africa* (1909), indulged in outright fakery. Chicago film producer William N. Selig, disappointed that Theodore Roosevelt did not take a filmmaker from Selig's company along on his 1909 safari, decided to make a film about the hunt anyway. Selig renovated his studio to resemble an African jungle, purchased an elderly zoo lion, and hired an actor who easily doubled for "T.R." and some black Chicago actors to pose as African porters. While the on-screen Roosevelt fired blanks, someone off-screen shot and killed the lion. When the real Roosevelt's first lion kill made the news, Selig released his film. *Hunting*

Big Game in Africa was an international moneymaker for Selig, prompting the studio to expand its jungle set and menagerie for future productions.[30]

The Selig film was far more successful than Cherry Kearton's authentic short film of the Roosevelt expedition, *Roosevelt in Africa* (1910), which failed to impress critics and audiences alike.[31] *Variety* ridiculed Kearton's project, lamenting that the first half, depicting tribal dancing and other human endeavors, might only be appropriate for classroom use, and that in the second half, much of the wildlife footage "is very poor." Still, the anonymous reviewer conceded that the film's few close-ups of animals "hold the attention strongly," and—erroneously—that its veracity would be certain if not for a " 'flashlight' of a lion taken from a painting or carved animal. This is the only suspicious incident in the entire film."[32] Failing to obtain usable motion-picture footage of lions in action, Kearton had spliced a still flash photo of a lion—a live, free-roaming lion, not a painting, a carving, or a cadaver—into the film.[33] Already primed to anticipate deception in a genre prone to overstating its realism, the writer found "nature-faking" in all the wrong places. The reviewers expected action—chases and kills by the renowned hunter-president—but were willing to settle for humorous outdoorsy exploits. Getting only unsatisfactorily soaked in whatever expedition ambience could be recorded under arduous field conditions, the *Variety* writer impugned Roosevelt's tough-guy image for having compromised the masculine expedition with a narcissistic filmmaking endeavor: "The idea of any man going hunting with a moving picture photographer to take count of his operations is funny enough to supply all of the comedy necessary."[34]

If the Roosevelt flop chilled the market for expedition shorts at all, as Kevin Brownlow argues, many subsequent expeditions undertaken by rich industrialists still took film crews in tow.[35] Most notably, Paul J. Rainey documented his expeditions with several shorts and at least two features, including *Paul J. Rainey's African Hunt* (1912) (also referred to as *Rainey's African Hunt*, or simply *African Hunt*), which was distributed by Carl Laemmele in a theatrical run that lasted fifteen months and earned half a million dollars.[36] The film opened in April 1912 as the popularity of both nonfiction and feature-length films were on the upswing, drawing to movie theaters the middle and upper-middle classes who shied away from other film genres that they perceived as too lowbrow. *African Hunt* drew both audiences, those interested in elite society and educational film, as well as "those who found amusement in the exotic, in spectacle and in the depiction of violence."[37]

Science or Sensationalism? A Genre in Uneasy Transition

By the 1920s, some wildlife filmmakers faced pressure to avoid fakery and to temper the sensationalism of their work with scientific accuracy and conservationist messages. The films of Martin and Osa Johnson are the most prominent examples. Martin Johnson, a young photographer from Independence, Missouri, sailed as a cook on Jack London's South Seas voyage aboard the *Snark*.[38] According to critical biographers Pascal James Imperato and Eleanor M. Imperato, Martin was heavily influenced on this trip by London's open belief in white superiority. Back home, Johnson partnered with a local drugstore owner named Charles H. Kerr to convert Kerr's drugstore into a theater to house long-running slide lectures based on photos from the trip, supplemented by images cribbed from other sources. The theater, called "The Snark" and designed to look like a ship, was so successful that they opened two more theaters; the chain boasted a total seating capacity of over 1,400. In 1910 Johnson married Osa Leighty, a high school student who once sang as part of the entertainment at the Snark theater.[39] The couple soon undertook an expedition to the New Hebrides, which resulted in their first film, *Among the Cannibal Isles of the South Seas* (1918). Refusing to slice the film into several ten-minute newsreels as requested by other interested exhibitors, Martin Johnson secured a booking with theater manager Samuel Lionel Rothafel to lecture and show the footage three times a day for a week at the Rivoli Theater in New York. Positive reviews helped ensure a profitable run. The *New York Times,* for example, congratulated Johnson and Rothafel for "[raising] the motion picture beyond the reach of those who would keep it trash."[40] The film's success attracted investors to the Martin Johnson Film Company (later called the Martin Johnson African Film Company), and encouraged the distributor Robertson-Cole to pick up a two-part, intertitled version, known as *Cannibals of the South Seas* and *Captured by Cannibals* (both 1918), which did not require the live lecture component.[41]

Praise for the film seems, in retrospect, deeply misguided. Reviewers understood the film as reliably educational, unaware that the Johnsons, seeking to appeal to large audiences who expected to be entertained, were often "distorting the meaning of what was actually being shown." In this film and subsequent projects, their interpretations of both cultural rituals and current events on the islands were shaped by stereotypes and their own fears of their subjects. They failed to recognize the role of Europeans in the Melanesians' poverty (often an effect of introduced diseases) and in provoking their sometimes-violent responses to outsiders. In their next release, a 1919 set of short films, Martin presented footage of mummification rituals and a simple pig roast by Espiritu Santo islanders as proof that they engaged in cannibalism.[42] Renarrativizing the practices of indigenous people so duplicitously was in itself nothing new. The specter of cannibalism had been evoked without meaningful evidence by explorers from imperial powers to confirm the inferiority and barbarity of populations subjugated by, especially, British colonizers, for centuries.[43] At the turn of the century, cannibalism persisted as a theme in essays on African life in U.S. magazines targeting both the middle class and new immigrant populations, reminding readers that America exemplified civilization, while the racialized, unassimilated Other represented "savagery."[44] The Johnsons transported this trope into their films. Despite their success, the Johnsons' own staff and their distributors were not convinced that a deep commercial market existed for films of the social practices of far-flung indigenous people, regardless of their ethnographic value (or lack thereof), and encouraged them to focus on the animals they encountered on their travels, to satisfy an already proven market.[45]

The Johnsons' first attempt to make a wildlife film was more arduous than expected, and they were often disappointed by the difficulty of tracking and filming elusive wildlife in the dense, rainy, shadowy forests of Borneo.[46] Still, they managed to release *Jungle Adventures* in 1921. By this time, Martin had met Carl Akeley of the American Museum of Natural History (AMNH) through the exclusive Explorers Club. (Osa certainly became acquainted with Akeley as well but she was not invited to join the all-male club.) Akeley, long an active filmmaker, had sold footage to Paul J. Rainey for use in *African Hunt* and worked as a scriptwriter on an ethnographic film by Rainey, *Military Drills of the Kikuyu Tribe and Other Ceremonies* (1914), but he had come to believe that wildlife filmmakers whose primary concern was trophy hunting encouraged extermination of many African species. He hoped that Johnson would redirect his photographic skills from entrepreneurial sensationalism to scientific purposes and promotion of the museum's agenda. Akeley persuaded Johnson to adhere to higher standards of accuracy, to become more sensitive to the need for conservation of African wildlife, and to help "populariz[e] Africa," which would facilitate the museum's efforts to raise funds for his Hall of Africa project at the AMNH.[47]

At Akeley's behest, the Johnsons traveled to East Africa, but four months before their first film featuring its wildlife was completed, the father-and-son team H. A. and Sydney Snow's *Hunting Big Game in Africa with Camera*

Osa Johnson rests at camp, served by locally hired staff. An Akeley motion-picture camera appears behind the breakfast table. Courtesy of the Martin and Osa Johnson Safari Museum.

and Gun (1923), a largely faked feature-length travelogue, opened to extensive and lucrative nationwide bookings.[48] Fearful that his opportunity to promote the Hall of Africa would meet a glutted market, Akeley became a vocal critic of the Snows' film; he worked with Rothafel to promote the Johnsons' *Trailing African Wild Animals* premiere at the Capitol Theater in New York, with lobby displays of trophy heads, skins, and photographs, and contributed laudatory quotes to press kits that reaped supportive coverage in women's magazines, newspapers, and the motion-picture trade press. The film was a box-office success, but the projected costs of the Johnsons' future expeditions were too large for them to depend on private investors seeking quick profit. Akeley, with the support of museum president Henry Fairfield Osborn, persuaded George Eastman (of Eastman Kodak, an avid philanthropist and big-game hunter) to contribute $10,000 seed money toward the Johnsons' next films; museum trustees raised another $125,000.[49]

One of the AMNH-supported Johnson films was *Simba*, a 1928 feature.[50] Viewers primed by the title to expect moving pictures of lions remain in suspense until the final quarter-hour of the eighty-seven-minute film, because the Johnsons encountered very few lions during the four-year safari undertaken to gather footage for the film. They managed only to collect a few still images of a lioness, photographed early in their trip, which were inserted into the first section of the film, solving the problem of a conspicuous lack of lions just as had Kearton in *Roosevelt in Africa*. The Johnsons did, however, encounter many other animals. In two early instances, they appear to be so much more concerned about filming in close proximity to an animal than about its safety that they provoke a rhinoceros and later an elephant into charging them. As if mimicking the turn-of-the-century "camera hunters" who snapped still images of charging animals just before their hunting partners brought the animal down, Martin keeps the camera rolling while Osa, hovering nearby with a rifle, shoots to kill each animal before it reaches her husband.

In the film's final act, hearing that nearby Lumbwa villagers plan to kill some lions that have been preying on their herd animals, the Johnsons set out to film the ritualized hunt. An intertitle introduces the method of hunting: "Sportsmen kill with high-powered rifles—for fun—but the naked Lumbwa fights with spear against fangs and claws." The Lumbwa men, who are not naked but wear a kind of loincloth, chase and close in on a lion, throwing their spears at the animal until it falls dead. They nearly corner a second lion, but this one escapes, only to charge the camera. In a cutaway, Osa aims her rifle—not entirely "for fun" but to protect the camera operator, presumably Martin. Her second shot appears to fell the lion. The Lumbwa hunters gather around the lion and Osa, who exchanges a few words and laughs with one of the men. If Osa performs in these films as fitting helpmate to an adventurer-husband, and sports-woman in her own right, she also appears on camera in a more traditional role. To celebrate the successful day of hunting and filming, according to another title card, "So that night we had apple pie." Shots of Osa rolling out the dough and preparing the crust, with servants lending a hand, are interspersed with more traditional long shots of the landscape in which the expedition has landed, at sunset, to end the film. The villagers and their livestock are safe from the now-dead lions; the long expedition, the filmed record of these travels, and the day itself are coming to apparent close; and Osa, once posed in the ambiguously gendered role of huntress, is reposed in the camp kitchen.

The compromise between scientific authenticity, to please the AMNH, and drama, to please exhibitors and, presumably, at least some segments of the movie-going public, that the Johnsons had to strike is evident in these scenes. Akeley demanded that films funded by the museum could not fake scenes or needlessly harm animals, but the agreement seems to have left plenty of room for interpretation of what constitutes fakery and needless harm. In *Simba,* cutaways of Martin cranking the camera and Osa taking aim were filmed *after* the incidents with these animals. Osa did on occasion kill animals for food or to protect Martin as he filmed, but she did not shoot the lion pursued by the Lumbwa men. That task was performed by an off-screen, hired sharpshooter, who was white. Their embellished reconstruction of a scene in which Osa's pretense is made to appear reliably naturalistic, by means of editing, recalls Selig's *Hunting Big Game in Africa,* faked in the studio, more closely than the staged narrow escapes of the late nineteenth-century camera hunters.[51] The cutaways—and an inserted nineteen-second clip of a Maasai spearing a lion by another filmmaker—add drama to the scene, as well as "proof" that the lion had to be killed before it attacked a human, but also suggest that narrative needs would often trump conventions of realism and the obligation to veracity.[52]

As well as exploiting African wildlife as resources for the taking, and mythologizing the Johnsons as a wholly self-sufficient husband-and-wife team conquering the wild, *Simba* demonstrates the racial ideology of the Johnsons' films and that of prevailing voices at the AMNH. In *Simba* indigenous Africans appear as comic relief, beasts of burden, oddities, or uncivilized savages, in each case closer to animal than human life. The film juxtaposes title cards remarking on the latest "flapper" styles with images of Lumbwa women wearing short garments or being introduced to tobacco, and cross-cuts scenes suggesting the similarity of nonwhite human and animal subjects, a commonplace convention of ethnographic films of the era, seen as Robert Flaherty's intercut scenes of Inuit actors and their dogs in *Nanook of the North* (1922) and in various conflations of human and monkey or ape subjects in the films of Cooper and Schoedsack, including *Chang* (1927), *Rango* (1931), and *King Kong* (1933).[53]

As for the AMNH, Imperato and Imperato note, "while the museum insisted on the validity of the wildlife sequences, it gave no thought to fostering a vision of equality among the races." At the turn of the century, the AMNH employed progressive anthropologist Franz Boas as a curator, but many of those in positions of power at the museum gave a great deal of thought to fostering a vision of *inequality* among the races. AMNH board president and paleontologist Henry Fairfield Osborn and trustees such as Madison Grant were active supporters of the eugenics and anti-immigration movements.[54] They believed that race was a fixed and immutable, not socially constructed, set of categories, and that those of Nordic descent were superior to other "races" in physical, mental, moral, and social capacities. Their AMNH projects and the representations they produced (such as the Hall of Africa and the Johnsons' films) were intended to shape the way that Americans would think of Africa and Africans. As Donna Haraway argues, to the Johnsons, and to those at the helm of the AMNH, "Africans had the same status as wildlife . . . the ultimate justification for [their] domination" by white Westerners.[55]

Madison Grant's book *The Passing of the Great Race* (1916) expresses such a racial ideology in no uncertain terms, in passages that articulate a vile racism based on discredited evidence: Grant believed that human races constitute "distinct subspecies" with a "perverse predisposition to mismate."[56] Grant, who was chairman of the New York Zoological Society as well as an AMNH trustee, promoted an absolute hierarchy of racial development and strict separation of the races, and displayed a dismissive ignorance of the cultural traditions of non-Europeans:

> There exists to-day a widespread and fatuous belief in the power of environment, as well as of education and opportunity to alter heredity, which arises from the dogma of the brotherhood of man, derived in turn from the loose thinkers of the French Revolution and their American mimics. Such beliefs have done much damage in the past, and if allowed to go uncontradicted, may do much more serious damage in the future. Thus

the view that the negro slave was an unfortunate cousin of the white man, deeply tanned by the tropic sun, and denied the blessings of Christianity and civilization, played no small part with the sentimentalists of the Civil War period, and it has taken us fifty years to learn that speaking good English, wearing good clothes, and going to school and to church, does not transform a negro into a white man.... Whether we like to admit it or not, the result of the mixture of two races, in the long run, gives us a race reverting to the more ancient, generalized and lower type. The cross between a white man and an Indian is an Indian.... The negroes of the United States, while stationary, were not a serious drag on civilization until, in the last century, they were given the rights of citizenship and were incorporated in the body politic. Those negroes brought with them no language or religion or customs of their own.[57]

Grant's disdain for nonwhites, especially people of African descent, and his willful ignorance of African cultural history influenced both the AMNH agenda and congressional legislation that instituted strict racial and ethnic quotas on immigration.[58] But this was hardly an isolated instance of exercise of eugenicist thought in public policymaking. The biologist Julian Huxley enthusiastically supported the eugenics movement, and called for its development as "part of the religion of the future...a sane outlet for human altruism," as well as a science applied to "the improvement of the human race by means of the improvement of its genetic qualities." Huxley also speculatively ranked races in terms of intelligence and, like Grant, his influence extended beyond the walls of the academy or museum: Huxley was the first Director General of the United Nations Educational, Scientific, and Cultural Organization (UNESCO) for the years 1947–48.[59]

Eugenics theory pervaded scientific and political thought and institutions, and crept into the common sense of dominant classes generally. Accordingly, the Johnsons persisted in sensationalized racial representations even when their ties to the AMNH crumbled. Seeking to secure their place in a film industry that was becoming increasingly consolidated, the Johnsons, like many independents, feared that their films would fail to find distribution and strove to work within the studio system, promising their next feature to Fox Film Corporation. The film, *Congorilla* (1929), subjected both African people and animals to exploitation and ridicule, both on and off screen, provoking controversies that had profound impact on the Johnsons' relationship with the museum. It was not the cruel tricks they played on local Africans they encountered in the course of filming that caused a rift with the museum, but rather their unethical actions regarding gorillas. To obtain a permit from the colonial Belgian government to capture a gorilla to use in the film, Martin Johnson claimed to be working for the AMNH. Then, instead of taking only one gorilla as specified by the permit, the Johnsons collected an adult and two infants, the latter by felling a stand of trees in which they tried to evade capture. After the expedition, the Johnsons brought the duplicitously obtained baby gorillas to the United States and donated them to the San Diego Zoo. In response to negative publicity for the AMNH and the Johnsons generated by zoologists (and competing filmmakers), the museum retracted its support of the Johnsons.[60] Withdrawal of AMNH support freed the Johnsons to concentrate solely on the entertainment value of their films. They remained at work on increasingly formulaic and sensationalizing fare including sound features (*Baboona,* 1935; *Borneo,* 1937). Martin died in a commuter plane crash in the United States in 1937; Osa continued to release films based on previously gathered footage such as *Jungles Calling* (1937) and *Tulagi and the Solomons* (1943).

If wildlife filmmakers seeking popular distribution dabbled with authenticity (largely, in the Johnsons' case, to secure AMNH funding and promotion), commercial success in animal films would depend on the degree to which they embraced sensationalism. While, ironically, André Bazin named *Congorilla* as one of several "travel-in-the-grand-manner" films that demonstrates "an authentically poetic quality which does not age and is admirably exemplified in *Nanook,*" he lamented that the wildlife genre and the travelogue in general had entered a "decline characterized by a shameless search after the spectacular and the sensational." Bazin singled out Paul L. Hoefler's nonfiction travelogue *Africa Speaks* (1930, referred to by its French title *L'Afrique vous parle*) and W. S. Van Dyke's dramatic adventure *Trader Horn* (1931) as particularly egregious examples of the trend in which "it was not enough merely to hunt the lion, the lion must first gobble up the bearers."[61] Both incorporated footage that was not collected in Africa to heighten dramatic aspects of the films. *Trader Horn* includes animal-attack scenes, in which lions kill an antelope and a leopard attacks a hyena cub, which were staged in Mexico.[62] In *Africa Speaks,* Hoefler and his sidekick, Harold Austin, pose in front of rear-screen projected footage of African wildlife and villages, implying greater proximity to their subjects than they may have actually obtained while filming during their expedition. As well, dialogue that takes place in these inserted scenes provides respite from voiceover narration that guides the viewer through most of the film. Promoted as the first of its genre to incorporate animal sounds recorded in the field,

Osa Johnson in *Jungles Calling* with "Snowball," a gorilla captured by the Johnsons in the Belgian Congo. Courtesy of the Martin and Osa Johnson Safari Museum.

dialogues and sound effects help to construct an illusion of naturalistic, synchronously recorded sound, even if the results are not always convincing.

Beyond its use of new sound technologies, *Africa Speaks* sports attributes of expedition films of its own era and subsequent generations. The film's first nontextual image, following the opening title, is an establishing shot focused on a map of Africa, locating for the viewer the presumably "exotic" setting in real geographic space. The map shot gives way to footage of the expedition's point of origin, a pan of a Niger River port city. Promptly, the film's narration incorporates a generalized insistence on the remarkable abundance of animals throughout Africa, despite decades of faddish trophy hunting and habitat-altering developments such as the railroad and telegraph, the latter said in narration to garrote an occasional giraffe. The persistence of healthy wildlife populations is proclaimed over a montage of quick shots of an array of species (storks, monkeys, cheetahs, zebras, among others), and again when showing animals, such as flamingos, congregated in large numbers. The robustness of Africa's animal populations is contested in a single scene, in which the narrator points to the trade in horns for traditional Chinese medicines as cause for the decline of the white rhino. Hoefler's narration strays into anthropomorphism uncharacteristic of the era only once. This indulgence is part of a sequence in which not only the animal, but also the African members of Hoefler's crew, and (presumably) American rubes not so sophisticated as these world-traveling adventurers, are targeted with ridicule. Scenes of a herd of giraffes cut to a pair of approaching lions, then to a shot of Hoefler and Austin at work. "Lions!," one proclaims, as the other cranks the camera—and two black men in the back of a truck leap, as if terrified, into a storage bin, closing the lid. The giraffes, too, seek safety, but the narration dismisses the danger: "These two lions are stuffed with food and lazy. They're just looking for a shady place to snooze. But Mr. Giraffe doesn't trust them. He's just remembered an important business engagement elsewhere." Drawing the viewer's attention to the film's soundtrack, the narrator continues, "Our microphone registers only the hoofbeats, for giraffes, having no vocal cords, cannot utter a sound. They're just naturally dumb. But not quite as dumb as the yokel who first saw one in the circus and said, 'there ain't no such ani-mule!'" The actions of the African men, certainly staged later, are not remarked upon.

Hoefler's cavalier response to the lions (or, more accurately, to inserted cutaways of lions) turns to foolhardy disregard for the lives of others in another encounter with lions. When members of a pride being filmed begin to eye the cameramen, Hoefler orders the Maasai boy who has helped carry their equipment to "get rifles from the motor car, quick!" On the way, the youth runs straight into harm, to be felled by a lion; at least, what appear to be human legs protrude from beneath a crouching lion. Hoefler and Austin fire handguns at other threatening lions; one leaps, twisting in the air when it is wounded, then eventually falls to its side on the ground. No longer threatened themselves, they stop shooting, noting that it is already "too late" for the boy. This is one of the many apparently staged scenes in *Africa Speaks,* but it tacitly devalues African human life as expendable, fueled by the same racist bravado that pervades the Johnsons' films. The shot of the dying lion lingers more plaintively than the film's treatment of the death, fictional but passed off as actual, of the Maasai youth.

Like other expedition films of the era, *Africa Speaks* is partly motivated by ethnographic pretenses. Encounters with "natives" are not confined to

the occasional hired hand. Elsewhere, Hoefler treats the range of indigenous African tribes his party meets as objects to be scrutinized for physiological and behavioral curiosities, just like the animals he captures on film.
At times, they are also subject to pseudoscientific racial categorization, as
when the narrator announces that the Pygmy king "and his subjects show
character and intelligence. In this way they differ from most of the other
African tribes.... According to scientists who have made a study of this
race, the Pygmy is not really a Negro." (What racial classification they may
belong to instead is not said.) Each ethnographic segment features a few
aspects of each tribal society, for example, the skillful archery of the Pygmies
and cattle-herding by the Maasai. Marriage practices of each group—such
as Maasai polygamy, or the easy dissolution of unsuccessful marriages
among the Pygmies—are mentioned in wry tones, underscoring these
titillating differences in social organization. The footage Hoefler collected
while visiting near villages in French West Africa (now Chad) is most striking in its focus on images of women; far fewer men or boys are depicted.

The introduction to this section indicates that they found the history
of the tribe they call "Ubangi" written, literally, on the faces of the women,
whose cheeks were scarified and lips extended through the insertion of
wood plates.[63] Over close-up footage of the women, clapping their hands
to the beat of an off-screen drum, the voiceover explains:

> The story of the Ubangi is as strange and tragic as any in the history of
> races. A few hundred years ago, these women were far-famed for their
> beauty. Now they are the most horrible in all Africa and made so by their
> own hands. The duck-billed women, apparently happy, yet they vie with
> each other for bigger and better lips. What won't a woman anywhere do to
> be in style? ... Necessity was the mother of the invention. Years ago when
> slaves were bought and sold all over the world, errant slave traders swooped
> down on the tribe at every chance and carried away the wives and daugh-
> ters to the slave markets at Timbuktu and Zanzibar, where they were sold
> to the highest bidder. The tribe diminished so rapidly that the chief
> schemed to make them frightful instead of beautiful to keep slave traders
> from taking them away.... The red rouge lips of our women are just as
> curious to the Ubangis as their [scarified] cheeks are to us.

Despite positing the practices as unique in their historical construction,
the narration in *Africa Speaks* likens rather than distances their acts to
those of "a woman anywhere ... our women," and while acknowledging
the practice's origins in one of history's worst tragedies, it is treated by the
film as fair game for derision.

Next, the film shows three girls dancing in the foreground of a large crowd. The narration reverts to a more conventional assertion of difference between African and American social practices, noting, "These little girls mature very early and are often married by the time they are ten. They are mothers when our youngsters are still in the third grade." Cutting to an image of two seated women, one holding a toddler, the narrator adds a hyperbolic punchline: "By the way, the little fellow in the foreground is still single." Suggesting that the French colonial government's ban on body modifying practices has shocked a marriage market in which women had traditionally represented, produced, consumed, and been converted into wealth for men, he continues: "Women without scars or big lips haven't much value, and the father sells them for whatever he can get." Tracking a young man's efforts to make a trade for one of the daughters of a fellow tribesman, the narrator goes on, "The father gets rid of the biggest eater first. Anyway the boy isn't particular. He's saving up to buy one with a nice big strong hip—I mean lip. This girl will do in the meantime. Without much ceremony he sends her out to rustle up something to eat." The boy gives the girl a basket; she places it on her head and exits the frame. While the narrator's script may betray his own cultural bias regarding what makes women attractive, it also reveals the presumed interchangeability of women whose value is both utilitarian and symbolic.

Africa Speaks used glimpses of the human body and hints of exotic behaviors to spice up an otherwise formulaic equatorial-Africa travelogue. Other films of the era abandoned entirely the assumption that pictures of far-off lands and their inhabitants, human or animal, would be enough to bring in audiences. The most controversial of the era, *Ingagi* (1930), produced by Congo Pictures Ltd. and distributed by RKO, premiered to crowds titillated by a publicity campaign that suggested sexual relations between African women and male gorillas, conflating a set of racist and misogynistic fantasies about the Others who might be objects of the colonial gaze. The American Society of Mammologists condemned the film for setting back newly organized efforts to protect the endangered species. Within a month, the Motion Picture Producers and Distributors of America (MPPDA) banned the film, not for its sexual and racial representations, but for what Gregg Mitman calls, borrowing a phrase from Teddy Roosevelt, its "nature faking." The purported African location was the Selig studio's zoo in Los Angeles, and the action was staged with an actor in a gorilla costume and white actresses in blackface, augmented by stock nature footage.[64] While the film industry, according to Thomas Cripps, responded in other genres to pressure from the MPPDA and the National Association for the Advancement of Colored People (NAACP) to forego racist stereotypes standard since *Birth of a Nation* (1915), "animal films" continued to feed an appetite for racist imagery: these films "not only failed to depict African life authentically and honestly; they became elaborate unconscious allegories for the 'black brutes' of the white Southern folklore."[65]

For a time, nonfiction wildlife film nearly vanished from theatrical distribution, with few exceptions, such as British Instructional Films' natural-history shorts *Secrets of Nature* by Percy Smith, Mary Field, and Bruce Woolfe from 1922 to 1933.[66] Another British film, *The Private Life of the Gannet* (1934), is noteworthy for its origins in both scientific and commercial interests. Julian Huxley wrote and narrated the short film about a breeding colony of diving birds located on Grassholm Island, off the southwestern coastal tip of Wales. Alexander Korda produced the film for release in a theatrical package with his own *Scarlet Pimpernel* (1934); the title associated the project with a trio of features directed by Korda: *The Private Life of Helen of Troy* (1927), *The Private Life of Henry VIII* (1933), and *The Private Life of Don Juan* (1934). Korda's cinematographer, Osmond Borrodaile, undertook most of the shooting, and the influential documentary filmmaker John Grierson shot the final scenes. Still, the film barely broke even, reinforcing industry doubt about the marketability of nonfiction animal subjects devoid of sensationalism, even though it won an American Academy Award in 1937.[67]

Huxley, writing some years later, acknowledged that observers of animals are often most fascinated by behaviors related to mating, and liberally anthropomorphize animals of all species, speculating about their motivations and feelings:

> We men like to see animals courting. It amuses us to see them thus imitating humanity, and throws something at once romantic and familiar into those dumb and hidden lives which they veil so closely from us. . . . Man is a vain organism, and likes to stand surrounded by mirrors—magnifying mirrors if it be possible, but at any rate mirrors. And so we read the ideas of our own mind into the animals, and confidently speak of "suitors" and "coy brides to be won" and "jealous rivals" and what not, as if birds or even spiders or newts were miniature human beings, in fancy dress no doubt, but with the thoughts of a twentieth-century inhabitant of London or New York.[68]

But the film resists most of the anthropomorphic techniques that would become commonplace in Disney's postwar nonfiction wildlife films and those to follow. Notably, Huxley does not individualize his gannet subjects, does not even identify which of a mated pair is male and which is female (assuming, of course, that it is not a same-sex pair). However, he does legitimate his choice of subject and follow a narrative trajectory in ways that would become genre conventions.

Like *Africa Speaks*, the *Private Life of the Gannet* begins with the camera focused on a map that spans the British Isles. The camera zooms in gradually toward tiny islands off the Welsh Coast and dissolves to aerial motion-picture footage of the actual island. The shot continues to zoom in, approaching the cliffs on which the birds gather, until birds in flight and eventually nesting birds become discernible. As the camera closes in on the film's subject, it provides a literal bird's-eye view, positioned as if it were a gannet soaring toward its island home. This is the only time in the film in which the viewer is asked to identify with the birds. Otherwise, the camerawork represents the point of view of the inquisitive, exploring filmmakers. Meanwhile, the narrator makes a pair of claims, both of which would be echoed by countless subsequent filmmakers, working in different settings and distinguishing different subjects. The first is largely implicit, regarding the filmmakers' heroic efforts to overcome the arduous conditions of this isolated location to collect these images from a "lonely outpost … without power or landing strips," the island's coves thick with "wrecked ships" of those who have tried to visit in the past. And for what? The narrator's second claim is explicit, establishing the extraordinariness of its subject, its superior physical and behavioral attributes that make the gannet special, perhaps unique: the gannet is the "largest and finest sea bird on the North Atlantic … its ability to fly home to its lonely breeding rock over thousands of empty miles of sea has established it as having the most uncanny sense of direction of any living creature."

After this overview, the film shows a man holding a live bird for the camera's examination: its beak, eye (unusual for a nonraptor in being placed for binocular rather than typically avian peripheral vision), webbed feet, and clawed middle toe are shown in extreme close-up. The one-reel short then moves at rapid clip through scenes of the gannet displaying a range of behaviors. The birds nest, court, and contend with pesky seagulls that visit the colony to steal food collected by the gannets. A time-lapse sequence shows the hatching of an egg and growth of a chick. Adult birds feed their young, the young teach themselves to fly and fish, and the film celebrates the "graceful motion of this handsome bird" with scenes of the flock circling in flight. Grierson's scenes show the birds dive-bombing from high in the sky into churning, glistening water for fish. Finally, the narrator remarks that Grassholm is one of only twenty gannet breeding rocks and speculates that the bird's population may not always enjoy its "present secure position," pointing out that they are threatened both by storms and by polluting oil spewed into the sea by ships. He tacks on a hopeful coda: "Nature and man may one day observe a truce with all such forms of wildlife, toward the continual prosperity of that which gives us pleasure because of its grace and beauty." A brief expression of concern for the bird's future, diffused by an expression of faith that conservationist values and the resilient adaptability of nature itself ("a truce") will prevail, accompanied by an assessment of the bird's worth in terms of human self-interest (its capacity to "[give] us pleasure"), became standard practices of wildlife filmmaking of the latter half of the twentieth century.

Following the dissolution of the expedition films in scandal, and the commercial disappointments of *Secrets of Nature* and *The Private Life of the Gannet,* wildlife films remained scarce in American theaters until Walt Disney reintroduced the genre a decade and a half later, recasting animal subjects as fully developed, individual, emoting characters, mirrors for their human audiences. Meanwhile, scientific and educational uses of wildlife footage, common since the 1920s, matured in the late 1930s and through the 1940s into vast and valuable collections utilized in specialized research and for the nontheatrical market, especially schools and universities.[69] Depression-era nonfiction filmmakers devoted themselves to representing human lived experience, to some degree, under the influence of John Grierson. In the United States, independent film and photography leagues emerged in various cities to document and help sustain the workers' movement.[70] Eventually, the federal government funded New Deal propaganda through the Works Progress Administration and the Resettlement Administration, such as Pare Lorentz's *The Plow That Broke the Plain* (1936).[71] When the United States entered World War II, another wave of filmmaking mobilized by the government absorbed Hollywood resources to produce propaganda, training films, and newsreels for the troops. Nonfiction nature and wildlife films remained largely out of fashion and off theatrical screens.

Elsewhere, in the 1930s and '40s, some remarkable wildlife filmmaking took place, even if it did not secure widespread distribution in the U.S. market. In France Jean Painlevé, a documentary and experimental filmmaker allied with the Surrealists, pioneered underwater cinematography with the shorts *The Sea Horse* (1934) and *Freshwater Assassins* (1947).[72]

With resources and labor redirected to other ends, and opportunities for leisure travel abroad on hold, nature filmmaking largely stalled during the war, except for in neutral Sweden, where Arne Sucksdorff completed *A Summer's Tale* (1941), *Reindeer Time* (1943), and the unnarrated *Gull!* (1944).[73] Only at the end of the 1940s, after nearly two decades of social and economic upheaval and war, would the wildlife genre return, in a new form, to popular nonfiction filmmaking in the United States.

The Disneyfication of Nature: The True-Life Adventures

Early wildlife film typically represented animals and nonwhite humans alike as expendable resources to be exploited and dominated from its origins into the 1930s. In the late 1940s, the most prominent examples of wildlife film for general audiences took a different approach. Disney's True-Life Adventures were innovative, ambitious, risky, and influential; they were also sentimental, anthropomorphizing, and steeped in postwar ideologies of progress and individualism, homeland prosperity, and so-called family values. And they returned the nonfiction wildlife film to movie theaters, with considerable success. But just how Walt Disney got into nature filmmaking is the stuff of multiple Disney legends. Disney's inspiration for the True-Life Adventures may have been wildlife footage on which Disney animators were to base their drawings for *Bambi* (1942). According to Robert De Roos, writing in 1963 for *National Geographic,* Disney told him,

> In *Snow White [and the Seven Dwarfs],* we had cute little animals, more on the fantasy side. In *Bambi* we had to get closer to nature. So we had to train our artists in animal locomotion and anatomy.... I sent some naturalist-cameramen to photograph the animals in their natural environment. We captured a lot of interested things.... Gee, if we really give these boys a chance, I might get something unique![74]

In another version of the legend, Walt Disney was on vacation in Alaska when it occurred to him that the American wilderness would be a fine subject for a new series of short films.[75] In any case, Disney hired Alfred and Elma Milotte, amateur filmmakers who owned a camera store, to make *Seal Island,* a half-hour film completed in 1948. Disney's intentions regarding the Milottes' work may not have been clear, and they set about documenting the infrastructural and industrial development of Alaska—road-building, mining, and the like—but he responded to each set of rushes the Milottes delivered with the telegraphed order, "More seals."[76]

Disney failed to secure a distribution contract for *Seal Island*, but persuaded a friend who owned a Pasadena theater to run the film for a week late in 1948—just long enough, and just in time, to qualify for an Academy Award nomination for short-subject documentary. After winning the award, the film returned to theaters in 1949 in a surprisingly lucrative wide release. To capitalize on the success of *Seal Island*, Disney undertook a series of short nature films under the title "True-Life Adventures." The next four entries in the series (*Beaver Valley*, also known as *In Beaver Valley*, 1950; *Nature's Half-Acre*, 1951; *Water Birds*, 1952; and *Bear Country*, 1953) also brought Disney short-subject documentary Oscars. *The Olympic Elk* (1952) and *Prowlers of the Everglades* (1953) completed the series of shorts.

Legends aside, economic considerations provided motivation for Disney's foray into nature filmmaking at least as much as serendipity. The turn to wildlife subjects provided a means through which the Disney Studio could redirect its nonfiction film-for-hire enterprise—for the government in wartime, and industrial films as a source of quick revenue after the war—into a genre that could be marketed as both educational and entertaining, allowing the studio to revitalize operations and maintain production during the postwar financial slump. Wildlife filmmaking required relatively small crews, and utilizing 16mm stock and nonsynch sound cost less than 35mm productions in terms of raw materials and equipment.[77]

While there was little faith among other Disney executives and associates that the True-Life Adventures would make money, Walt Disney was committed to the project for another reason: the immeasurable value of his product's distinctive brand identity. In the 1940s theater owners still regularly played short films before the feature presentation. If the studio released a feature but did not simultaneously release a new short title, theater owners would book it with a short from another studio. Walt Disney preferred to package a Disney short with a Disney feature, typically one live-action, the other animated, as in the pairing of *Nature's Half Acre* (1951) with the re-release of *Snow White and the Seven Dwarfs* (1937).[78]

Further, the True-Life Adventures may have formed a synergy with representations of animals at Disneyland itself. Disneyland opened on July 17, 1955. Among its early features was the Jungle Cruise attraction in Adventureland, in which visitors rode a boat around an artificial lagoon populated by robotic (or, in Disney's language, "Audio-animatronics") animals of various species, a white male explorer, and stereotypically caricatured Africans posed to threaten viewers or seen scampering away from pursuing animals. The experience offered, according to Steven Watts, one of

Disneyland's many "populist political emblems that further reinforced an American way of life ... with its playful pacification of the Third World."[79] In a segment of the television series *Disneyland* called "A Trip Through Adventureland" and first aired February 29, 1956, Walt Disney narrates a tour of the Jungle Cruise: "It all started with an idea that sprang from our True-Life Adventure films. We would duplicate in Disneyland park actual scenes and settings from this nature series. Of course we knew that our biggest job would be recreating the actors of the wildlife dramas."[80] Disney references those animal "actors" by naming and cutting to footage from the True-Life Adventure *The African Lion* (1955), which was in production for three years while Disneyland was being built and released about eight weeks after the park opened.

The True-Life Adventures quickly settled into two primary narrative forms. The first followed the life cycle of a particular species; the other took an episodic structure to examine various forms of life in a specific area. *Bear Country*, written and directed by James Algar, who had worked as an animator and sequence director on films such as *Fantasia* (1940) and *Bambi*, with photography credited to Alfred R. Milotte, James R. Simon, and Tom McHugh, typifies the former style.[81] It begins with a brief on-screen introduction by narrator Winston Hibler, a Disney writer and producer, who explains that bears once "ranged from coast to coast" but have been driven to limited ranges by the growing human population. The camera zooms into a globe toward the western United States; this sequence and similar openings for other True-Life Adventures follow the map-to-locale convention established in early films such as *Africa Speaks* and *The Private Life of the Gannet*. Thereafter, Hibler's presence is only in voiceover. The globe shot dissolves into a hand-drawn scene of snowy mountains, which in turn dissolves into actual film footage of, according to the narrator, the early springtime Rocky Mountains. The camera comes to rest briefly on a ridge of snow that might be covering the bears' den, as Hibler announces that this is the bear's habitat. Making an implicit claim for why the bear is a worthy subject, Hibler notes that the bear differs from other animals in these mountains because it has hibernated through winter, living on stored fat, while other species search for scarce food, evidenced by successive shots of a moose and a deer, each knee-high in snow and nibbling on bare branches. A bird identified only as a member of the crow family attacks and carries off a field mouse that has left its nest to forage, while the camera lingers on the spot where the mouse's tracks end in a flurry of impres-

Mother and cub in the Walt Disney Company's True-Life Adventure *Bear Country.*
Courtesy Disney Publishing Worldwide. © Disney Enterprises, Inc.

sions in the snow left by the bird's beating wings, accompanied by funereal chords.[82] The bird's next encounter, with a more sizable and toothy pocket gopher, is less successful.

These opening scenes introduce some of the species that share the bear's territory. Further setting the stage, a shot of a thawing stream, indicating the arrival of spring, prefaces footage of a bear emerging from her den, appearing for the first time nearly five minutes into the film. An eight-week-old cub slides down a snowbank, holding a chunk of ice in its front paws; the mother follows. The voiceover continues: "Mother always keeps a close watch over her youngster, for if she were to let him travel alone at this age, he'd be vulnerable to enemies," as tension in the soundtrack rises and the scene cuts to a shot of a mountain lion. "When she's in charge, however, even the mountain lion gives the family wide berth," underscoring the need for constant parental authority.[83] The camera lingers as mother and cub engage in what is apparently affectionate play. With the next scene, the film begins to track the activities of another female bear and her two young cubs at play, in encounters with other species, and in hunting and gathering lessons. Occasionally, for comic or dramatic effect, the camera strays from the little family and incorporates footage of other bears, as in a scene lasting a minute and forty-five seconds, containing two dozen shots of bears scratching themselves, in rhythm to a see-sawing musical score, and in scenes of bears fighting during mating season. The film follows the family until the mother, having mated again, abandons the cubs to prepare for the next hibernation on their own. In the film's snowy final shot, the bears, entering their den, "end their True-Life Adventure as they began it, deep in sleep... until the time of easy living comes again to bear country."

Bolstered by the True-Life Adventure shorts' success and prestige, Disney expanded the series to include several feature-length films. Several of the True-Life features took episodic form to explore a bioclimatic zone, as in *The Living Desert* (1953) and *White Wilderness* (1958), or theme, as in *Secrets of Life* (1956). *The Living Desert*, directed by James Algar (from a script by Algar, Hibler, and Ted Sears, and principal photography by N. Paul Kenworthy Jr. and Robert H. Crandall), interweaves conflictual meetings between animals of various species. These interactions fall into two basic categories, linked in the narration as part of the overarching "struggle for existence" by animals in a landscape that is variously described as "wasteland... eternal desert... incredibly ugly yet fantastically beautiful, seemingly without purpose, without meaning, without life," but shown to be full of plant and animal species well adapted to the environment. One set of behaviors is predatory (a coatimundi digs up a scorpion to eat, toads gulp down passing insects, squirrels evade predators while foraging); the other, reproductive (scorpions engage in a courtship dance set to square-dance music, male tortoises spar over a female). The film returns again and again to a tarantula, once to observe her being courted by a male who literally knocks on the "door" of her burrow, and elsewhere to watch her battle attackers and potential prey. The tarantula is identified as a "lethal lady" of great predatory skill; even so, most of the creatures that pass by her nest (a pocket mouse, a centipede, and a beetle) escape unharmed. As potential prey herself, she manages to rebuff a rattlesnake, but near the film's end, a wasp kills the tarantula because it needs her body to lay its eggs in, situating this species and others as part of an interdependent and endlessly renewable eat-or-be-eaten ecosystem.

Secrets of Life, which was also written and directed by Algar (and photographed by Stuart V. Jewell, Robert H. Crandall, Murl Deusing, George and Nettie MacGinite, and a dozen other credited photographers) foreshadows a distinctive preoccupation with animal reproduction that becomes commonplace in wildlife programming of the 1980s. (It also briefly

"Duel in the Desert": Pepsis wasp and tarantula in the Walt Disney Company's True-Life Adventure *The Living Desert*. Courtesy of the Academy of Motion Picture Arts and Sciences. © Disney Enterprises, Inc.

examines other behaviors.) About a third of the film depicts the reproductive techniques of plants, from the self-planting maneuvers of species such as milkweed and wild oats, to the literal dissemination of pollen. Many of these scenes are detailed in lush time-lapse sequences. The rest of the film contains lengthy sequences on the lives of bees and ants, and a more rapidly visited series of animals, from single-celled protozoans to stickleback fish (notable for the male's role as primary caretaker of eggs), and other fish, mollusks, and insects.[84] These sequences end with a few shots of waves crashing on craggy shores, which cut away to scenes of volcanic explosions, glowing-hot diversions from the watery cool rationality of the previous orderly scenes. As the image shifts from water to fire, the narrator intones:

> Like the tides, Nature's world is ever restless, as turbulent as the elemental
> energies that shape her globe. . . . The volcano is the most spectacular, a
> force constantly remaking the very planet on which life must exist. In its
> fiery furnaces, we find the final miracle in our story of nature's secret world.

In *Secrets of Life*, nature is, not surprisingly, personified as female, always-changing, and teleological (but never quite explicitly *evolving*), controlled by mythic elements and rife with miracles.

Elsewhere, nature appears to be more intensively subject to Disney's conventional commitments to character development, dramatic tension, and humor, and not to Darwin, but to the ideological distortions of Social Darwinism. *White Wilderness* (written and directed by Algar, with photography by James R. Simon, Hugh A. Wilmar, Lloyd Beebe, Herb and Lois Crisler, and six others), combines biographical and episodic strategies, surveying the tundra's diverse wildlife, from beluga whale and caribou to wolf and wolverine, while revisiting throughout the film the antics of a pair of polar bear cubs and their reliance on the steady care of their mother. Like *Bear Country*, *White Wilderness* opens in springtime, includes an early scene in which the cubs emerge from their den for the first time, and ends with the return of winter. As well, the feature, just as much as the short, intersperses the comic—the slipping and sliding of the cubs on snowy and icy slopes—with gravely dramatized scenes of animal predation. Not all the chase-and-kills are successful. A lemming, one of a countless population migrating vulnerably across open tundra, loses a "desperate battle" against an especially stealthy jager bird, but a loon escapes from the still youthfully clumsy polar bear cub.[85] Wolves, tracking the fringes of a huge caribou herd, take down "laggards," a tactic described as "nature's way of culling out the herd. Generally speaking, the predators pull down the cripples and the weaklings, and one by one the unfit come to the end of the trail." Throughout this narration, the adult wolves and pups mill about a half dozen kills.[86] Each felled animal appears to be an adult caribou, at least four of which sport large racks of antlers. In the Disney view, nature may be red in tooth and claw, but not too red: underdogs sometimes overcome; the individual effort, skill, and experience of the hunter (read: worker) lead to triumph; the dawdling, untrained, and inattentive bring disaster onto themselves; and prey are expendable, deserving of their fates. While there is no visual evidence that the animals killed by the wolves are "cripples" or "weaklings"—in fact, each appears to be large, and at least one still struggles against the pack—the narration represents the events of the sequence as a model for a kind of natural eugenics that could be relied upon to shape the future of the herd and the species for the better.

Oliver Wallace's *White Wilderness* score, and perhaps most notably Paul Smith's scores for *The Living Desert, Secrets of Life,* and other True-Life Adventures, strive to reinforce narrative or visual information, even the Disney ideology of nature. According to Carl Plantinga, "In *The Living Desert,* the musical interludes reinforce the film's depiction of nature as organically unified and fundamentally benign."[87] Elsewhere in the True-Life Adventures, musical flourishes accentuate humor in the visual images, as when a group of female seals comes ashore in *Seal Island* to the tune of "Here Comes the Bride." Reviewers for *Time,* the *New York Times,* and *The Nation,* among others, ridiculed these films' use of melodrama and humor, perceiving its recognizably "Disneyesque" worldview and cinematic strategies as undermining the film's documentary ethos.[88] Despite the critical disdain, audiences and the industry embraced *The Living Desert.* The film, which cost about $300,000 to produce, seems to have earned between $4 and $5 million in its first domestic theatrical release.[89] It also won the Academy Award in the documentary feature category. But while *The Living Desert* earns its place in film history due to its role in repopularizing the wildlife genre in feature form, it also marks, at least as importantly, a shift in the Disney corporate structure. RKO Radio Pictures had distributed Disney's films since 1936, handling twenty of twenty-one previous Disney features. When RKO refused to take on a feature-length documentary, assuming that it would fail to attract an audience, Walt Disney's brother Roy organized an in-house office christened Buena Vista to distribute the film.[90] Buena Vista operated at about half the cost of an outside contractor, leaving little reason for Disney to retain RKO's services for any of its films. Disney's relationship with RKO ended in 1954.[91]

The series' next release, *The Vanishing Prairie* (1954), went into production while *The Living Desert* was being edited.[92] Its success proved that neither the box-office earnings of *The Living Desert,* nor the capacity of Buena Vista to distribute nonfiction features, were flukes. *The Vanishing Prairie*'s release earned $1.8 million, or as much as fifteen times its production costs.[93] The film's box office may have gotten a boost from publicity generated when the New York State Board of Motion Picture Censors threatened to ban the film, unless Disney removed footage depicting the birth of a buffalo calf. Censors rescinded the order after intervention by the American Civil Liberties Union.[94]

True-Life Adventure shorts and features brought Disney financial success during a recession in the film industry, prestige within the industry in the form of awards, and impetus to vertically integrate by launching its own distribution concern. The series also popularized the wildlife film to a degree preceded only by some early big-game hunting newsreels and expedition travelogues. However, there are a number of important differences between most prewar variations of the genre and the postwar True-Life Adventures. The significance of the True-Life Adventure series lies in both its formal innovations in regard to how wildlife is represented and its relevance to dominant experiences and ideologies of nature and humanity's relationship to animals. As Margaret King points out, the series abandoned the representational strategies of most previous popular wildlife films and established new conventions for the genre: a reconceptualized "plot structure, anthropomorphism, animal biography, species hierarchy, and stock technical effects (such as stop motion and time lapse) . . . all predictable traits of subsequent nature series."[95] Likewise, Derek Bousé notes that the True-Life Adventures contributed heavily to codifying what is now widely regarded as the "classical" wildlife film, "having a strong central [animal] character and a biographical structure," often in the form of coming-of-age stories.[96] That is, the wildlife narrative is no longer structured by human activities, such as tracking, photographing, or hunting. Under Disney's control, the classic form of the wildlife film shifted from that of a travelogue to that of a coming-of-age movie, using animals as allegorical ciphers in place of human actors.[97]

But these are not Disney's only contributions to reformulating and reinvigorating the wildlife genre. On a note closely related to King's and Bousé's emphases on the wildlife film as biography, Disney's foremost structuring feature was the removal of human subjects. In Martin and Osa Johnson's *Simba,* which is arguably paradigmatic of intrawar expedition films, the protagonists are not lion but human. The lion is the film's rarely seen antagonist, depicted as the elusive enemy and rightful prey of humanity, object of the human gaze and human action—but the protagonists of *Bear Country* are bears. This strategy was not entirely unprecedented, but most theatrically distributed wildlife films prior to the True-Life Adventures were human-driven adventure-and-expedition sagas. Excising human protagonists displaces the viewer's identification onto the animal, mapping human motivations onto animal behaviors. Many critics have derided the

True-Life Adventures on the grounds that such anthropomorphism distorts the reality of animal life. Indeed, animals in True-Life Adventures are sometimes treated as, in Erik Barnouw's words, "burlesque humans"; excessive anthropomorphism has been one of the most common and virulent charges against the films.[98] At the same time, in granting the bears subjectivity, the film appears to argue what many scientists and philosophers have long believed: that at least some species experience feelings, desires, and other mental states.[99]

Some of the tactics of anthropomorphization—the recognition of animals as distinct individuals, and speculations about their emotions and motivations for their actions—are not only representational strategies of filmmakers, but have long been utilized, and contested, by those who study animals. Eileen Crist demonstrates that in the writings of Charles Darwin and those influenced by him, "animals are acting subjects" to which we can attribute will, emotion, language, intelligence, and pleasure.[100] These naturalists were not engaging in metaphor or in linguistic accidents but intentionally anthropomorphized animals to emphasize their continuity and similarity, rather than their dissimilarities, between human and animal life. Still, critics of both representational and scientific strategies agree that some uses of anthropomorphism may be counterproductive. If Disney filmmakers framed and edited bear footage in order to create an allegory of human motherhood, according to Randall Lockwood, "there is no recognition of the true biological needs and adaptations of the animals involved . . . the animals that are used to portray some personal, symbolic message . . . are flesh and blood beings who may suffer in the process"; misunderstandings take place if observers "interpret an animal's behavior or temperament on the basis of surface qualities that are unrelated to those that actually regulate it."[101] Alongside the film itself, promotional materials for *Bear Country* employed just the kind of assumptions that such critics of anthropomorphism object to, extracting moral lessons from the animals' behaviors.

Further, Disney popularized North American wildlife and landscape as appropriate subject matter for the genre. Watts links the True-Life Adventures' preference for American locations and the Disney penchant for a view of nature that revels in the survival of the fittest with the liberal ideology of individualism and surging Cold War–era nationalism.[102] Alexander Wilson sees Disney's turns to wildlife subjects found on home shores during the period in which suburbanization rapidly consumed much of America's countryside True-Life Adventures as both "transparent allegories

"Mr. and Mrs. Ground Squirrel" appear in the Walt Disney Company's True-Life Adventure *The Living Desert.* Courtesy of the Academy of Motion Picture Arts and Sciences. © Disney Enterprises, Inc.

of progress, paeans to the official cult of exploration, industrial develop-ment, and an ever rising standard of living . . . metaphors about economic growth." Flowers bloom "only to the point of 'perfection'" in Disney films (namely, *The Living Desert;* also *Secrets of Life*), they rarely wither or decompose, and each new generation of beaver explores a bit further down the river than its parent in *Beaver Valley.* True-Life Adventures may appear to claim an isomorphic correspondence between postwar prosperity and these features of the natural environment, but Wilson notes that they also provided a reassuring "utopian fantasy" of stability and "balance" for view-ers displaced socially, geographically, or psychically by widespread social reorganizations of this period.[103]

If earlier interest lay in collecting and disseminating images of faraway worlds inaccessible to most, the turn to wildlife subjects found on home shores expressed American ideologies of patriotism and progress. Further, aiming the camera at our own national parks and backyards (and excising from them all human images) may have been both economically and politically strategic. Gathering footage in the deserts of Arizona or the national parks of Wyoming would be far cheaper than sending crews to other continents and may have allowed Disney wildlife filmmakers to evade potentially controversial representations. When most of the True-Life Adventures were made, in the 1950s, many colonized nations of sub-Saharan Africa were engaged in struggles for independence.[104] At the same, in the United States in the 1950s, the antisegregationist civil rights movement was under way. Rather than respond to the contemporary social reality, Disney avoided settings and representations—such as demeaning representations of people of African descent—that might have broached politically and socially volatile territory. Exceptions were few—the Jungle Cruise at Disneyland Park, safely situated within the ostensibly depoliticized, fantasy-driven, consumerist amusement park, and *The African Lion,* shot on location in the national parks of South Africa, Kenya (at the time a British colony), and Tanganyika (then under British and United Nations control, now part of Tanzania).

Finally, filmmakers such as the Johnsons had usually taken for granted that the "nature" they found in far-off places was there for the taking. In contrast, the True-Life Adventures wistfully acknowledge that nature, especially North American nature, is precious and that it is at risk, but that risk is always paired with reassurances that the threat is contained, and the future is full of hope; the animals at hand, safely populous, offer their images as proof. In *The Private Life of the Gannet* two decades earlier, the narrator acknowledged the birds' vulnerability, then pointed optimistically to their hopefully bright future. Likewise, Hibler acknowledges that bears once "ranged from coast to coast," and that, with the continent's growing human population, "the bears retreated deeper and deeper into the backwoods," but the significance of the decline in their habitat or population is quickly glossed over: "here [in Yellowstone National Park] the American black bears still exist in plentiful numbers." As Watts argues, whatever conservationist messages these films contain is muted by the requisite happy ending, a Hollywood device that invites the audience to return day after day, or week after week, to the same ticket lines and time-slots.[105] Typical films in this series maintain that no matter what we do to nature (log the forest, or hand-feed bears marshmallows, as shown in *The Yellowstone Story*), it is ultimately resilient. Like the cycles of rain and drought, birth and death, that the wildlife genre is so often structured around, True-Life Adventures assure us that, just as the bears' biological capacity to store fat and their instinctive compulsion to hibernate allow them to survive harsh winter storms and food shortages, life goes on, and winter always turns to spring. As Stephen Mills acknowledges, audiences expect and want to be entertained, pushing the wildlife filmmaker to present habitats and species as far more resilient than they actually are: "Nature is disappearing. If he says too much about that he loses his audience."[106] The conservationist message of the True-Life Adventures would be echoed, adapted, and elaborated upon in wildlife film and television of the 1960s, '70s, and beyond.

While Disney eventually abandoned the True-Life Adventures, favoring instead fictional films with animal actors and animated animal characters, Disney rhetoric about the films emphasized their "found" qualities, as if filmmakers only stumbled across and documented events in nature without mediating factors such as the selection of subject matter, editing decisions, and staging scenes they could not capture "in the wild."[107] William R. Koehler, a Disney animal trainer, differentiates the nonfiction True-Life Adventures from the fictional projects on which he worked:

> Walt Disney gave fans two kinds of animal pictures; both of which did more than entertain.
>
> One kind is the pure, unplotted, true-life film, such as *The Living Desert*. For those productions the studio hires individuals or teams, who are qualified as patient naturalists with great skill as cinema photographers, to go into an area and photograph a subject's actions in any order they occur until nature provides them with material which, when shown in proper sequence, will be a true-life drama.[108]

The "other kind" of animal picture utilized some wildlife filmmaking techniques to gather footage for scripted animal dramas. For example, *Perri* (1957), released under the short-lived series title "True-Life Fantasy," did not pretend to document natural history facts in telling the story of a female squirrel from the time of her birth to her own first mating. Like Disney's animated *Bambi*, *Perri* was adapted from a novel by Felix Salten. Subsequent films in the same style (*Nikki, Wild Dog of the North*, 1961; *The Legend of Lobo*, 1962) depended on trained animals and the animals' interactions with humans. While these films are openly scripted and fictional,

Koehler claims that the content of Disney's nonfiction animal films was "pure," "unplotted," filmed "in any order," even a resource that "nature provides," but, paradoxically, a resource that must be reordered in "proper sequence." Storytelling, of course, was Disney's specialty, and its conventions applied as strictly to nonfiction as to fiction genres.

As the Walt Disney Company reinvented the wildlife film and returned it to theatrical distribution, its innovations were so readily conventionalized that many later observers would not hesitate to claim that "the modern era of wildlife films began ... with Walt Disney."[109] Some, such as David Payne, would lament the True-Life Adventures' influence, citing the distorted representations in "Disney-inspired nature narratives that fill the curricula of our Public Broadcasting Stations" that have replaced lived experience of nature for many viewers.[110] But Disney was not the only source of filmed representations of wildlife in this period. Swedish filmmaker Arne Sucksdorff completed *The Great Adventure* in 1953, a dramatic feature in which a farm boy raises an otter and then must release it back to the wild. He followed the film with several dramatic wildlife shorts, most with hunting themes: *Shadows on the Snow* (1954), *The Hunter and the Forest: A Story Without Words* (1956), and *Shadows of the Hunter* (1957). In direct competition with the True-Life Adventures, *The Sea around Us* (1953), based on Rachel Carson's book of the same title, won the 1953 Academy Award for documentary feature. *The Sea around Us* was released as an RKO Radio Picture, an ironic turn given Disney's split with RKO over the matter of documentary distribution. It surveys, with bombast uncharacteristic of the book, the ocean as a source of food, other resources, and recreation; as a site of both cooperative and violently predatory species; and as an impetuous danger.[111]

Jacques-Yves Cousteau also contributed to this renewed presence of nonfiction nature theatrical films, with his examinations of oceanographic life, *Le Monde du silence (The Silent World)* (1956), sponsored by the National Geographic Society and filmed by a very young Louis Malle. The film opens with a series of undersea scenes, and the narrator's first line (at least, in its English-dubbed version), "This is a motion-picture studio," referring to the marine setting. And a spectacular studio it is: much of the footage in *The Silent World* is luscious. Fluttering sea anemones, a sparkling, surfing school of porpoises, and the mostly well-muscled, often shirtless crew all glow in luminous Technicolor. But *The Silent World* is less a wildlife film that one might expect to relay natural-history facts about undersea life encountered by an adventurous filmmaking crew than it is a film about an adventure undertaken by men living off the sea's consumable resources. The *Calypso* crew observe divers harvesting live sponges; they dig into an abundant lunch of freshly caught lobster; the unusual behavior of flying fish goes unremarked, but the ship's chef gathers them off the deck at dawn to fry for breakfast. A crewmember catches a ride from a sea turtle, grabbing onto its shell; others sit and try to ride on land tortoises when the boat anchors at an island. Cousteau explains that the crew can legally dynamite a coral reef (though it would be illegal for fishermen to do so) so as to collect and census the fish, declaring the task impossible without killing the fish. The men pile dead fish on the beach, but the film does not report the findings of their census. A puffer, having survived the blast but bloated with water in its typical response to stress, is tossed atop the heap, spewing water as it deflates and squirms.

When the *Calypso* encounters a pod of sperm whales in the Indian Ocean, a baby whale becomes separated from its mother, crossing underneath the boat in what Cousteau refers to as "childish carelessness." It is slashed by the *Calypso's* propellers. Someone harpoons the wounded creature, whose body spews blood, so that it can be held still and close to the boat until a rifle is found and it is "put out of its misery." Sharks approach, drawn to feed on the whale carcass. Cousteau's men jab the sharks with hooked poles, dragging several onto the deck to clobber them with an axe. Cousteau explains that the men seek to "avenge" the young whale, an utter irony given that its death is not attributed to the sharks but only to the ship's entry into whale territory, its unfamiliar veerings through the habitat of a naturally curious and social animal. Eventually, the crew's cameras capture footage of two fish of different species that swim together as constant companions. Cousteau wonders if humanity and marine life can be so harmoniously "intimate." After his crew's ludicrous attack on the harmlessly feeding sharks, it is difficult to imagine an optimistic answer to the question he poses. *The Silent World* won the Palm d'Or at Cannes and an Academy Award in the documentary category; a later film, *Jacques-Yves Cousteau's World Without Sun* (1964) earned Cousteau's second Oscar.

Alongside this surge in the commercial presence and prestige of the wildlife genre, animal subjects also appeared in several types of nontheatrical media in the postwar era, including ethnographic and corporate film. Ethnographic filmmaking, which had come to a near halt in many parts of the world during the Depression and the Second World War, resurged. As in the interwar period, when *Nanook of the North, Chang, Grass,* and other early landmarks in ethnographic filmmaking were made, such productions often dwelt on human uses of animals, as in *Hippopotamus Hunt* (1946) and *The Lion Hunters* (1965) by Jean Rouch, the great innovator of cinema verité, direct cinema, and ethnographic filmmaking practices.[112] Animals also occasionally appeared in postwar industrial films, such as Shell Oil Company's *Atomization* (1949) and *The Greatest Enemy* (1955), depicting insect life, infestations, and the benefits of insecticides.[113] And in the 1940s, even before Disney released *Seal Island,* small but ever-growing numbers of television viewers received moving images of animals, both domesticated and wildlife species, in their own homes.

By the time that the Walt Disney Company turned its attention to wildlife filmmaking, some seventy-five years had passed since Charles A. Hewins became the first known person to successfully photograph a wild animal, and since Eadweard Muybridge went to work for Leland Stanford capturing images of a horse in motion. It had been over half a century since Thomas Alva Edison's first short films played for viewers' amusement on Kinetescope viewers, and later, in nickelodeons and traveling film exhibitions. Early photographers and cinematographers had faced similar problems when they selected animal subjects: standard equipment was cumbersome and ill-suited to field conditions. Their efforts were not, however, fully determined by technological constraints; rather, their innovations—Muybridge's rapid shutters, Shiras's flash kits, Akeley's switchable lenses, among others—helped to shape photographic and cinematic technologies.

Likewise, both photography and cinematography were adopted for multiple purposes, by individuals and institutions with divergent goals. Some sought visual evidence for scientific research, to educate an interested public about the natural world, or to promote the nascent wildlife conservation movement. Others sought visual evidence of their adventures, power, and trophy kills; to profit from entertaining audiences; or to legitimate prevailing and exploitive colonial relations and racial ideologies. In the first few decades of cinema, the latter set of interests dominated until the wildlife genre collapsed under the weight of formula and scandal around 1930. Almost two decades passed before Disney revamped the genre so that it would not only appear to educate as it entertained, but also to retell value-laden stories recast as natural history. As the practice of wildlife filmmaking found an outlet in the new medium of television, those who took up Disney's innovations and added their own faced many of the same problems as early wildlife photographers and filmmakers: technological constraints that motivated invention; a mission that teetered between education and entertainment, between ecological concern and adventurist, consumerist impulses; venerable traditions of allegorizing the family and the nation in tales about animals, and the demand for scientific accuracy; and the genre's fragile financial viability within the context of a largely profit-driven industry.

2

The Quest for Nature on the Small Screen

I'm going to like this place. It's my own *National Geographic Special*.
—Harper Pitt (Mary-Louise Parker),
in *Angels in America*

In the postwar period, while the Walt Disney Corporation set about producing True-Life Adventure wildlife shorts and features for theatrical distribution, American audiences saw the commercial introduction and expansion of a new medium: television. Early television borrowed most of its programming ideas from radio's genres, both the fictional, including situation comedies, dramas, and melodramatic serials, and the nonfictional, such as news, sports, variety, quiz shows, and talk. The new medium's visuality allowed the nascent television industry to develop new genres as well, including educational and instructional media in a "show-and-tell" format, which would include early TV's wildlife and pet programming. With some innovation, hybridization, and lots of repetition, this range of genres has continued to dominate television production. Accordingly, nonfiction animal content has maintained a presence since TV's early broadcast days. Still, that presence has varied considerably over the course of television's history in terms of the quantity of wildlife TV on the air, its place in network programming strategies, and its transformation from simple show-and-tell, studio-based programs putting captive animals on close-up display to elaborate representations of the daily lives of free-roaming animals in their natural habitats.

In 1945 Marlin Perkins, then director of the Lincoln Park Zoo, began taking animals to a Chicago TV station for occasional local broadcast appearances. He became one of American wildlife TV's first celebrities, but his earliest appearances depended on studio settings that removed animals from their natural habitats. This staid format offered few of the genre's currently expected visual pleasures—vast landscape vistas, freely moving animals—but a great deal of explanatory chatter, and prying close-ups of animals handled by humans. In the 1950s and 1960s, Perkins, David Attenborough of the British Broadcasting Corporation (BBC), their oceangoing counterpart Jacques-Yves Cousteau, and others remade the genre once again as a masculine adventure saga reminiscent of expedition films of the 1910s and '20s in its predilection for action and the exotic. These filmmaker-hosts—the new *auteurs* of the genre, always white, always American or European, and regularly male—sought out animals (and, occasionally, indigenous peoples of the lands in which they filmed) as objects of the camera's gaze rather than quarry of the gun. Rather than making a fast and clean break between pre- and postwar versions of the genre, the films and TV shows they appeared in carried into the postwar period some aspects of ideologies of race, sexual difference, and the exploitability of nature that were present in works by earlier generations of filmmakers. While few women—foremost the primatologist Jane Goodall—lent scientific credibility to the genre, they usually appeared as ethereally feminine exceptions to an authoritatively masculine rule that depended on feats of increasingly spectacular mastery of visual technologies. Shooting on location around the world, using lenses capable of greater focal length and depth of field, tiny endoscopic lenses, infrared lighting used to illuminate nests and dens without disturbing their inhabitants, and other technological developments, these programs produced ever more intimate views of the daily lives of familiar and little-known species. They allowed the audience to enjoy the visual illusion of approaching the animal a little more closely, immersing the viewer a little more fully in the represented habitat with each innovation.[1]

Marked by dramas of conflict between animals, the novelty of discovery, and the heroics of conservationists, wildlife TV may in retrospect seem comfortably compatible with the goals of the commercial networks and early visionaries of the medium. As Lynn Spigel's studies of the incorporation of television into the postwar suburban home indicate, the medium promoted itself as a form of armchair travel and a wealth of vicarious experiences. In 1946, according to Spigel, programmer Thomas Hutchinson lauded TV for providing a "window on the world" through which "the outside world can be brought into the home." This claim was echoed by early TV theorist Charles Siepman, who wrote that "television...is bringing the world to people's doorsteps."[2] While nonfiction nature and wildlife programming may seem to have satisfied these ideals—as well as the positivist faith in direct and untroubled relationships between real and represented worlds, between scrutinized subjects and interpretive texts—its presence on broadcast TV was marked by fluctuation rather than continuity. For a variety of political-economic reasons, the networks abandoned virtually all documentary production by the late 1960s. The wildlife genre might have virtually disappeared, but new Federal Communications Commission (FCC) regulations, which required the networks to use some programming produced by non-network sources in primetime, spawned a surprising flurry of independently made wildlife series in syndication in the 1970s. When this trend played itself out under a combination of economic and regulatory conditions, the Public Broadcasting System (PBS) began to make a place for nature programming, first only occasionally, but by the early 1980s public television briefly but almost entirely controlled the U.S. market for wildlife TV.

Animals on Early TV: Out of the Studio, Into the Zoo

Cataloging all televisual representations of animals, "wild" or otherwise, would be an impossible task due to a dearth of evidence about the earliest broadcasts and the massive quantity of TV images produced, among other factors. Although limited local broadcasting experiments date back to the 1930s, few early broadcasts were kinescoped, and fewer of the kinescopes remain extant. There are virtually no filmed records of live TV broadcasts dating from prior to 1948, but the Ampex videotape recorder (VTR) and magnetic videotape, introduced in 1956, would definitively reverse the ephemerality of early television.[3] However, it is clear that at least domesticated animals appeared on television by the 1940s. Photographs show that trained horses and dogs appeared on variety shows of the 1940s, on stations from W6XYZ on the Paramount lot in Los Angeles, to WRGB in Schenectady, New York.[4] Programming devoted to companion animals and specimens borrowed from local zoos were soon to follow. Economic and technological constraints on early TV shaped a preference for studio settings that could provide necessarily bright lights and bulky equipment, contributing to the development of show-and-tell formats in which trainers, veterinarians, and zookeepers displayed and discussed their charges from stages and tabletops at local stations.

The show-and-tell format was compatible with the quality of image production in early television—black-and-white, low resolution, and low contrast—which influenced a televisual aesthetic described by John Ellis as "stripped-down, lacking in detail," and forming the basis of "the TV emphasis on close-ups of people."[5] Close-ups of animals allowed viewers to discern the pictures being transmitted to their homes, whereas visual styles copied from wildlife filmmaking, with its preferences for panoramic landscapes and long shots of groups of animals, as seen in expedition filmmaking of the 1920s, may have been unintelligible on the small screen in its early days. At many early TV stations, the studio was the only possible source of transmittable programming: ironically, at the BBC's studio in Bristol, later renowned for its cinematographic wildlife work, the first nature shows took place entirely in the studio because the network lacked the means to transmit prefilmed material.[6]

In the United States, the best-known household name in wildlife TV was Marlin Perkins, a largely self-taught zoologist and then-director of the Lincoln Park Zoo who launched his TV career in the show-and-tell format. He first appeared on the air in Chicago in 1945 in fifteen live, half-hour studio-based shows on WBKB, at a time when there may have been as few as 300 active television receivers within the station's range.[7] He would transport an animal from the zoo's collection to the station's studio and discuss its characteristics on the air, giving viewers "tabletop views of animals with chalk talks," using a blackboard to amend his verbal description.[8] Production of Perkins's show ceased in 1947 when he asked for mobile equipment dedicated to the project so that broadcasts could originate from the zoo; WBKB declined the request. Two years later, Chicago's NBC affiliate WNBQ fulfilled Perkins' wish.[9] *Visit to the Lincoln Park Zoo* continued to take a show-and-tell format, but on location, and weekly rather than only occasionally. The show, cohosted by Perkins and newscaster Jim Hurlbut, was a promotional tool for the not-for-profit zoo (run by the city's Parks District), produced at the expense of the station.[10]

By spring 1950, NBC changed the show's name to *Zoo Parade* and secured commercial sponsorship from Jewel Food Stores and Quaker Oats' Ken-L Ration dog food to expand the show to more than two dozen other network stations.[11] The series was one of WNBQ's numerous award-winning children's series, and part of an overall schedule acclaimed for its originality and quality.[12] Unlike Disney's True-Life Adventures, which delivered to the viewer cinematic sightings of seals, bears, lions, and other species on their home turf, Perkins believed that *Zoo Parade* was appealing precisely because the animals were removed from natural—or even naturalistic—habitats and behaviors: "I had encouraged the keepers to make

pets of their animals whenever possible."[13] Using the show-and-tell format, Perkins familiarized audiences with the zoo's residents, making some
of them, such as a gorilla named Bushman, celebrities in their own right.[14]
Individualized and tended by keepers and trainers, the Lincoln Park Zoo
animals that appeared on *Zoo Parade* demonstrated the capacity to which
wild animals could be domesticated, but did not provide the glimpses
at the daily lives of free-roaming animals—their natural feeding, hunting,
herding, mating, and reproducing behaviors—that became staples of the
genre once it left the studio and went into field production a few years
later.

Zoo Parade did provide a virtual tour of the Lincoln Park Zoo's collection, throughout which Perkins offered observations about animal behavior and utility. In a 1951 episode based in the Zoo's Buffalo Barn, local
television personality Tom Duggan substitutes for Perkins's regular cohost.
Perkins and Duggan meet in a pen that houses a water buffalo named
Fatima, who eats from a crib of hay throughout the segment. Cameras on
either side of the animal switch from close-ups of her head, which is
topped with horns that meet in a heart-shaped curl, to medium shots of her
entire body. Perkins discusses the animal and at times interviews Duggan
about his knowledge of it. The discussion is sufficiently revealing about
their attitudes toward animals and toward the range of social settings in
which they may encounter animals as to warrant quoting at some length:

> PERKINS: She comes from India, Indochina, down through the Malay
> onto the Islands, into the Philippine Islands and off down, uh, oh, into
> the islands in the Dutch East Indies down through that country there.
> And over there, they're used as a semi-domesticated beast. There's
> some wild ones, but they're called the carabao in the Philippines. Were
> you over there, Tom, in the war?
>
> DUGGAN: Yes, I was, I was in the Marianas. Saw some of them working
> over there a bit.
>
> PERKINS: Mostly in rice fields, weren't they?
>
> DUGGAN: Yes.
>
> PERKINS: And, any, see any of the children on the back of any of them,
> native children?
>
> DUGGAN: I did once or twice, and saw them pulling carts, but we never
> got as close as I would have liked *not* to.
>
> PERKINS: I think that's very good reason because they're quite friendly
> with the people they know, at least those out there in that country are,
> and they're not so friendly with strangers, particularly foreigners. I
> don't know why it is but a little native child can ride on the neck of

Marlin Perkins and Jim Hurlburt, on location at the Lincoln Park Zoo in *Zoo Parade*. Courtesy of the Lincoln Park Zoo.

one of these animals and loll across the horns and the animal is per-
fectly gentle and docile and just as easy as it can be with the child. And
yet a foreigner comes around, someone the animal doesn't know, and
they can be quite vicious.

While Perkins and Duggan talk, Fatima continues to eat, ignoring both
the guests in her pen and the cameras around her. The World War II theme
recurs twice more in the episode: first, when a keeper brings a donkey into
view, Perkins explains that it has been donated to the zoo from Italy in
recognition of the American role in postwar reconstruction.[15] When the
donkey is led away, Perkins greets the director of the Tokyo Zoo, introduced only as Mr. Koga.[16] Perkins interviews him briefly:

PERKINS: How about your zoo at home? Have you many animals there?

KOGA: Not so many animals.

PERKINS: The war perhaps?

KOGA: Yes, the elephant castle burned, by bomb [inaudible]. Also, animals died during the war.

PERKINS: "What a shame. I suppose you're building up again?

KOGA: Yes, we have many visitors, and after the war, we have enlarged the place . . . and we're going to make new houses for the animals.

PERKINS: Well, that's wonderful, I know that you get big crowds and that just shows that everybody likes animals all over the world.

Perkins's manner is brusque. He appears eager to sidestep the twin unhappy topics of animal death and the destructiveness of war. He bids the visitor farewell and resumes his tour of the Buffalo Barn, stopping at pens holding American bison, a camel, a Brahmin calf, a waterbuck, eland, yak, and llama. Only when discussing North American animals (the bison and the pronghorn) does Perkins focus on their size and speed, respectively, pridefully assessing the animals aesthetically and athletically. When attention turns to other species, they are evaluated pragmatically in terms of their economic value as sources of labor, food, and fiber for clothing. While pointing to the gentle temperaments of most zoo residents, Perkins adopts a different tone alongside the waterbuck, one of only two animals from sub-Saharan Africa included in the episode. He is firm in his resolve that the species is so irredeemably antisocial that it requires strict segregation from others and is unapproachable by humans. He calls the waterbuck "a demon . . . as are almost all of the waterbucks I've seen. We never go in with that animal." The waterbuck frets his horns against the wall of his enclosure while the camera rolls. The Lincoln Park Zoo takes the shape of what Michel Foucault once called a heterotopia, an institutionalized site containing representations of the whole world within its collection.[17] The world it represents, immediately postwar and in the early stages of a civil rights movement, is one in which the war-torn are understood to be grateful to a heroic America; Africa is referenced as a source of untamable threat; and despite what is postulated as universal human love for animals, a xenophobic territorialism is naturalized in the animals (the foreigner-loathing water buffalo; the "demon[-ic]" waterbuck) themselves.

By the mid-1950s the show-and-tell format, whether rendered from a studio, or constrained by zoo barriers, may have seemed quaint and static in comparison to the major networks' fictional action-adventure series, some of which, like *Rin Tin Tin* (1954–59, ABC) and *Lassie* (1954–71, CBS; 1971–74, syndicated), were based on theatrical films featuring animal stars. Jewel and Quaker Oats withdrew sponsorship in response to both *Zoo Parade*'s declining audience share and to redirect their involvement in television away from children's programming.[18] During the series' last two seasons, 1955–57, Mutual of Omaha took over the role of sponsor, and *Zoo Parade* produced some of its first prerecorded episodes on location at zoos throughout the United States. These final seasons also included episodes filmed during Perkins's first trips to East and South Africa, which became the boilerplates for his next television project, *Wild Kingdom,* developed in collaboration with *Zoo Parade*'s producer/director Don Meier. Still, it would be several years before *Wild Kingdom* went into production. In the meantime, Perkins left Chicago (in 1962) to become director of the St. Louis Zoo.[19]

During Perkins's tenure as host of *Visit to the Lincoln Park Zoo* and *Zoo Parade,* other producers developed short-lived nonfiction programs about animals using the show-and-tell format. At least three featured advice on care of companion animals: *Animal Clinic* (1950–51, ABC), a Saturday morning series; *Your Pet Parade* (1951, ABC), aired on Sunday afternoon; and *The Pet Shop* (1951–53, Dumont), a primetime series that originated at WNBQ in Chicago.[20] The in-studio format that brought animals into the station for live show-and-tell persisted on local noncommercial educational television stations at least through the late 1950s. For example, KQED in San Francisco welcomed animal visitors to their studios for *Who's Who at the Zoo.*[21] Short-lived network series *Saturday at the Zoo* (1950, ABC), and *Meet Me at the Zoo* (1953, CBS), broadcast on Saturdays from the Philadelphia Zoo, used the same format as Perkins's shows based at the Lincoln Park Zoo.

Meanwhile, throughout the 1950s, some producers working in the wildlife genre conformed footage shot in more naturalistic conditions, in more exotic locations, to television formats. A handful of nature-travelogue series reached syndication, a booming market after the FCC resumed licensing new stations in 1952, and especially after the Dumont network ceased operations in 1955. Most new stations and former Dumont stations were not yet affiliated with other networks, and they depended heavily on filmed, syndicated programming rather than locally produced, live content to fill their schedules.[22] *Osa Johnson's Big Game Hunt,* a series of twenty-six half-hour shows, was syndicated to independent television stations in 1950.[23] *Big Game Hunt* recombined footage, edited at a rapid clip and emphasizing action scenes, from the Johnsons' films of the 1920s and '30s. Osa herself introduces the episode "Rhinoceros: The Horned Terrors of the Jungle," showing off paintings of African animals and tribal peoples that decorate her home. A male voice narrates the rest of the program, in which, twice, Osa shoots and kills charging rhinos. Once, she shoots and misses an animal that is clearly in retreat. The episode also traverses the Johnsons' encounters with lions, elephants, baboons, and a group of American Boy Scouts who join the expedition briefly in Mombasa. Other episodes were introduced by nature writer (and later, investigator of unexplained phenomena) Ivan T. Sanderson. "Return to Adventure" begins with Sanderson displaying a live aardvark in a studio setting. The rest of the program contains a series of excerpts from films including the Maasai lion hunt from *Simba* (1928), the scene in which the Johnsons introduce Pygmy villagers to cigar-smoking in *Congorilla* (1929), and segments from *Borneo* (1937), as well as footage implying, fallaciously, that the filmmakers are briefly endangered by Solomon Island "headhunters...every one of them an agent of death."

More syndicated expedition programming followed later in the decade, including *Jungle Macabre* (1953), *Kingdom of the Sea* (1956), *The Michaels in Africa* (1959–60), which was filmed and narrated by George and Marjorie Michaels and reprised later as *B'wana Michael* (1966), and *Safariland* (1963). These programs provided viewers with images of companion, captive, and wild animals (and sometimes images of indigenous tribespeople, in the case of the Johnson series, culled from hoary prewar footage rife with racial stereotypes), but American television networks made little room for such material. *Zoo Parade*'s network run was the exception to this rule, and it was the work of independent rather than in-house network producers. In contrast, the BBC began experimenting with animal television programming in 1953, and soon launched *Look* (1954–67), hosted in-studio by Peter Scott. BBC nature programming long retained a sedate tone, more "chatty" than action-packed, which may be attributed not only to its originally limited resources but also to the fact that in Britain, wildlife TV developed from wildlife *radio* programming, which the BBC had launched in 1946 with Desmond Hawkins's *The Naturalist*.[24] In 1954 the BBC added another nature series, *Zoo Quest* (1954–64), the first of many programs to be hosted by David Attenborough. Attenborough undertook quests to far-off places—some of his first episodes were set in South America and Borneo—around the same time that Marlin Perkins began to experiment with location shoots in the final years of *Zoo*

Parade. By 1957 the BBC devoted resources to a separate BBC Natural History Unit that would, in years to come, produce huge quantities of nature content, which since the 1980s has been exported regularly to American public television.[25]

The Walt Disney Company kept wildlife on network TV—at least occasionally—after *Zoo Parade* went off the air in 1957. *Disneyland* premiered on ABC in 1954 to promote the eventual opening of Disney's theme park in Anaheim, California. The series was one of a handful of new productions that marked the film industry's entry into the business of TV and the relocation of network TV production from New York to Hollywood.[26] *Disneyland* established Disney's presence on television as movie attendance was declining dramatically, providing untold promotional value for the park and upcoming theatrical releases, as well as a new outlet for Disney's film library. Theatrical shorts and features, including the True-Life Adventures, were edited to conform to television's one-hour-minus-commercials format, with new production costs limited to brief introductory bumpers for each segment. *Seal Island* (1948) appeared on the third episode of *Disneyland* (aired November 10, 1954), the first to feature a True-Life Adventure or other natural history content.[27] *Disneyland,* which was renamed *Walt Disney Presents* at the start of the 1958–59 season, aired an average of one or two True-Life Adventures each season until the fall of 1961, when the series moved to NBC.[28]

Once *Walt Disney* changed networks, the nonfiction nature films appeared less frequently. In 1963 Marlin Perkins's *Wild Kingdom* premiered on NBC; the network may have sought to eliminate even slight overlap between otherwise distinctive series.[29] The final True-Life Adventure feature, *Jungle Cat* (1960), was broadcast in 1964, and the 1963 short *Yellowstone Cubs* aired in 1965. Since part of the purpose of the Disney presence on TV was to promote its theatrical releases, the True-Life films were predictably shelved once that series ceased production. However, animal protagonists became even more commonplace. Disney had long used animals in its animated features, in *Dumbo* (1941), *Bambi* (1942), *Lady and the Tramp* (1955), *One Hundred and One Dalmatians* (1961), and *Jungle Book* (1967), but in the 1960s the studio turned emphatically to fictional, live-action animal stories. Many featured canines and felines, both domesticated breeds and trained specimens of species usually thought of as wild, as in *The Incredible Journey* (1963), *That Darn Cat!* (1965), *The Ugly Dachshund* (1966), and *Charlie the Lonesome Cougar* (1968), usually as companions for humans.[30] In an exception to Disney convention, *Never Cry Wolf* (1983), a dramatized version of ethologist Farley Mowat's book of the same title, shows wolves as research subjects rather than companions or characters.

In theatrical release, these films entered a market targeting children and families alongside competition such as *Born Free* (1966) and *Living Free* (1972), both the popular dramatic adaptations of Joy Adamson's nonfiction books about a lion pride and its matriarch Elsa, and *Animals Are Beautiful People* (1974), directed by South African filmmaker Jamie Uys. The latter uses many of Disney's most anthropomorphizing techniques in its study of the diversity of animal life in the Namib and Kalahari Deserts.[31] The film's narration liberally imputes human emotion and motivation to animals. A hyena is "lazy"; a mother duck is "a very clever actress"; an ostrich's mate is his "ladylove"; a warthog bathes on his "wedding day" because he "wants to look nice for his bride-to-be." Rhythmic editing and flourishes of familiar classical music dramatize or add humor to scenes.

Marlin Perkins's *Zoo Parade* and Walt Disney's True-Life Adventures sought to entertain viewers with glimpses of animals presented as curious objects and friendly subjects. If the viewer learned something, all the better, so long as scientific veracity and educational intent didn't muss with an appealing presentation or a good story. Still, in the mid-1950s, Disney aired nonfiction wildlife content only sporadically, and *Zoo Parade* struggled to retain sponsors. Meanwhile, a new style of wildlife television program emerged to establish a more secure and prestigious niche for the genre in the United States. These shows would reinscribe the expedition travelogue with new emphases on scientific activity and innumerable facts about animal species, beginning with the first of many documentaries on oceanographic life by Jacques-Yves Cousteau aired on the Ford Foundation–sponsored series *Omnibus* on January 17, 1954.[32]

The Expedition Film, Returned

As nonfiction representations of nature gradually faded from Disney films and TV programs, and as television in general gained greater capacity to leave the studio and engage in field production, two distinct paradigms emerged for wildlife TV of the 1960s. The organizing principle of both was a quest—for a particular animal, and for observations about it from which knowledge could be produced—undertaken by an intrepid naturalist-host, like Cousteau or Perkins, or by a celebrity scientist such as Jane Goodall. One variation on the wildlife-quest program contained the hour-long, occasional specials by Cousteau and by the National Geographic

Society. The other took the form of weekly half-hour series, beginning with *Wild Kingdom* and eventually followed by an array of network and syndicated series. The place of both forms of wildlife TV would be subject to fluctuating demand from television programmers, resulting from the major networks' inconsistent commitment to documentary production.

Cousteau's work, and that of other nature-special producers to follow, was part of a brief torrent of documentary production that peaked in the early 1960s. In the late 1950s broadcast networks began to pour unprecedented resources into documentary production, seeking to deflect regulatory scrutiny and public criticism of industry practices, the vapidness of its content, and its inattentiveness to public affairs. Much of the criticism contended that television ought—in fact, was obligated by the Communications Act of 1934—to serve the public interest but, operating largely within a free-market logic, would be more likely to emphasize light or sensationalistic entertainment. By 1962, capping a brief period sometimes lauded as the "golden age" of the TV documentary, production peaked as ABC, CBS, and NBC produced a combined total of 387 documentary programs in the form of both specials and series. Many, shaped by Cold War politics and paranoia, took as their subject the supposed global "Communist threat" to the "free world," and the superpower standoff.[33]

After 1963 the networks pulled sharply away from documentary production, for an array of possible reasons: unspectacular ratings; disinterest from sponsors and advertisers; the networks' turn to less controversial, higher-rated, less costly "breaking news"; and changes in the political climate and foreign policy after the assassination of President John F. Kennedy.[34] A few science and nature documentaries emerged to fill the gap, such as CBS's *National Geographic Specials* in 1964, and ABC's *Undersea World of Jacques Cousteau* in 1968. Ideologically, their exploration, discovery, and adventure themes reiterated American and Western European dominance of global resources. The era of broadcast critique of establishment views and goals, however brief and anomalous, and however constrained by the networks' commercial imperatives, was over.

Cousteau's first *Omnibus* segment, "Undersea Archaeology," led to regular Cousteau features on the series during the 1956–57 season. Cousteau, who is credited along with Emile Gagan for inventing the aqualung, a device for underwater breathing, conducted expeditions on his ship, the *Calypso,* with funds from the French government and the National Geographic Society. The long-running, irregularly scheduled series of specials *The Undersea World of Jacques Cousteau* premiered with "Sharks" on ABC in

1968. Later, Cousteau produced limited-run series for other networks, including *Cousteau Odyssey* (1977, PBS) and *Cousteau Amazon* (1984, TBS). Whereas Disney eliminated people from the wildlife film, Cousteau returned to the nature genre a human protagonist, transformed since the early twentieth century from a trophy hunter armed with a camera instead of (or in addition to) a gun to a man (and occasionally woman) of science, but in either case an explorer delving into little-known territory to capture—or capture images of—exotic creatures.

Despite the ostensible educational value of Cousteau's adventures, Alexander Wilson points out that in many of his films, "The scientific purpose of the voyages is never all that clear. The crew do basic field work, such as collecting specimens and observing animals, but Cousteau spends a large part of the edited programs on . . . sightseeing: boating, diving, and underwater photography."[35] Similarly, Chandra Mukerji has noted that "basic exploration" of terrain with visual appeal is sometimes

> more interesting to the general public than to the state or science. It is not so absorbed in the world of science as to be inaccessible to outsiders, and it can easily be contextualized in a tradition of romantic storytelling, placed in the popular realm, not just the public one. For many television viewers, Jacques Cousteau made the act of exploration very compelling in just this way. . . . There is excitement, personal glory, and even money to be made by explorers like Jacques Cousteau and his counterparts in this country. . . . But it is not the science that gets the most attention in the social world of scientists because it has limited use in expanding the domains of science.[36]

TV audiences may have enjoyed the adventure and aesthetic qualities of Cousteau's work, even if the data he collected had little or unknown scientific value. Still, Wilson argues that Cousteau's importance goes beyond his innovations in diving and underwater cinematography technologies. The Cousteau formula—"travelogue cum scientific documentary—became the model taken up by National Geographic and other filmmakers in the 1960s and after . . . his style became an industry norm."[37]

Marlin Perkins returned to television in a new format that was similar to Cousteau's travelogue/scientific documentary hybrid. In *Mutual of Omaha's Wild Kingdom* (1963–71, NBC; 1971–88, syndicated), Perkins, accompanied by a cohost, traveled the world for encounters with wild animals. Perhaps the best known of Perkins's sidekicks, Jim Fowler (cohost, 1963–68) was a former professional baseball player whose knowledge of falconry and rare birds of prey were the basis of *Wild Kingdom*'s pilot. Many of their animal quest objects would be tranquilized and tagged for scientific and conservation projects (nicknamed in the industry the "drug-and-tag" film), or rescued from manmade dangers such as floodwaters created by a new dam or other intervention.[38]

The insurance company Mutual of Omaha gained, through its sponsorship of *Wild Kingdom,* a relatively inexpensive means of keeping its name in the public eye, associating itself with a series believed to contain some educational value, and exploiting the genre's tropes of risk and danger to try to prompt in the viewer a mood receptive to the promotion of insurance products.[39] From a set furnished like an office or den, adorned with expedition souvenirs, including a leopard skin stretched across a back wall, Perkins and his cohost introduced each commercial break from the set with a pitch linking something that had just occurred in the program with a Mutual of Omaha product. In the episode "To Catch a Giraffe" (1969), shot in the Wankie (now Hwange) National Park in Zimbabwe (then Rhodesia), Perkins makes the following transition from a chase scene, in which a giraffe to be relocated to another area is lassoed by park rangers riding in a truck, to advertising: "Catching a giraffe is no easy job, and as you've just seen, very complex and extremely difficult. On the other hand, looking for help in choosing the right health insurance protection is easy, as easy as opening the May issue of *Reader's Digest.*" At this point, Perkins takes the magazine from a bookshelf, opens it to a Mutual of Omaha advertisement on the inside front cover, and points out some of the ad's highlights.

Perkins also launched and closed each episode from the set. In "Chase by Copter" (1963), Perkins announces, "Jim and I have just returned from two exciting hunts in the wilds of Canada," and points to their destinations in Ontario and the Canadian Rockies on a map of North America. It is possible that Perkins utilized this visual device in an effort to avoid rambling geographical monologues, like that describing the water buffalo's natural habitat in the "Buffalo Barn" episode of *Zoo Parade,* or because it was already an established convention for launching expedition and wildlife narrative from an image of a map, previously known in *Africa Speaks* (1930), *The Private Life of the Gannet* (1934) and the Disney True-Life Adventures (1948–60). Cutting to location footage, Fowler joins park rangers seeking to tag moose with devices that will allow them to monitor the movements of the animals (Perkins does not appear in these scenes). With the helicopter skimming the lake's surface and closing in on a moose in the water, the park ranger perches on one of its pontoons, leaning out to grasp the fur on the animal's neck and clip the tag to her ear. Fowler tries to tag the next moose pursued by the helicopter pilot, but she swims too close to shore for the aircraft to follow safely; the ranger fails to tag a large male, unable to reach around the rack of antlers to a taggable ear. Pursuing another female, Fowler is successful on his second try, and he concludes the scene in voiceover, "This is a great way to tag moose. All this tagging helps scientists study animal movements and habits more thoroughly. Vital research for all those who live in the animal kingdom." He does not elaborate on what kinds of data might be culled from a record of the animals' movements, and overlooks the fact that the technique seems to be "a great way to tag" only the antlerless female moose, and is impractical for tagging antlered males.

Throughout the episode, the pleasurable excitement of adventures among wildlife are interwoven with the insurer's offer of products associated with financial security: vicariously experienced risk is resolved via a safety net cast to viewers in the comfort of their own homes. In the second segment, Perkins and Fowler meet park rangers in the Rockies, where they intend to capture mountain goats for "scientific study," the purpose of which is explained only when the program switches back to the office set for a word from the sponsor. Fowler begins: "Conservationists at the Alberta game farm will study the mountain goats so that they can learn more about how to care for them and how to help them survive in the wild." Perkins adds, "Care is important to our survival, too. And Mutual of Omaha and Mutual's life insurance affiliate United of Omaha really care." Later, to conclude the episode, Perkins joins a helicopter pilot who tries to herd goats "like an aerial sheepdog" down the mountain. A ranger catches one of the goats by its horns and wrestles it to the ground. Perkins's narration segues to another message from the sponsor: "Trapping mountain goats takes the skill of an expert. Planning your health insurance needs takes the skill of an expert from Mutual of Omaha."

Perkins and his sidekick-of-the-season often appeared on location and interacted physically with animals in what the series called "involvement shows" like "Chase by Copter," but about a third of all *Wild Kingdom* programs, those dubbed the "ecology shows," examined a habitat "without any visible evidence of people."[40] For example, in "Tigers of Sariska" (1966), Perkins and crew are shown scouting locations from which to film tigers at Sariska Wildlife Sanctuary in India, escorted by park rangers. The remainder of the footage focuses on interactions among animals, rather than interactions between animals and humans. These scenes (the mother tiger and her cubs, the mother tiger's several attacks on prey, the cubs and the potentially dangerous cobra and pesky palm civet that they must learn to avoid) are captivating, both in the charming depictions of the inquisitive cubs, and in the deft use of suspense when they or their mother faces adversaries. With important exceptions, *Wild Kingdom* minimized representations of people of color in its frequently African and also Asian-Pacific and South American settings, as if it were possible to accurately represent a human-inclusive ecosystem without considering the impact of humans. Rendering indigenous populations invisible, wildlife TV presented these lands as untroubled, untouched, unaltered nature—and as attractive tourist destinations.[41]

When *Wild Kingdom* did train its attention on indigenous peoples, the scripted narrations often ascribed an endemically primitive nature to its subjects, rendering them as incontrovertibly distinct from and distinctively inferior to Euro-Americans. In the "People That Time Forgot" (1968–71?), Perkins visits an aboriginal tribe in Arnhem Land in Australia's Northern Territory. Much of the episode extols their skills in painting, music, weaving, and hunting, and explores their narrative dance traditions that engage participants in an elaborate dreamworld, but casts them as oddities, even animal-like in their choice of food, their nomadism, and their relative lack of material possessions. Framing the aborigines as premodern seems to allow them to be represented in ways that would usually be disallowed by broadcast standards under other circumstances: that is, women, in skirts, appear bare-breasted; children are naked.[42] (Men wear a loincloth said to be a recent influence of the dress of nearby islanders.) They appear throughout most of the episode as observed subjects, are never shown to engage in conversation with Perkins or the film crew, and interact as peers only when Perkins enlists one of the men to help him try out the throwing stick known as the woomera.

Perkins concludes by informing viewers that the Australian and regional government agencies are striving to help the aborigine "scale the ladder of civilization" through modernization in health care, education, and the rights of full citizenship. This episode was filmed soon after Australia's historic 1967 constitutional referendum that assigned the Commonwealth the power to override state laws, which had exerted total control over aboriginal reservations. These laws effectively barred most aboriginals from exercising their right to vote. They had also allowed for the forcible removal of aboriginal and mixed-descent children from their parental homes for assignment to missionary schools, domestic work, and foster care with white families. It had been long believed by policymakers that these reassignments would facilitate assimilation and, eventually, the managed disappearance of aboriginals as a distinct ethnic group through intermarriage within the white majority population. This eugenic policy produced what is now known as the "Stolen Generation." The Arnhem Land site and its citizenry that Perkins and crew visited were then in the midst of transformative reform of institutionalized racism reaching back into prior centuries, but neither this legacy nor the landmark referendum get a mention. In fact, Perkins voices skepticism about the capacity of these "primitive" users of "Stone Age" tools to wholeheartedly integrate into modern multicultural Australian society: "In time, the aborigine almost certainly must adopt the ways of the modern world. Yet I suspect that whatever external changes he makes, he will in his dreams always remain a true creation of the wild kingdom." Thus consigning the aborigine to the "wild" world of nature rather than to human civilization and culture, *Wild Kingdom* exhibits vestigial traces of the racial ranking that pervaded— maybe even motivated—many prewar examples of the genre.

Not long after the premiere of *Wild Kingdom*, the National Geographic Society began to produce television specials, at a rate of about four per year, first for CBS (1965–73), and then for ABC (1973–75). Founded in 1888 as a club for amateur scientists, the National Geographic Society published a magazine that boomed in circulation after it began using photographs in 1896, adding color in 1926. *National Geographic* grew along with the positivist movement in science, which held that one could learn the truth of the natural and social worlds through observation, and which had incorporated photography and filmmaking as scientific knowledge-gathering technologies.[43] Explorers whose voyages were sponsored by the National Geographic Society carried motion-picture equipment as early as Anthony Fiala's Arctic expedition of 1903; the footage they gathered illustrated live lectures at the Society's headquarters in Washington, D.C.[44] Circulation of the magazine held steady in the 1930s and 1940s, while, true to its stated policy of "avoidance of controversy," the magazine ignored the effects of the Depression but devoted a great deal of coverage to supporting the war effort.[45] Spiking from 2 million in 1957 to 7.2 million subscriptions in 1971, the magazine evaded the civil rights movement and avoided coverage of contemporary Vietnam in favor of archaeological finds in the region.[46] Readers in this period subscribed in great numbers; they began to see the world through National Geographic's eyes on television, too, with the Society's contributions to the series *Omnibus,* and then with its own self-branded *Specials.*

The *National Geographic Specials* covered a broad range of natural history, anthropological, archeological, adventure, and exploration themes.[47] The very first *Special* was *Americans on Everest,* which premiered September 10, 1965. The second was *Miss Jane Goodall and the Wild Chimpanzees* (December 22, 1965), which was filmed by the Baron Hugo van Lawick, who had married Goodall in 1964. Introducing the *Specials* in an issue of the magazine that would reach subscribers just prior to the broadcast of *Americans on Everest,* Melville Bell Grosvenor, then president of the Society and editor of the magazine, promised readers the same high-quality product they expected from other National Geographic endeavors: films to be televised in color "at their brilliant best," under the supervision of "one of the industry's ablest young producer-directors, Robert C. Doyle." Grosvenor pointed out that Doyle is "Harvard-educated," and that he enlisted "award-winning" David L. Wolper Productions in the project, further distinguishing the state-of-the art *Specials* from National Geographic's black-and-white *Omnibus* efforts, endorsing the Ivy League educational capital and the industry credentials of his own staff and their collaborators, and thus reinforcing the Society's status as authority on all matters scientific and aesthetic.[48]

Grosvenor established the *National Geographic Specials* as not only quality television, but also as a kind of visual experience virtually exchangeable with direct experience of the natural world, echoing the "window on the world rhetoric" of early writing on TV. On cinematographer Norman Dyhrenfurth's footage, Grosvenor writes,

> We had seen some of the most extraordinary motion-picture sequences ever filmed. More than that—for such is the power of moving pictures—we felt that we ourselves had climbed Mount Everest.
>
> Every member of your family can share the Everest adventure just as fully on September 10—and succeeding programs will have the same universal appeal.[49]

As lavish as Grosvenor's claims for the series may appear, substantial audiences seem to have agreed. An internal National Geographic Society memo reports that, according to Arbitron ratings, "It is estimated that the film 'Miss Goodall and the Wild Chimpanzees' was viewed in 12 million homes by 25 million people," with a 32 share of the total viewing audi-

Jane Goodall with chimpanzee in *The New Chimpanzees* during the early years at the Gombe National Park in Tanzania.

ence.[50] These numbers are competitive figures for any broadcast, even in the precable TV decades of the three-network oligopoly, and especially impressive for a documentary. In response to the Goodall broadcast, National Geographic received stacks of correspondence—thank-you notes, really—from grateful viewers. Some of the letters comment on both the magazine and the *Specials*:

> I can't tell you how much we enjoy the N.G. and much help it is to our children in their school work.... We much prefer looking at your type program than most of the slush on T.V. —Michigan, January 11, 1966

> Your T.V. Programs sure are wonderful. —California, January 13, 1966

> We immensely enjoyed both of the Society's T.V. offerings this year.... Too often the trash of T.V. is offered early in the evening and the better programs are on after they retire. —Ohio, January 14, 1966

The T.V. program of the Baroness that lived with the chimps produced
5 new members. . . . I believe it [the magazine] should be in every home,
especially where there are school age children. —Pennsylvania, n.d.[51]

The praise heaped on the *National Geographic Specials* by these viewers
has been tempered by criticism. Herb Schiller, for example, has written
that while the Society (and many other American information and
education-oriented institutions) strive to "present themselves as nonideological," such a stance is untenable, and contradicted by a history of implicitly political representations of historical events, people of color, the
environment, animals, and science itself not only in the *Specials*, but in the
Society's immense experience in producing photographic images on these
subjects for over a century.[52] Likewise, Donna Haraway, writing on the
Specials within a larger study of primatology, also describes the *National
Geographic Specials* as sites in which ideologies of postcolonial dependence, race, gender, nature, and science are represented and reinforced.

Haraway understands National Geographic's depictions of "western
scientific primatology as travel and quest literature, wherein the individual hero brings back a prize valuable for the whole community," suggesting that National Geographic's representational strategies are firmly
rooted in nineteenth- and early twentieth-century expedition photography
and film.[53] For example, *Monkeys, Apes, and Man* (1971), which visits several primate research projects led by women, shows how Biruté Galdikas's
three years of habituating Indonesian orangutans to human observation
pay off when a male named Nick approaches the researcher, and, conveniently, the camera, by his own volition. Previous encounters required that
the humans carefully approach the ape. Nick's approach is the climax of
the film's segment on Galdikas, who achieves her prize—a habituated
orangutan—and presents it to viewers on film.

Haraway also demonstrates that *National Geographic Specials* have engaged at times in a pattern of disturbing racial representations and omis-
sions. She points out that indigenous Africans are regularly assigned a status legible to the viewer as subhuman, while the "selfhoods" of higher
primates are lovingly elaborated. Haraway describes a shot in *Monkeys,
Apes, and Man* that shows Dian Fossey in the company of "an African man
playing a wind instrument for her and his wife and child," while the
voiceover narration claims that Fossey is the "one human being" at her
mountain gorilla sanctuary. Throughout the film, white researchers are
carefully identified, and it is clear that naming and constructing biog-

raphies for primates is key to the project, but Rwandans working at the sanctuary remain mostly nameless figures in the background.[54]

Haraway offers *Gorilla* (1981), filmed at the Mountain Gorilla Project in Rwanda, as further evidence of the struggle between scientific and conservationist goals that have become dependent on ecotourist income for subsistence, and a "latent logic of racism" that either ignores indigenous Rwandans altogether or treats local farmers as pests "encroaching" on gorilla habitat.[55] Primatologists Amy Vedder and William Webber of the Bronx Zoo's Wildlife Conservation Society founded the Mountain Gorilla Project in the 1970s, which is sustained by ecotourist dollars as a means of protecting their habitat against logging and agricultural expansion.[56] In *Gorilla*, Vedder escorts tourists into photographic range of the gorillas, and Webber lectures Rwandese schoolchildren, "none of [whom] has ever seen a gorilla," on the importance of conservation. Haraway describes the film's final image, "a little white child's hand reaching through the mesh netting of a cage to touch a tiny black gorilla baby inside," as positing white intervention as the gorilla's only hope for survival. According to Haraway, the image "recodes the colonial discourse of race onto a post-colonial restrained African animal and an exploring Western human." The gorilla occupies the complex and contradictory role of Other, a figure so "primitive, authentic," and "wildly free," so charismatic, so dangerous, and yet so fragile that she must be subordinated.[57]

National Geographic followed *Miss Goodall and the Wild Chimpanzees* with another full-length documentary on Jane Goodall's research, *Among the Wild Chimpanzees* (1984). (It was Goodall's third appearance in a *National Geographic Special,* as she was one of the featured primatologists in *Monkeys, Apes and Man.*) *Among the Wild Chimpanzees* reuses footage from the earlier programs to construct a biography tracing her interest in animals to childhood, and even to a favorite toy, a stuffed chimpanzee. Haraway describes Goodall's transformation from an innocent "white girl scientist" who arrived at the Gombe Game Preserve (later a national park) with her mother as chaperon, and, as her mentor Louis Leakey demanded, "unbiased" by scientific training. She gained acceptance from both local villagers and the chimpanzees, becoming both "virgin-priestess" and "priestess-scientist" with an almost magical capacity to transcend cultural differences and make herself part of the Gombe environment so different from her London upbringing.[58] Haraway observes that in *Monkeys, Apes and Man* Goodall's "virgin-priestess" status gave way to her image as legitimate scientist (having gained a Ph.D.), a wife with a noble title (having married the Dutch baron and wildlife filmmaker van Lawick), and a mother raising her son in the same environment in which her research subjects also struggle to raise their young chimps. By the third film, Goodall is also a woman who has survived tremendous heartbreak, as her beloved chimps have suffered a polio epidemic, and several violent episodes result in the deaths of several adult and infant apes.

Haraway's analysis of the Goodall *Specials* as documents of an idealized feminine intimacy with nature, and a web of emotional relationships and fantasies, is persuasive. The *Specials* popularized not only Goodall as celebrity-scientist with a mythic stature that Haraway describes as a combination of "Girl Guide," "virgin-priestess[-scientist]," and "Wise Woman" tropes.[59] They also delivered to mass audiences Goodall's discoveries about the chimpanzee, the primate most closely related to humans, its diet, communication, tool-making and -using, and aggression. Audiences were obviously fascinated by this new knowledge, if uncertain regarding how to use it other than as a form of distinction, proof of our own good taste in reading material and television programs. Despite that distinction, audiences were perhaps, inured to the sometimes troubling racial and gendered representations that still remain conventionalized within a genre that was then and is now largely the work of First World professionals in Third World settings. (A subsequent generation of wildlife filmmaking, discussed in chapter 4, provides a more explicitly instructional model for the recasting of knowledge about nature and nonhuman animals into insight into ourselves.)

Despite new and often spectacular innovations within the genre by Disney and later, Perkins, Cousteau, and National Geographic, some short-lived wildlife programs of the 1960s continued to follow *Zoo Parade*'s show-and-tell paradigm. For example, *Zoorama* broadcast from the San Diego Zoo in 1965, first only locally, and later on CBS, with host Bob Dale.[60] *Wild Cargo* (1962–63, syndicated) explored how animals are captured for zoos, bridging the "at the zoo" and "in the wild" models; the series returned in 1965 under the title *Capture*. Still, these shows, mostly filling half-hour timeslots, remained relatively rare until the FCC codified Financial Interest and Syndication Rules (Fin-Syn, or FISR) and Prime Time Access Rules (PTAR) that took effect in 1971. The "Fin-Syn" rules, intending to introduce new competition into a tightly oligopolistic industry, required part of early primetime to be filled by shows produced by nonnetwork sources, unless that hour could be filled with network-produced educational programming.[61] Under the new rules, syndicated programming flourished; to producers seeking to ride the swell of environmental awareness being embodied in both grassroots activism (such as the first Earth Day, 1970) and public policy (the Marine Mammal Protection Act of 1972, the Endangered Species Act of 1973, and the Convention on International Trade in Endangered Species of Wild Fauna and Flora of 1973), wildlife programming seemed a timely content category to develop.

The wildlife series that flourished during the syndication boom not only fulfilled new regulatory obligations and trends in potential audience interests, but did so at relatively low cost. Some, like *Wild Kingdom,* usually sent film crews on assignment. Others reduced costs by cobbling together footage purchased from independent film crews or from stock footage archives.[62] Reportedly, one of the most prolific producers of syndicated wildlife series, Bill Burrud, completed some half-hour episodes for "as little as $12,500" each.[63] These cost-cutting strategies impacted the kinds of narratives that these shows could contain. In response to criticism of the True-Life Adventure style from scientific communities—and to keep production costs down—most of the footage made for television depicted general animal behaviors and environments, rejecting Disney's expensive and time-consuming method of following a specific animal group for months or years to accumulate enough footage to create anthropomorphized portraits of individualized animals. Filmmakers "found it easier to produce scientific documentaries than to try to do what Disney had done," although the balance between "science" and drama in the final product often tilted toward the latter.[64]

Wild Kingdom was both the first and the most successful of the half-hour nonfiction wildlife shows that used location footage on the regular basis. The series enjoyed a lengthy network connection before entering the syndication market, and in syndication achieved relatively high ratings and wide distribution. In 1982, for example, it was the fifth-ranked syndicated program in the United States and sold to TV networks in thirty-seven other nations.[65] However, it was not the only series in this format, nor the only series whose premise depended in part on the credibility of its host as an authority on animals. *Animal Secrets* ran for a single season on Saturday afternoons (1966–67, NBC) and was rerun well into 1968. Like *Wild Kingdom*'s Marlin Perkins, *Animal Secrets*' host was a credentialed expert in the field, Loren C. Eisley, an anthropologist from the University of Pennsylvania. Each episode investigated a phenomenon of animal behavior, such as migration or communication. The Audubon Society, which like National Geographic (and, decades earlier, the American Museum of Natural History) drew on its institutional reputation as a source of information on animals and conservationist sensibility, produced seventy-eight episodes of *Audubon Wildlife Theatre* (1971–72, syndicated) as a joint venture of ABC and Twentieth Century–Fox. Other incarnations of the half-hour nonfiction format featured the recognizable voices of popular male actors in place of on-screen, expert hosts.[66] Many did not send crews on assignment, but depended heavily on stock footage. They replaced the familiar, Perkins-style authority who may have actually been on location where footage was collected with a usually unseen and invariably masculine voice of authority, disconnected from but responsible for giving coherence to the images on screen.

During the same period, several fictional adventure series featuring wild animals also appeared. In *Flipper* (1964–67, NBC) and *Gentle Ben* (1967–69, CBS), a dolphin and an American black bear, respectively, became the companions, even helpmates of families headed by a game warden or park ranger, each a kind of unusual equivalent of *Lassie*. *Daktari* (1966–69, CBS), starring Marshall Thompson as a veterinarian at a conservation park in Tanzania, and *Cowboy in Africa* (1967–68, ABC), in which a rodeo star played by Chuck Norris took up a wildlife management career in Kenya, offered fictional protagonists enjoying many of the same heroic adventures as Marlin Perkins. Ivan Tors Productions, an independent film and television company specializing in adventure themes, developed many of these shows, as well as feature films including *Flipper* (1963) and the sequel, *Flipper's New Adventure* (1964). While *Daktari* and *Cowboy in Africa* were set in Africa, both shows were filmed at Africa, U.S.A., a private animal park co-owned by Tors near Los Angeles. On the coattails of these successful series, the Australian production *Skippy, the Bush Kangaroo* (1966–68) entered syndication in the United States in 1969.

By 1980 demand for wildlife filmmakers' product from television programmers had declined. The boom prompted by the Fin-Syn and Prime Time Access Rules lasted only about a decade while the rules themselves persisted until the early 1990s.[67] Steinhart points to several causes:

> For one thing, the cost of making wildlife films has increased while the cost of some competing forms of entertainment has gone down. For another, the ratings game has become more serious. And perhaps most important, wildlife films are so good and have increased so much that it is harder and harder to produce new and interesting material.[68]

Still, the networks did not abandon wildlife programming entirely; they tried to fold it into other genres. Celebrities, more than wildlife, were the focal point of *Those Amazing Animals* (1980–81, ABC), a primetime series on animal behavior hosted by Burgess Meredith, Priscilla Presley, and Jim Stafford, with regular appearances by Joan Embrey of the San Diego Zoo, Jacques-Yves Cousteau, and the underwater cinematographers Ron and Valerie Taylor. A few years later, Alan Thicke hosted *Animal Crack-ups* (1987–90, ABC), a game show featuring celebrity panelists and animal footage from the Tokyo Broadcasting Station.

Going Public: Televisual Nature, PBS Culture

While the commercial networks scaled back their commitment to the wildlife genre and to documentary in general, science, nature, and exploration programming found a home on public TV. With its founding in 1967 PBS became "the principal broadcasting outlet for documentaries," which had been rapidly disappearing from the commercial networks.[69] By the early 1980s virtually all television documentary, including representations of nature and wildlife, that explored their subjects in any depth were aired on PBS affiliates, beginning with the science-oriented *NOVA*, launched in 1974. Later, the *National Geographic Specials*, which had begun on commercial television, moved to public television, as a project of WQED in Pittsburgh, from 1975 to 1994.[70] The *Specials* reigned as one of PBS's most successful projects: when the series celebrated its twenty-fifth anniversary in 1990, it could claim twenty of the top twenty-five highest ratings ever scored by PBS.[71] In 1982 naturalist and BBC executive David Attenborough's series *Life on Earth* aired over the course of several weeks, followed by his *The Living Planet: A Portrait of the Earth* in 1985 and *The First Eden* in 1987.[72] Also in 1982, two new PBS series, *Nature* and *Wild America*, began to provide regular weekly timeslots for nature and wildlife programming. After the genre became almost fully concentrated on public television, in the mid-1980s commercial TV activity in nature began to renew, escalating in the 1990s. In the meantime, public television provided audiences with most of the available nature programming and documentary of all kinds for several years.

PBS's first science-oriented series, *NOVA*, debuted in 1974. A project of WGBH in Boston, *NOVA* remains the longest-running series in the documentary format to appear on U.S. television. Producer Michael Ambrosino of WGBH, working temporarily for the BBC in London and already experienced in exploration and science specials for PBS, was inspired by programming strategies on the BBC-2 channel, which made science content a priority; bringing this value stateside would remedy what Ambrosino called PBS's "appalling gap." Second, it organized a flexible scheduling regime dubbed a "strand" for its new science series *Horizon. NOVA* copied the strand format (as did subsequent PBS series), interspersing within a season's programming both new titles and some previous seasons' reruns, and solo productions alongside coproduced and acquired titles.[73] Under the format, which allows for flexible budgeting and cost-sharing, WGBH has produced about ten original *NOVA* hours per year, supplemented with acquired titles. The BBC provided not only a model for the series but also, through ongoing coproductions and programming exchanges, some of its content. *NOVA*'s premiere program, "The Making of a Natural History Film," was produced for *Horizon;* WGBH acquired its rights for broadcast in the United States. The film showcased the methods of the production company Oxford Scientific Films in their contract work for the BBC.[74] Nature and wildlife topics would occupy a constant presence among *NOVA*'s wide-ranging menu of subject matters, from anthropology to airline safety and psychology to physics.

Whereas the *NOVA* series and National Geographic's handful of *Specials* each year addressed a range of science and natural history subject matter, PBS's *Nature,* which premiered in 1982, defined its content parameters more narrowly. Scheduled weekly in an hour-long timeslot and produced by New York City's PBS affiliate WNET, *Nature* has enjoyed a long-term contract guaranteeing U.S. rights to its choice of four BBC Natural History Unit programs, out of about twenty produced annually.[75] *Nature* has frequently been touted as the locus for the very best wildlife filmmaking, as in this *New York Times* review of *Nature*'s six-hour series *Realms of the Russian Bear* (coproduced by the BBC, 1992), couched within acknowledgment of the genre's frequent reiteration of visual clichés: "Even people who feel that if you've seen 10 snowpeaked mountain ranges or 20 fish-filled lakes you've seen enough should find themselves impressed by the fine photography that has distinguished 'Nature' from its beginning."[76]

Rather than mimicking National Geographic's focus on scientific projects involving animal observation, or human-animal interaction, *Nature* often borrows a strategy rendered "classic" in Disney's True-Life Adventures and recapitulated in *Wild Kingdom*'s "ecology shows": remove people from nature. The absence of visual cues, such as vehicles, clothing, or hairstyles that might lend a dated quality to the footage, aids in constructing the footage's timelessness, both ensuring its reusability in future projects and helping the filmmaker evade controversies over land use or issues like human poverty that might turn away audiences looking to be entertained or uplifted. According to Jennifer Price, *Nature*'s premiere program, a three-part series on the Andes called *Flight of the Condor* by Hugh Miles, begins with an introduction by narrator George Page, who describes its setting as "an empty land . . . as still as if it were the beginning of time." In "human-free" *Nature*, Price argues, nature is not only "unchanging" and "timeless," but it is taken for granted that it is the same everywhere: Page's introduction was filmed on a Southern California—not Andean—mountain.[77]

The preference for unpeopled landscapes also bolsters an implicitly positivist belief in the veracity of direct observation, that is, in the camera's capacity to represent reality. This idea is contrary to critical analysis spanning several decades which argues that photo- and cinematography depend on selection, point of view, framing, narrativization by means of editing, and interpretation. Despite the on-screen participation of both series host Page and Moscow State University natural history professor Nikolai Drozdov as "tour guide" for *Realms of the Russian Bear,* Charles Siebert argues that in *Nature* the "makers' hands are kept out of the frame so as not to break the tension . . . between the indifference and apparent arbitrariness of occurrences in the natural world and our own civilized stays against it."[78] In other words, rather than representing relationships, conflictual or otherwise, between natural environment and human society, the strategy of minimizing human presence in wildlife film seems to invite viewers to forget that their view of nature is mediated, even as the very act of nature spectatorship underscores its distance and unfamiliarity.

While many *Nature* programs have utilized the "classic" unpeople form, others programs present their subjects through the experiences of a scientist or filmmaker. *Echo of the Elephants* (1993), directed and photographed by Martyn Colbeak, is based on the observations of Cynthia Moss, director of the Ambroseli Elephant Research Project in Kenya. The *Christian Science Monitor* praised the film as "truly a story about elephants, not about someone studying elephants."[79] *Incredible Suckers* (1995), directed by Robin Brown for Oxford Scientific Films as a coproduction of Thirteen/WNET and the BBC, does not attempt to mask, downplay, or ignore the role of the observing filmmaker. In fact, it celebrates the nature filmmaker as an explorer and a master of mediating visual technologies. Michael deGruy photographed and coproduced the film, which comprises an anthology of encounters with cephalopods, the genus that includes octopus, squid, and cuttlefish. *Nature*'s host/executive producer George Page, standing on a dock, introduces the program with commentary that acknowledges the work of deGruy and the work of his photographic extensions:

> Mike deGruy is one of *Nature*'s most intrepid filmmakers. He'll do almost anything to get the shots he wants, especially if they've never been filmed before. But when he decided to document the lives of squid and octopus, he faced a special challenge. They're hard enough to find, much less film. Mike came back with some incredible pictures. But so did this machine.

As Page ends these remarks, "this machine"—a camera contained within a submarine—is pulled vertically out of the water by a crane. After opening titles, Page's voice introduces over a montage of images of various cephalopod species.

The camera lingers on a nearly silhouetted image of deGruy, in diving gear, swimming among fish, then around the submerged camera, apparently testing its controls. DeGruy describes his relationship to the visual apparatus in more detail:

> I've always been passionate about cephalopods, and twenty years ago, that passion first brought me here, because Palau is where nautilus live. Not up here near the surface but down there, a thousand feet into the abyss. It's impossible for me to dive that deep. But Homeboy can. This remote-controlled camera vehicle was last used to explore the sunken *Titanic*. Homeboy's job is to bring back the first pictures of nautilus, the living fossils, in their natural surroundings. Homeboy's unique images travel up the little sub's umbilical cord to our support boat a thousand feet overhead.

DeGruy and partner Bruce Carlson continue to refer to the camera by its nickname "Homeboy" (a choice rife with connotations of racialized camaraderie and territorialism) as they operate the control panel in their boat's hull, directing the trajectory of the camera and monitoring the footage it collects.

Homeboy operates as the filmmakers' visual prosthesis, a proxy that enters previously unseen waters, an extension of their bodies that ventures safely into dark waters where their physical bodies could not survive. DeGruy acknowledges the distance between himself and the camera— while he dives "*up here* near the surface," the camera reaches "*down there*, a thousand feet into the abyss." The camera and boat are connected not by an audiovideo cable but by an "umbilical cord"—a live connection from the possessor of the gaze to the technology enabling it. DeGruy's display of Homeboy's images of the nautilus, staged as if the scene were being broadcast live, is interrupted when suddenly the boat begins to take on water and quickly sinks. The accident is documented in a series of still photographs apparently taken from another boat; the narrator explains that a nearby fishing boat rescued DeGruy and his crew. DeGruy claims, "We lost everything, including the unique nautilus footage," causing a six-month delay in the project while they replaced lost equipment and retook the nautilus footage.

DeGruy's next location is off the Australian coast, where he seeks to document cuttlefish behaviors. Again, he frames this sequence as his quest for new knowledge recorded as evidence on film. The crew manages to film cuttlefish mating practices, in which the male passes a sperm sac into the female's mantle cavity near her oviduct. She does not use the sperm immediately but rather stores it until she becomes fertile, and the male remains with her to protect her from advances by other males. When the male whose sperm the female carries loses a battle with a challenger, the new male uses one of his ten arms—the hectocotylus, referred to in the program as, more colloquially, his "funnel"—to reach into her cavity and sweep it clear of her previous mate's sperm before depositing his own. Bits of white sperm from the defeated male's sac, which bursts as the new male disposes of it, disperse in the water around the cuttlefish pair. Positing the practice of filmmaking as an important means of observing animal behavior, deGruy calls the practice a "shrewd maneuver [which] no one knew about until we filmed it." But he is at least as amazed by what happens afterward: "I was surprised by the touching and caressing from the male cuttlefish. Are these animals more complex than they seem?" he asks, as the final shot of this sequence shows the male hovering just above the female, his tentacles stroking her gently. DeGruy commends the male's drive to mate, to reproduce, and to prevent other males from reproducing, so strong that it may entail aborting a prior insemination, as "shrewd," implying clever, strategic self-interest, but he doesn't seem surprised by it. The male's behavior is framed as normal if previously unknown in this species, an event that deGruy is simply pleased to have discovered and documented. In contrast, the animal's capacity to pair-bond, engage in nonsexual physical contact, or protect its investment of sperm for a period of time after the act of mating, astonishes deGruy. He leaves the cuttlefish

Male cuttlefish begins to transfer his sperm sac into the female's mantle cavity in *Incredible Suckers*.

segment without answering the questions it raises regarding animal drives, intelligence, or emotion; the documentary offers striking images, but not necessarily illuminating interpretations of them.

Later, deGruy films squid near the Cayman Islands with a custom-made camera that has infrared-light capability and intensifies the scarce light at great depths. Again, he credits these technological innovations for the crew's ability to observe and document "behaviors that were virtually impossible to record before." He then joins marine biologists at the Monterey Bay Aquarium Research Institute, on California's Pacific Coast, aboard a boat equipped to monitor a camera mounted within an unmanned submarine, capable of submersion nearly a mile to the floor of the nearby Monterey Canyon in the Pacific Ocean. DeGruy addresses the scientist directing the submarine's movement as if the camera has become a cybernetic extension of their bodies. When the camera locates a particularly interesting species, deGruy asks, "Shall we hang out here and see how it behaves?" The men seem to sense that their visual reach, displayed on a series of video monitors above the control panels that guide the sub, is as easily mediated by a camera submerged over 1,200 meters below the boat, as by a camera they would usually control with their hands or hoist on a shoulder. "Here," where "we hang out," is not their physical location in the hull of the boat but the place to which their vision is displaced. In this sequence, as in others, *Incredible Suckers* foregrounds, even personifies, the specialized technologies of underwater cinematography as a tool of exploration and discovery, producing data of unknown value to marine biologists. Perhaps their findings, as Mukerji suggested of Cousteau, are primarily of potential appeal to the general public who may be amazed by the visual spectacle or the oddity of these species, or excited by the drama of both the failed and successful expeditions.

In the mid-1990s, as if the visual spectacle of the animal kingdom were not enough to attract viewers, *Nature* began to feature an occasional celebrity-driven wildlife filmmaking series. When *Nature* was first broadcast in 1982, it faced little competition. After the Discovery Channel launched on cable in 1985 with nature and science as flagship programming themes, the wildlife genre began to return to commercial networks. The audience for wildlife programming, once constrained to public television as virtually the sole outlet for the genre, now had many more options; movie stars may have been an incentive to keep them loyal to PBS stations. The series, *In the Wild,* is made by Tigress Productions, a company based in London and Bristol, as a joint venture of WNET, the BBC, and ITV. Over the years, its titles have included *Wolves with Timothy Dalton* (1994), *Pandas with Debra Winger* (1995), *Orangutans with Julia Roberts* (1998), *Baby Animals with Whoopi Goldberg at the San Diego Zoo* (1999), *Wild Horses of Mongolia with Julia Roberts* (2000), *White Elephants of Thailand with Meg Ryan* (2002), and *Polar Bears with Ewan MacGregor* (2002), among others.

While *Nature* has sought out species ranging from the rarest (*The Panda Baby,* 2001), those most difficult to film *(Incredible Suckers),* the most farflung (in the two-part *Antarctica: The End of the Earth I—Katabatic* and *II—Iceberg,* 1999), and the nearest to the constituency of its sponsoring local PBS affiliate, WNET (*The Wild Side of New York,* 2001), another PBS series long devoted particular attention to the wildlife of the United States. *Wild America,* produced and hosted by wildlife filmmaker Marty Stouffer, is unique in the history of wildlife-oriented animal shows in its emphasis on locations and species found in the United States, focusing even more intensively on North American animals than Disney's True-Life Adventures. The series began appearing regularly on PBS-affiliate stations about the same time as *Nature,* in 1982. PBS paid $14.85 million for rights to 110 half-hour episodes, renewed in 1994 at a cost of over $3 million.[80] "The Babies" episode, aired in March 1987, earned a Nielsen rating of 14.7, ranking it among PBS's highest-rated shows to date.[81]

The episode *Wild Dogs* (1982) typifies *Wild America*'s didactic approach.[82] Appearing on-screen in a snowy woodland that seems to be the setting of the program's first segment, Stouffer addresses the viewer directly as he introduces the wild dog family as misunderstood, unnecessarily feared, and sometimes exterminated. Voiceover narration begins as, in long shot, he strides through the snow toward his animal quest object. The next shot shows a coyote standing in a clearing, then cuts to an image of Stouffer, who has found his subject, peering through binoculars at it. The half-hour program contains brief segments on the coyote and several species of wolves and foxes. Most scenes depict hunting or caring for pups, and Stouffer points out social behaviors that liken wild species to domestic breeds, seeking to render them more familiar and less threatening. When discussing their parenting behaviors, which appear to include affection, social learning, and play, Stouffer cautions that his interpretations "may be giving this wolf human traits," alerting the viewer to the possibility that humans fancifully project themselves into interpretations of animal behavior. This self-reflexive statement about anthropomorphizing or allegorizing animal behavior in human terms suggests that Stouffer is striving to consider animals on their own terms, and to avoid describing them in the human terms for which the Disney True-Life Adventures were often criticized.

Elsewhere, Stouffer articulates quite another point of view, extrapolating readily from animal to human behavior, a tactic common to the sociobiological methods of theorizing that dominated the animal sciences by the early 1980s. Without qualification, he describes the wolves' social hierarchy as a paradigm universal to all living creatures, presumably humans as well as nonhuman animals: "just as in any group, there are leaders and followers. In the wolf pack, an individual's status is constantly displayed by dominant or submissive body language." Like Mike deGruy's interpretations of cuttlefish behavior in *Incredible Suckers*, Stouffer's reactions to exertions of power and self-interest are treated as natural and inevitable and universal, but nurturing—even if it can be understood as benefiting one's offspring, rather than true altruism—elicits surprise and uncertainty. The episode ends with Stouffer indoors, again using direct address to make a plea for the protection of wild dogs.

In less than forty years, from Marlin Perkins's first appearance on a local Chicago station, to the early 1980s, by which time PBS's *NOVA, National Geographic, Nature,* and *Wild America* aired most of the wildlife content found on television, the genre underwent a series of transformations shaped largely by aspects of the television industry itself. Emerging in the 1940s and 1950s in a show-and-tell format confined to the studio or a static set at a zoo, wildlife was an inexpensive and incidentally educational diversion for early TV audiences. As the profit imperative reformulated the schedules of the commercial networks in the next decade, and changing political and regulatory climates brought the short-lived, so-called golden age of the public affairs documentary to an end in 1963, variations of the wildlife paradigm became established TV genres. In the form of both half-hour, often syndicated series, and hour-long network specials, wildlife in the 1960s tended to be based on the exploratory and scientific quests of the likes of Perkins, Jacques-Yves Cousteau, Jane Goodall, and other scientists, naturalists, and conservationists afield in their subjects' habitats. These quests would grant the celebrity-scientists, filmmakers, and media brands associated with them rarefied status as mediums through which viewers experienced or imagined themselves to be experiencing adventures in the natural world from the comfort of their living rooms. The status of this realization of the genre would become a commonly shared cultural referent, immediately available to viewers. In HBO's adaptation of Tony Kushner's play *Angels in America* (2003), Harper Pitt (played by Mary Louise Parker), struggling with Valium dependency, hallucinates herself into an Antarctic setting that she recognizes as so immensely pleasurable—and familiar—that it could only be her very "own *National Geographic Special.*"

While the quest version of the genre was never abandoned, and carried forward new versions of the gendered and racialized dimensions of the genre's prewar expressions, since the 1970s TV's wildlife producers turned toward views of nature that often excised humans. If Disney's True-Life Adventures two decades prior used this technique to encourage viewers to identify with their films' animal protagonists, resulting in more emphatically anthropomorphized animal characters and more biographical narratives, the independent producers selling to the bullish syndication market had an added incentive: they could slash production costs by assembling programs from stock footage, rather than filming each episode anew based on the host's recent travels. When the syndication boom collapsed, most wildlife programming—and most documentary of all kinds—could be found only on public television. A range of wildlife formats was now fully codified—the show-and-tell, the scientific quest, and the classic form, with its timeless, unpeopled animalscapes—but their near-disappearance from commercial TV would soon be reversed. By the mid-1980s, a television revolution of sorts was underway, one that would require huge quantities of new, rerun-able, and inexpensive programming as channel capacity increased in the United States, and as formerly public or state-run television systems worldwide privatized and commercialized. The deployment of animal genres, which return with a new generation of celebrity-naturalists, as a means of both niche programming in the national market and expansion into global markets in the last two decades of the twentieth century, is the subject of the next chapter.

3

Wildlife, Remade for TV

> GRACE: To be honest, I'm not really a big fan of
> the museum. The Louvre.... I went through
> that sucker in a half hour at a dead run. Give
> me *The Pet Psychic* any day of the week.
> ELEANOR: Is that, uh, some sort of a cartoon
> where a dog can read minds?
> GRACE: What, do you live under a rock? *The Pet
> Psychic* is—okay, wait, I don't want to
> oversell this. It is the greatest TV show *ever!*
> —*Will and Grace*

In the 1970s and well into the 1980s, nonfiction wildlife filmmaking reached American television audiences largely in the form of low-cost, syndicated half-hours such as *Mutual of Omaha's Wild Kingdom,* and highbrow series and specials such as *Nature* and *National Geographic,* featured by the Public Broadcasting System (PBS). That is, wildlife constituted a marginalized segment of TV production and distribution that could be found by viewers only on the fringes of an industry dominated by three commercial networks. By the end of the 1980s, the cable network Discovery Channel had proven that documentary could become the centerpiece of an innovative and profitable program line-up. Surprisingly, the wildlife genre itself would not only be a flagship of Discovery's programming strategy, but also part and parcel of a widespread proliferation of animal TV in various forms. This new array of televisual representations of animals would contain an equally wide array of meanings written with the animal image, and even contain competitive and conflicting meanings in which the animal would be deployed variously as object, as agent, and as malleable sign.

The new prominence of animals on TV resulted substantially from a matrix of changing conditions in the television industry that influenced how both broadcast and cable networks financed, scheduled, and distributed TV programming and, even more broadly, how they conceived of TV form and content. In the 1980s and 1990s cable and satellite-TV subscriptions increased at a rapid pace in the United States.[1] The mass broadcast audience, once clustered around a few oligopolistic channels, fragmented into an array of audiences served by networks targeting particular demographic niches. Many, relative to the broadcasters, were small and small-budget operations that depended on economical means of acquiring or producing vast new quantities of programming to fill the new networks' schedules. The venerable broadcasters lost viewers—and therefore advertising revenue—to these new competitors, leading them to try to cut costs.[2] Cable and broadcasting alike turned in varying degrees to nonfiction genres, including so-called reality formats, that typically cost a fraction of dramatic and comedy series; many networks also sought to expand into newly privatizing media markets abroad.

Discovery played a large role in repositioning nonfiction, in developing hybrid reality subgenres, and in recommodifying wildlife programs that commercial broadcasters had all but phased out as irreversibly formulaic and unprofitable; the company also participated vigorously in the trend toward media globalization. Following suit, in the 1990s, other networks resuscitated and revamped animal programming across the TV spectrum. Most prominently, in 1996 Discovery teamed with the BBC to launch Animal Planet, devoted entirely to companion animals and wildlife. The channel features pet-care shows and classic wildlife filmmaking, but much of its programming casts animals in game shows, talk shows, talent shows, athletic contests, and docudramas. A year later, in 1997, National Geographic countered with its own channel featuring science, nature, environmental, and adventure programming, first in the United Kingdom, then moving quickly into other global markets, including the United States in early 2001. Broadcast networks and cable-programming systems not previously associated with animal genres experimented with reality-based series, miniseries, and specials and turned at times to animals, for *The World's Most Dangerous Animals* (1996–97, CBS), *When Animals Attack* (1996–97, Fox), *Man vs. Beast* (2003, Fox), *Miracle Pets* (2001–4, PAX TV), and *Wildboyz* (2003–, MTV).

Animal TV settled into its new status as a significant popular culture trend, frequently referenced in other genres. Nickelodeon based a children's cartoon—*The Wild Thornberrys* (TV series, 1998–2003; feature film, 2002)—

on the adventures of a wildlife-filmmaking family. Daughter Eliza (voiced by Lacy Chabert) enjoys the ability to communicate with animals, especially a chimpanzee named Darwin (Tom Kane). In 2002, the sitcom *Will and Grace* (1998–, NBC) incorporated a tongue-in-cheek commendation to Sonya "The Pet Psychic" Fitzgerald's Animal Planet series (2002–4). In the episode "The Needle and the Omelet's Done" (Nov. 14, 2002), Grace (played by Debra Messing) declares to her fiancé's mother, Eleanor (Judith Ivey), that *The Pet Psychic* is "the greatest TV show *ever!*" Feature films have also pointed to the new ubiquity of animals on TV. In the low-budget thriller *Open Water* (2004, directed by Chris Kentis), a harried urban couple is left adrift by all-too-relaxed charter-boat guides who muddle the headcount at the end of a scuba-diving tour. After their first shark sighting, a frightened Susan (Blanchard Ryan) begs husband Daniel (Daniel Travis) for wildlife TV–derived knowledge: "What do we do if it comes back? Do we splash or do we stay still? You're the one who watches 'Shark Week.'" And the comedy *The Life Aquatic with Steve Zissou* (2004, directed by Wes Anderson) stars Bill Murray as a very Cousteau-like oceographer-filmmaker. These intermedia-textual references would be grasped by audiences even casually familiar with a new generation of animal TV that mingles real-life and staged encounters between humans and animals to distinctive ends, perpetuating wildlife filmmaking's displays of (mostly) masculine physical prowess, knowledge, and control over the natural world in an era that spans both the celebration of a tough-guy paradigm (in action films, in rap and rock music, and in U.S. military policy) and the backlash emergence (if less widespread throughout American society) of the metrosexual.[3] Complementing the masculinist bent, *The Pet Psychic, The Wild Thornberrys,* and some representations of Jane Goodall's ongoing celebrity within the genre return to a melodramatically feminine proximity to nature's secrets.

While animal programming boomed on TV, Hollywood produced a spate of feature comedies with animal themes. In some, anthropomorphized and animated animal characters live out very human narratives, including *Antz* (1998, directed by Eric Darnell and Tim Johnson for Dreamworks), *A Bug's Life* (1998, directed by John Lasseter and Andrew Stanton for Pixar/ Disney), and *Chicken Run* (2000, directed by Nick Park and Peter Lord for Aardman Animations). Alternatively, human lives became unusually entangled with animals, as in *George of the Jungle* (1997, directed by Sam Weisman), in which Brendan Fraser plays a live-action version of a raised-by-apes cartoon character; Disney's lushly animated *Tarzan* (1999, directed by

Kevin Lima and Chris Buck), the forty-eighth film version of Edgar Rice Burroughs's 1914 novel; and *The Animal* (2001, directed by Luke Greenfield), in which a bumbling Rob Schneider becomes a kind of superman after receiving transplants of animal organs. While these themes suggest the cross-species identification that intensifies in wildlife filmmaking during this period, they reach the traditional big screen only in fictional forms. Nonfiction wildlife ventures in theatrical distribution remained scant, with the exception of an emerging specialty market. In the 1970s the IMAX Corporation introduced a new large-format cinema, based on a 70mm frame that can be projected to reach the proportions of an eight-story building, and launched a chain of specially designed and equipped theaters. The large-format excels at the sweeping land- and seascapes conventional in the nature genre, and many films using IMAX technology have featured wildlife, exploration, or ecological subjects, such as *Beavers* (1988), *Blue Planet* (1990), *Everest* (1995), *Island of the Sharks* (1999), *Jane Goodall's Wild Chimpanzees* (2002), and the 3-D *Bugs!* (2003), but its compatibility with wildlife film is institutional as well as aesthetic. Many IMAX theaters are located in institutions with educational and conservationist missions, such as the American Museum of Natural History in New York City (associated with popular wildlife film since funding films by Martin and Osa Johnson in the 1920s), the Reuben H. Fleet Science Center in San Diego, and the Apple Valley Minnesota Zoo outside of Minneapolis. Long-time nature-film producer National Geographic began to invest in large-format films and theaters in 1996.

As animal TV proliferated, and nature subjects found new outlets in large-format cinema, a dramatic film, *L'Ours* (*The Bear*, 1989) by Jean-Jacques Annaud, brought an animal protagonist to the big screen using many of the techniques of the nonfiction wildlife film. *The Bear* employed Bart the Bear (who also appears in *Legends of the Fall* [1994] and a dozen other films) as an adult male who take an orphaned cub into his care as the two try to evade hunters. The plot was entirely a fiction; in the wild, males never provide parental care and pose a threat to orphans. Many of the film's features derived from classic Disneyana. For example, in *Bambi* (1942), hunters kill the fawn's mother early in the film; the cub's mother dies part way through *The Bear*. Just as in *Bear Country* (1953), the cub is threatened by a cougar and protected by his mother, *The Bear* cub is rescued from the same threat by his adoptive father. These parallels suggest just how entrenched these themes of peril and protection, the privileging of fatherhood and the expendability of females, remain.

Only a handful of nonfiction feature films enjoyed theatrical releases in the 1990s and early twenty-first century. The French *Microcosmos* (1996), produced by Jacques Perrin and directed by Claude Nuridsany and Marie Pérennou, earned $1.4 million in the United States. As trivial as that figure may be by Hollywood standards, it overwhelms the earnings of Discovery's *The Leopard Son* (1996; under half a million) and the Swedish *Kestrel's Eye* by Mickael Kristersson (1999, about $50,000). *Winged Migration* (2002), which was directed by Perrin, earned a relatively substantial $10.7 million in the United States, but it was far outpaced by *March of the Penguins* (2005) by Luc Jacquet, a nonfiction feature earning $70 million within three months of its U.S. release. Despite these exceptions, nature remained a predominately televisual genre.

A genre that only a decade and a half earlier could be found on U.S. television almost exclusively on PBS had become available around the clock, on several competing channels, to the majority of American homes and to millions more throughout the world. Now, viewers worldwide could at any given moment experience a representation of what may sometimes *seem* to be "the totality of the world," simply by channel-surfing between images of crocodiles in Australia, wolves in France, or manatees off the Florida coast.[4]

The Discovery Channel and Its Wild Discovery

On June 17, 1985, the Discovery Channel's premiere reached only 156,000 homes, in an improbable, undercapitalized entry into the competitive cable market. Within a decade, it became one of the most widely distributed cable-programming services and the cornerstone of a mid-sized media conglomerate. Discovery Communications Inc. (DCI) now controls four analog and nine digital-cable channels in the United States. Variations on these services distributed abroad to a combined total estimated at one billion subscribers in 160 countries; a chain of retail stores; home video, book, music, and multimedia publishing interests; and more.[5] But the growth of Discovery is not just a tale of the little network that could. As a cable channel and as a media conglomerate, Discovery is both typical and exceptional, conducting business-as-usual in terms of the standard practices of the cable-television industry, and contributing to innovations in industry structure and practices. One of those innovations would be the centrality of wildlife in the brand-identity of a commercial network.

Discovery entered the cable marketplace during a period of rapid growth and change in the industry, marked as different from cable's other offerings by its then-unique reliance on the documentary form and on natural history, science, exploration, and related content believed by most programmers and potential investors to be irretrievably unprofitable. No other network, not even PBS, devoted so much of its schedule to documentaries, or to the content categories that were Discovery's mainstays. In 1988 journalist Peter Steinhart estimated that a third of its programming involved nature subjects.[6] In contrast, in 1993 science and nature constituted only 6.1 percent of all programming hours distributed by PBS's National Programming Service to its affiliates.[7] Some industry professionals have touted Discovery as an example of the best that television has to offer: Ajit Dalvi, a Discovery board member and vice-president of Cox Cable, once commended Discovery for offering "educational programming . . . in the true sense," and TCI senior vice-president John Sie boasted that the network would "repatriate science and technology" to a general public lacking in knowledge of these subjects.[8] But Discovery has not always represented itself as an educational programmer. According to DCI executive Chris Moseley, "[Education] isn't why people are drawn to our brand."[9] Instead, Discovery strategically cultivates the entertainment value of nonfiction, in nature and in its other content categories.

In 1982 Discovery founder and chairman John S. Hendricks began to orchestrate an increasingly complex partnership that would finance the network's launch (Hendricks also served as chief executive officer until 2004). Attracting investors was difficult, since the scant presence of documentary on television at the time seemed to prove that the form lacked commercial value. According to industry lore, Hendricks's breakthrough came when he secured a letter of support from the legendary newscaster Walter Cronkite, who had hosted the recently canceled, science-oriented documentary series *Universe* (1980–82, CBS).[10] In Discovery's first (but short-lived) vertical affiliation with a carriage provider, Westinghouse's Group W Satellite Communications acquired a 6 percent share in exchange for $3 million worth of marketing and satellite-transmission services.[11] The channel offered twelve hours of programming daily, much of which was older product previously aired by National Geographic or PBS.[12] Charging no affiliate fees to cable systems that agreed to put Discovery on the air, the channel depended solely on advertising revenue.

In 1986, a year after launch, Hendricks brokered an innovative deal with Tele-Communications Inc. (TCI), United Television Cable Corporation,

Cox Cable Communications, and Newhouse Broadcasting Corporation (later Advance/Newhouse). Each of these multisystem operators (MSOs) acquired a 10 percent stake in Discovery and agreed to carry the channel.[13] The deal brightened Discovery's prospects on three accounts. First, the injection of cash allowed for the acquisition of new programming, including, for the first time, shows not yet aired on other channels.[14] Second, the MSOs' commitments to carry the channel led to regular non-ad revenue in the form of fees when, in 1987, Discovery began to charge cable systems two to five cents per month per subscriber; larger affiliates paid the least, privileging the systems vertically affiliated with Discovery. Third, the deal pushed Discovery into another 13.5 million homes, surpassing the threshold over which the A. C. Nielsen Company would, at the time, begin to monitor a channel's viewership, making Discovery far more intelligible and appealing to advertisers, thus enhancing another income stream.[15] Vertical affiliation all but guaranteed Discovery's viability.

Why did the MSOs risk investing in a fledgling network? In short, they had both power and motivation to assure that Discovery would attain carriage sufficient to attract significant numbers of viewers and advertisers, therefore raising the value of their investment. Some observers gloated that the MSO bailout of Discovery was "one of the brighter moments in cable history," and (erroneously) "the industry's first equity alliance between programmer and operators."[16] But Discovery's successful exploitation of these vertical affiliations demonstrates the potential anticompetitive hazards of a market in which such affiliations are now commonplace: MSOs are most likely to add channels in which they invest to their systems, and to favor them in placement, pricing, and promotion over unaffiliated networks or those owned by competitors. In MSO hands, Discovery became the fastest-growing cable network in 1987 and 1988, and as Discovery grew, the MSOs increased their investments until they controlled some 97 percent of its equity.[17] By 1994 Discovery, with 60.5 million U.S. subscribers, ranked among the six most fully distributed networks, along with CNN, ESPN, TBS, TNT, and USA Networks. Four of these top six networks benefit from vertical integration, suggesting that these alliances are important means of achieving market power. The Discovery Channel continued to grow as cable and satellite subscriptions gained additional market share, and by 2003 it reached 86.5 million homes in the United States.[18]

While Discovery developed a niche audience and MSO executives gloated about its virtues, some critics thought of Discovery in its early years as "a repository for off-PBS reruns, a showcase of stale fare that nevertheless managed to attract an audience."[19] But as the network's finances stabilized, it became less dependent on acquired material.[20] Its first original production, *Ivory Wars* (1989), a documentary about elephant poaching, was coproduced with the World Wildlife Fund, garnered healthy ratings and positive reviews, sold well overseas, and was one of Discovery's first successful home-video titles.[21] Another early original Discovery production, *In the Company of Whales* (1992), premiered as a two-hour special that garnered a 2.7 share, twice the network's average in its timeslot.[22] Discovery's success with these programs and the annual boost from "Shark Week" to typically lackluster August ratings positioned wildlife as a centerpiece of the Discovery brand identity and programming schedule.[23]

For the 1995–96 season, Discovery consolidated its archive of nature programming under the title *Wild Discovery*, offering viewers daily access to wildlife programming that had thrived for the network in the form of specials. The hour-long series was stripped five nights per week in prime time and repeated in late-night hours. During the first month of the season, Discovery's Nielsen ratings in the timeslot increased by 50 percent to a 1.5 average.[24] In many ways, *Wild Discovery* served as the channel's flagship during this season, with its eponymous title and desirable timeslot. Discovery found its animal programming so exploitable it gave the genre a whole network of its own the following year, but would not excise wildlife from its own schedule, which continued to sport *Wild Discovery* timeslots and the annual "Shark Week." In fact, post–Animal Planet launch, the Discovery Channel would at times expand its own animal hours. In 2000–2001 and 2001–2, Discovery doubled its daily wildlife programming, scheduling two daily *Wild Discovery* hours back-to-back but shifting them to the early fringe of prime time.

Still, the questions remain: why did Discovery bank so heavily on the wildlife genre? What advantages did wildlife present over other documentary themes? Observers within the television industry have pointed convincingly to two clusters of largely economic factors: costs (relative to potential revenue) and shifting audience profiles. Documentaries, especially those with nature or wildlife subject matter, are inexpensive, durable, and flexible products, compared to many other TV genres. Their budgets vary tremendously but are typically only a fraction of the cost of fictional TV genres: "no expensive actors, directors, writers, or sets. The animals and plants are nonunion, not entitled to residual payments, and work for nothing."[25] Unlike newsmagazines or documentaries on topics in which knowledge and practices change frequently, such as medicine and health, or current public affairs, nature documentaries have unusually long "shelf life"; they are rerun season after season without losing audience.[26] Further, wildlife footage can be archived, disaggregated, and sold for reuse in new contexts.

The genre's audiences complement its low costs and recyclability. While modest in size, audiences for animals on TV have been reliable and appealing to advertisers, which is commensurate with industry trends accommodating smaller but more homogenous audiences. Ratings even increased mid-decade, not only for the *Wild Discovery* timeslot: audience share for TBS's *National Geographic Explorer* grew almost 50 percent in 1995, and, for PBS's *Nature* 30 percent in 1996.[27] But numbers of viewers don't tell the whole story; the genre's small audiences often sport demographic characteristics attractive to advertisers. In 1996 *Forbes* described the audience for *National Geographic Specials* as "male viewers aged 25 to 54, a typically tough crowd to reach with TV."[28] General social trends, such as increasing "interest in the environment" or "growing green consciousness," also paved the way for cable programmers to embrace the wildlife genre in the late 1980s and early 1990s.[29]

Many of the programs offered to audiences in *Wild Discovery* timeslots have exemplified classic wildlife filmmaking. Like Walt Disney's True-Life Adventures and *Wild Kingdom*'s ecology shows, *Wild Discovery* selections often avoid depictions of human life, except in voiceover narration (usually intoned by a masculine voice). In the narrative model developed by precedents ranging from *The Private Life of the Gannet* (1934) to the premiere episode of *Nature,* titled *Flight of the Condor* (1982), many typical *Wild Discovery* programs follow members of a single species—usually a specific herd, pack, family, or other grouping—throughout a year-long cycle that includes mating, birth, raising young, and separation of mother and young, as in *Wild Dogs: A Tale of Two Sisters* (1990). *Wild Dogs,* made in Tanzania by Hugo van Lawick for Partridge Films, is largely a story of the brutality of nature and the remarkable, but not infinite, resiliency of animals. In the film a pack of African wild dogs, led by two females, endures interpack squabbles over a new litter, fluctuating availability of prey, and threats from predators. At the end of the film, the narrator discloses that after filming ended, the entire pack died from distemper passed from dog to dog through their elaborate licking behaviors, described earlier as essential to grooming and bonding between pack members. As this tragic turn is revealed, the final scene shows the pack trotting, literally, into the sunset. In this case, the film documents the activities of members of a species not from birth to maturity, but from birth to death.

Alternatively, *Wild Discovery* programs may, like Disney's *Nature's Half-Acre* (1951) or *The Living Desert* (1953), examine a bioclimactic zone. For example, *The Big Wet* (1993), a coproduction of the Australian Broadcasting Corporation and Discovery, surveys the lives of reptiles, birds, marsupials, and others throughout seasons of drought and fire, rain and flood in Australia's Kakadu National Park. Occasionally, a *Wild Discovery* episode focuses on a particular cross-species set of animals, as in *The Wonder of Baby Animals* (1996), by KEG Productions of Canada. Like the species-specific model, many examples of these alternative narratives forego representations of human life; others feature on-camera presenters.

Settling into a newly comfortable financial situation, with this kind of content featured prominently, Discovery began to seek further growth, first through diversification of its domestic television activities. In 1989 Discovery joined other networks and some MSOs in developing Cable in the Classroom, an educational media-transmission service, and in 1991, striving toward horizontal integration in basic cable, purchased The Learning Channel. At the same time, DCI set its sights overseas, its eagerness to become a player in global media fulfilling the logic of commercial media that, as Nicholas Garnham argues, seeks to expand not by providing viewers with new choices but by finding new markets to saturate with its product.[30] In television, global expansion became possible only with the widespread deregulation of national electronic media markets beginning in about 1980. According to Dan Schiller, "unremitting U.S. pressure, supranational initiatives within the European Union and the World Trade Organization, shifting affinities among national elites after the fall of Soviet socialism, and hardly least, the explosion of Internet systems" motivated the trend.[31] In the United States, deregulation allowed for more concentrated and cross-media ownership, and lifted public-interest content obligations such as the Fairness Doctrine. In public and state-controlled markets, especially in Europe, "deregulation has mainly taken the form of relaxing monopolies and ownership rules together with increasing the number of television services available . . . connected to the increased funding of television by commercial means in preference to forms of taxation" in response to the incorporation of new technologies into the mass-media economy, a trend toward allowing the market to determine public interest, and consumer demand.[32] These trends facilitated the growth of media generally, and eased the entry of entities like Discovery into global markets.

In 1989 DCI launched Discovery Channel–Europe, losing money for six years, but allowing Discovery to test programming and modify marketing strategies in territories where cable and satellite services then reached only a small percentage of potentially huge markets.[33] In 1992 a new DCI division, Discovery/International, organized to expand beyond Europe through global partnerships with established networks in Asia and the Americas. This strategy lowers barriers to entry by facilitating cost-sharing for new productions, accessing a staff already experienced in local culture, and opening the door to markets where foreign investment is limited by law.[34] Hendricks's boast, "We hope to blanket the world by late 1995 or early 1996," was hardly an exaggeration.[35] By 1997 Discovery self-reported on its website that the channel reached cable- and satellite-service subscribers in 145 countries.

In some markets Discovery encountered relatively weak barriers to entry. In 1993 the United States, Mexico, and Canada enacted the North American Free Trade Agreement (NAFTA), and the venerable Mexican broadcaster Televisa entered into a joint venture with DCI to produce a version of the Discovery Channel for Latin America. American media corporations had invested in and sold programming to the Mexican media market since the early years of radio, and by 1996 provided 90 percent of all cable and satellite signals imported by all Iberoamerican countries. But these signals reach only elite subscribers, an upper-class niche market that consumes large amounts of foreign programming; most people in these markets receive only broadcast signals. Canada, having negotiated a "cultural exemption" to NAFTA, kept in place media regulations designed to protect Canadian economic and cultural sovereignty, especially from dependence on the United States.[36] Discovery partnered with the Labatt Brewing Company to launch a network, its equity share restricted by law to only 20 percent.[37]

Discovery adapted its launch model to situate itself as broadly as possible. Discovery Networks Asia, based in Singapore, launched in 1994. It was ranked as "Asia's No. 1 cable channel . . . [most] watched by adults ages 25 to 64" each year from 1997 to 2002, according to surveys conducted in Tokyo, Jakarta, Manila, Bangkok, Taipei, Hong Kong, Sydney, and other urban centers where viewers—especially the economically elite top 10 to 15 percent sought by advertisers—are concentrated.[38] Other markets resisted, at least incrementally, trends toward privatization, commercialization, and foreign investment. In China, which was poised to become "the biggest cable television market in the world," Discovery found a gradually privatizing but still relatively closed television market, where the Ministry of Radio, Film, and Television still attempted (not always successfully) to limit the entry of foreign programming, despite Rupert Murdoch's vigorous efforts to launch his StarTV network.[39] Seeking to establish early ties with a potential lucrative market, Discovery developed a season-long campaign around a programming exchange with the state-run China Central Television (CCTV).[40]

Discovery launched in India in 1995, initially in English, then adding a parallel programming feed in Hindi, and adapting its translation style to the findings of market researchers. According to Discovery Communications India's managing director, Deepak Shourie, "We researched it and consumers said, 'First we used to watch, now we understand.' Our language in Hindi was seen to be too technical, and so we made it colloquial."[41] Eventually, Discovery also began to provide a daily programming block revoiced in Tamil, and would continue to consider new feeds in other languages. In this instance, the channel largely retained its globally distributed content, but sought to render that programming increasingly accessible to subscribers by adjusting its speech style and enlarging its audiences' menu of linguistic choices.

In several sub-Saharan African nations that have provided the setting for countless wildlife (and ethnographic) films, Discovery established the Discovery Channel Global Education Fund in 1997. If commercial entry into these markets might not be profitable, corporate donations in these areas might produce other rewards. Collaborating with other corporate and foundation donors, NGOs, local government agencies, the World Bank, and other partners, the Fund set up over six dozen "Learning Centers" at schools and community centers in South Africa, Tanzania, Uganda, and Zimbabwe, supplying each center with a TV set, VCR, cable hook-up or satellite dish, solar power where electricity is otherwise unavailable, and access to programming from Discovery networks and other sources. In Zimbabwe the project also runs mobile media centers and libraries, transported by truck or donkey cart. Television reaches relatively small portions of these countries' populations, especially in rural areas—for example, only a quarter of Zimbabwean households own sets, concentrating access among the urban middle class.[42] But Discovery's donations train rural teachers in the use of media in the classroom and acclimatize rural populations to media use in anticipation of eventual economic development and growth in these markets.

"All Animals, All the Time": Spinning Off a Cable Hit

In 1996, seeking to expand by means of product differentiation, Discovery undertook another growth spurt in both domestic and global markets, launching a raft of digital channels and the basic-cable network Animal Planet, promoted in ad campaigns as the channel on which to find "all animals, all the time."[43] Animal Planet's first airdate reached a modest three to four million homes in the United States.[44] Its expansion depended on DCI's ability to divert funds from the profitable Discovery Channel and The Learning Channel to buy Animal Planet's way into carriage, offering MSOs $5 to $7 per subscriber to make room for the channel on their analog tiers in 1996 and 1997.[45] Growth also depended on an alliance between Discovery and the BBC, which gave the venerable British public entity's commercial division for global activities, BBC Worldwide, a 20 percent interest in the U.S. version of Animal Planet, and 50 percent of the network in other markets.[46] These strategies worked: less than two years after launch, Animal Planet reached 37 million subscribers, averaging 200,000 viewers in primetime and occasionally, a Nielsen rating of 0.5, surpassing more established channels such as VH1 and MSNBC.[47] In 2004, seven years after launch, Animal Planet reached as many as 85 million U.S. homes, and 126 million in other countries.[48]

Animal Planet programming extends the success that Discovery had with wildlife and incorporates elements of other TV genres. Most daytime programming focuses on breeding, pet care, and training, in shows like *Adoption Tales, Breed All about It, Good Dog U, Pet Story, Petsburgh USA,* and *That's My Baby.* Animal Planet's mostly short-lived game shows have included *Zoo Venture,* a children's program and the network's first original production, taped at the San Diego Zoo in 1997, the primetime *You Lie Like a Dog,* premiered in 2000, and *Pet Star* (2002–). A talent show that takes the form of an elaborated, less ironic riff on the *Late Night with David Letterman* routine "Stupid Pet Tricks," *Pet Star* features celebrity judges, many of whose credits link them to other animal-themed media, such as Lindsay Wagner, who played the director of the Los Angeles County Zoo on the CBS series *Peaceable Kingdom* (1989, CBS), and Tim Curry, one of the voices of *The Wild Thornberrys*. As throughout much of TV, game shows morphed into reality challenges: in *King of the Jungle* (2003–4), contestants vied to host their own one-hour wildlife special. The contest was based on displays of knowledge about animals, skills in animal handling, and success in performing tasks much like those on reality competitions in which the environment provides playing field and raw material for physical stunts, such as *Survivor* (2000–, CBS). In primetime, dog shows and agility contests appear frequently as special events, and the network has experimented intermittently with fictional projects, many of them remakes, including a serialized version of *Call of the Wild* (2000), based on the novel by Jack London, and the made-for-TV-movie *Gentle Ben* (2002), based on the boy-and-pet-bear TV series of the same name (1967–69, CBS).

Animal Planet uses wildlife most frequently in primetime. "Classic" wildlife filmmaking occasionally appears, as in the new *Mutual of Omaha's Wild Kingdom*, revived in 2002 in the form of one-hour specials produced under the advisement of Peter Gros, who, along with Jim Fowler, hosted the original *Wild Kingdom*'s final season of new shows after Marlin Perkins retired in 1985. But most Animal Planet wildlife programs feature on-screen presenters, such as Mark O'Shea, an uneffusive herpetologist from the British Midlands who has produced series and specials for the Discovery Channel, Animal Planet, and Channel Four under the title *O'Shea's Big Adventure* (1999–2004), and Nigel Marven, a longtime BBC Natural History Unit producer and director associated with several of David Attenborough's projects and his own *Nigel's Wild Wild World*, a series launched in 2001 and continued in the form of specials. Rather than pristine nature, unpopulated by humans, these action-adventure series update conventions established in early expedition filmmaking and persistent through the "drug-and-tag" era of the 1960s–'70s. They feature personable naturalist-hosts, men—and occasional women—who not only observe but often interact with wild animals, rescuing or relocating animals in trouble, collecting specimens for scientific study, or handling their quest-objects while exhibiting their findings to the viewer. In contrast with wildlife filmmaking projects undertaken by crews with lengthy field commitments and even lengthier lenses, allowing cinematographers to document the behavior of undisturbed animals from afar, this new generation of naturalist-hosts specializes in close proximity, and sometimes physical contact, with their animal quest-objects.

The most successful of these shows, in terms of longevity, ratings, the celebrity achieved by its host, and its exploitability across product lines, has been *The Crocodile Hunter,* featuring Australian Steve Irwin and, in an irregular supporting role, his American wife, Terri Irwin. Launched in 1996 and filmed in locations around the world, the series has been one of Animal Planet's top-rated, setting a record of one million viewers for the first night of a week-long "Croc Week" marathon in 2000.[49] Drawing on Steve Irwin's experience in wildlife relocation, and on his family's experience in operating the for-profit Australia Zoo in Queensland, the Irwins wrangle crocodiles that have outgrown their habitats or become dangerous to humans or livestock; they criss-cross Australia and traverse the globe to collect footage of snakes and other animals. At each location, Irwin locates and displays a sought-after animal, points out some of its physical features and behaviors, and returns it to captivity or its natural environment. In episodes from the show's earliest years, Irwin's bravado is tempered by his generally serious and thoroughly sincere, even awestruck response to the animals and environments he encounters. He restrains the volume of his voice when a potentially dangerous animal is nearby; a single camera tracks his actions in the field.

Nevertheless, even early *Crocodile Hunter* episodes employ age-old wildlife filmmaking techniques, such as constructing narratives from pools of footage derived from different sources. In "The Ten Deadliest" episode (1996, Partridge Films, Ltd.), Irwin seeks ten species ranked as possessing the venom most dangerous to humans, all conveniently located in his native Australia. He saves snakes from people and people from snakes: en route to the first deadly snake location, he stops to move a carpet python off the road so that it cannot be run over. In another scene Irwin hikes Mount Chapel Island, off the coast of Tasmania, in search of tiger snakes. Cutting from a long shot of Irwin to a close-up of a snake scurrying into a hole in the ground, to Irwin's boots hitting the ground as he walks, and back to the snake, the editor assembles an argument: the snake is aware of, perhaps frightened by, an intruder and seeks to avoid a confrontation. But the illustrating images don't match: in videotaped footage, Irwin is surrounded by vigorously windswept dune grass; in the inserted shots of the snakes, the air is still, grasses undisturbed. When Irwin does make contact with dangerous quarry, exposing himself to free-roaming venomous snakes, they tend to slither out of frame rather than strike. On occasion, he resorts to editing tricks when real risk is null. Telling the viewer that "this island is absolutely riddled with burrows . . . we'll just have a little look down here," he reaches into a hole in the ground, jerks his hand back, then reaches in again. The image cuts to an interior shot of an underground burrow serving as a mutton bird's nest, suggesting that Irwin's hand was pecked by the chicks, or worse, as the narrator informs viewers that tiger snakes often adopt empty nests as their own dens. Inferred risk aside, the scene was obviously (if harmlessly) staged, and there is no evidence that the hole Irwin reached into was occupied at all.

As the popularity of the show and Irwin's performance style and celebrity status became established, episodes occasionally forayed into the Irwins' personal lives. In the episode called "Steve's Story" (1999), clips from other episodes are interspersed with family snapshots and recreations of Steve's childhood, home video of his early crocodile captures, reminiscences by his father, and scenes taped during the birth of Steve and Terri's daughter, Bindi Sue. In separate interviews for the episode, Terri and Steve describe how they met when Terri, visiting Queensland from Oregon where she was also involved in conservation, happened upon Australia Zoo and lingered after Steve's croc-feeding demonstration to chat. They weave a portrait of a family whose public and private personas, their encounters with wildlife and with one another, are, at least in representation, deeply entangled.

In later seasons Irwin maintains a hyperactive enthusiasm, becoming a kind of wide-eyed parody of his earlier persona and of stereotypically rough-and-tumble Australian masculinity, risking life and limb to get good footage, peppering his speech with regional slang (such as his trademark exclamation "Crikey!"). He presents if not a wholly impenetrable body, then at least one indifferent to pain, appearing to regard the occasional broken finger or other wound as an acceptable occupational hazard. Most episodes feature at least one close call; quarry lunge and strike as if on cue. In the otherwise informative "Outlaws of the Outback" (2000), an episode focusing on the overwhelmingly negative impact of introduced species on native Australian habitats and species, Terri endures a stunt worthy of the reality-competition *Fear Factor* (2001–, NBC), crouching on the floor of an infested barn as hundreds of mice scurry around—and on—her, which she describes as "icky." The shot ends after she tells Steve one has gone down her shirt. Later in the episode, Steve falls from a truck while chasing down a feral camel. He makes a joke about Terri's driving, but ignores a bloody gash to his ear. In another segment, after blurting "ow" several times while being bitten through gloves and on the wrist by a rat, Irwin adjusts his grip, lifts the rat up near his own face, and grins into the camera. To reframe his loss of control over the animal, he directly addresses the viewer with an almost endearing dismissal of the irritation: "They're little naughty ones, aren't they?"

Steve Irwin plants a kiss on the head of a komodo dragon in *The Crocodile Hunter Diaries'* "Living Dangerously."

In other instances, real danger is cultivated and its outcomes, elaborated in some detail, and invoked when danger dissipates without causing actual harm. The episode "Graham's Revenge" (2001) features encounters with a particularly aggressive captive crocodile named Graham (including his attack on one of Irwin's colleagues that resulted in serious injuries, filmed up close while the man recovers in a hospital room, and reenacted later by Irwin and the attack survivor). Before a crowd at Australia Zoo, Irwin, in Graham's enclosure, tempts the crocodile out of a pond with fish, the huge reptile snapping at the tips of his fingers. Irwin slips as he backs too close to the edge of a second pond. The crowd gasps audibly in anticipation that he will fall and Graham will attack. Irwin regains his footing, and the animal does not lunge. In voiceover, Irwin recasts the anticlimactic stumble—"The crowd loves it when I nearly die"—rendering risk, real, exaggerated, or staged, that has typified the genre for over a century, self-reflexively explicit.

Following the completion of dozens of *Crocodile Hunter* episodes that could be aired in more or less constant rotation, spinoffs continue to feature the Irwins in slightly varied concepts. *The Crocodile Hunter Diaries* (2002–) has been set almost entirely in the Australia Zoo, offering a behind-the-scenes glimpse at zookeeping. In the third season, Steve Irwin pays visits to other zoos in episodes such as "British Gorillas" (2004), just as in latter seasons of *Zoo Parade* (1950–57), having exhausted Lincoln Park Zoo locations, Marlin Perkins tours other zoos and conservation parks. Episodes of a children's version of the show, *Croc Files*, were produced in 2003 for the Discovery Kids digital channel and Discovery Kids' Saturday morning block on NBC. The *Crocodile Hunter* property is also exploited throughout Discovery's conglomerate endeavors, in t-shirts and videos sold on-line and at Discovery Stores, in licensed merchandise from action figures to temporary tattoos, in appearances on talk shows from *Oprah* to *Larry King Live*, and in the feature film *The Crocodile Hunter: Collision Course* (2002, directed by Irwin's frequent TV director, John Stainton). The film, which was released by MGM, was produced for $12.5 million, modest by Hollywood standards, and grossed $28.5 million in domestic box office. Steve and Terri Irwin play themselves, going about their business of nonfiction wildlife filmmaking, showing off to the camera various animal specimens; in a fictional plotline, Steve and Terri seek to wrangle and relocate a troublesome croc that has been menacing livestock, but stumble into an adventure based on international espionage.

After years of carefully crafting this celebrity based on goofy fearlessness and good will toward animals, Steve Irwin drew unflattering attention to his practices as both filmmaker and parent. In January 2004 an Australia Zoo visitor captured Irwin on video, entertaining a crowd by feeding a large crocodile with one hand while he held his one-month-old son, Bob, with the other. The tape made the news worldwide and prompted investigations of the Irwin children's exposure to potentially dangerous animals. Six months later Irwin faced allegations that he had failed to keep regulated distances from marine mammals and birds in a region of Antarctica governed by Australia while filming encounters with animals for the already-broadcast episode "Ice Breaker." Scrutinizing agencies, from local Family Services to Australia's Department of the Environment and Heritage, cleared Irwin of all charges in both incidents.[50] Irwin's relationship with Animal Planet appeared unchanged. (In the fall of 2005 he began to host a new series, *New Breed Vets*.) His reputation has been only a bit sullied for having joined the long slate of wildlife filmmaking scandals, and the incidents, tempered by Irwin's admired enthusiasm for wildlife and his obvious expertise in animal handling, have been framed as a kind of just-over-the-line recklessness.

After all, proximity to animals forms a pillar of Irwin's version of wildlife nonfiction, an approach that self-consciously discards classic wildlife filmmaking techniques in favor of intrepid contact, whether in the course of pest control and animal rescue (relocating dangerous or endangered animals), data collection (capture-and-release programs, in which animals are fitted with radio collars for scientific research), or simply to engage in the adventure of locating the quest animal and sharing it, along with some facts about it, with a viewing audience. "Steve's Story" closes with the following monologue, which frames his work as a calling, an almost spiritual mission with an evangelical component that entails appealing to viewers through action-adventure and coaxing them toward conservationist values (which, of course, many viewers may already hold; Irwin could be preaching to the already converted). The scene begins without musical accompaniment; Irwin gestures with his hands throughout and appears to speak to an off-camera interviewer, punctuating his remarks by shifting to a direct-address gaze into the camera intermittently toward the end:

> In my life dealing with wildlife, I've been gored, clawed, chomped, bitten, savaged, jumped on, whacked, peed on, even groped. And every single time, it's been my fault. If I get bitten, I've made the mistake.... Have a look at my hands. Virtually scars on scars. You can't see the last bite because it's scar on scar. And this isn't some giant ego trip. Uh-uh. [Plaintive musical score rises.] It's just that, I've gotta get the camera, I've gotta be right in there, I have to get right there, smack into the action. Because this day has come where the audience—you—need to come with me and be there with that animal. If there's whales dying on the beach on the western side of Tasmania, I want to share that with you. Because if we can touch people about wildlife, then they want to save it. If you go to SeaWorld and you get to have an encounter with a dolphin, you want to save dolphins.
>
> Gone are the days of sittin' back on the long lens on the tripod and lookin' at wildlife way over there. Uh-uh. Come with me. Share it with me. Share my wildlife with me. Because humans want to save things that they love. My job, my mission, the reason I've been put onto this planet is to save wildlife and I thank you for coming with me.

Pumping his fist in the air, his all-the-while earnest expression brightening toward his signature wide-eyed pluck, Irwin concludes, "Yeah, let's get

Jeff Corwin and bear cub in the "Extreme Encounters" episode from *The Jeff Corwin Experience.*

'em," with an affirming nod to the audience, capping off this unusually sentimental reflection with a glimmer of Croc Hunter bravado.

Another Animal Planet wildlife series, *The Jeff Corwin Experience* (2000–), follows Irwin's model of combining the format of an on-screen host who undertakes animal quests with action and humor. Corwin, formerly the star of *Goin' Wild with Jeff Corwin* (1997–99) on the Disney Channel, shares Irwin's intrepid adventurism and self-effacing affability, and has achieved a modest degree of celebrity based on boyish, all-American looks that landed him on *People* magazine's list of fifty most beautiful people for 2002. He also vies with Irwin in terms of marketability. In 2003 Discovery culled a children's show, *Corwin Unleashed*, from *The Jeff Corwin Experience* footage. The show ran briefly on NBC's Saturday morning Discovery Kids block before moving to the Discovery Kids channel. Also in 2003, Corwin began to host Animal Planet's reality show *King of the Jungle*, in which contestants compete to host their own wildlife show, and guest-starred as himself on an episode of CBS's *CSI: Miami*, consulting on a case in which forensic evidence is found in an alligator's stomach. In 2005 he launched a new series, *Corwin's Quest*, on Animal Planet.

While Irwin usually wears a loose khaki uniform, Corwin favors pec-clinging t-shirts and is more likely to sneer sensitively at a foul odor than to engage in a macho plunge into harm's way. He bursts into song—show tunes now and then—and slips easily into camp impersonations, from Cousteau's French lilt and Elmer Fudd's lisp during the episode "Louisiana: Call of the Cajun Wild" (2000), to Arnold Schwarzenegger's Austrian-accented growl while manipulating the forelegs of a bulky South American bullfrog into bodybuilder poses in "Extreme Encounters" (2001). If Corwin's presentation in this genre seems atypically theatrical—that is, *queer*—he goes to lengths to deflect such a reading by making occasional references to his wife (though, unlike Terri Irwin, she does not appear as part of a wildlife filmmaking couple), and in narrative tangents with sexual undertones. In the Louisiana episode Corwin appears throughout as himself but also, clad in overalls and scraggly wig, as a *Deliverance*-inspired banjo-player who seems to stalk the naturalist-Corwin, inspiring a homosexual panic that drives the show's host to flee his backwoods döppel-ganger. In the episode's final scene, Corwin enters a local club, where a band plays and he dances with some of the women, reiterating his heterosexuality, legitimating his role within a conventionally masculinist genre. In "Extreme Encounters" he holds a bear cub that eagerly licks his ear. Corwin murmurs, "That's kinda, kinda nice," then shifts his tone to one of indignation: "Stop that! I'm a married man, please." A wedding ring is plainly visible on his pale hand, close to the camera and clasping the cub's dark fur.

Out of the Cable Box: Discovery Pictures and *The Leopard Son*

While Discovery diversified its cable operations and partnered with broadcasters, it also extended its brand into other media, beginning with home video in 1990, then book, CD-ROM, and music publishing; a website and on-line shopping; a chain of Discovery Channel stores; travel and athletic/adventure competitions; toys; and, in 2001, live shows based on Animal Planet themes at Universal Studios theme parks in Hollywood and Orlando.[51] Discovery's brand extensions were not in themselves unusual, except for their scope and scale. As most media conglomerates with brand-based stores, including Disney and Time-Warner, struggled and scaled back, or like Viacom's Nickelodeon closed entirely, Discovery moved into notoriously risky retail and to degrees unprecedented by other cable networks.[52] Hendricks announced another Discovery experiment in a non-cable market, the formation of Discovery Pictures in 1994. For its first project, *The Leopard Son* (1996), Baron Hugo Van Lawick and his crew spent two years in the Ngoromgoro Conservation Area of Serengeti National Park in Tanzania. They gathered thirty hours of film and ninety hours of sound. Its $3-million budget, 35mm film stock, and eighty-four-minute running time distinguish it from the 16mm format, under-an-hour length more typical of the genre, but its thematic and narrative concerns are consistent with others of its type. Following a brief theatrical release, the film was recast by Discovery as a *Wild Discovery Special Event* aired on May 10, 1998 (not coincidentally Mother's Day), a home-video release, and the subject of a behind-the-scenes short, "The Making of *The Leopard Son.*"

The Leopard Son is narrated from the point of view of the filmmaker, the well-known van Lawick (the script, by Michael Olment, is read by Sir John Gielgud) rather than an anonymous and omniscient voiceover. In many other aspects, it is typical of classic wildlife filmmaking. As documentary footage edited to dramatize the everyday life of an animal, *The Leopard Son* embraces a number of strategies conventionalized by Disney's True-Life Adventures: simultaneous emphasis on the preciousness of wildlife and its resilience despite the brutality of nature; a narrative structured around that resilience through a story of parental devotion and a youngster's coming of age; exhortations toward human-animal identification in an unpeopled landscape; and, frequently sumptuous visuals of the land and its inhabitants. Its opening sequence is especially reminiscent of *Bear Country.* The film begins with a montage lasting over a minute of twelve black-and-white photographs of van Lawick at work, aging over three decades. Closing this review of his career and credentials of lengthy intimacy with the Serengeti and its animal inhabitants, a close-up of van Lawick dissolves into a full-color long shot of the plains, as the narration announces that this film depicts "a tale of coming of age and exploration I will never forget." The camera lingers over the expansive landscape as van Lawick declares, "This is my Serengeti," framing the film as being from his point of view, and recalling century-old proprietary relations of white Europeans over colonized Africa.

A sequence lasting just over three and a half minutes follows the landscape long shot. It montages images of wildebeests, gazelles, cheetahs, vultures, and other animals, setting the stage for the introduction of the film's

Hugo van Lawick at work in *The Making of the Leopard Son.*

main character-species. The "one animal always hovering on the edge of my vision and dreams... the unbelievably elusive leopard" appears first only as a tail undulating through tall grass, then in portrait-style close-up. Van Lawick testifies to his special relationship with his subject, referring to the adult female leopard he has found: "From that first day, I almost felt that she'd singled me out somehow. It was as if she had a secret she wanted to share with me alone." After the main title, two shots—one of a new moon; the other, a giraffe, grazing in the light of dawn—precede the first image of the male leopard cub. Van Lawick is triumphant: "In the crook of an old tree, I discovered the future," but one which is immediately marked as full of "dangers" with a cutaway to a male lion. Observing the female leopard watching over her cub, van Lawick continues, citing his close identification with the animals, his respect for conservation-park prohibitions against interfering with wild animals, and, implicitly, his belief in familial responsibility and division of labor (the leopard father is never mentioned, taking no role in parenting): "Watching her I suddenly knew that I was watching every mother, my mother even, scanning the bush for any and every threat. Still, I worried every time he left the safety of his tree to go out into the wild world. But I could not teach him. That was his mother's work."

"In the crook of an old tree, I discovered the future": a cub in *The Leopard Son.*

Here, the cub approaches his mother, who licks her cub and tussles with him playfully. Over the course of the film, the cub matures and learns to hunt, eventually gaining independence. Near the film's end, his mother bears twin cubs in the same tree and is shown going off to hunt for food. While she is gone, the leopard son, now two years old, exhibits a behavior the narration claims is previously undocumented: he returns to his birthplace. Despite concern that he will harm the cubs, he pays them little attention, but finds his mother's carcass. She has been killed by lions that will prey on other carnivores to reduce competition for food. With the newly orphaned cubs squeaking helplessly in the tree, the newly adult son finds in this scene a "new beginning"—a young adult female leopard. The film ends melodramatically with the two meeting in silhouette at sunset.

Narrative and formal similarities between *The Leopard Son* and *Bear Country* abound. One of the first tasks of the narrator in *Bear Country* is to legitimize the bear as a worthy subject; van Lawick establishes the importance of his project, citing the difficulty of capturing images of the "unbelievably elusive" leopard. Later he claims to document previously unheard-of behavior when the two-year-old returns to the tree.[53] *Bear Country* reveals its main subject over four and a half minutes into the film, after introducing six other species that share its territory. *The Leopard Son* depicts an adult leopard after eight other species, almost four minutes into the film, and the cub more than a minute later. Both films immediately precede the first images of their title subjects with an animal-free landscape shot, as sort of a visual-palette cleansing device. (This technique was already well established. The animated *Bambi* precedes the first peek at deer with a multiplane pan of the forest and visual inventory of the animal species found there, almost four minutes into the film.) Both opening sequences include an act of predation: in *Bear Country* a bird snatches up a field mouse; in *The Leopard Son* cheetahs chase down a gazelle. Both films are preoccupied with birth, maternal care for young, and growing up. These processes are represented as taking place within functional nuclear families defined by a marked sexual division of labor; yet the male's contribution consists only of his appearance for mating once every year or two. Neither depicts the act of mating, although in the 1990s footage of animals' sexual behaviors had become commonplace in the genre. *The Leopard Son*'s omission of such a scene reinforces its marketability as a family film. Both films quickly introduce a threat to the cubs' safety (for the bear cub, a cougar; for the leopard, a lion), but both films follow shots of the threatening species with sequences of the mother engaging in defensive behavior, then lavishing her offspring with affection. Each sequence ends with playful behavior alleviating the ominous threat. While the bear mother does not die at film's end, she turns her attention away from her maturing cubs in order to bear a new litter, as the leopard mother requires her son's independence to breed again.

The films differ primarily in the strategies they use to narrate their stories and to anthropomorphize their animal subjects. *Bear Country*'s narrator is omniscient, while *The Leopard Son*'s story is told by an observer on the scene who openly identifies with the animals he is filming. Where *Bear Country*'s abundant use of humor helps Disney personify animals as gentle pranksters, humor is almost entirely lacking in *The Leopard Son*. Instead, van Lawick anthropomorphizes the leopards through his sentimental identification of the cub as his own son, and the leopard mother as his own mother. While the film ends with the cub's triumphant entry into independent adulthood, he finds himself alone because his mother is dead. As in *Bambi*, the son is prompted to become a "man" (a term the narration uses in reference to the leopard) because he no longer has a mother to infantilize him.

The narration makes regular analogies between the animal and the human, displacing its emotional rendering of the female leopard's devotion to her cub onto a nostalgic privileging of fatherhood, in the form of van Lawick's recollections of raising his son in the same landscape. Human motherhood is, like leopard fatherhood, invisible. Observing that the cub spends days alone in a tree while his mother hunts, Gielgud-as-van Lawick notes, "the cub's secluded life reminded me of my son, who grew up with us in the wild. Like the cub, he played alone, and shared his world with wild and sometimes dangerous creatures." Except for the oblique reference to "us," there is no mention of van Lawick's son's mother (Jane Goodall).[54] Instead, *The Leopard Son* renders mothers not as subjects in their own right but rather as intermediate bodies, temporary staging grounds on which the male is nurtured to maturity and through which he will produce his own offspring.

While many of the generic conventions found in *The Leopard Son* are familiar borrowings from the genre's classical paradigm, other contemporary representations were less often deriving storylines from venerable literary traditions like the coming-of-age saga. Still, *The Leopard Son's* form—as an especially spectacular 35mm feature-length production—evidences Discovery's own coming of age as a media conglomerate with pockets deep enough to conduct costly experiments in new markets. In this instance, the risky new venture failed to reposition in theatrical distribution what Discovery had successfully commercialized on cable TV. Meanwhile, new channel acquisitions and launches and forays into digital cable and global markets proved greater successes for a company that had shrewdly exploited the conditions into which it launched: the expansion of channel capacity, the fragmentation of the mass audience, the rise of niching, a relaxing regulatory environment in the United States, and rapidly privatizing television industries abroad.

New Sensationalisms: "Fang TV" and Nature Faking Redux

Defying industry wisdom that an all-documentary format could never succeed, Discovery's global marketing was applauded by some and decried as crass commercialization of its educational mission by others. In Discovery's early years, industry observers noted that the network allowed critical analyses (especially on environmental issues, as in Michael Tobias's 1989 *Black Tide,* on the Exxon Valdez oil spill) that were usually absent from programming dependent on advertising, corporate sponsorship or government funding.[55] But by the 1990s, Discovery and its competitors in the nature and wildlife genre were at the center of a debate in the popular press about the televisual trend toward sensationalism. "Industry consensus," according to *Variety*, holds that viewers flock in largest numbers to nature programs featuring top predators such as sharks, tigers, crocodiles, and grizzly bears, fascinated by the "violent natures" of the most spectacularly "fanged and clawed" species.[56] Discovery drew on this assumption when it regrouped *Wild Discovery* episodes featuring predators under a new title, *Fangs!*, weekly for the seasons 1995–98. The series, which a front-page *Wall Street Journal* article called a "bloodbath," was Discovery's highest rated in 1995.[57]

The escalation of scenes of predation and aggression in the nature genre can't be attributed solely to Discovery. The controversial trend attracted the attention of television critics in 1991 when the Turner Broadcasting System (TBS) premiered *Trials of Life*. The series, a project of Sir David Attenborough coproduced by TBS, the BBC, and the Australian Broadcasting Corporation, consists of twelve thematic hour-long programs examining different aspects of animal behavior. Human representations are mostly absent, except for explanatory narration, Attenborough's occasional intervening appearances, and musical score. Episodes ranged from "Homemaking," an exploration of the types of structures birds, insects, and other animals build, to "Hunting and Escaping," often singled out in the press as containing particularly explicit scenes of predation.[58]

The Trials of Life's scenes of mating and predatory behaviors elicited press coverage that was sometimes puritanical in tone, and that interpret the series as sensationalistic and prurient, potentially corrupting, rather than knowledge-producing, or visually and narratively pleasurable. Criticism focused on explicit scenes of killing and mating, and, in particular, the emphasis on violence and sex, especially in promotional material for the series, which a *New Yorker* column described as "a cross between 'Jaws' and '9-1/2 Weeks.'"[59] Media professionals defended interest in these themes in a 1992 *New York Times* article. Tim Cowling, a Discovery executive producer, cited the role of "improved technologies . . . better film stocks, smaller cameras, the ability to shoot with less light" and the skills of trained naturalist-filmmakers, in contributing to the trend toward increasingly explicit footage of select natural behaviors. Candice Carpenter, president of Time-Life Video and Television, said that the *Trials of Life* campaign emphasized predation in a conscious attempt to expand the viewership for wildlife film "beyond the PBS audience to the action-adventure audience."[60] A year later, a *Christian Science Monitor* editorial decried the sensationalism of recent nature programs, recognizing in recent wildlife documentaries an easy identification between humans and animals and a Social

Darwinist framework, and assumed that the media has an instrumental effect on viewers, influencing our values and prompting viewers, especially children, to imitate what we see on the screen.

> The subtler message . . . is that humans themselves are merely part of a Darwinian natural order in which the only value is survival, kill or be killed. It's an old seductive message: Man wants to be civilized but, despite our best efforts, we are finally just animals. . . . We need to make sure we and our children don't become what we watch.[61]

Criticism seems to have had little effect on producers and programmers. Within a few years, the major broadcast networks were also hybridizing emergent forms of so-called reality-based television with "fang and claw" themes. The results, such as the miniseries *When Animals Attack* (1996–97, Fox), *World's Most Dangerous Animals* (1996–97, CBS), and *When Good Pets Go Bad* (1998–99, Fox, which ranks among reality producer Mike Darnell's early credits), compile amateur footage shot on the scene where some pet, stray, performing, or wild animal turns on a human, along with re-creations of such scenes. Each spawned sequels in subsequent seasons. One of the least expensive forms of television production, these shows repeat scenes during the same episode, or exchange footage with other reality-based shows. In Nash Entertainment's *When Good Pets Go Bad 2*, home-video parade footage, in which four Clydesdale horses break their harness and rush through rows of lawn chairs left empty by a fleeing crowd, is shown no less than seven times in succession. Episodes of both *When Animals Attack* and *When Good Pets Go Bad* use the same footage of a trained bear mauling a bystander in a TV studio and a panda batting at a man who leans against the bars of its cage. A *When Good Pets Go Bad 2* scene featuring a housecat's pounce onto a tourist in a New York City drugstore was reframed as a humorous "blooper" in another show.[62] The cat scratched Linnea Cohen's face, which was said to require thirty-eight stitches. The incident is reenacted on rapidly edited and grainy black-and-white, rollickingly handheld footage; Cohen appears in cutaways to a still color photo of her blood-streaked and bandaged face, and in a taped interview in which she wears a tiger-striped blazer.

In these shows animals are barely containable threats to human safety, driven by instinct toward vicious and seemingly random attacks; the co-existence of animal and human life is rendered as perpetual, life-threatening tension. Sometimes the instinct is recognized as self-preservation, in cases where tormented animals seek to escape their circumstances or redress their abusers; here, both human treatment of animals and the natural animal response are equated as unfettered and unfetterable brutality. Over a montage of bullfight scenes, the exceptionally deep-voiced narrator intones, "No country treats bulls more savagely than Spain. It's no wonder that sometimes these good bulls go bad." The visuals cut to pallid, jumpy camcorder footage, and the narrator continues, "In one event, the crowd taunts a confused bull. The poor creature can't stand the abuse, and tries to run." The bull jumps into the stands "in a monstrous display of fury" and tramples a couple of children before the scene ends. While this image and others—of, for example, a rodeo cowboy slamming headfirst into a fence, and a montage of stallions compelled to fight one another as sport—are graphic, others mine these encounters for irony. Over a lengthy scene that concludes *When Good Pets Turn Bad 2*, when a typically placid reindeer attacks a South Dakota man playing Santa Claus, the narration is peppered with Christmas references. A reenactment (involving the actual victim and, apparently, a stand-in reindeer), is embellished with actual 911 audio. Santa is treated for his wounds in an ambulance, and viewers learn that the animal has died of heart failure. Finally, the narrator makes an ominous announcement: "even more shocking than the attack is what happened next." Cut to a shot of steaks sizzling on a stove, as the animal converts from trusted companion, to brutal force of nature, to—if unexpectedly—a source of food.

While media watchdogs fretted over depictions of animal behaviors that they found more prurient than educational, others charged wildlife filmmakers with using unethical methods to represent animal behaviors realistically. Much of this concern focused on Marty Stouffer. In the early 1990s, without obligation to produce new *Wild America* episodes, Stouffer focused his attention on wildlife product for the home-video market, with titles including *Dangerous Encounters* (1993), which takes animal attacks on humans as its subject; *Fantastic Follies* (1996), which humorously presents animal mishaps; the polar bear film *Queen of the Ice* (1997); and *Wacky Babies* (1997), in which animals "speak" through cute human voiceovers.[63] Early in 1996, when Stouffer was negotiating with PBS for a contract to produce ten new *Wild America* episodes, the *Denver Post* claimed that he had used trained animals in scenes purported to depict wild ones in *Dangerous Encounters* and other projects. The story also contended that Stouffer had tethered prey to posts in order to film attacks by predators.[64] Stouffer admitted to staging "factual recreations" but denied outright fakery or cruelty.[65] A PBS investigation "found fault" with fifteen *Wild America* episodes and dropped the series, but cited financial rather than ethical reasons.[66] In 1998 *Wild America* returned to television in commercial syndication, distributed by Rysher Entertainment.[67]

The controversy suggested a degree of historical continuity in methods between early, openly exploitive cinematic representations of animals and more contemporary examples where exploitation is concealed and fakery well masked. Stouffer presented himself as unfairly victimized, and admitted that unethical practices are widespread when he told reporters at the 1997 Jackson Hole Wildlife Film Festival, "I was crucified for the sins of many."[68] In fact, he was not the only target of criticism. For example, cinematographer Wolfgang Bayer and others claimed that the late Marlin Perkins had endangered animals for solely dramatic purposes, charges that went largely uninvestigated; *Wild Kingdom* was long off the air and there were no financial interests at stake.[69]

Going Global: Animals in the Global Television Marketplace

In the 1990s televisual representations of animals proliferated not only in the United States but also globally, and not only on the Discovery Channel and Animal Planet, but also from a new competitor, the National Geographic Channel. The same economic advantages that spurred the wildlife genre's surges in the syndication boom of the 1970s and the cable boom of the late 1980s played roles in the globalization of the genre, as did the assumption that its content is culturally nonspecific; that is, nature (and representations of nature) transcend ideology. According to Animal Planet's general manager, Clark Bunting, "There is interest in the Siberian tiger whether you're in America or Cuba or Czechoslovakia [sic] or anywhere in-between.... It crosses borders and media platforms better, and more economically, than any other form of TV."[70] Just as Leo Braudy argues that generic "portability"—the production of stories for an American population so diverse that they also appeal to audiences in other nations—facilitated the globalization of Hollywood film, TV executives point to wildlife as universally appealing, especially when the programs lack or minimize human presence and require only the translation and rerecording of voiceover narration.[71]

The assumption of the universal appeal of nature and wildlife themes (and related science and adventure themes) shaped National Geographic's decision to develop a twenty-four-hour cable channel featuring nature, science, exploration, and adventure programming, announced not long after Discovery Communications Inc. and the BBC made public their plans for the global joint venture Animal Planet.[72] The National Geographic Society had considered but rejected the idea of launching a U.S. cable network in the early 1980s, even before Discovery's launch; new leadership revived the plan in the 1990s.[73] National Geographic enjoyed advantages that eased its entry into crowded cable markets. Through its partnership with the National Broadcasting Corporation (NBC) the channel gained access to global TV markets. Furthermore, the National Geographic brand was already widely recognized—and revered—due to circulation of the English-language *National Geographic Magazine* (published continuously since 1888) and its longtime television presence.[74] The high-profile, high-prestige *National Geographic Specials* aired on the major broadcast networks from 1964 to 1975, and then on PBS until 1994. In 1995, the nonprofit National Geographic Society reorganized its television unit as a for-profit, taxable enterprise in 1995 to separate commercial activities and therefore protect the tax-exempt status of its core operations.[75] After two decades on PBS, the new unit, National Geographic Television (NGT), promptly returned the *Specials* to NBC.[76] NGT also placed *Really Wild Animals* (1995–97), a series originated a year earlier for British television and narrated by actor Dudley Moore, into CBS's Saturday morning children's block, and eventually moved *National Geographic Explorer,* which had first aired on Nickelodeon (1985–86) and then on the superstation WTBS (1986–99), to NBC's cable news channels CNBC and MSNBC (1999–).[77]

The first joint launch by NBC and NGT, whose international wing became known as National Geographic Channels Worldwide (NGCW), was the National Geographic Channel UK in September 1997, followed within a year by channels established in Australia, Ireland, Finland, Poland, and throughout Scandinavia.[78] To secure widespread carriage, the NBC-NGT venture turned over a 50 percent stake in its U.K. and Scandinavian launches to News Corporation's British Sky Broadcasting (BSkyB).[79] NGCW president Sandy McGovern (a former senior vice-president of international development for Discovery) denied that her channel was entering a saturated market, speculating that with the availability of additional "high-quality programming," people "will probably just view more TV" rather than shift their loyalty from one network to another. Further, she expressed confidence in the venture's globalization project, claiming, "This kind of programming transcends borders. It's not considered American or British or whatever. Unlike general entertainment or comedy, it goes easily from country to county."[80]

Not long after the U.K. launch, NBC, facing disappointing ratings abroad for its situation comedies and talk shows, including *The Tonight Show,* turned over most of its channel space in Europe and all of NBC Asia to National Geographic in July 1998. The revamped channels, featuring a block of NBC news but dominated by programming provided by National Geographic Channels Worldwide, immediately reached 11 million subscribers in Europe and 7 million in Asia. NBC retained channels for its own programming in some European countries, such as Germany, where the market in television advertising was at the time surpassed only by the United States.[81] Some cable launches were coordinated with introduction of *National Geographic Magazine* in the local language.[82] Before the commercializing reorganization it was published only in English and Japanese; new editions including Spanish, Greek, and Hebrew quickly rose to first or second most popular among subscription magazines in Spain, Greece, and Israel.[83] Four years after launch, the National Geographic Channel claimed to reach 160 million households in 160 countries worldwide.[84]

In light of the capacity of multinational media corporations to engage in a kind of cultural imperialism, by flooding new markets with product that suits economic agendas more fully than it satisfies consumer demand, it is difficult to assess with certainty the degree to which these networks have been embraced by diverse populations worldwide. Thus, the question remains, not fully answerable here: to what extent are television viewers in global markets exercising consumer sovereignty, and to what extent are they choosing among a constrained set of formats and contents imposed without regard to local relevance? For Discovery and National Geographic, global TV launches have required tweaking on local levels, so that globalized content is distributed according to market-compatible modes of address. National Geographic's perspective on ease of entry into global markets echoed Animal Planet executives' assumptions that Anglo-American aesthetics and values are universal, and that the points-of-view of off-screen narration, on-screen hosts, and behind-the-scenes filmmakers are un-inflected by their own cultural experiences. In India, where National Geographic first launched in 1998, the channel airs in English and in Hindi, and, following Discovery's lead in serving regional language groups, provides at least a four-hour programming block in Tamil. Zubin Gandevia, managing director for National Geographic Asia, said that this strategy offers audiences "global product with a local packaging," acknowledging that whether or not the content appeals to local audiences is not under discussion, but that "how well you present the product to viewers determines your success."[85] Presentation includes scheduling as well as revoicing; most global versions of the National Geographic Channel feature thematic evening programming blocks (for example, wildlife on Tuesdays), and each differs from most other National Geographic channels in taking its own culture as subject of one evening's theme.

An American version of the National Geographic Channel faced a scarcity of open channels on which to launch. Eventually, NGCW and NBC assigned a one-third stake in the U.S. venture to a subsidiary of the powerful media conglomerate that had joined its launches in other markets, News Corporation's Fox Entertainment Group, and the National Geographic Channel found carriage on U.S. cable systems early in January 2001. Like Animal Planet, National Geographic places nature and wildlife prominently in its schedule, featuring series such as *Reptile Wild with Dr. Brady Barr,* a weekly primetime series launched in December 2001 with a title touting the academic credentials of its resident herpetologist, differentiating Barr from the proudly self-trained star of Animal Planet's *Crocodile Hunter.* In response to Discovery's aggressive launches of Animal Planet throughout markets targeted for the National Geographic Channel, executives at NGCW sought to differentiate their network by invoking National Geographic's prestigious history as a noncommercial entity devoted to scientific discovery and education—and by disparaging the competition. NGCW president McGovern, when asked to compare National Geographic's fact-checking procedures and standards to Discovery's, responded, "I *know* they don't do it" (emphasis in original). National Geographic Ventures head Rick Allen (another former DCI employee) boasted that "We have a level of authenticity and substantive involvement that no one else does," in the *Washington Post.*[86] (One wonders how they might have answered questions about Discovery's trustworthiness while still in their employ.)

But National Geographic did not brand its channel solely on the basis of scientific legitimacy. The channel also turned to charismatic (and sometimes already familiar) hosts, as in the Kratt Brothers' *Be the Creature* (2003–), and to elaborate displays of technological expertise, in *Crittercam* (2004–). Both series comprise quests for animals in the wild with which to interact and to exhibit to television audiences in ever-more intimate visual frameworks. A coproduction with the Canadian Broadcasting Corporation, *Be the Creature* features Chris and Martin Kratt, a cheerfully preppy pair of brothers who appeared previously on children's wildlife shows *Kratts' Creatures* and *Zoboomafoo,* launched on PBS in 1996 and 1999 respectively. The Kratts intermingle with their animal subjects, providing the animals' point of view, mimicking animal behaviors, and placing themselves among animals. When the subject is banded mongoose in Uganda, Chris and Martin count and recount young pups, appearing to fret when one goes missing as much or more than members of the mongoose pack. When the low-to-the-ground animals cross a field of tall grass, the Kratts crawl on their stomachs so that their camera mimics the animals' point-of-view. When a young mongoose learns to break an egg by hiking it against a rock, a Kratt tries the technique as well. And when Martin reclines in the show's final scene, the mongoose, well habituated to humans through contact with nearby villagers and researchers who have radio-collared one of the pack before the Kratts' arrival, crawls on him as if to groom insects off his body, a service they sometimes provide (in exchange for the bugs, which they eat) for napping pigs. Instead of trying to groom Martin, the animal scent-marks his back with a spray of urine, as it would a member of its own pack. Martin reacts with ambivalence about the meaning of the behavior, brushing off the animal and stripping off his shirt in apparent disgust, but exclaiming with satisfaction, "Now I'm really one of them."

The gadget-centric *Crittercam* goes even further than the Kratts to create images from the animal's perspective. Using a compact video camera designed by biologist Greg Marshall, the show's host, Dr. Mike Heithaus (another wildlife adventurer with foregrounded academic credentials), collaborates with scientists seeking footage of animal behavior that will reveal, as the introduction claims, "what happens when nobody's watching." The "Crittercam" is a visual technology that enables the science and film crews to capture images that they themselves cannot see with their own eyes or approach with cameras conventionally controlled by hand, a visual prosthesis much like Mike DeGruy's Homeboy, which was used to gather deep-sea footage for *Incredible Suckers* (1995), discussed in chapter 2. The Crittercam shows not what the filmmaker saw but, strapped or glued to fin or fur, the device approximates the animal's point of view. For underwater projects—such as an episode seeking to compare nurse sharks' mating behaviors in easily observable shallow waters with behaviors in deep water that have never been observed—the animal is captured, the camera attached to a fin; released, the shark unwittingly conducts its own surveillance. The device is designed to release automatically when six hours of video have been recorded, so that it can be retrieved with the help of radio signals, reviewed by researchers, and edited for television (land-based camerawork incorporates wireless video transmission). While legitimated by National Science Foundation funding and the presence of credentialed scientists who profess gratitude for means of accruing new data, the show teeters unevenly between the concerns of workshop tinkering, as clasps and harnesses for attaching the camera to different species are adapted, and a reality-based novelty that produces footage that is, for the most part, no more and no less compelling than the footage collected for the show (or any other) by more conventional means.[87] (For its part, Animal Planet countered with a special called *Spy on the Wild*, a BBC coproduction, in December 2004, in which various animal species are outfitted with cameras of their own.)

Not content to contain its media activities to a single cable channel, National Geographic Television's investments sprawled. In 1996 National Geographic Television became a partner in Destination Cinemas, which coproduces and distributes large-format films, and operates National Geographic–branded theaters at tourist sites: the Grand Canyon; Niagara Falls; Hearst Castle in San Simeon, California; and Victoria, British Columbia. NGT coproduced its first large-format film, the dramatized *Mysteries of Egypt,* starring Omar Sharif, in 1998 in collaboration with Destination Cinema, NOVA and WGBH-Boston, the Chicago's Museum of Science and Industry, the Canadian Museum of Civilization in Quebec City, and Centex Investment Ltd. A record-setting hit for the format, grossing nearly $100 million, NGT followed *Mysteries of Egypt* with *Lewis and Clark: Great Journey West; Roar: Lions of the Kalahari* (2003) directed by prolific wildlife filmmaker Tim Liversedge; and *Forces of Nature* (2004), which was funded in part by Amica Insurance and the National Science Foundation. National Geographic also invested in the feature film *K-19: The Widowmaker* (2002, directed by Kathryn Bigelow), and licensed nonmedia products to the Museum Store, J. C. Penney, First USA Bank, K-Swiss, and others that earned for National Geographic $200 million in 2001 alone; the sum constituted a ninefold increase since the cable launch.[88]

In Asian markets National Geographic sought to cultivate local production as a source of new content for its television channel, engaging the press in efforts to publicize a call for digital video submissions to a new adventure-oriented series to be called *Up for It.*[89] In December 2001 NGCI and the Singapore Economic Development Board announced a new joint venture, the National Geographic Channels International–Economic Development Board Documentary Production Fund, designed to make awards to young Asian filmmakers and Asian production companies. The assistant managing director, Tan Chek Ming, told the press that the project would "groom local talent . . . build Singapore into a media hub . . . [and] distinguish ourselves as a centre for factual programming."[90] In fall 2003 NGCI began to air the first ten completed documentaries funded by the program and renewed the project for another four years. Broaching a range of cultural topics, some of the funded films took on human-animal interactions: *Operation Hot Pursuit,* directed by Nikhil Alva, tracks conservationist Vivek Menon's largely undercover investigation of the illegal ivory trade from India to markets in Taiwan and Japan; *Beetle Battles: Kwang Bang,* directed by Karina Holden for the Australian company Becker Entertainment, explores the Thai practice of beetle fighting.[91] By the third season, the NGCI-EDB call for submissions in categories suggested a shift in focus away from National Geographic's conventional approaches and toward action-oriented, reality-based adventurism, stunts and the paranormal: "disaster . . . riddles of the dead . . . killer instincts. . . . What we're not looking for: factual educational story-telling."[92]

These choices were not National Geographic's alone but symptomatic of trends throughout a television industry depending evermore heavily on reality concepts and competitions, ranging from the *Crossing Over with John Edward* (2001–3, syndicated), a psychic foray into the afterlife; the daredevil- and gross-out challenge *Fear Factor,* which regularly features animals in stunts that subject contestants to immersion in tanks of rats or snakes, and provides live insects for contestants to consume; *The Swan* (2004, Fox), a hybrid cosmetic-surgery makeover show and beauty contest; and the provocatively titled *Wife Swap* (2004–, ABC, based on a British version of the show launched in 2003), which in actuality comes off as a moralistic "family values" tract with the basic message "there's no place like home." As National Geographic's competitor Discovery continued to brand itself more aggressively as entertainment rather than education, industry observers condemned some of its programming risks as tarnish on its reputation and abuse of the documentary form. According to *Broadcasting and Cable* editor-in-chief Harry A. Jessel:

> TV is awash in UFOs, alien abductions and just about every other para-normal phenomenon you can think of. But one of TV's greatest unexplained mysteries . . . is why such programming dreck has found homes on networks like Discovery and The History Channel. . . .
> [Recently] Discovery aired an hour on the afterlife (with zombies!) that careened so violently between fact and fiction that it made you want to question every claim on every show on the network.[93]

Once a darling of industry executives eager to claim cable's worth in the public interest, Discovery, with National Geographic on its heels, strayed far from its original mission in the course of a global ratings war fought conventionally with spectacle and sensationalism.

All Reality, All the Time: Animal TV and Generic Hybridity

In the early twenty-first century, television's heterotopic displays of the animal world became available not just daily but around the clock and on multiple competing channels in multiple global markets, in an industry recently retooled to sustain an unprecedented number of hours of nonfiction programming. Some of these programs followed tried and true traditions. For example, in *Jack Hanna's Animal Adventures* (1993–, syndicated), Hanna, director of the Columbus (Ohio) Zoo from 1978 to 1992 and a regular guest on *Good Morning America* and *The Late Show with David Letterman* since the 1980s, visits conservation parks and other locations worldwide, in a format familiar since the old *Wild Kingdom*. In a twist on the format, Hanna's cohost is his daughter Kathaleen. Likewise, most Discovery Channel, Animal Planet, and National Geographic animal programming follows conventional paradigms—minor variations on instructional pet care, presenter-featuring animal-quest adventures, and classic wildlife film-making—but Animal Planet also moved heavily into developing "reality" concepts with animal themes, blending genres generally, and blurring the boundaries of fiction and nonfiction.

These shows exemplify the pervasive industry logic that a network can never have enough of the latest good thing, and will copy and combine successful formulas from other genres and networks to try to remain competitive. *Animal Court* premiered in fall 1998, featuring Judge Joseph Wapner, formerly of the syndicated *People's Court* (1981–93), hearing cases involving breeding rights, neglect, boarding bills, and other animal-related disputes.[94] Early in 1998 the network set the reality series *Emergency Vets* in a Denver animal hospital to follow stories of injured or ill animals during their treatment. The series duplicated the prior success of veterinarian-featuring reality programming by the BBC. *Animal Hospital,* set in a Royal Society for the Prevention of Cruelty to Animals clinic in North London, drew some nine million viewers to its second broadcast in 1994 and sustained popularity throughout its ten-season run. The show was followed by *Vets' School* (1996) and its spinoffs, *Vets in Practice* (1996–) and *Vets in the Wild* (1998–99). Animal Planet general manager Clark Bunting claimed that despite generic innovations, "We never laugh at the animals," but another variation on an inexpensively produced format appeared on the channel in 1999, *The Planet's Funniest Animals,* based on home videos submitted by amateur camcordists.[95]

Other series explored unconventional aspects of animal and human relationships, using animals as ciphers onto which any number of meanings with distinctive ideological ends can be projected. *Animal Miracles,* for example, depends on trends in a syndication market optimistic about the capacity of animals to hold viewers' attention, and on a turn toward dramatic content inflected with sometimes-vague spiritual concerns, or sometimes not-so-vague nonsecular Christian content.[96] A series of thirty-nine one-hour shows produced by Peace Arch Entertainment Group of Canada, *Animal Miracles* was sold in 2001 to Animal Planet, and is also run regularly by the family-oriented broadcast network PAX TV under the title *Miracle Pets.* Typical episodes feature four segments. In each, an animal performs a feat that saves a human life or that can be interpreted as a moral lesson. Canadian actor Alan Thicke introduces each segment and provides voiceover; real-life humans who have experienced animal "miracles" appear in interview footage, while actors recreate their stories. In a segment called "The 78th Floor," a guide dog named Roselle accompanies her master, Michael, down dozens of flights of stairs at the World Trade Center (WTC) following the terrorist attack on September 11, 2001. Scenes taped in a generic office set and stairwell lack exterior shots of Lower Manhattan, the WTC, or the post-crash fires on the upper floors. The collapse of the tower, shortly after Roselle, Michael, and a coworker reach the ground floor and exit the building, is reenacted as a cloud of dust that envelopes the actors while the real Michael recalls the sounds made by the falling skyscraper. In "Moses and Cassie," a Massachusetts couple discuss home-video footage of a stray kitten that frequented their yard for months, always accompanied by a crow that fed it by mouth as if it were a hatchling. In voiceover, Thicke suggests, "Perhaps there's a lesson we can all learn from this incredible relationship"; a local veterinarian's assistant adds, "If you're able to gain trust in someone or something or each other, then anything is possible." In yet another "miracle," a woman seeks treatment for abdominal pain following an unexpectedly rough horseback ride; her doctor discovers a malignant ovarian tumor: "that horse jumped Pam right into early detection of this deadly disease." Each incident is represented as inexplicable through analyses of instinct, intelligence, training, or as coincidence, but only as human-helping miracles.

In *Animal Precinct* (2001–2) and *Animal Cops* the table is turned. Rather than faithful helpmates, animals are all too often victims of individuals who fail in their role as stewards of nonhuman forms of life; saviors arrive in the form of law enforcement officers. *Animal Precinct* quickly became, alongside *The Crocodile Hunter,* one of Animal Planet's top-rated shows.[97] The series, in the style of Fox's long-running reality series *COPS* (1989–, Fox), sends a camera crew along as officers employed by the Humane Law Enforcement division of the New York City American Society for the Prevention of Cruelty to Animals (ASPCA) answer calls about neglected, abused, or abandoned animals, dog- and cockfighting, which typically result in the arrest of abusers and rescue of their victims. In 2002 Animal Planet added *Animal Cops: Detroit,* later followed by *Animal Cops: Houston* in 2003, *Miami Animal Police* (2003–4), and *Animal Cops: San Francisco* in 2005, for more of the same in different settings.

In yet another reality-animal hybrid, animals are neither our rescuers nor our victims, but rather our beloved if often misunderstood companions. *The Pet Psychic* became one of Animal Planet's highest-profile phenomena during its two-season run (2002–4). British-born Sonya Fitzgerald, a former model and etiquette consultant, hosts the show, lending to animals a sympathetic ear and conveying to befuddled owners the real reasons behind pets' strange behaviors. Fitzgerald plays interspecies mediator, showing off telepathic "skills" to astonished pet owners of dogs, cats, snakes, and other animals, and couples-counseling troubled human and animal companions back to mutual satisfaction. The second season took Fitzgerald out of the studio and onto locations, which included visits to celebrities and their pets.

Live animals would be absent from some of Discovery's highest-profile programming, collaborations with the BBC such as *Walking with Dinosaurs* (1999), *Walking with Prehistoric Beasts* (2001), and *Walking with Cavemen* (2003). Animals and humans appearing in these series are mostly fabricated using computer-generated imagery (CGI), constituting not so much natural history or even factual evolutionary theory but exercises in spectacular animated speculation.[98] Discovery's *Animal Face-Off* (2004–, Natural History New Zealand) draws on the same interest in high-tech tinkering pitched to male audiences in Discovery and The Learning Channel hits such as *Junkyard Wars* and *Monster Garage.* The show is bloodsport gone virtual: a typical episode begins with zoologist David Salmoni's presentation to a so-called international team of scientists, designers, and engineers (introduced members of the team hail only from the United States, England,

and Australia), which huddles around a crocodile skull: "All right, guys . . . who's gonna win in a fight between a saltwater croc and a great white shark?" To answer the question, the cast splits into two teams, each of which designs and constructs computer and animatronic models of top predators and pits them against the others in both mechanical and CGI-battles. While much of the show is devoted to displays of technical exper-tise—sculpting of polystyrene models, forging aluminum casts at a foundry, testing robotic motion—the mission is less means than end, neither how-to nor treatise on animal behavior. Instead, it returns again and again to the question of who will win, which is debated in dim-lit tête-à-tête inter-ludes between the two team's lead scientists. Predicting the outcome of these battles is also fodder for polls and games on the official website for the show.

Such programming has veered away from the animal itself, allowing the living animal to recede into geographic and historic, replaced by the mechanical, the electronic, and the imaged animal. This move was fore-shadowed by John Berger's account of the explosion of animal imagery in late modernity, as urbanization, industrialization, and mechanical reproduc-tion lessened daily human contact with animals and increased the number of representations of animals in circulation.[99] But perhaps the oddest twist on the wildlife genre, *Wildboyz* (2003–, MTV) relocates reality-based stunts into wildlife and ethnographic filmmaking tropes, situating presenter/filmmakers in immersive encounters with human and animal Others. The series, reuniting *Jackass* (2000–2002, MTV) creator Spike Jonze, director Jeff Tremaine, and performers Chris Pontius and Steve-O, abandons urban and suburban American settings, sites for stunts involving shop-ping carts and portable toilets, and drops its cast and crew into foreign lands for challenges both culture and nature that make the nose-to-nose tactics of Steve Irwin and the Kratt Brothers appear quaintly restrained. In India, often bare-chested, showing off tattoos (Steve-O's back is filled with a large image of his own face and signature), clad in dhoti and turbans while many of the Indian men they encounter wear jeans and button-down shirts, Chris and Steve firewalk, lie on a bed of nails, pierce Steve-O's cheek, and lick the bare feet of strangers.

While many segments place Chris and Steve-O among people, where they witness or experience challenging or exoticized and unexplained cul-tural practices, the show is largely promoted as the "boyz'" adventures in nature, a kind of wildlife-filmmaking-gone-wild, just as early twentieth-century filmmakers such as Martin and Osa Johnson were largely promoted and are largely remembered as *wildlife* filmmakers despite the regular presence of footage recording their encounters with indigenous African and South Pacific peoples in their films. In the India episode the "wildboyz'" first interact with animals among snake charmers. Steve-O hides in a corner much of the time. Chris cackles joyfully at first sight of the snakes but calls for the scene to end when a cobra strikes at the flute he tries to play. They wrestle sloth bears until Steve-O's ribcage is striped with claw marks; they join elephant polo teams but disrupt play when Steve-O throws elephant excrement at Chris. To conclude the episode Steve-O crouches beneath an elephant and waits for it to urinate. Soaked, he tackles the show's director, then gags in disgust, the third time he vomits or nearly vomits in a half-hour episode.

A trip to South Africa includes a brief visit to a Zulu village, where Chris and Steve-O are introduced to local smoking, dance, and marriage traditions, but most of the episode is spent among animals. Frequently, they expose themselves to animal attacks. Dressed in a two-man zebra costume, Chris and Steve-O are attacked by a lion that trots off with the cloth zebra head while they retreat. In another scene Chris holds scorpions in place to sting Steve-O's buttocks, a favored target of *Wildboyz* stunts generally; in an episode set in Belize, Steve-O holds a banana "in [his] ass" to be snatched away by a tapir. While more traditional wildlife-TV counterparts strive to present *impervious* bodies, ever in control of themselves and of nature (and, like Steve Irwin, downplaying real injuries that do occur when control is lost), Chris and Steve-O are exhibitionists constantly testing their own abject *perviousness,* albeit staged and temporary: they are regularly pelted with excrement, gashed open and bloodied by animal claws, or injured in other ways. Their bodies, often nearly naked, come into intimate contact with one another. They are scrutinized in extreme close-up by the camera, and penetrated by objects. And sometimes they engage in explicitly sexual behaviors. In Belize, Chris, feminized by wearing a bright red flower behind his left ear, introduces a kinkajou as it licks his nipple, which is smeared with a substance that glistens like honey. Then, Chris, with the left side of his face shown in profile, eyes closed, open-mouthed, allows the animal to lick his chin, lips and tongue, groaning softly over a romantic musical cue. In the next shot, Chris has turned, literally, away from the scene and walks with the right side of his body to the camera in medium shot, so that the flower in his hair is no longer visible. He addresses the camera with chagrin: "I feel kinda weird. I don't know if it's because I made out with an animal or because I made out with a *male* animal," then grins mischievously and laughs to end the scene.[100] These events are typical of the series, each an exercise in subjecting one's own body to pain and the grotesque, relieved by the capacity to walk away from too-arduous rituals without understanding their meaning, to flirt with danger until the threat of serious injury becomes too real. If in daily experience, most contact with "the wild" has been lost, in *Wildboyz* it is a voraciously consumed and disposable backdrop for the exhibition of white, masculine physical prowess and cultural mobility.

Shifting paradigms in the wildlife genre expressed the heated competition among television networks in the 1980s and 1990s. Commercial networks had little use for wildlife programming after the syndication boom of the early 1970s. But as channel capacity expanded, audiences fragmented, and advertising revenue dispersed, the genre—slow to go out of date, relatively inexpensive, recyclable in a variety of contexts—fulfilled network needs for product to fill schedules amid a proliferating number of channels competing for advertisers' dollars. Nature migrated with ease from its prestigious but small presence on PBS to its strategic deployment by cable networks such as TBS and, on a more regular basis, Discovery, to broadcasters such as CBS and Fox. Eventually, in efforts to develop new networks with coherent brand identities, niched audiences, and global reach, Discovery teamed with the BBC to launch Animal Planet, a round-the-clock source of representations of animals, and National Geographic, a competitor in natural history and adventure programming, partnered with NBC and News Corporation subsidiaries to found its own cable channel. Following industry trends, these leading producers and outlets for wildlife programming did not constrain their activities to their domestic markets, but entered television markets worldwide.

During this period of recommercialization and globalization, dominant practices within the genre downplayed classic wildlife filmmaking tropes of pristine, unpeopled, and timeless nature, and called upon ideologies of nature as both a brutal force and as a resilient resource worthy of, even requiring, human stewardship. New examples of the wildlife genre emphasized scientific discoveries, the urgency of conservation efforts, and the consumer potential of nature. Representations of animals increasingly took the form of action and adventure sagas, in their preoccupations with predatory behaviors, or in the form of human encounters with nature, returning many of the strategies of early wildlife expedition films to its contemporary version. Masculine identity formations proliferated, displacing the stoically self-made authority embodied by the late Marlin Perkins and the by-now-grandfatherly David Attenborough, and the patrician control of Hugo van Lawick, with the hands-on, blokey machismo of Steve Irwin and the Kratt Brothers; the sporting technophilia of the folks behind *Animal Face-Off* and *Crittercam;* and the ironic indulgences of Jeff Corwin and the *Wildboyz* crew. Channels featuring nonfiction animal programming also veered sharply, as did other TV networks, toward cheap reality-based formats hybridized with all manner of other TV genres: game shows, talent shows, police-chase shows, court TV, talk shows, psychic readings, and stunt competitions. While these generic offshoots treated the animal variously as economic asset, as victim, as threat, as savior, as companion, as playmate, and as individual subject vis-à-vis a relationship to humans, simultaneous trends in the genre took their cue from new and sometimes controversial scientific theories about animal—and human—biology and behavior. Perhaps most provocatively, animal programming continued (as have several of the films and television programs examined in some detail thus far, such as *Bear Country* in chapter 1, *Incredible Suckers* in chapter 2, and *The Leopard Son* in this chapter) to maintain an interest in animal mating and reproduction.

4

Animal Sex

> HORSE: Listen, just think of the most boring
> thing you can come up with. That should
> keep it well in order.
> GERALD: Like what?
> GUY: . . . Nature programs.
> GERALD: I *like* nature programs.
> GUY: Ah! But they don't give you a hard-on,
> now do they? Do they? Blimey!
> GERALD: Oh, shut up! It's not funny, it's
> medical.
>
> — *The Full Monty*

What is it that we see when we look at images of animals? More specifically, what it is we see when we look at images of animal courtship and coupling? Elizabeth Grosz suggests that we hope to see a bit of ourselves:

> Animals continue to haunt man's imagination, compel him to seek out their habits, preferences and cycles, and provide models and formulae by which he comes to represent his own desires, needs and excitements. The immense popularity of nature programmes on television, of books on various animal species, beloved or feared, and the work of naturalists recording data for scientific study, all testify to a pervasive fascination with the question of animal sex: how do animals *do it*? How do elephants make love (the standard old joke: very carefully)? How do snakes copulate? What are the pleasures of the orangu-tang, the gorilla, the chimpanzee?[1]

A great deal of televisual evidence suggests that Grosz is right. Part of the human fascination with images of animals is voyeuristic, deriving from curiosity about sexual activity, theirs and ours. Indeed, images and explications of animals' mating practices have entered the standard repertoire of scenes in wildlife narratives. They have become so commonplace that other mass-media genres have occasionally speculated on how viewers might put these images to use. In a scene from the feature film *The Full Monty* (1997, directed by Peter Cattaneo), the character Gerald (played by Tom Wilkinson) fails to hide from his friends Horse (Paul Barber) and Guy (Hugo Speer) that he becomes aroused while watching animals—inferentially, animals mating—on television, but tries to distinguish this response ("it's medical!") from other kinds of stimulation. In the song "The Bad Touch" by Bloodhound Gang (1999), lyricists offered images of animal sexual behavior as erotic inspiration ("let's do it like they do on the Discovery Channel").

Another handful of pop-culture references to wildlife films suggests that when we look at animals—including animals on TV—we understand their behavior as it correlates with our own. We may hope that through animal images we can make better sense of the bewildering behaviors of our partners. In *Bridget Jones' Diary* (2001, directed by Sharon Macguire), a televisual depiction of lions mating reminds the despondent, channel-surfing Bridget (Renée Zellweger) of the demise of her fling with Daniel Cleaver (Hugh Grant). She grimaces as the narrator describes the scene: "the male penetrates the female and leaves. Coitus is brief and perfunctory."[2] Changing the channel, she lands on another film in which animals play a part in human psychosexual dynamics, *Fatal Attraction* (1987, directed by Adrian Lyne): a woman (Glenn Close) exacts revenge on the adulterous husband (Michael Douglas) who jilted her by boiling his daughter's pet rabbit. In *Someone Like You* (2001, directed by Tony Goldwyn), the coincidentally named Jane Goodall (Ashley Judd) can't figure out why her relationships don't seem to last. After a few weeks of passion, Jane's current boyfriend, Ray (Greg Kinnear), sabotages their plan to move in together and stops returning her phone calls. Jane finds his behavior inexplicable. Then, she recognizes his actions in a wildlife TV program:

> Throughout the animal kingdom, prey species have developed a wide array of escape behaviors. Freezing is a common response to predator alarm. Sensing danger, many animals assume a rigid statue-like position. Fleeing is another popular method. Some species will simply try to outrun their captors while others take an erratic zigzag course in the hope that sudden direction shifts will eventually tire the predator, causing her to give up the chase.[3]

Ray freezes, he flees, he zigs, he zags, just like the warthog, giraffe, rabbits, ostriches, and other freezing, fleeing, zigzagging creatures that appear on

Jane's TV screen. Jane tires, gives up the chase, and embarks on a study that results in her "new cow theory." Learning that in some species, a male animal will refuse to mate with any female he has mated with before, she assumes that Ray has a short sexual attention span and has found someone new. Jane looks to animals for what Grosz might call "the models and formulae by which [she] comes to represent [her] desires, needs and excitements"—and those of her lovers.

Someone Like You's Jane watches wildlife as a source of insight into human sexuality, but wildlife filmmaking has, historically, used images of animals to somewhat different ends. As noted in previous chapters, the wildlife genre's "classical" form has frequently contextualized animal behaviors in narratives that allegorize them as lessons in sex roles and parenting. The "classical" wildlife film typically features an individual, anthropomorphized animal protagonist, and is often constructed as a "coming of age" story. Its theme is the ultimate resiliency of nature, despite its occasional brutality and hardships that may be imposed by human activity. During the arduous trajectory from birth to maturity, the animal experiences a series of dramatic conflicts but eventually reaches adulthood, which is represented as the opportunity to mate and reproduce. A common variation follows an animal group throughout a yearlong cycle of seasons, also marked by births, struggles, and triumphs. The Walt Disney Company conventionalized these thematic and narrative conventions in the True-Life Adventures series, beginning with the short *Seal Island* in 1948 and ending with the feature *Jungle Cat* in 1960. They persist in more recent wildlife films, from Jamie Uys's *Animals Are Beautiful People* (1974) to Discovery Pictures' *The Leopard Son* (1996) and *Africa's Elephant Kingdom* (1998). In the classical mode, not only is the protagonist animal rather than human; humans are virtually erased from sight, even if human presence lingers in the form of omniscient, interpretive voiceover narration and nondiegetic music. The near-absolute separation of animal and human life reinforces the nostalgic view of nature as an idealized past and as a representational field of malleable signs from which allegories may be gleaned.

Wildlife nonfiction made for television often takes a less allegorical and more directly didactic approach, deriving many of its associations between animal and human behaviors from recent trends in the sciences, rather than allegories constructed in venerable literary traditions like the coming-of-age story. To a great extent, wildlife TV has abandoned its old habit of explaining animal behavior by reference to human social identities and relationships. Instead, the genre increasingly explains human behavior by means of correlation to seemingly homologous animal behaviors. Drawing on new theories produced since the emergence of sociobiology in the 1970s and its disciplinary progeny, narrations scripted for wildlife television programs now frequently extend interpretations of observed animal behaviors to human social phenomena, especially the process of mate selection, the extent of pair-bonding, and the care of offspring.[4]

In the 1980s wildlife television programs begin to feature explicitly represented sexual behaviors, serving as entertainment in a TV environment that in this period expanded rapidly and required the production of unprecedented programming hours, much of it in nonfiction genres, and in which human sexuality was being represented with greater frankness than in prior decades. The genre's once-predominant focus on the animal family becomes a "pervasive fascination" with animal sex, alongside commensurate shifts within other TV genres and paradigm shifts in animal-observing sciences. Accordingly, representations of animals' reproductive behaviors have been rendered with increasing visual and rhetorical explicitness, and the genre has begun to pay scant but significant attention to the controversial subjects of animal "rape" and same-sex sexual activity. Such representations map the boundaries of the normative and the nonnormative onto behaviors understood as the reproductive and the nonreproductive, for animals and by extension, for humans.

A Televisual History of Animal Sex: Genre Contexts and Conventions

Human fascination with other species' mating habits is more than a voyeuristic glance at the ways of animal-Others, whose bodies may be similar to our own (as in the case of primates) or different, to greater or lesser extents (as in the cases of snakes, insects, elephants). It is also a search, as Grosz argues, for explanations of our own desires and justifications for our deeds. Wildlife television has provided a steady stream of images of mating and other social behaviors that provide just these explanations. Derek Bousé, in *Wildlife Films,* reminds his readers that this preoccupation is essentially a postwar trend: "the pervasiveness of mating, reproduction, and the rearing of young in wildlife films today make it easy to forget that these were not always mainstays of the genre. In its earliest years they were not even present." He mentions a few exceptions among early ornithological films by Oliver Pike; dramas featuring animal characters such as *Call of the Wild* (1923) and *White Fang* (1925), both based on novels by Jack London; Cherry Kearton's fancifully newlywed penguins in *Dassan* (1930); and some scientific (not popular) nature films of the 1940s.[5] As well, Jean Painlevé's short *The Sea Horse* (1934) depicts a male that seems to give birth, releasing the hatching eggs that he has carried since the female deposited them in his pouch upon fertilization. But the predominant prewar wildlife film-making style—the expedition film, undertaken by both big-game hunters and "camera-hunters"—emphasized human encounters with animals rather than relationships among animals, sexual, familial, or otherwise. Later, these themes became commonplace for reasons that can be found among larger trends in television content and competition, and in the genre's development of new forms of spectacle and articulations of new scientific claims.

Once television became the primary outlet for wildlife nonfiction, the centrality of the family and, later, sex should come as little surprise. Television has been a mechanism for engineering and imaging the American family since its widespread popular acquisition from 1948 to 1960. The television industry, as Lynn Spigel's work on the period shows, promised to bring the family together by situating a new form of entertainment in the home, frequently in genres oriented toward the family in various forms.[6] In situation comedy alone, examples are far too numerous to mention more than a tiny sample: the nuclear family appears in *Ozzie and Harriet* (1952–66, ABC), *All in the Family* (1971–83, CBS), *The Cosby Show* (1984–92, NBC), and *That '70s Show* (1998–, Fox); single moms, in *Julia* (1969–71, NBC) and *Kate and Allie* (1984–89, CBS); and male parenting teams, in *My Three Sons* (1960–65, ABC; 1965–72, CBS), *Full House* (1987–95, ABC), and *Two and a Half Men* (2003–, CBS). Likewise, mate selection, pair-bonding, and care of offspring play large roles in representations of animals, evidence that thematic trends, representational strategies, and viewers' expectations may spill across TV's fictional and nonfictional genres. The concerns of many classic wildlife films—for example, *Echo of the Elephants* (1992, directed and filmed by Martyn Colbeak, written by David Attenborough and Cynthia Moss for BBC Bristol), which observes the close relationships between a clan matriarch, her sister, and their offspring—is the stuff of much of television, transportable from wildlife film to made-for-TV movie to serial melodrama or sitcom with only changes in cast and setting.

When the wildlife genre intensifies its attention to mate selection, this trend is commensurate with trends in other TV genres. By the 1970s, the once-almost-exclusively domestic and typically prudish sitcom had begun to branch out of the home and into workplace settings, with characters drawn from peer rather than family groups. Dating became an increasingly primary theme of shows such as *I Dream of Jeannie* (1965–70, NBC), *Mary Tyler Moore* (1970–77, CBS), *A Different World* (1987–93, NBC), *Seinfeld* (1990–98, NBC), *Friends* (1994–2004, NBC), and *Sex and the City* (1998–2004, HBO). "Reality-based" TV has only dabbled in observations of family life, as in its *cinéma-vérité* precedent *An American Family* (1973, PBS), or *The Osbournes* (2002–5, MTV). But matchmaking game shows, such as *The Dating Game* (1965–73, ABC), *Love Connection* (1983–93, syndicated), and *Singled Out* (1995–97, MTV), and so-called unscripted entertainment have been saturated with examinations of how the human species selects its mates: *Blind Date* (1999–2003, syndicated), *Who Wants to Marry a Multi-Millionaire* (2000, Fox), *Temptation Island* (2001–2, Fox), *elimiDATE* (2001–3, syndicated), *Taildaters* (2002–3, MTV), *The Bachelor* (2002, ABC), *The Bachelorette* (2003–5, ABC), and *Joe Millionaire, Married by America,* and *Mr. Personality* (all 2003, Fox), among many others. These shows scrutinized (and sometimes satirized) the process through which participants evaluate one another as potential sex partners, second dates, or longer-term commitments. Meanwhile, wildlife filmmakers have tackled much the same material, utilizing more explicit representations of animal sexual behavior than permissible within representations of humans.

Depictions of animal sex reach the viewer-as-voyeur in venues where their human counterparts are unrepresented, such as the primetime family TV hour, or the G-rated IMAX movie, which reaches school groups and families in theaters typically located in science museums and tourist destinations, but not always without controversy. A famous example of a controversial image in a popular American wildlife documentary was the depiction of the birth of an American bison calf in Disney's True-Life Adventure *The Vanishing Prairie* (1954). To date, birth scenes had been limited to eggs hatching. In response to the bison-calving scene, the New York State Board of Motion Picture Censors banned the film temporarily.[7] American television resisted depictions of explicitly sexual behaviors for nearly three decades. CBS excised a mating scene from *The Family That Lived with Elephants* (1974, Survival Anglia Ltd.), and even when PBS permitted a scene of wild pigs mating in a 1983 episode of Marty Stouffer's *Wild America,* some local affiliates edited it out.[8] Now, scenes of births and sexual behaviors have become commonplace throughout nonfiction animal programming. Watching animals' reproductive behaviors is framed as ironically wholesome, both entertaining and educational, both feel-good and good for you. As Jane C. Desmond has pointed out, in regard to the tourist experience of watching live animal sex during mating-season tours of the elephant seal colony at Año Nuevo State Park in California, "Were these humans, of course," she writes, "the site would be closed down immediately. But sex among animals is nature at its most natural."[9]

In the early 1990s the genre's increasing attention to mating (and to violence) caught the attention of journalists and editorial writers, some of whom pined for gentler and more genteel representations of nature. Some network executives defended the shift as attributable to technological advances in filmmaking and to new scientific knowledge. Thus, hunting, killing, sex, birth, and death could be seen, in the words of *Nature's* longtime host and producer George Page, as simply "relevant to the film, to explaining how the natural world works." Others admitted that competition played a role, as networks vied to grab and hold the attention of television audiences that dispersed in the 1980s and 1990s as cable-channel capacity expanded and new consumer technologies were introduced. Fred Kaufman, *Nature's* executive producer, told the *New York Times*, "we're all trying to come up with the next dolphin film, the next cat film, the next blockbuster."[10]

Still, many wildlife films continue to avoid representations of mating behaviors that might be considered sexually explicit. Some concentrate so intently on courtship that its outcome garners little attention, and so intently on male behavior that little is shown (or seems to be known) of the female. For example, *Flying Casanovas* (2000), a BBC production written and hosted by Sir David Attenborough and aired on the PBS series *NOVA*, explores how male bowerbirds, found throughout Australia and Papua New Guinea, attract mates. As Attenborough explains, "Instead of showing off their bodies, they use inanimate objects that they collect and arrange in special ways.... No other male animal woos his mates by displaying inanimate objects in this way. Except, of course, us." Each species in the bowerbird family has its own style of bower-building, and each male seeks to attract females to inspect his bower, for the female will mate only with the male with the most elaborate bower in her vicinity. The only purpose of these structures appears to be as entries in the annual competition for reproductive opportunities (they serve as neither shelter for adults nor nests for offspring), and the designs are elaborate. Western bowerbirds display their collections of all-white bones and shells in front of freestanding archways built from twigs. Instead of an arch, the Macgregor bowerbird constructs a Maypole, which he adorns with pendants shaped from caterpillar droppings and surrounds with a fence made of moss and fungus. The reproductive stakes in this competition are high: only one in ten males gets selected for mating, and those few males mate with virtually every female in the area. Attenborough visits several bowers and demonstrates the birds' commitment to particular designs and color schemes by fiddling with their structures. When the birds return from scavenging, they distress over the changes and correct the damage. The program is almost entirely fixed on the sculptural labors of males. The females appear rarely, and only to briefly consider a potential mate's bower-building prowess; their mating, her care of their offspring, and other aspects of her daily life are not depicted.

Other examples of the genre move directly from scenes of courtship to birthing, skipping the sex act and the intervening months of pregnancy. In *Wolves at Our Door* (1997) by Dutcher Film Productions for the Discovery Channel, the narrator explains that a pack's alpha male is about to select a new mate. He vocalizes and approaches the chosen female. She licks his face, and he follows closely as she meanders throughout a stand of bare trees as snow falls, resembling nothing so much as a courting couple on a romantic stroll. She sprawls on her back in the snow; he nuzzles her head and neck as the narrator declares the pair bonded—and facing portentous responsibility: "Attention turns to affection. Usually, only the alpha pair mate. The future size and fate of the entire pack will depend on the ritual of breeding they now begin." The image of the courting pair, at rest on the ground with the female in a submissive pose, dissolves to a post-pairing family portrait. The alpha male, the new alpha female, and her sister stand shoulder-to-shoulder-to-shoulder in a profile composition that evokes the solidarity of kin and strength of leaders, in contrast to prior shots of the languid lovers. The film cuts from this portrait to footage of the female trotting to the den she has prepared, about to give birth. While she gives birth and begins to care for her young alone, members of the pack mill about "with an air of celebration," awaiting the occasion when the mother brings the puppies out of the den for the first time. She introduces the litter to other members of the pack, who are said to be eager to "baby-sit": "all wolves adore puppies." Their aunt, shown in close-up, licks one of the tiny puppies to end the scene. The interval between mate selection and the emergence of the two-week-old litter from the birth den is collapsed into a two-and-a-half-minute sequence that contains more information about the pack's cooperation as a reproductive unit, an extended family comprised of more helpers than breeders, than about the biology of wolf reproduction itself. Representations of copulation, of events throughout the three-month gestation period, and of birth itself are simply

An alpha male selects a new alpha female in *Wolves at Our Door.*

omitted, as if too messy, too indelicate, too extraneous to a narrative that leaps from picturesque canine pair-bonding to the first peek at a litter of furry, squealing, stub-nosed pups.

Flying Casanovas and *Wolves at Our Door* illustrate two typical narrative trajectories in which treatments of the reproductive lives of animals confine their interests to behaviors that precede or follow copulation. However, the trend since commercial proliferation of the wildlife genre in the mid-1980s has been away from such narrative ellipses and toward increasingly explicit depictions of sexual (and predatory) behavior. As Marty Stouffer has noted, "During the Disney era, you couldn't show killing or copulating.... Then with Perkins's 'Wild Kingdom' you could show killing but no copulating. Today, you can show both."[11] Significantly, explicit mating scenes don't definitively reposition particular programs as adult content, especially when such scenes are brief or diffused through some kind of visual interruption. A scene that shows male and female pandas mating in NHK's *Giant Panda Sho-San and His First Year* (1995, produced by Tazuhiko Kobayashi, filmed by Masaki Watanabe) lasts under half a minute. In a medium long shot, the pandas' bodies fill much of the frame. The male clasps the female's hips with his front paws and mounts her; the shot lasts some twenty seconds. A five-second, extreme long shot of the pandas in the same position follows. Unlike the kinds of close looking provided by pornography—which makes identification between viewer and performer possible, bringing the viewer into the act so that seeing substitutes for touching—the shot imposes distance between the scene of animal sex and the viewer.[12]

Likewise, in Discovery's IMAX movie *Africa's Elephant Kingdom,* an intercourse sequence lasts fifteen seconds. It is preceded by several shots of male elephants in combat, as the narrator (actor Avery Brooks, whose lines are written from the point of view of the eldest bull in the clan) intones, "The winner receives as his prize a fertile, sometimes reluctant female." The picture cuts to an extreme long shot of a small adult female dashing across the frame with the much larger bull in pursuit. In the next shot, over the course of about ten seconds, the male, who faces away from the camera, mounts the female. The viewer sees only his backside as he rises on hind legs. A third elephant approaches from the left and begins to obscure the mating pair. In a five-second sideview, the third elephant blocks the camera's view of the mating pair's pelvic areas, reasserting a family-friendly discretion over the peek at animal sex just provided. Reminding the viewer that the act depicted produces offspring, Brooks continues, "Twenty-two months later, if they have chosen their mates well, these females will have strong and healthy babies, just like their fathers." The film cuts to a new scene on another topic.[13]

These scenes, as Grosz suggests, operate as sources of sexual knowledge, both as means of satisfying our polymorphic curiosity about how all kind of bodies, not just those who are our sexual objects, might "make love," and as means of understanding our own desires by looking at other species' practices. The usual brevity of these scenes signals that most of these programs are not *about* mating, but one of many animal behaviors in a sequence of events that constitutes a narrative of animal life. By this measure, mating footage in *Brother Wolf* (1996), by the French company Mona Lisa Productions, aired on *Wild Discovery,* seems unusually abundant. As members of a pack of European wolves interact in a snowy forest clearing, three brief attempted matings take place, but in each case, the male is driven away from the female by other wolves. Once all challengers are repelled, the alpha male mounts the alpha female; a brief long shot cuts to a fifteen-second medium long shot of their copulation. The narrator notes that the event (which he calls a "physical tie") might last thirty minutes, then explains that while usually only the alpha pair mate and reproduce, subordinate wolves (betas) may reproduce if the alphas reach an advanced age. During his monologue about the complexities of pack hierarchy and contingencies on breeding rights, the male tries but cannot dismount. Unable to withdraw his penis, the pair is stuck together. Having struggled to separate, both male and female now stand on all fours, facing opposite directions; the rest of the pack mills about. This shot lasts a full fifty seconds, then cuts to a quick long shot in which they part and walk away from one another. The narrator does not comment on the reproductive advantages of their inconvenient postcoital position, ignoring the visual event.[14] Instead, he tacks on new information about research showing that sometimes betas as well as alphas breed, about interpack breeding, and about the fate of alphas whose mates die. This dissonance between image and narration is surely an example of how, to borrow Craig Owens's phrase, "fragmentary, intermittent, or chaotic" the relationship between the one text that doubles the other, between captured image and attached explication, may be.[15]

Elsewhere, narration and image resonate more closely, the voiceover or on-location host's monologue drawing viewers' attention to physiological or behavioral characteristics and offering explanations of what can be seen. Narrators frequently point out sexual signs such as the swollen, reddened buttocks of the macaque, in *Wild and Weird—Wild Sex* (1999, Natural History New Zealand/The Discovery Channel, produced and directed by Mark Ferris; written by Nigel Zega) or the temporal gland that seeps behind the bull elephant's eye when he is in musth, a cyclical phase in which the male's testosterone level spikes and he becomes prone to aggressive behavior toward other males and the pursuit of nearby fertile females, in *Echo of the Elephants*. Other signs, like the elephant's penis, which nearly reaches the ground as he approaches a female in *Echo,* are frequently visible but less-often remarked upon.

While scenes depicting acts of mating tend to be brief, they can, in some program formats, be frequent. *Giant Panda Sho-San and His First Year, Africa's Elephant Kingdom,* and *Brother Wolf* all incorporate at least some of the elements of classic wildlife filmmaking; each concentrates on a particular group of animal kin over a long term. In these films, mating is just one of many behaviors—a seasonal one, at that—depicted. In contrast, some made-for-TV wildlife programs take the form of compilations, assembling mixtures of new and virtually ageless and therefore endlessly recyclable stock footage from various sources, to survey a particular set of behaviors across many species rather than concentrating on a single animal group.[16] If the theme is sexual behavior, the compilation program may include dozens of scenes in which sexual behavior is not elided, but rather collected and compared in abundant, and sometimes redundant, scene after scene, and explicated by scripted narration. Usually, these programs undertake comparative analyses of biological and social aspects of sex among animals (sometimes including humans).

Explaining Animal Sex: Sociobiology's Impact

Images of animal sex became commonplace in the wildlife genre not long after new theories about sexual behavior, both human and animal, had begun to emerge from the biological sciences into popular discourse. As Roger N. Lancaster demonstrates, ever since *Time* magazine first ran a cover story on sociobiology in 1977, science journalists have covered countless provocative studies of animal and human behavior—with particular relish for those suggesting that women are by "nature" nurturing and monogamous, while men are both promiscuous *and* protective of their mates—all too often in a speculative form that Lancaster chides as "sociobiology lite." These arguments quickly crept into other popular culture forms—such as dialogue from the courtroom "dramedy" *Ally McBeal*—and into popular discourse.[17] If this new life science, especially its preoccupation with why and how we "do it," and with whom, is delineated and debated in newspapers, magazines, and on TV, why not in wildlife TV? On one hand, wildlife was a genre already loaded with natural history facts, preoccupied with reproduction (if historically given to consigning the reproductive act to the viewer's interpolative imagination), and through its anthropomorphizing legacy, rife with loose associations between animal and human behavior. On the other hand, in the late 1970s and early 1980s, the genre was near a nadir. It had been all but shooed off the commercial networks, save for a few family-friendly syndication packages, and it was still establishing a foothold on PBS. Thus, just out of sight, it was also ripe for reinvigoration as a genre with commercial potential and potential appeal to the new audiences formed throughout the 1980s by the booming cable TV industry and the IMAX film phenomenon.[18]

Of course, this wasn't the first time that knowledge about animals would be mined for insight into human life, and, vice-versa, that animal life would be explained through reference to familiar human identities and social relations. As Eileen Crist shows in a wide-ranging study, scientists of various disciplinary orientations, from Charles Darwin to the sociobiologist, have utilized anthropomorphizing language to draw analogies between animal and human behavior.[19] Some of Darwin's own writings contain some of same saccharine metaphors that Disney and Uys would later employ: "pigeons . . . rarely prove *unfaithful* to each other. Even when the male does *break his marriage-vow,* he does not permanently desert his mate" (emphasis added). Thus Darwin appears to impose on the avian pair-bond the sentiments of human romantic and legal relations.[20]

Later, parallels drawn between animal and human behavior would derive less from the invocation of social conventions as explanatory frameworks than from the development of theoretical models based on observations of animals and extended to humans. Some of the best-known transformations of observations of animals into theories about human behavior appeared in the 1960s. In *On Aggression,* published in Germany in 1963 and first translated into English in 1966, ethologist Konrad Lorenz attributes the human impulse to consider ourselves distinct from animals as deriving from pride, contempt for animals, philosophic traditions, and "our reluctance to accept the fact that our own behavior obeys the laws of natural causation . . . the justifiable wish to possess a free will."[21] Drawing on Darwinian and Freudian theories, Lorenz argues that human violence— the capacity to murder, to engage in warfare—arises from instincts like those found in animals, and are doubly strong for being reinforced by cultural heritages. Still, Lorenz concludes by enthusing that rationality can overcome destructive impulses. Desmond Morris takes a different approach in *The Naked Ape,* which first appeared in 1967. Instead of applying findings about animals to humans, he attempts to observe and describe humans as simply another animal species with its own peculiar patterns of mating, child-rearing, procuring food and shelter, resolving conflicts, and interacting with other species. In every instance he emphasizes the biological processes associated with these behaviors, concluding that some (perhaps Lorenz) believe that "our intelligence can dominate all our basic biological urges . . . [but] this is rubbish." Morris argues that human survival and quality of life depends on "submitting" to biological or instinctive urges, rather than suppressing them.[22]

Lorenz's and Morris's attempts to explain human behavior from models built on animal observations were part of a new wave of research soon to coalesce as the new field of sociobiology. In 1975 the first edition of Edward O. Wilson's *Sociobiology: The New Synthesis* was published.[23] This cornerstone text amasses research findings in the behavioral-biological sciences—ethology, behavioral ecology, and population biology—in an encyclopedic volume ranging from colonial invertebrates (coral, the Portuguese man-of-war) to nonhuman primates (lemurs, baboons, chimpanzees).

Wilson defines sociobiology as "the systematic study of the biological basis of all behavior," concerning primarily nonhuman animals, but also extending its interest to "the social behavior of early man and the adaptive features of organization in the more primitive contemporary human societies."[24] In his first chapter, Wilson excludes the social behavior of modern humans from the sociobiologists' purview, leaving it to sociology.[25] But he makes thoroughly modern *Homo sapiens* the subject of his final chapter, suggesting that many apparently cultural practices—art, music, war, gendered division of labor, to name a few—are biologically motivated. He surmises, without regard for the parameters he has set for the discipline earlier in the book, that sociobiology will eventually reveal "the genetic bases of [human] social behavior." In other words, the new field of study will lead to widespread recognition of the true dominance of "nature" over the illusory power of "nurture." However, Wilson is pessimistic about what may be found: potentially, the evolutionary inevitability of natural selection toward an increasingly less cooperative, more bellicose population.[26]

In 1976, a year after the publication of Wilson's hefty, scholarly tome, the first edition of *The Selfish Gene* by Richard Dawkins followed. While Dawkins takes up many of the same themes as Wilson, redressed for a general readership, he also argues against what he believes is a common misconception about evolutionary theory: that the purpose of reproduction is to perpetuate species. Instead, he contends, the motivation for reproduction is the replication of genetic material: "the fundamental unit . . . of self-interest, is not the species, nor the group, nor even, strictly, the individual. It is the gene." An individual, according to Dawkins, is a "survival machine," a "gene vehicle," "gene machine," or "selfish machine," programmed to do whatever is best for his genes as a whole."[27] Although Dawkins reminds readers that his language is metaphorical, not literal, he anthropomorphizes genes themselves. He occasionally reflects on his use of language:

> If we allow ourselves the licence of talking about genes as if they had conscious aims, always reassuring ourselves that we could translate our sloppy language back into respectable terms if we wanted to, we can ask the question, what is a single selfish gene trying to do? It is trying to get more numerous in the gene pool. Basically it does this by helping to program the bodies in which it finds itself to survive and to reproduce.[28]

In other words, the purpose of life—not partly, not predominately, but solely—is to make more life, and the kinds of bodies in which we do so and the behaviors undertaken with them are simply bells and whistles, accessories and gimmicks, with which to entice others to make more life with us, if our species requires such partnerships. If the meaning of life can be parsed to the level of the individual gene and its sphere of action, pared down to the reproduction function, then, it would follow, what is learned about one gene-comprised, reproducing species applies to others as well.

To many, the totalizing breadth of these new theories reiterated, consciously or not, ideological—specifically traditional—values. As a result, theoretical models derived in research among this species or that might be extrapolated, more liberally than the evidence might support, to the realm of human social relations, diminishing or dismissing out of hand the often-staunchly intransigent *cultural* reproduction of norms, as well as the view that gender differences are to a significant extent socially constructed.[29] Within the scientific community criticisms focused on the broadness of sociobiology's claims, its tendency to reduce behaviors to solely biological functions and to excise culture entirely, its too-easy extrapolations from animal data to human conclusions, and the metaphorical language through which some of its claims have been staked. Dawkins himself, in later volumes, further explained (and perhaps somewhat tempered) his views of the genetic bases and powerful environmental influences on behavior, without the excitedly deterministic language that helped sensationalize sociobiology in the popular press and public imagination. Stephen Jay Gould, the evolutionary biologist and prolific writer about science for lay audiences, contends that sociobiologists too readily assume that adaptive behaviors "must have a genetic basis, since natural selection cannot operate in the absence of genetic variation," overlooking the vast and rapid changes produced by learned behaviors in the context of human culture. Sandra Harding, a philosopher of science, argues that sociobiological perspectives are of limited value in understanding human sexuality, which is influenced by a variety of factors, including "parental expectation" and other environmental forces. Biologist Ruth Hubbard and others have called into question the "reductivist" scientific trend away from the study of whole complex organisms, toward its elemental components, as in molecular biology, as well as the implications of genetic information and gene-based theories, some still quite speculative, on social institutions such as education, criminal justice, other kinds of public policy, psychology, and the pop-psychology of the huge self-help market.[30]

Scientists (and those who document their work, such as journalists and wildlife filmmakers), like the rest of us may be biased in their interpretations of animal behavior by their dependence on their own human experiences for linguistic resources with which to name and explain non-human behaviors, and by ideological and scientific standpoints, explicit and implicit, conscious and unconscious. As Jennifer Terry argues, "laboratories, like zoos, are sites of voyeurism. We look to the sexual behavior of animals to give meaning to human social relations, and by doing so, we engage in imaginative acts that frequently underscore culturally dominant ideas about gender and sexuality." According to Terry, biologists and neuro-anatomists search for a supposed cause of human sexual orientation in the genes of fruit flies and in hormonal influences on the brains of rats because they see "animal behavior as a 'natural' and elementary foundation for understanding human behavior." That is, they see human and animal—rodent, insect, or other—anatomy *and therefore behavior* as unproblematically homologous, despite evidence that is sometimes uncertain or contrary.[31]

Evolutionary biologist Marlene Zuk likewise challenges all-too-easy extensions of knowledge about animal behaviors to humans, arguing that our biases—prejudices, stereotypes, and cultural traditions—inflect our interpretations of animal behaviors. Paying particular attention to masculinist biases that privilege male subjects and male agency in science, Zuk undertakes an illuminating feminist analysis of principal findings in sociobiology's disciplinary offshoots, behavioral ecology and evolutionary psychology. Noting that while sometimes animal studies of the ubiquitously studied *Drosophila* (fruit fly), even, but more often of primates are relevant to human physiognomy or behaviors, Zuk argues that sometimes knowledge about an animal is simply knowledge about an animal. The presence or absence of any number of behaviors among animal species should bear not at all on our attitudes toward such behaviors among humans, which can be understood and evaluated independently: "There is not a moral to every story in animal behavior. Sometimes a snake is just a snake, and sometimes snake sex is only about sex in snakes, or sex in egg-laying reptiles."[32]

Niles Eldredge, in a related critique, refuses the tendency of "selfish gene" theories to define all behavior as bells and whistles contributing directly or indirectly to reproduction. He offers a correctively balanced view of organic life as a compound of both "economic" activity ("making a living" for oneself, by which he means eating, drinking, respiration, and fulfillment of other life-sustaining needs), and "reproductive" activity (which produces new life but is nonessential—if desirable, sometimes achingly so—for the sustenance of one's own life). Eldredge reminds the reader that for humans (and for our close relative the bonobo), sex is both an economic and reproductive behavior. Too often, he argues, behaviors without reproductive consequence and entwined with social status and other resources have been underestimated, since "gene-centered" evolutionary psychology "has increasingly swept over both academic and general cultural thinking about who we are and what we do."[33] As Evelyn Fox Keller warns, genetic origins of behaviors are all too often no longer grappled with as scientific questions or recognized as entangled with ideological contests but rather accepted as the "common sense" presupposition among science professionals and in lay opinion.[34] In wildlife television, such a view has become an almost unquestioned paradigm, articulating and circulating to mass audiences theories of human behavior derived from animal observations.

Showing and Telling Animal Sex

By the 1990s explanations of behaviors that drew on the theories of behavioral and evolutionary genetics replaced familiar wildlife storylines. Debate continued among scientists regarding the extent to which the findings of research on animals might be extrapolated to humans, and the extent to which genes determine animal and human behavior.[35] Despite cautionary critiques from within the sciences, a great many wildlife films treated what Wilson called "the new synthesis" as irrefutable fact. Many wildlife programs embraced the point of view expressed by biologist Randy Thornhill in a National Geographic Television program called *Animal Attraction* (1997): "It is not a leap at all to talk about humans in relation to scorpionfly behavior, or scorpionfly behavior in relation to human. It is all a matter of biology."

Throughout the 1990s and the first few years of the twenty-first century, mate selection and sexual behavior became the subject of an unprecedented number of nonfiction wildlife programs in the form of compilation documentaries. Some, like the series *The Trials of Life: A Natural History of Behavior* (1991, written and hosted by Sir David Attenborough), constrain most of their claims to nonhuman animals. Others, such as *Wild and Weird—Wild Sex* and "The Mating Game" episode of a six-hour series optimistically called *Triumph of Life* (2001, co-produced by Devillier Donegan Enterprises of Washington, D.C., Green Umbrella Limited of Bristol, and Trebitsch Produktion International GmbH of Hamburg, for PBS-affiliate Thirteen/WNET New York's series *Nature*) assert contiguity between animal and human behaviors by means of subtle rhetorical tactics. Still others—*The Most Extreme* "Lovers" episode (2002, coproduced by Natural History New Zealand and Animal Planet), and *When Animals Attract* (2004, by National Geographic for broadcast by the Fox network)—take explicitly comparative approaches to animal and human mate selection, at times incorporating footage of humans engaged in the social rituals of courtship and coupling.[36]

The Trials of Life stirred controversy regarding its frank depictions of mating and predatory practices, especially in its aggressive advertising campaign, and enjoyed a lucrative broadcast and home-video release (see chapter 3). Four of twelve episodes address aspects of reproduction: "Courting" examined the diverse displays, scents, and songs that animals use to attract mates; "Continuing the Line," the mating act itself; "Arriving," giving birth; and "Growing Up," the care of young. Early in "Continuing the Line," Attenborough appears on-screen to state that this program will examine "the problem that all animals will face if they are to be a biological success: how to pass on their genes to the next generation. But though the problem is always the same, the solutions are amazingly varied." Indeed, in over twenty species, from butterfly to spear-nosed bat, Attenborough finds quite a range of methods by which genetic material is combined, and he largely (but not entirely) avoids the temptation to renarrativize the acts of other living things according to human values, expectations, and desires.

The final sequence in "Continuing the Line" begins with a long shot of a grassy hill that slopes toward a shoreline. The landscape, initially devoid of human or animal bodies, inserts a shift in tone from the high drama of the scene that precedes it (in which a male elephant seal crushes a seal pup) to pensive calm. Wordlessly, Attenborough walks into the scene from the left side of the frame, and a large, as-yet-unidentified bird streaks across the frame, just over his head. The picture cuts to a shot of the bird gliding in flight, wings outstretched and virtually still, as only its feet beat in rudderlike motion. The camera seems to tag along behind the bird. In the next shot, Attenborough walks toward the camera, beginning the narration:

> So, the number of different ways in which males and females can come together and raise their young is huge. I, because of the particular species to which I belong and the particular society in which I happen to have been reared, tend to think that the monogamous pair, one male, one female, husband and wife, staying together long enough to share responsibility of

raising the young, is the norm. But actually in the animal kingdom at large it's very, very rare, and one of the few creatures that off-centers that is this beautiful bird, the royal albatross.

As Attenborough finishes this sentence, his voice softens and he kneels. The camera pans downward, revealing a large, starkly white bird that now dominates the screen-left foreground. Attenborough, clad in khaki and posed against dry grass, recedes into background. He has finally encountered the object of his quest: an apparently monogamous animal, instead of so many whose behaviors suggest that monogamy is rare among sexual behaviors. The next shot is an extreme close-up of the heads of a mated albatross pair. In voiceover, Attenborough explains that this pair mated twenty years ago, when they were five years old; they breed and raise a single chick each year. Each of these lifelong companions takes a turn tending their nest while the other undertakes lengthy feeding excursions.

The camera lingers on a final shot of the albatross pair, and Attenborough's closing monologue begins in voiceover: "If you watch animals objectively, for any length of time, you're driven to the conclusion that their main aim in life is to pass on their genes to the next generation." In the next shot, he faces the camera, a lighthouse visible over his shoulder on another grassy hill, indicating that he is still in the albatross's habitat. He continues:

> Most do so directly, by breeding. In the few examples that don't do so by design, they do it indirectly by helping a relative with whom they share a great number of their genes, and inasmuch as the legacy that human beings pass onto the next generation is not only genetic but to a unique degree cultural, we do the same. So animals and ourselves, to continue the line, will endure all kinds of hardships, overcome all kinds of difficulties, and eventually the next generation appears.

As he finishes these lines, the clacking sound that the albatross makes with her beak is heard, and the picture cuts from Attenborough to the albatross. The camera pans downward and cuts to a shot of a hatching egg. In the final scene of the program, Attenborough sits by the bird, which he says is a thirty-year-old grandmother who has "faced the trials of life and triumphed. For her little two-day-old chick, the trials are just beginning." In long shot, he stands and walks out of the frame; the bird and chick remain on the nest. Credits roll over footage of two adult birds preening and billing, nearly in silhouette, as the sunset glints on dark waters beyond the shoreline. Attenborough's presence is temporary; the animals remain as evidence of nature's enduring persistence and cyclical resilience.

Sir David Attenborough, albatross, and chick in the "Continuing the Line" episode of *Trials of Life*.

In "Continuing the Line," Attenborough trains his attention on the "trials of [reproducing] life" faced by nonhuman animal species, extending cross-species generalizations to humans only occasionally, and reserving for humans measures of both cultural and biological influences on behavior. He comes closest to likening animal and human behaviors in accounting for the reality of nonbreeding individuals, assigning helper roles to nonreproducing individuals (including animals but especially humans) as means of "indirectly" passing on related genes—and cultural traditions—so that the behaviors of those of us who do not reproduce can also be explained by means of the presumed selfishness of our genes.[37] Other programs that stick primarily to animal subjects purposefully stake broader claims through a variety of rhetorical strategies: through the use of adjectives or modes of address that by definition reference human social structures or the human viewer, as in *Wild and Weird*—*Wild Sex*, or through exceptional but explicit links drawn between particular observed animal behaviors and theorized human behaviors, past or present, as in *Triumph of Life*'s "The Mating Game."

Wild Sex presents dozens of short scenes, each devoted to a particular species' mating practices. While mating scenes are regularly incorporated into wildlife films programmed as family entertainment, this program, a compilation of mating scenes, is about sex and pitched as adult entertainment. When *Wild Sex* aired on *Wild Discovery*, the Discovery Channel prefaced the episode with the warning, "The following program contains scenes which some audience members may find disturbing. Viewer discretion is suggested," which was then repeated at the program's midpoint.[38] After the series' standard title sequence, the episode begins with nine quick clips from scenes that appear later in the program. As this montage unfurls, the narrator engages the viewer: "Tonight, a world of orgies, sex changers, and female impersonators. Sex in the wild is more than the birds and the bees. The rituals and dangers of wild sex, now on *Wild Discovery*." While *Wild Sex* does not include footage of humans or theorize overtly about human behaviors, the narration draws subtle comparisons between its animal subjects and human viewers through liberal use of analogies borrowed from specifically human ways of life to describe the circumstances in which animal behaviors take place.

In *Wild Sex*, a fifty-second segment on the Southern right whale begins with a scene shot underwater, showing three whales swimming close together. A tail swoops across the frame close to the camera's position, then the picture cuts to a side view as the narration begins: "In terms of sheer size, the record-holding male is a whale. Southern rights have a ten-foot penis and half-ton testicles, and they use them for a most *unusual* competition." In the next shot, the penis of the whale in the lower half of the frame moves toward the whale in the center, touches and penetrates her. The narrator explains, "Rather than fighting for possession of a female, males will take turns to mate with her." Shots of the shiny black bodies of the whales breaking the water's surface alternate with underwater images of the animals, still copulating. As the narrator concludes, snidely, "It's a very civilized ritual," the three whales continue to swim, the camera's angle displaying their bodies in vertical tandem, their flukes at the top of the screen, their bodies extend below the edge of the frame, the withdrawn penis still visible.

The narration's framing of the right whale's mating practices shifts from "unusual" to "civilized" in the course of just a few sentences. The claim that any particular animal behavior constitutes a "civilized" act is itself unusual (especially when applied to animals other than primates). The practice is positioned as "unusual," not only because it defies both the traditional norms of many human societies and human expectations for animals in its inclusion of multiple individuals in a single sexual encounter.

It also qualifies as "unusual" because, instead of fighting or engaging in a spectacular display, the males "take turns" and do not attempt to prevent one another from mating. The order in which they mate with the female is determined through a negotiation that is either left unexplained or is not understood. The possibility that mating order is determined by selections made by the female is not considered. In fact, she is barely present in the narration, except as a receptacle for consummation of what counts as real sex, while ecstatic same-sex behavior among males counts as a form of competition. Paradoxically, this substitution of cooperation for combat also qualifies the behavior as "civilized." This shift in frame is represented visually as well as in the narration. So long as the behavior is categorized as "unusual," the three whales share the screen. But in the final postcoital shot, after the behavior is repositioned as "civilized," only two—presumably or at least symbolically the two that have last mated—are shown, erasing from view the other male who has either already mated or will mate next. Shot from above water, the backs of two of the animals hover at the surface, leaves the scene with an image of a whale "couple," reestablishing an expected pairing after this peek at an unexpected sexual behavior.

Triumph of Life's "The Mating Game" almost entirely avoids drawing *explicit* conclusion about humans derived from animal models. An exception points to the promiscuity of apes—and studies (now largely discredited) suggesting that sperm literally go to war if they encounter the sperm of another male; that is, if the female has mated with more than one male, the sperm may compete within her just as her suitors may have competed to be selected for making in the first place.[39] Here the narration distinguishes carefully between the biological bases of aspects of a theorized human past and the experienced human present of multiple influences on behavior. Still, the boundaries of the claims in the "The Mating Game" are not always precisely defined, especially when the program focuses on the unequal contributions of males and females of many species to the work of reproduction. The narrator declares, during a segment on lions,

> Except for sex, it often seems that females could raise families on their own.... Many females seem to get a bad deal out of life for the sake of sex. But they are simply being driven by their genes. The females instinctively make sacrifices in order to breed.... Throughout the animal world, equality rarely has a place in sex.

Here, does "animal" mean nonhuman animal, or does the animal world include humans? The parameters of the naturally unequal status of the sexes remains undefined, left to interpretation by the viewer.[40]

The Most Extreme series goes further to render explicit parallels between animals and humans. Each episode of the series comprises a top-ten list relative to some physiological or behavioral theme ("Builders," "Jumpers," "Gluttons," "Cheats"), juxtaposing footage of animals and humans for each entry on the list. The "Lovers" episode begins with the Tasmanian devil, ranked at "number 10 in the countdown, because when it comes to courtship, these guys make war, not love." A male approaches a female's den, and their screeches replace the narrator's voice. An exterior shot shifts to footage collected by a camera within the burrow; the devils claw and bite at one another, continuing to screech, then assuming a mating posture. The narration returns:

> The Tasmanian devil really pushes the battle of the sexes to the extreme. Their courtship may be short and violent, but it's enough to establish them as a couple.... Unlike Tasmanian devils, humans usually take a more subtle approach to dating. But biologically speaking, there's still a battle when a man meets a woman. That's because men and women have very different needs.

A vintage cartoon replaces images of the devils: Betty Boop compares pictures of two suitors, and discards one, as the narrator explains, "According to evolutionary theory, a woman is looking for the kind of man who can protect and provide for her and her children." But Betty isn't the only one looking. A half-dozen women chase the desired male down through city streets, while the narrator continues: "Men are looking to sow their genetic seed as widely as possible." Inexplicably, this apparently superior male runs into his house and slams the door on the pursuing women. The sequence is amusing, to be sure, but contradicts the theory of sexually different reproductive imperatives presented by the narrator. If males are eager to "sow their genetic seed as widely as possible," why does this one flee from willing females? The incoherence of the sequence remains unaccounted for, but is displaced by another piece of footage, in which (live, not animated) humans mingle at a party. Spotlights fall on a man and a woman, who make eye contact, approach one another, and converse. Eventually, cartoon thought-bubbles appear above their heads, indicating their "very different needs." Above the woman's head, we see footage of the couple at their wedding. Above the man, the two appear locked in an embrace, kissing; her hands stroke his bare back. Despite the real differences among the kinds of evidence presented, a model of female selectivity and commitment to high-quality mates and the male's search for reproductive opportunities in quantity with little commitment links these segments, however loosely. The remainder of the countdown proceeds in much the same fashion, comparing, for example, the role of the sense of smell in rhino mate selection to our own scent preferences, and the self-fertilizing whiptail lizard female, with B-movie fantasies of all-female Amazon societies. Each analogy, it would seem, is more fanciful than the next.

Like *The Most Extreme*'s "Lovers," *When Animals Attract* takes for granted that there are substantial similarities between the ways that animals and humans choose mates. With a title that was clearly a play on Fox's reality-based specials *When Animals Attack* (1996–97), the Fox network broadcast *When Animals Attract* on February 13, 2004, not coincidentally, the eve of Valentine's Day.[41] Early in the program, the narrator assures the viewer that "there's nothing like mother nature for inspiration." Opening scenes, cut to the beat of the 1975 hit song "You Sexy Thing" by the British funk band Hot Chocolate, juxtapose shots of people (for example, a man lifts weights, a woman applies lipstick) and animals (displaying plumage, grooming one another), visualizing variations in means of attracting mates, from the peacock's tail to ballroom dancing, as roughly equivalent outcomes of sexual selection.

When Animals Attract also invites identification with the animals on screen by regularly addressing an implied male, heterosexual viewer in the second person ("So now you've serenaded her, danced until you're foot-sore, bought her dinner and trinkets; now maybe you'll get to the good part, right? Not so fast"). Despite the program's attention to the active roles of females in selecting among suitors, the female viewer is most frequently alluded to as an object to be cajoled and conquered by competing males. She is not directly addressed until the close of the narrator's monologue, which begins with a review of lessons learned from the animal behavior observed over the previous hour. His lines, which are almost interchangeable with the summary messages delivered by the cast of the reality-makeover series *Queer Eye for the Straight Guy* (2003–, Bravo), are heard over another montage in which images of animals alternate with shots of human couples, many kissing, to the tune of "You Sexy Thing":

Human animals imagine fulfilling their "very different needs" in *The Most Extreme* "Lovers" episode.

Boys, just remember what Mother Nature's telling you. Work on your presentation, your song and dance. A good bluff is better than getting rough. Get in touch with your feminine side. And show her how much you appreciate her. Girls, the ball's in your court when it comes to the choosing, so choose well. Tall, dark and handsome may be immediately appealing, but don't forget to consider more subtle attractions. [Here, an image of a strutting silverback gorilla gives way to an extreme close-up of a lizard's claws stroking the body of another.] And never forget, in the romantic, sometimes bizarre contest to get our genes into the future, it takes all kinds.

The music fades out during the penultimate shot, in which two small monkeys embrace, one mouthing the other's neck. The final shot—a frontal view of Galapagos tortoises copulating, the large male's front claws grasping the female's shell just above her head, while she appears to look directly into the camera—lingers in silence, until the sound of a woman's sigh is matched to the palpitations of the female tortoise's fleshy throat, which throbs as she breathes. Following a program's worth of models culled from other species, men might render themselves more attractive to women by tending to their appearance, learning a few dance steps, substituting strategy for fisticuffs when rivals threaten one's own chances to mate, and giving appropriate gifts. Women are reminded to keep their expectations in check, to accept their partners in all their human variety. *When Animals Attract* not only includes humans within its purview, it also derives from animals a couple-counseling coda and employs the animal as a teaching tool in the self-help and conciliatory discourses found more commonly on makeover and quasi-therapeutic talk TV. The realities of nonhuman animal life here recede from view, in favor of a string of animal-signs.

The Rape Wars and Wildlife TV

While much interest in sex, animal and human—in society at large, in science, and in media—focuses on so-called normative heterosexual courtship, pair-bonding, and reproduction, other kinds of sexual behaviors also garner substantial scrutiny and study, their motives and ramifications subject to heated debate. For instance, in the 1970s, feminists and some sociobiologists turned their attention to rape. Feminists launched a movement to reform rape laws, to found support groups for rape survivors, to teach self-defense, and to counter stereotypical assumptions about rape that blamed the victim. As Sarah Projansky and Sujata Moorti have shown, various media genres (dramas, soap operas, talk shows) represented the ensuing contest between feminist analyses of rape and what they have generally represented as traditional patriarchal attitudes toward rape.[42] Meanwhile, some sociobiologists sought to understand what motivates rape among humans by observing instances of forcible copulation among nonhuman animals. New scientific theories of rape appear to have been overlooked in most popular genres, but forcible copulation among animals became a topic of interest in wildlife film, sometimes extrapolated, implicitly or explicitly, to human behavior.

The feminist analysis of rape asserted that rape is a markedly un-natural, specifically social human act. In *Against Our Will,* one of the landmark feminist texts of the era, Susan Brownmiller writes,

> No zoologist, as far as I know, has ever observed that animals rape in their natural habitat, the wild. Sex in the animal world, including those species that are our closest relatives, the primates, is more properly called "mating," and it is cyclical activity set off by biologic signals the female puts out.... At other times there is simply no interest.... Zoologists for the most part have been reticent on the subject of rape. It has not been for them an important scientific question.[43]

Brownmiller argues that rape is an act of intimidation and control, disengaged from sexual desire and reproductive instinct: "rape is not a crime of irrational, impulsive, uncontrollable lust, but is a deliberate, hostile, violent act of degradation and possession on the part of a would-be conqueror." She treats pregnancy as a generally unintended consequence with the exception of slave-breeding.[44]

In 1977 David P. Barash first published an article describing instances in which male mallard ducks abandon typical courting behaviors and "rape" resistant females whose mates are absent. He also observed in field studies that when a "raped" female's mate returns, he too will forcibly copulate with her, foregoing the courting behaviors the pair would otherwise perform.[45] Barash went on to say that forced copulation is motivated by the drive to reproduce in the absence of willing females. That is, rape—among ducks or humans—is a shortcut through which the male—especially a low-ranking male unlikely to be selected by females for consensual intercourse—seeks to maximize the chance that his genetic material will survive without enduring the time-consuming practices of courtship and pairbonding. In 1979 Barash introduced these ideas to mass-market readers in *The Whisperings Within*. In 1980 Randy Thornhill published a study on behaviors he called "rape" among scorpionflies and, in collaboration with Nancy Wilmsen Thornhill, began to apply these findings to humans.[46]

With Barash's and Thornhill's publications, animal "rape" became an important sociobiological question, and sociobiology became a vocal counterdiscourse to the feminist analysis of rape. Barash writes,

> In her book *Against Our Will*, Susan Brownmiller claimed only human beings engage in rape. The facts are otherwise. Rape is common among the birds and bees, and is epidemic among the mallard ducks.... When mallards pair up for breeding, there often remain a number of unmated males in most of the species.... These bachelors have been excluded from normal reproduction, and so they engage in what is apparently the next best strategy: raping someone else's female.... Perhaps human rapists, in their own criminally misguided way, are doing the best they can to maximize their [genetic] fitness.[47]

Barash, then, recasts rape as an evolutionary adaptation, a (male) reproductive strategy developed to overcome female choosiness. Criminal, yes, Barash adds, even as he almost commends the rapist for fashioning an alternative, "next best" strategy when social norms fail him, and excuses him as "misguided...doing the best [he] can."[48]

Almost immediately, some behavioral biologists began to critique the use of human social categories by sociobiologists to describe animal behaviors. Animal behaviorists Daniel Q. Estep and Katherine E. M. Bruce suggested the use of the term "resisted mating," arguing that the term "rape" in regard to nonhuman animals is "sensationalistic [and] imprecise."[49] Patricia Adair Gowaty also argued against sociobiologists' use of language that applies "anthropocentric value judgments of the activities of nonhuman animals," on grounds that it may indicate scientific bias and "exposes a hidden agenda which I fear has little to do with the communication of science." Pointing out that sociobiologists sometimes redefine terms to fit their research interests (for example, Thornhill used "rape" only when insemination took place, a condition not required in its current human-legal sense), she endorsed the term "forced copulation" as a more neutral descriptive substitute for "rape" (as well as "kleptogamy" and "one-male social unit" rather than "cuckoldry" or "adultery" and "harem"). A possible negative outcome of imprecise language, she warns, is that scientific knowledge can influence other cultural realms, even when the scientific theory is not yet proven, or its meaning misapplied or misunderstood. "The possibility of transference of the sociobiological idea to the legal realm," in the case of rape, for example, could reconfigure its legal sense to require ejaculation, even impregnation.[50]

While in intervening years, sociobiological theories of rape have not remade rape law, there is some evidence of the incorporation of data supporting the status of rape as a natural behavior, whether adaptive or maladaptive, into legal thinking.[51] Debates over the motives of rapists have continued between biologists and social scientists, and among biologists themselves. In 2000 Randy Thornhill and Craig T. Palmer published a controversial book, *The Natural History of Rape,* which elaborated theories of rape as either a direct evolutionary adaptation or a "by-product" of other adaptations (that is, a kind of side effect, a behavioral consequence of other presumably evolutionary adaptations: in short, male aggression plus reproductive instinct).[52] In an essay that previewed a chapter of the book, the authors summarized their argument:

> Since women are choosy, men have been selected for finding a way to be chosen. One way to do that is to possess traits that women prefer: men with symmetrical body features are attractive to women, presumably because such features are a sign of health. A second way that men can gain access to women is by defeating other men in fights or other kinds of

competitions—thereby gaining power, resources and social status, other qualities that women find attractive.

Rape can be understood as a third kind of sexual strategy: one more way to gain access to females. There are several mechanisms by which such a strategy could function. For example, men might resort to rape when they are socially disenfranchised, and thus unable to gain access to women through looks, wealth or status. Alternatively, men could have evolved to practice rape when the costs seem low. . . . Over evolutionary time, some men may have succeeded in passing on their genes through rape, thus perpetuating the behavior.[53]

Thornhill and Palmer, like Barash before them, instruct readers that "by categorizing a behavior as 'natural' and 'biological' we do not in any way mean to imply that the behavior is justified or even inevitable," and they assert that the social sciences, neglecting to acknowledge evolutionary influences on psychological as well as physiological attributes, have failed to explain the phenomenon of rape or to develop effective measures to stop it.[54] Some critics have argued that Thornhill and Palmer failed to establish that rape is fitness-enhancing, that is, its reproductive "benefits" (measured in sheer numbers of offspring, irrespective of degree of paternal certainty or parental involvement, or trauma exerted on the victim) to the rapist outweigh the potential costs, such as retribution, and that re-examining the data suggests that rape is far from an efficient reproductive strategy.[55]

Others have pointed out inadequacies in Thornhill and Palmer's accounting for rapes without reproductive potential (rapes of preadolescent and postmenopausal women, homosexual rapes, rapes and sexual assaults not involving penile-vaginal penetration and ejaculation), and the speculative features of the project and evolutionary psychology generally, in terms of nonexistence or uncertainty of data on behaviors in the prehistorical evolutionary environment.[56] Clashes between these authors and their critics have surfaced from time to time in popular media and, occasionally, biological explanations of forcible copulation among animals— from which the evolutionary-psychology studies regarding rape among humans took inspiration—appear in the wildlife genre.

When wildlife filmmakers have interrogated sexually coercive behaviors among animals, they have bypassed Barash's and Thornhill's primary research subjects, the scorpionfly and the mallard duck. Instead, they have frequently observed a similar behavior among spectacularly hierarchical and polygamous species of pinnipeds (sea lions, elephant seals) of which large amounts of footage has been gathered. Attenborough's *Trials of Life* took up the sociobiological theory of rape in "Continuing the Line." Its narration naturalizes Barash's theory that rape is a natural impulse, a "next best" reproductive strategy undertaken by males "doing their best" when the system denies them access to willing females.[57] One of the most provocative scenes depicts the social and sexual relations of sea lions that gather annually on Patagonian beaches. The segment introduces a huge male as the master of a "harem" of females, who arrive at the beach to give birth and become "sexually receptive" just a few days later. The dominant male moves throughout the herd, mating with one on the beach, the next in the frothy shorebreak. Meanwhile, younger, smaller males without access to females remain at the margins of the herd. One challenges the "harem-holder's" dominance; other males approach the females who are unprotected while the master is distracted by the fight, a commotion depicted in slow-motion. As a male seal drags a female across the sand, Attenborough narrates: "An intruding male tries to abduct a female. He will rape her if he can." The scene cuts rapidly between the males' battle and new conflicts throughout the herd as females resist the young males. Attenborough concludes this segment's narration: "The violence spreads. A young male who has still not mated works off his frustration on a pup," clutching it in his jaws, flinging in the air, biting it several times after it falls. Attenborough does not make any claims about human actions based on the seals' behaviors, but its treatment of rape as the natural outcome to male sexual frustration is clear.[58] The camera lingers on the male seal's torment of the pup, and the music, which has risen dramatically during their battles, as the scene cuts abruptly to a new location, a grassy, sloping shore in which no animal appears.

Subsequent programs revisit the same or related species with similarly dramatic and similarly interpreted results. In *Elephant Seals: Those Magnificent Diving Machines* (1994, WNET/Thirteen), which aired as an episode of *Nature*, another marine mammal species appears in footage collected during the colony's annual gathering at Año Nuevo State Park in Northern California. Each year, the males arrive first to the beach, to establish dominance hierarchies and territorial claims. They are followed by females who arrive at this "war zone" a few days away from giving birth, after which they will become almost immediately fertile and mate with a dominant male. Males unable to secure their own willing females, according to the narration, suffer "intense sexual frustration" and "mount anything that comes their way" despite the risk of retribution by senior bulls, often selecting small pups for these "misdirected mating attempts" with no possibility of reproductive outcome, given both that the pups are not yet sexually mature and that they are often injured or killed in the process; females under attack by rogue males cry out to their mates for protection from unwanted sexual intercourse. *Triumph of Life*'s "The Mating Game" elaborates on this aspect of these complex interactions among elephant seals: when a bachelor intrudes, females deflect his advances, refusing to mate with a male so inferior that he has not won his own "harem" in battle. The females alert the "beachmaster" to the intruder's presence, and the younger male is chased out to sea. In the last shot of this scene, the beachmaster has returned to the harem and mounts one of the females; the narrator refers to the females as "willing concubines." It is impossible to tell if it is the same female that the bachelor tried to mate with, or even if this scene occurred immediately after the encounter with the intruder. But the scenes are edited to indicate a rapid sequence of events, consistent with Barash's thesis that if a female is forced by a nonmate to copulate, her partner will respond to the event by mating with her, perhaps forcibly, too.

Wild and Weird—Wild Sex uses footage similar to that in *The Trials of Life*, gathered at a colony somewhere in the Southern hemisphere. During scenes in which male elephant seals spar, challenging one another to territory and the females in it, the narrator explains that males who do not control territories may sneak up on vulnerable individuals: "defeated bulls sometimes vent their sexual frustrations on half-grown pups" who may be crushed to death in the process. In medium long shot, a huge bull lumbers toward and clambers atop a tiny pup; two others escape, darting toward the camera. In the next shot, the faces of the large male and the struggling pup nearly fill the screen in close-up for nearly fifteen seconds, interrupted by the pup's piercing cry. After a quick shot from behind the male's bulky body, which obscures the pup from view, the scene cuts to seagulls tearing at its dead body. The narrator continues, "Rampant male hormones can destroy life instead of create it. . . . But it doesn't have to be this way. There are many other ways of breeding." The male's behavior is treated as the natural outcome of a social system that prevents some males from mating, typical to this species (and perhaps to others in which breeding opportunities are unequally distributed) but not inevitable across species.

While the sea lion and elephant seal scenes in all of these programs, in pacing, in the narrators' tones, and in musical scores, are dramatic, ominous, even poignant, *Wild Sex* takes a slightly different approach when the attacking male is not a hulky creature with a gruesomely bulbous face like the seal, but rather one of the animal kingdom's most cuddly and gentle-looking members. "When a female koala's call to a senior male goes unanswered, an opportunist steps in. Despite her protests, he forces her to copulate." The female struggles but the low-ranking "opportunist" holds her in place by his teeth and claws. "The commotion attracts the dominant male, who leaps into action"—in a scene run in dramatic slow-motion— to break up the encounter by attacking the low-ranking male. The narrator points out the viciousness of the attack, especially the aggressive bites to the genitals of the low-ranking male, and offers the viewer a word of warning: "If you're going to be sneaky, it pays not to get caught." The joke engages the viewer to identify with the scene and reminds viewers to conduct their violations of group norms with discretion, just as *Bear Country* or *The Leopard Son* offered mothering lessons. Recalling Barash's and Thornhill et al.'s theories, it would seem that the young koala is simply pursuing his genetic compulsion to reproduce within a social system that makes it difficult for him to do so. The same logic, and the same permission to try to get away with it, is extended by the narrator to the male viewers invited to identify with him, exemplifying the kinds of quick slips between animal and human behavior that Gowaty and others viewed as dangerous rationales for criminal behavior among humans.

Does the winking aside to the presumed male viewer constitute a tacit agreement with the viewer that, as the old saying might be updated to say, "boys have evolved to be boys," and will "naturally" seek reproductive opportunities in the absence of female consent? A cagey dismissal of the trauma, psychological and physical, experienced by victims of rape, and a recasting of rape as a crime against the female's male partner, rather than against the female herself? In the impoverished discourse of "pop sociobiology," unfortunately so. In seeing the human animal only as animal—in reducing the complex interactions of biological and social imperatives, and the complex diversity of human behavior, to the singular force of the reproductive drive, attempts to account for the existence of rape among humans through solely biological motives will surely tell only part of the story and offer less than adequate solutions. The insistence on seeing the causes of human behavior as fully articulated in easily observed animal behaviors suggests a dangerously reductive trend toward oversimplifications derived from potentially spurious and superficial likenesses. In the words of evolutionary geneticist Jerry A. Coyne, "surely it is absurd to assume that rape may be a reproductive strategy in humans because it is a reproductive strategy in flies or ducks."[59] Or marine mammals or marsupials.

"Gay" Animals and the "Gay Agenda"

Wildlife television programs have infrequently incorporated footage of sexual behaviors other than heterosexual courtship and copulation. On these exceptional occasions, casual invitations to viewers to understand their own sexuality through animal models are virtually absent. Gay-rights advocates and those who would seek to limit the rights of gay men and lesbians have for decades clashed over whether homosexuality constitutes a natural and moral variation within human sexuality, an unnatural and immoral choice, or an intolerably animalistic deviance—a clash with implications for legislation and public policy with material consequences for those of us who are queer.[60] Meanwhile, a television genre preoccupied with other kinds of sexual behavior has remained virtually silent on the matter. In the 1990s and early twenty-first century, evidence of homosexual behaviors and pair-bonds in many species accrued in scientific literature and garnered some media attention. A very few wildlife programs have begun to acknowledge such behaviors.[61] Perhaps television's most unabashed recognition of homosexuality among animals cropped up in another genre.

On March 11, 2004, *The Daily Show with Jon Stewart* (Comedy Central) aired a segment that leapt into ongoing debates over the causes and consequences of homosexuality. The half-serious, half-satire talk show approached the matter with typically facetious provocations riffing on current events. Stewart introduced the segment, when it was rerun on September 23, 2004, with remarks about a flurry of state referendums to ban same-sex marriage going before American voters later the same fall (there were eleven, all of which were approved). Turning the segment over to "correspondent" Samantha Bee, Stewart asks, "Would such laws leave room for a loophole?" Bee finds that loophole at New York's Central Park Zoo and Wildlife Center, whose "gay penguins" had recently been in the news.[62] Feigning shock, Bee interviews Dr. Dan Wharton, director of the zoo, who goes along in knowing good humor with her off-kilter questions. He quietly explains that the zoo has two male pairs of chinstrap penguins and one female pair of Gentoo penguins that have established long-term bonds, and, he adds, homosexual behavior is observed among the zoo's seals and snow monkeys, too. When Bee interjects in mock disapproval, "Just because it happens in nature does not make it natural!," Wharton barely suppresses a smile as he corrects her ("I think by definition it actually does") and corrects her again when she refers to the chinstrap species as "strap-ons."

Later in the segment, Dr. Paul Cameron—a professionally discredited but nevertheless visible spokesperson with a decidedly antigay agenda— flatly denies Wharton's claims: "There is no such thing as a gay penguin. This is just propaganda. If you believe that there are gay penguins, you're buying the gay agenda."[63] Prompted by Bee, he agrees that the zoo's acknowledgment of same-sex behavior among its animals sends a message to children that homosexuality is natural, normal, and acceptable, obviously a message he believes to be dangerously tolerant of queerness. After allowing Cameron to have his say, Bee leaves him befuddled when she asks how his no-gay-animals thesis can account for the undermining existence of Chip and Dale—Disney's cohabitating cartoon male chipmunks—and Garfield the comic-strip cat, each of whom Bee describes as embodying stereotypical gay characteristics. And she has the last word, peering with a now-speechless Cameron into the penguin exhibit: "Okay, I'm with you on the male penguins—deviant and disgusting. But girl-on-girl penguin sex? That is hot."

The Daily Show mined the gay-rights debates for laughs, poking fun at gay-lifestyle clichés and especially at the extreme leaps of logic undertaken by gay-rights detractors. But the substance of the argument remained no laughing matter, as gay-rights advocates and the opposition grapple with the significance of homosexual behaviors among animals as means of understanding human sexuality. The "gay agenda" to which Cameron refers is a caricature of the broad civil rights campaign waged by advocates for gay and lesbian communities in the 1980s and '90s, a political movement reactivated in part by the urgency of organizing around issues related to the HIV/AIDS crisis. The "gay agenda" has been depicted in the far-right media as an organized attack on traditional family values, a predatory attack on the nation's youth, a creeping infiltration of social institutions (including marriage), and a devious grab for "special rights." Through videos, books, and sermons raging against "the gay agenda," the Christian right has rallied its constituency against a wide range of efforts to protect gay men and lesbians from discrimination (in schools, at work, in the military, in immigration).[64] Much of this antigay-rights rhetoric has been predicated on the belief that homosexuality is *un*-natural and that it is a *choice* that can be changed through psychiatric treatment or prayer, rather than a value-neutral social identity whose members are fully entitled to equal protection under the law. To many *anti*-gay rights activists, who had long assumed that animals engaged only in heterosexual sexual behaviors for the purpose of reproduction (recall Cameron's claim, "There is no such thing as a gay penguin"), scientific data on homosexual behaviors among animals posed a vexing problem that had to be dismissed as what Cameron called "propaganda" in support of the "gay agenda."

Wildlife TV, for all its preoccupation with animal social life and sexual behaviors, has not readily taken on the question of same-sex pair-bonds and homosexual activity among animals. Most wildlife films posit heterosexual mate selection as not only typical but inevitable and without exception. The acceptability of mating scenes suggests an underlying assumption, shared by producers, programmers, and audiences, that peering at behaviors with reproductive outcomes contains a legitimate educational or moral component. Other kinds of behaviors seem to all-too-readily remind us that peering at sexual behavior is also, potentially, a source of voyeuristic pleasure, or a target of moral outrage. The genre's history is marked by its simultaneous provision of entertainment and education, but it is a history that has been careful about the content of its lesson plans.

As debates unfold about the origins of homosexuality, evidence of its commonplaceness accumulates in the scientific and popular-science literatures, if not in wildlife film. Bruce Bagemihl, in his encyclopedic *Biological Exuberance,* compiles evidence of behavioral diversity that he claims has usually been underestimated or explained away in animal studies, cataloging research that recounts same-sex sexual behavior, including courtship, "kissing," masturbation, oral-genital contact, "lesbian" mounting, anal intercourse between males, and temporary or long-term pair-bonding among hundreds of mammal and bird species.[65] While these behaviors take place in nature, and are sometimes documented in the scientific literature, wildlife filmmakers have paid little attention to them. On the rare occasions that homosexual behaviors are represented, they are typically explained as a ritual of dominance, a form of combat, sometimes a prelude to heterosexual coupling, but rarely as evidence of natural variation in sexual relations.

Historically, prevailing generic formulas—wildlife filmmaking's classical form, especially the predominance of "coming of age" themes, as well as the expedition-style "quest" film—leave little room for narrative problems that might be posed by displays of nonprocreative sexual behavior. The classical form requires a heterosexual mating to produce the young that are typical protagonists. Films in this form usually end just as the featured animal becomes sexually active. In the quest film, a naturalist seeks and finds an example of some rare, elusive, or particularly interesting species, showing it off to the camera and moving along to the next quest-object; animal behaviors are treated only fleetingly. Further, commercial television as a whole has historically shied away from homosexual characters and themes, in order to avoid offending conservative viewers with sympathetic representations, to avoid offending gay and lesbian audiences with negative representations, and to retain advertising contracts with corporations that might withdraw from controversial programming.

When television networks have depicted homosexuality, it has most often been as a phase, or as a problem. Advertisers have sometimes shied away from material that could be perceived as endorsing homosexuality (and much controversial content generally), and audiences have behaved erratically. One of the earliest series to include a gay or bisexual lead character, *Soap* (1977–81, ABC), featured Billy Crystal as Jodie Campbell, a young man seeking sex reassignment to please his closeted football-player boyfriend. The relationship ended and Jodie canceled his surgery, but he never overcame his ambivalence about being gay, and eventually engaged in sexual relationships with women, married, and had children. In 1997 the "coming-out" episode of *Ellen* (1994–98, ABC) achieved exceptionally high ratings. Subsequently, the once-popular series failed to hold audiences' interest.[66] To some, Ellen DeGeneres and her character's self-same queerness was an unwelcome revelation. To those who didn't mind, Ellen Morgan-the-character preached tolerance to the already-accepting. To others (and perhaps especially gay and lesbian viewers), she wasn't "out" enough. Both previously loyal and potentially new queer viewers avoided the show in droves, leading to its cancellation. There are, of course, some exceptions to the rule that television approaches queerness rarely and cautiously, and inarguably, queer characters appear with relative frequency in the post-*Ellen*, ever-expanding multichannel TV era.[67] But historically and on the whole, television has underrepresented queerness, or represented it as a problem, a curiosity, or comic relief.

Similarly, the wildlife genre has been structured almost exclusively by heteronormativity. *Wild and Weird—Wild Sex* downplays—even avoids—same-sex behaviors in the cavalcade of animal sexualities it frames as varied. A near-exception appears in the form of an Australian wasp in a segment on animals that employ deceptive practices to lure mates. A male wasp mounts a receptive female. A competing male approaches. When the first male finishes inseminating the female, she walks away, and he assumes the submissive female posture. "Confused," the interloper mounts this male who has just successfully mated. By the time he "realizes his mistake," dismounts, and scurries toward the female, she is no longer willing to mate, and rebuffs her second suitor. The scene does not depict a homosexual act so much as what the narration calls a "female impersonation" that buys time for the male who seeks to assure paternity.

In the *Triumph of Life* episode, "The Mating Game," intercourse among hermaphroditic species is not only heterosexualized but also represented as a battle over which participant will take "male" and "female" roles. The narrator introduces the aquatic flatworm:

> Each sex has its own rules in the game, even those curious creatures that play on both sides. . . . Some animals are both male and female, hermaphrodites. These flatworms produce both eggs and sperm, but they don't fertilize themselves. They need new genes to mix with their own, so they must cruise the reef in search of sex. When they meet, an expected move might be for one to play male and the other female. But flatworms have their own game plan. Each tries to be male, stabbing at the other with a harpoonlike penis that can pierce any part of the other worm's skin. In this strange duel, the rules of engagement are simple. Stab. And avoid being stabbed.

Meanwhile, the camera lingers on a lavender pair, each with a red-and-white stripe down its back, dueling with the "harpoons"—both weapons and sex organs—that grow from their snowy white undersides. Switching to a maroon and black pair, frilled with yellow and white edges and sporting double-harpoons, the narrator continues, "In every contest there has to be a loser but there's triumph in this defeat. The loser's eggs will be fertilized by sperm with winning genes." One of each pair of flatworms is shown penetrating its partner's skin. The winner penetrates, or "plays the male"; the "female," impregnated and consigned to nurturing energy-consuming eggs, is deemed a "loser."[68] Sexual behavior, other than heterosexual pairings in which males dominate subordinate females, is simply unimaginable here. A pairing that does not in many ways fit the normative human template described in *The Trials of Life*'s "Continuing the Line" by Attenborough as "the monogamous pair, one male, one female, husband and wife," is narrativized so that its participants mimic sexual difference, becoming the pair, the male, the female, husband and wife if only in our fleeting glimpse at them.

In an exception to the general absence of images of sexual behavior other than the procreative, *The New Chimpanzees* (a *National Geographic Special* aired on NBC in 1995, directed by Cynthia Moses and written by

Takayoshi Kano of the Kyoto University Primate Research Institute watches bonobos in *The New Chimpanzees.*

Catherine McConnell) approaches the sexual behavior of the bonobo with a refreshing matter-of-factness.[69] The program, which surveys the findings of a post-Goodall generation of primate researchers, devotes about seven minutes to a group of bonobos at a research station near Wamba in the Democratic Republic of the Congo, which was established by Takayoshi Kano of the Kyoto University Primate Research Institute. The segment begins as Kano's research team leaves a treat of sugarcane stalks in a forest clearing, which attracts the bonobos and brings them into view. The narrator (actor Linda Hunt) points out some of the physiological characteristics that render the bonobo more similar than other apes to humans: its slender frame and adeptness in walking upright on two legs. But the primary emphasis is on how different the bonobos are from other chimps behaviorally. Prior segments have focused extensively on violent behaviors among chimpanzees, such as the capacity of dominant males to control females and subordinate males through intimidation and threatening displays; Jane Goodall's observations of a four-year-long "war" between factions of a previously unified group that resulted in the violent death of every adult male in one of the factions; Craig Stanford's studies of the selfish behavior of male chimpanzees in group hunts for Colobus monkeys; and incidences—rare but not unique—of infanticide and cannibalism. Turning to bonobo, the program also turns, explicitly, away from violence, and posits the bonobo as a different model from which humans might seek inspiration.[70]

Among bonobos leadership is shared among males and females. Fighting is rare. Food is regularly shared, and alliances are forged and conflicts alleviated through sexual behaviors. According to the narration, a male bonobo remains in his mother's group for a lifetime and enjoys rank in the group hierarchy commensurate to the status she has achieved. When a high-ranking adolescent male is taunted by an orphan who lacks maternal protection or privileges, another high-ranking male rallies to his side, but not to protect his kin or join in harassing the interloper, but to distract and comfort him, embracing and then mounting his distressed friend for brief sexual contact. Hunt narrates: "Instead of fighting, bonobos use sex to diffuse aggression in this genuine make-love-not-war society. Bonobos have largely divorced sex from its reproductive role." As she speaks, the film shows two youngsters playing; then one mounts the other. The narration continues, while another pair stands back to back, rubbing their buttocks together: "Sex is used by all bonobos regardless of gender or age to form bonds and mitigate tension."

While bonobo sons stay with their mothers as adults, adolescent females leave their families and join other groups before they begin to breed. The group being filmed is visited by a young female, named Shin, who is seeking a new home. Hunt explains that Shin will form bonds with the group through sexual behavior, not only with the males, but also with females: "Female bonobos also use sex to form strategic alliances with each other." Meanwhile, an adult female with an infant clinging to her back crouches atop another female, who lies on her back and wraps her legs around the other female's waist, positioning herself so that their vulvas touch as they thrust against one another. (The behavior is typically referred to in scientific literature about the animals as genito-genital, or GG rubbing.) Shin mates with one of the group's males, sliding smoothly into the same face-to-face "missionary" position while the pair continues to chew on sugarcane stalks. But her new place in the group is secured only when she "is embraced by a high-ranking female who will act as her sponsor." Shin literally returns this embrace, her arms encircling the torso of the female who accepts her, clutching her underside so tightly that she is lifted entirely off the ground as they rub their bodies together.

The scene of this encounter operates as a kind of *social* (if not sexual) climax to the segment. We are not told if the bonobos' sexual behavior is orgasmic; we can only observe that at least some of it takes place during

Bonobo youngsters play at sex in *The New Chimpanzees*.

meals, seems to accompany food-sharing, and is often sustained for only a few seconds per contact. We know that Shin has used sex to forge new social bonds, and that her entry into the group has been successfully consummated. These pieces of knowledge provide narrative rationale and closure to the sex sequence. As the bonobos finish their meal and begin to move back into the forest, the segment draws to a close: "With equality between the sexes, and the substitution of sex for violence, the social lives of bonobos are very different from that of their sibling species, the chimpanzee." The camera tilts skyward, panning the tall trees that form the forest from which the bonobos have emerged, and rests atop the forest canopy in a transitional shot typical of the genre, one that allows us to rest our eyes on the landscape in which the animal subjects we are leaving reside before cutting away to a new location or new species.

At this juncture, with only treetops and open sky on screen, the tone of Linda Hunt's narration alters slightly, as she shifts from dispassionate explication of depicted behaviors to a just-slightly wistful and laudatory farewell: "While chimps may wage war, the gentler lives of bonobos show that violence, although part of our primate inheritance, is not inevitable." As the narration describes an evolutionary future less prone to aggression that was once or may still be possible for humans, the gravity in Hunt's reading of these lines imbues them with a sense of sadness, as if she feels too strongly that at a long-ago fork in the evolutionary road, humans followed the chimpanzees' path rather than the bonobos'. Instead of concluding on this plaintive note, *The New Chimpanzees* offers another segment, this time surveying new research on chimpanzees' tool use and evidence of culturally developed practices (rather than only instinctive behaviors) such as signaling the desire to be groomed through an apparently symbolic gesture made with a leaf. If the persistence of violence among the chimpanzees, our estrangement from the social benefits of the bonobos' large range of sexual expressions, and the endangered status of both species, have cast a somewhat grim pall, this evidence of culture—that is, teachability, the capacity to learn—among chimps represents an optimistic turn, even a genre-typical happy ending.

The narration during the bonobo segment focuses on the social benefits of sex, but the program avoids likening bonobos and humans, even though it is in our sexual behaviors that our species share some of our most significant similarities: year-round sexual behavior, unconfined to the briefly seasonal fertile periods during which females are receptive and males aroused among most other species; a reproductive rate similar to other apes despite this regular sexual activity, much of which involves kissing, masturbating, oral-genital contact, and nonorgasmic genital stimulation; same-sex, intergenerational, and juvenile sexual activity; and genitals more frontally oriented than other species so that intercourse is possible in a face-to-face position.[71] In other segments, we are likened to apes at critical junctures—for example, to engage the viewer during the program's first scenes with close-ups of the animals' faces and the reminder that humans and chimpanzees "share more than 97 percent of our genes, and it shows."[72] The program avoids this strategy when such a likening would require staking a claim that homosexual behavior is "natural" at a time that beliefs about the origins and morality of homosexuality are hotly contested by an antigay Christian right and determined but hardly unified gay-rights activists.

While among bonobos, *The New Chimpanzees* explains same-sex sexual behavior as a means by which the animals "form bonds and mitigate tension" and, in doing so, have "divorced sex from its reproductive role," homosexual behavior among another species is explained as not well understood, but perhaps a means by which animals compete for reproductive advantage. *Killer Whales: Wolves of the Sea* (1999, produced by David Parer and Elizabeth Parer-Cook as a joint venture of the Australian Broadcasting Corporation, the National Geographic Society and TBS), begins off the coast of British Columbia. The killer whales in these waters live in pods of about twenty individuals, typically including three generations. Because they are kin, mating does not take place between males and females within a pod. Rather, multiple pods meet in what the narration refers to as "social gatherings" late each summer during which females mate with males to whom they are not closely related. These annual events are described over a series of images of whales, alone and in pairs, their coal-black dorsal fins jutting into the air, tail flukes smacking the water's surface, interspersed with murkier images shot underwater of whales swimming so close together that they "rub shoulders, literally."

The narrator puts forward that not all sexual behavior that takes place at these "social gatherings" has direct reproductive consequences: "But unexpectedly, many of the sexually active groups that form during these big assemblies consist entirely of males. This is one, swimming upside down in the mating position." John Ford, who is affiliated with the University of British Columbia and the Vancouver Museum and has been consulted in a previous segment on whale vocalization and echolocation, takes over the narration: "One of the more peculiar behaviors of killer whales is the sexual play that goes on among males in pods and males from different pods when pods are traveling together. This may go on for hours at a time, with males rolling over each other, usually with erections." The image that appears on screen as he speaks has been made by an underwater camera that trails behind a male who glides through the water on his back. The tail is foregrounded and white belly clearly visible, as is the long thin penis that is usually contained internally and extrudes through a genital slit when the animal is sexually stimulated. A second whale swims nearby and briefly presses its tail atop the base of the first male's penis.

Cutting away from this image to another series of shots of whales at the surface, Ford continues, "We don't really know what the function of the interactions are [sic] but it seems to be where the big mature bulls, through various sexual displays or physical displays, demonstrate that they are dominant over others that might be competing with them for access to breeding females." Here, the narration ceases for the remainder of this segment of the program, replaced by notes of a mournful musical passage. During the unnarrated moments, another underwater shot shows two males. Again, one touches his tail flukes to the penis of the other. These two whales swim downward, diving toward the ocean's depths during commission of a little-understood act that the film has called "unexpected ... peculiar." The visual cue of downward motion, bolstered by these Othering adjectives, nudge the image toward a connotation of deviance, a meaningful and morally questionable, if not damnable, status, despite its found-in-nature naturalness. The scene concludes with a series of three successive long shots in which whales—presumably males from the "sexually active" group—perform breaches, undertaking powerful leaps that shoot their bodies, which can reach nine or ten meters in length, almost vertically and fully out of the water. Each of the three breaching whales lands on the water's surface on his side, resembling nothing so much as a series of images of penises rapidly becoming erect and then rapidly losing tumescence in a frothy splash. When the trio of breaches begins, the funereal music that accompanied the shots of same-sex genital touching ends; the audio portion of the program returns to diegetic sounds, the climactic explosion of water being displaced by the whale's huge and surging bodies, the crashing and splashing that accompanies their fall back into the sea.

Following the breaching sequence that signals the end of the program's inquiry into apparently homosexual acts, the program makes an awkward transition to the next segment, striving to reset a mood that had been turned plaintive with somber music, periods of silence, and the composition of shots containing downscreen exits of whales from view. The narrator announces, "After a hectic bout of socializing, some of the whales will often head for a particular rocky beach on Vancouver Island." *Socializing,* however, is not a euphemism for the ecstatic, homosexual, orgiastic behavior just observed. In cetacean observation, the term indicates a period of interactive, playful displays under and above-water. The narrator's tone is jocular, resetting the mood by excising the sexual aspect of the behavior in question (his tone would be just as suited if the line was rewritten as "after the ballgame, a few of the guys head to the neighborhood bar"). The whales frequent this beach because the floor of its shallow waters is made up of small, smooth stones. Apparently, "rubbing themselves along these rocks creates a most delectable sensation." The whales skim the pebbled floor on their sides, brushing their skin against the stones just as in prior scenes they brushed their bodies against one another, minus the erections. The whales are said to obtain pleasure ("a delectable sensation") by rubbing their bodies on these stones, but pleasure is almost inconceivable as an ingredient of sexual activity among these animals in the previous scene. Do contests not yet visible to human observers in these "interactions" determine who among the males will have access to fertile females, as Ford implies? Do whales derive pleasure from this "sexual play" that "goes on for hours" among the males? This latter possibility goes unstated. Gratification achieved by touching one's skin to rocks is conceivable; the idea of gratification achieved through same-sex physical contact is unutterable. In the *Killer Whales* narrative, as in most of wildlife TV, same-sex behaviors do not provide the group-wide social harmony observed among the polymorphous bonobos, or the coupled satisfaction observed in the Central Park Zoo penguins. Homosexuality is, within the bounds of wildlife TV, not a natural act to be understood on its own terms, but a phase of foreplay prior to the real reproductive deal, an assertion of power, or an experience through which one risks subordination. Pleasure, for these creatures, is strictly on the rocks.

Same-sex bonds and sexual behaviors in the natural world remain largely unrecognized, explained away. When they are represented, they have thus far been spared the freewheeling associations between animal and human behavior that can be found elsewhere in the wildlife genre. Even so, evidence of same-sex behaviors among animals and genetic influences on homosexuality among humans is used as ammunition in battles waged over gay rights for which advocates might be better off relying on other discourses through which civil rights are claimed. Such evidence remains inconclusive, uneasily generalizable across species, subject to wildly divergent interpretations, and likely to fail the endeavor of understanding animal behavior on its own terms. It is also as readily turned against the agenda it is claimed to support: one observer's found-in-nature-and-therefore-natural is twisted by another into a congenital defect to be treated, punished, corrected, or excised. As Marlene Zuk argues, "Whether or not animal homosexuality is widespread or occasional, whether it occurs more often in some species than others, should not influence our public policies and decisions about legal protection against discrimination for homosexuals."[73] Biology, that is, is neither moral guide nor master narrative, but rather a set of discourses that are part and parcel of the political contests that define our time.

This chapter begins with a quote by Elizabeth Grosz, who speculates that we look at animals, and especially animals' sexual behaviors, to satisfy our curiosity about their worlds, and to gain insight into our own. Animal sciences of the last forty years have done the same. In the 1960s ethologist Konrad Lorenz, known for his work on fish and birds, and Desmond Morris, a zoologist and author of popular books on snakes, apes, and pandas, turned their attention to their own species, examining human behaviors from biological perspectives. In the 1970s sociobiologists Edward O. Wilson, Richard Dawkins, David Barash, Randy Thornhill, and others developed new theories about human behavior from their observations of the animal kingdom. Wildlife documentaries absorbed their formulations and offered viewers nearly endless arrays of animal pairings, each rendered as unusual in its own way, interpreted in narratives that explicitly or implicitly suggested that how animals "do it"—by force, in groups, as winners of competitions—provides insight into human sexual relations. Sociobiological discourse assumes not only difference but inequality between the sexes as a genetically determined fact; naturalizes male promiscuity and normative heterosexuality; contains the female sex drive as not only choosy but also motivated only by reproductive efficiency and otherwise disinterested, resistant; and locates an explanation for rape in evolutionary biology. The scope of nonreproductive sexual behaviors, for both humans and animals, and the pleasures of sex—especially for humans, but documented in some other species—fade from view as trivial.

Half a century earlier, Walt Disney began allegorizing the postwar American household, idealized conservatively as a dominant male-breadwinner, a stay-at-home mother, and disciplined children, through representations of animal "families," like those in *Bear Country,* consisting of helpless, long-dependent offspring, a devoted mother, and an errant father who appears at intervals to perform familial duties. This narrative trope has survived into the present in an array of variations, in wildlife films such as *The Leopard Son* and *Africa's Elephant Kingdom,* which are also typified by the genre's preoccupations with kin groups, parenting, and the nurturing of young. Their values are reiterated in strains of the sociobiological discourse that has privileged the male sex drive and celebrated male aggression; naturalized the female who is choosy in mate selection, fiercely devoted to offspring and otherwise subordinate; and assumed that heterosexual sexual behavior is the only kind that counts. The wildlife genre embraced these assumptions, showing that social norms shape science as well as media. In descriptive and interpretive practices, research and representation, we are apt to find in nature, cast for the retelling, the stories that we ourselves wish to see and hear.

5

The Giant Panda as
Documentary Subject

Ling-Ling: she must mate so you can build
a wing on the zoo. So they go to China and
they anesthetize a panda, which is kind of
redundant...
> —Robin Williams,
> *Robin Williams Live on Broadway*

R epresentations of animals mating—whether cinematic or televisual—usually emphasize the ease, the *naturalness* with which sex
takes place. Whether sexual behavior takes place according to the rule-
bound rituals of the wolf or the whale, or following an elegant courtship
display such as the bowerbird's, or with the decisive force of the elephant
seal, or within the polymorphous sexual economy of the bonobo, animals
seem to know what they are doing. They are represented as both equipped
and compelled to reproduce, thanks to genetic heritage that determines
their physical characteristics and influences their behavior. With few exceptions (foremost, human's close relative, the bonobo), they are understood to engage in sexual behavior only to reproduce. Inexperience, incompetence, and misunderstandings are of little import to those who are
doing what comes naturally. Representations of one particular species,
however, suggest that ineptitude runs rampant among some members of
the animal kingdom. The discourse of mating and reproduction associated with the giant panda suggests the consequences of failing to achieve
the "natural" destiny of one's gender.[1]

While biological reproduction of the species has been tenuous, its status
as a media darling, its "compensatory... reproduction in images" has become assured.[2] Indeed, the animal and its dual reputation—for, on one
hand, malaise (reproductive and otherwise), and, on the other hand,

167

seemingly unbounded charm that translates into skyrocketing gate and concession receipts for zoos hosting pandas—have become familiar as the butt of jokes in all kinds of comedy. Robin Williams could send up both aspects in the standup routine filmed in 2002 for HBO (quoted in the epigraph), and the Will Ferrell vehicle *Anchorman: The Legend of Ron Burgundy* (2004) could take a jibe at local newscasters who treat the birth of a panda at the San Diego Zoo as "the biggest story of the year." Alternatively, the animal's apparent placidity appeared as one of many targets of rage in David Fincher's *Fight Club* (1999), in which the narrator (played by Edward Norton) seethed, "I felt like putting a bullet between the eyes of every panda that wouldn't screw to save its species."

Wildlife filmmakers began contributing to this discourse only in the 1980s, when for the first time they gained access to the panda's natural habitat in China. They found an animal that had been exploited as a diplomatic tool since the 1940s but most vigorously since the 1970s, pushed close to extinction by poaching and habitat loss, and both dangerously neglected and subjected to heroic conservation efforts, many in the form of aggressive breeding projects. Thus the panda became an object of negotiations between world-power governments, global nongovernmental organizations (NGOs), Western and Chinese zoologists and zoological societies, and adoring audiences (and some detractors) wherever the animal or its image appeared. The state of these negotiations influenced how the media would represent the animal as a precious resource misunderstood and undervalued by the Chinese, but potentially redeemable through American intervention and the enculturation of American values.

Most documentaries about giant pandas employ the conventions of the "quest" or expedition sagas of the wildlife genre, one of its earliest variations, dating back to the hunting films of early cinema and the wildlife travelogues of the 1920s. In the postwar era, while Disney developed the allegorical, unpeopled animal narratives that would set standards for subsequent generations of wildlife filmmakers, Jacques-Yves Cousteau and others rehabilitated the expedition film. They substituted scientists, conservationists, and explorers who showed interest in the study of nature and in conservationism for the big-game hunters and adventurers of the expedition film's early twentieth-century form. In this generic variation, a quest for interaction with animals propels the narrative forward, as a human protagonist seeks to observe some rarely seen species or previously little-known behavior. He or she records these observations on film (or video) in order to distribute this new visual experience as a commodity to audiences. The audience, in turn, gains access to rarefied visual experiences, glimpses of unfamiliar creatures and places, that bestow a kind of knowledge-based cultural capital on the viewer, through which one distinguishes oneself from those less knowledgeable.[3] Among animal-subjects of wildlife filmmaking (and zoological exhibition), there may be many species that are actually rarer than the giant panda, but few have been as touted as especially endangered and especially inaccessible. Knowledge of this animal, then, acquired either through direct experience or through observation of captive specimens or images of the animal in the wild (or more, typically, in protected areas), represents exceptional distinction for the Western scientists and filmmakers who have worked with the animal in its natural habitat. This distinction—the panda's designation as special—extends (proportionately diluted) to the zoo-goer or television-viewer who encounters it in exhibition or representation.

Frequently, wildlife quest films provide visual access to animals that exceeds the capacity of the unassisted human eye. Wildlife filmmakers have long used macro- and telephoto lenses, slow motion, time-lapse, and other photographic technologies to render the invisible visible. Similarly, wildlife professionals have used devices such as radio signal-transmitting collars to monitor the movements of animals far from visual range. These projects have been regularly documented by wildlife filmmakers, especially in the genre's drug-and-tag era, the 1960s and 1970s, when Marlin Perkins and his colleagues staged capture, collar, and release projects as action-packed chase scenes. More recently, medical imaging technologies complement the genre's expected vistas of animals and landscapes with views of what Valerie Hartouni calls the "bioscape," or scenes of the body's interior. Documentaries about "the wondrous workings of the human body," she notes, bring "hidden processes to light—the video extends our vision, technologically, beyond the everyday apparent through the use of prosthetic imaging devices."[4]

The panda emerges from these historical conditions of extreme rarity, popular appeal, and symbolic overdetermination as a favorite subject of wildlife filmmaking. News coverage familiarized many Americans with the animal during the 1970s, and positioned the animal as the object of sexual curiosity. Later, television documentaries situated the giant panda in the context of changing political and economic conditions under which pandas and images of pandas circulated in the late 1980s, 1990s, and early in the twenty-first century, as they continued to be exchanged by political and institutional rivals in contests over ideology, trade, and conservation. These representations mark the animal's physiological and behavioral attributes and its habitat as inscrutably unique; its diplomatic currency as invaluable; and its need for heroic interventions by (mostly) American scientists and conservationists (and their West-influenced Chinese counterparts) to save this rare species, acute. Consequently, they are infused with a kind of textbook Orientalism, always mediated through exoticizing and controlling gazes. As an example of what Edward Said called "a system of representations framed by a whole set of forces that [bring] the Orient into Western learning, Western consciousness, and later, Western empire," these images are a record of (especially) American inquisitiveness and acquisitiveness, extended through thickets of bamboo and into the body of the animal, extracted as natural resource and reproduced in new commodity forms.[5]

Panda News

The giant panda is critically endangered. While its exact numbers are unknown, estimates in two decades of news coverage hover around a thousand in the wild and another hundred in captivity.[6] The necessities of breeding efforts in its homeland and controversies regarding their presence in zoos have kept its captive population outside China relatively low. Pandas have been removed from China only when they have been exported as diplomatic gifts, or rented to zoos in exchange for funds to support conservation efforts in the animal's native habitat. Zoos have been eager to acquire pandas, which are widely considered one of the most crowd-pleasing of all animals.[7] In fact, the species attracts virtually fanatical attention from some admirers. When the Bronx Zoo hosted two of the animals for six months in 1987, a million people came to see them, including an Oneonta, New York, woman with great fondness for the panda. A reporter wrote:

> A typical day, she happily confided, might find her clad in her panda sweater, panda slippers and a panda hat. Her house is crammed with stuffed pandas, panda cookie jars and panda pictures. She and her husband, Ken, have seen pandas several times at the Washington zoo. "We have a whole room decorated panda," Ken said grimly.[8]

Despite the species' current widespread recognizability, little has been known outside of China about pandas until the last century, although historical records indicate that pandas were kept along with other rare and treasured animals in the emperor's gardens of the Han Dynasty over two thousand years ago. Western interest in the species was sparked only in 1869 when the French natural historian and Lazarist missionary Abbé Armand David acquired a specimen killed by hunters in his hire during an expedition in China. He sent several pandas to Paris, possibly to the Jardin des Plantes or the Natural History Museum, but historical records fail to confirm if any of them survived for a time or if he managed to deliver only carcasses. Following Abbé David, Western explorers who sought the panda succeeded only in purchasing pelts from local hunters. Then, in 1929, two of President Theodore Roosevelt's sons, Theodore and Kermit, organized an expedition sponsored by the Chicago Field Museum of Natural History. Assisted by Lolo trackers in the Hsifan mountains, they shot and killed a male panda. The museum stuffed and displayed the animal, inspiring other museums to send teams to collect specimens.[9]

The difficulties of maintaining and breeding captive pandas became apparent as soon as live specimens began to reach Western zoos. The first known panda to survive for any length of time outside China arrived in San Francisco on December 18, 1936, an event documented by photojournalists and newsreel-filmmakers. Ruth Harkness had collected the young animal, which she named Su-Lin, from the wild with the help of hired hunters. Harkness's husband had died during an earlier, failed panda expedition; she traveled to China to retrieve his ashes but undertook his mission instead. Harkness "donated" Su-Lin to the Brookfield Zoo in Chicago in 1937 in exchange for the zoo's sponsorship of her next panda-collecting expedition to China. She delivered a second panda to Chicago in 1938.[10] Brookfield acquired a third panda in 1939; the Regents Park Zoo in London acquired five in 1938 and 1939; and the Bronx Zoo acquired one in 1938, another in 1939, and two more, gifts of Mrs. Chiang Kai-shek, in 1941. This first wave of pandas to reside in zoos outside of China tended to suffer premature deaths; of the first nine, only three survived more than two years.[11]

Pandas at these zoos became popular attractions.[12] Perhaps the London pandas, during their short lifetimes, received the most intense adulation. Their presence prompted visits from royalty, newsreels of their activities, and a huge trade in souvenirs. The BBC conducted an early experimental remote-television broadcast from the zoo, in which one of the pandas, Ming, appeared.[13] The other London pandas died of various illnesses by 1940, but for much of the war Ming helped bolster Londoners' spirits—a newsreel shows her wearing a soldier's helmet and clutching a small Union Jack in her paw. Eventually, she began to exhibit physical and behavioral

In *Save the Panda,* Ruth Harkness deplanes with Su Lin, the first live panda in the United States, in 1936.

symptoms of stress. The zoo removed her from public exhibition and she died in 1944.[14]

Ironically, this specifically Chinese animal became a symbol of British hope, humor, and power. If in the nineteenth and early twentieth centuries hunting trophies, photographs of hunting parties, and skins mounted in natural history museums were representational evidence of colonial conquest and the wealth of resources acquired from far-off lands, live animals in zoos have served much the same purpose.[15] Ming and her exotic companions of other species offered living proof of the extent and success of the British empire. She served as a reminder, in her zoo habitat and in the newsreels that delivered her image to other audiences, that someday the bombing would stop, the war would end, and England would regain its former global stature, through which it had garnered tributes such as this rare and mysterious animal.

Then as now, zookeepers hoped to breed their exotic charges, but were thwarted in matching pairs by the difficulty of sexing pandas through visual evidence. Many of the first exported pandas were misassigned until post-mortem exams, as sexual dimorphism—the differences between male and female in size, shape, and other aspects of general appearance—in pandas is less distinctive than in similar species (such as members of the bear family, to which pandas are related).[16] The Brookfield Zoo, for example, thought that its first two pandas, Su-Lin and Diana, were female but, at their deaths, discovered that both were male. Also, according to Ramona and Desmond Morris, the male's penis is, at under three inches in length, "ridiculously short for so large an animal." Since it emerges only during intercourse and panda testes are buried in body fat rather than descended in an external scrotum, male and female ano-genital areas appear remarkably similar. Further complicating captive breeding, the female's estrus cycle occurs only once a year, and she is willing to mate only two to seven days during the period, so the timing of staged mating encounters (or insemination) is critical.[17]

While pandas attracted huge crowds to the few zoos that obtained them, China halted international trade of the animals for over three decades, during wartime and after the Communist Revolution in 1949, with the exception of animals sent to London in 1946 and 1958, Moscow in 1957 and 1958, and Pyongyang in 1965 and 1971.[18] The next wave of what has sometimes been ridiculed as "panda diplomacy" began in April 1972.[19] The People's Republic of China gave two to the United States to commemorate President Richard Nixon's meeting with Mao Zedong. In return, the United States sent two musk oxen to the Peking Zoo.[20] In an Animal Planet documentary, *Meet the Pandas* (2001), Julie Nixon Eisenhower recalls that the gift stemmed from a conversation between First Lady Patricia Nixon and Premier Chou En-Lai at a state dinner. When Mrs. Nixon admired images of pandas adorning a cigarette dispenser on their table, "The Premier said, 'Oh!,' he said, 'well, I'll give you some.' Mother said, 'Cigarettes?' And Chou En-Lai said, 'No, pandas.'" (Apparently President Nixon was less enthralled. He never went to see them.) The pair lived at the National Zoo in Washington, D.C., where they produced five cubs, none of which survived more than a few days. The female, Ling-Ling, died in 1992, and the male, Hsing-Hsing, in 1999.[21]

Ling-Ling and Hsing-Hsing's sexual and reproductive behaviors (or, their lack of these behaviors) were scrutinized not only by National Zoo staff but also by the press. Reporters for major newspapers and wire services covered their story as a melodrama with implications for human understanding of sexual behaviors and misbehaviors. In news coverage of the pandas' activities, reporters made abundant analogies between human and animal life, which may, in some researchers' views, sensationalize animal behaviors for a popular audience at the cost of accurate description and explanation.[22] Reporters (and other panda-watchers) regularly described the animals and their behaviors in terms culled from the lexicon of human sexuality—"virgin," "lover," "rape," "wife-beater"—that situated those roles and behaviors within value-laden social and legal contexts. Some journalists took their zoo-news assignments as opportunities to extract moral lessons from news events, allegorizing panda behaviors in terms of contemporary human social issues and mores, just as Walt Disney's True-Life Adventures of the 1950s couched interpretations of animal behavior within dominant marital and childrearing ideologies of their time.[23] Even more glibly, the narration of wildlife footage in Jamie Uys's *Animals Are Beautiful People* (1974) describes animal courtship, mating encounters, however brief, and pair-bonds in terms of the human rituals of love and institutions of marriage.

News coverage of the Washington pandas was intensely preoccupied with their sexual and reproductive capabilities. After years of vain attempts to mate Ling-Ling and Hsing-Hsing, zoo personnel began to believe that Hsing-Hsing might never mate successfully, given his general disinterest, poor technique, and low sperm count.[24] While the general public may have assumed that China had given the United States a mated (or mate-able) pair of pandas, the press set about dispelling that notion as the zoo began to pursue other means of impregnating Ling-Ling. In 1980 Dr. Robert Hoage of the National Zoo told the *Washington Post* that Ling-Ling had been artificially inseminated because Hsing-Hsing persisted in his "ineffective mating posture. He can't do it. We don't know why." The reporter wondered if Ling-Ling was still "a virgin," even though she might have been pregnant; Hoage tossed off the question as irrelevant but admitted "technically," this assessment was accurate.[25]

A follow-up article announced that Ling-Ling was not pregnant, describing her as "still the liberated woman and quite childless."[26] "Liberated" seems an ironic term to apply to a captive zoo animal being watched around the clock on closed-circuit television; some moral philosophers and animal-rights activists would argue that such an animal would be liberated only once returned to a cage-free existence in its natural habitat, where it can define its own territory, gather its own food, and associate with other animals at will rather than according to zoo schedules.[27] At the same time, the reporter's use of the term "liberated woman" caricatures feminism as organized around refusing to have sexual relations with men or to bear children, which were hardly tenets of the second-wave liberal feminism, or the "women's liberation" movement, of the 1970s. The reporter, intentionally or unintentionally, satirizes coupling and childbearing as oppressive conditions that Ling-Ling should be congratulated for having narrowly escaped once again.

In the same article, the reporter laments Hsing-Hsing's failure to impregnate her yet again—either on his own or by the use of his sperm in an artificial insemination—as part of his "sad sexual history... his sorry track record."[28] For the male, failure to breed is not a sign of liberation but a sign of failure, dishonor, and weakness, grounds on which he might be ridiculed. Another *Washington Post* writer reported that the zoo concurred that Hsing-Hsing had "fizzled as a lover," again borrowing a term used to describe a human relationship that seems ill suited to accurately conveying panda couplings.[29] "Lover," like "liberated woman," is more fanciful and metaphorical than descriptive, intended to dramatize the story and promote readers' identification with the pandas. If "lover" suggests, among humans, one who feels and acts on a passionate sexual impulse toward another, it may overstate the role of just about any panda in a sexual encounter. According to most accounts, female pandas in estrus can be more irritable and resistant than receptive, both in captivity and in the wild; males in captivity are typically passive and indifferent, even to receptive females. Adult pandas show virtually no affection, let alone ardor, for one another, and do not establish pair-bonds.[30]

In any case, the National Zoo remained determined to reverse Ling-Ling's "childless" state, which some reporters pointed out was not solely caused by Hsing-Hsing's incompetence. Al Kamen wrote, "It is not at all clear that the problem has been entirely his," as Ling-Ling "rolls over whenever Hsing-Hsing makes one of his rare amorous advances." Hoping that a more virile male—and some competition between males over her—might hold Ling-Ling's attention, the National Zoo tried to stage a natural breeding with another panda, a male named Chia-Chia loaned by the London Zoo. This male, while still a "virgin" himself, was thought to be both more assertive and to have a higher sperm count than Hsing-Hsing.[31] Chia-Chia and Ling-Ling, however, refused to mate. A *New York Times* article described their encounter as "90 minutes of swatting and shoving," in which he "tore at [her] fur" and she "batted him back." The same article quoted a zoo official who attributed their failure to mate to the fact that "Chia-Chia didn't care for Ling-Ling, and Ling-Ling didn't care for Chia-Chia."[32]

Subsequent *New York Times* news items, in which the reporter is bound by the conventional journalistic obligation to be objective and to tell "both sides" of the story, recalled the event as marked by "mutual antagonism."

But the *Times* editorial page consistently framed the incident as spousal abuse, ascribing bad behavior only to the male, calling Chia-Chia "a wife-beater," a "brute," "belligerent," and "macho," as if it were an opportunity for the paper to launch thinly veiled condemnations of domestic violence. In contrast, the *Washington Post*, the pandas' hometown paper, always cast the outsider as the aggressor: "Chia-Chia roughed her up considerably"; "Ling-Ling . . . was sore from bites and abrasions for two days"; the male visitor was "a real stud" who "beat her up." The *Post* embraced her as an abused local darling; its editorial page lamented that she was "subjected to a succession of public indignities—including exposure to that roughneck lover-boy from London—which no decent female should have to endure."[33]

When Hsing-Hsing successfully mounted and ejaculated into Ling-Ling during her 1983 heat, the *Washington Post* celebrated with a front-page article and photo. The journalist covering the event, Ken Ringle, claimed in his lead paragraph that the pair "finally consummated their too-long Platonic union yesterday, proving perhaps, that one should never give up too soon on a troubled relationship." The lesson Ringle drew from the panda mating seemed to be a plea for patience with lovers whose sexual performances are impaired by indifference, impotence, or ineptitude. While National Zoo staff who hoped the pair would produce a cub celebrated, and continued to watch Ling-Ling for signs of pregnancy—or, failing insemination, for signs of her next fertile period—some members of the D.C.-area public began to call on the National Zoo to cease trying to breed the pandas. The leader of the protests, Elizabeth Irvine, told the *Washington Post*, "It's like being raped. She doesn't like him. . . . Her life has been hell for the past 10 years, believe me." In Irvine's account, Ling-Ling appears as the passive object of masculine determination; she seems capable of neither rejecting a mate nor participating willingly in a sexual encounter; she is only a body whose history depends entirely on how it is used by males, both panda and human. The *Post* reporter suggested another interpretation. Ringle divided responsibility for the pandas' failure to mate between "an uncertain and ineffectual Hsing-Hsing" who was "cowed and confused by the demands of an impatient and aggressive mate [Ling-Ling]."[34] In his account, Ling-Ling is at fault for emasculating her mate, overwhelming him with her demands. Hsing-Hsing deserves our sympathy and encouragement, just as in the same reporter's 1983 piece that commends efforts to give the male panda more chances to prove his prowess. Reporters—and editorial writers—covering the latest exploits of Hsing-Hsing and Ling-Ling chose frames of interpretation that allowed them to expound their views on human sexual and social relations and the ongoing battle of the sexes as much as they attended to the battle to reproduce the endangered species. One wonders if they occasionally exposed quite a bit of themselves, even as they sought to reveal life lessons, culled from animal observations, for their readers.

Panda Television

If the panda's "biological reproduction" is a delicate and often unsuccessful endeavor, its "reproduction in images" is assured.[35] While in the 1970s, several pairs of pandas left China as gifts to foreign governments, pandas in China itself remained off-limits to foreign researchers and film crews. In the late 1970s the World Wildlife Fund (WWF) initiated negotiations with the Chinese agencies responsible for environmental protection to study pandas at one of the several established panda reserves. Project Panda was the first time that the WWF actually engaged in panda research and protection, even though its logo had been a picture of a panda since the organization was founded in 1961. Eventually, China granted the WWF researchers access to the panda reserves, in exchange for a $1-million contribution toward the construction of a permanent research center at Wolong Nature Reserve in southwest Sichuan Province.[36] In addition to construction of the center, Project Panda would focus on caring for pandas in case of food shortages, and on collection of data about the behavior of the then-little studied animal, under the supervision of George B. Schaller of the New York Zoological Society and Hu Jin-chu of Nanchong Teachers College.[37] And Chinese officials began to grant permission to foreign filmmakers to visit the reserves and to collect footage for television documentaries.

To be sure, the press continued to cover the breeding exploits of the National Zoo pandas, their health, and eventually, in the 1990s, their deaths. Ongoing threats to the species' survival, negotiations that led to the arrival of pandas at the San Diego Zoo and the survival of their first- and second-born, China's subsequent export of pandas to Atlanta and Memphis, and a new pair for Washington, were also newsworthy events. But another medium began representing giant pandas regularly in the early 1980s. Wildlife filmmakers gained access to pandas in China for the first time. Whereas reporters and editorial writers for the *Washington Post*, the *New York Times*, and other major newspapers had used the pandas to articulate views about sex roles, courtship, impotence, and domestic violence, wildlife filmmakers relied less on metaphorical language and allegorical narratives.

Instead, they repositioned the panda and its conservation as quest objects of Western scientists and Western audiences.

The National Geographic Society, the PBS-affiliate WQED Pittsburgh, and the WWF coproduced one of the first documentaries on the giant panda, *Save the Panda* (1983; Miriam Birch was both producer and writer; Norris Brock, director of photography). Just over a decade later, National Geographic released a follow-up, *Secrets of the Wild Panda* (1994, directed by Mark Stouffer, produced by Mark Stouffer and Adrian Warren for National Geographic). While National Geographic has long presented itself as politically disinterested, engaged only in documenting nature and culture through lenses purportedly uninflected by ideology, both *Save the Panda* and *Secrets of the Wild Panda* articulate Western ownership of environmental values and the superiority of Western science and technology, situating the fate of the panda in the hands, literally, of American zoologists. *Save the Panda*, which premiered during PBS's annual fundraising campaign, garnered a glowing review by the *Washington Post*'s nationally syndicated TV columnist and an enthusiastic plug on the *Christian Science Monitor*'s opinion page. A few years later, the *New York Times* reviewed its home-video release with more reserve, noting, "The visuals are slow and colorless, not up to National Geographic's high standards." The setting contributed to the impression: gloomy skies and stark snows cloaking the mountaintop reserve at which much of the program was filmed, and the preponderance of interior scenes contrast with the expansive, idealized vistas often favored by the genre.[38]

Instead of anthropomorphized animal subjects in apparently pristine nature, *Save the Panda* depicts expeditions into panda habitat and expeditionary interventions into the reproductive processes of the animal itself. Its pandas are not free-roaming subjects but rather the quarry of hunters and biologists, captive in either urban zoos or enclosed conservation parks. Its protagonists are not the animals themselves but the leaders of American research teams: principally Schaller, along with Devra Kleiman of the National Zoo and Emil P. Dolensek, chief veterinarian of the Bronx Zoo. *Save the Panda* shows the viewer more researchers than pandas, and demonstrates the animal's popularity with scenes of crowds formed at airports to greet newly imported specimens, and bigger crowds observing them at zoos. The Chinese researchers appear as onlookers and assistants eager to learn from the U.S. teams, and as providers of manual labor—preparing food for the animals, for example—rather than as providers of knowledge about their habits and habitat.

Wildlife filmmaking's classic form, rooted in Disney's True-Life Adventures, conventionalized narrative structures based on seasonal or life cycles, but *Save the Panda* is less cyclical than episodic in its structure. The National Geographic crew visited the Wolong Nature Reserve for about three months, concentrating on the researchers' activities rather than following an animal group over the course of an annual cycle, as in the genre's "classic" mode requiring lengthy field commitments and high shooting ratios.[39] *Save the Panda* begins with an introductory historical overview, then documents current activities at the Wolong Reserve. Three breeding projects comprise major segments of the documentary, with other activities interspersed throughout: Kleiman attempts to stage a "natural" breeding; the research team traps and places a radio collar on a male panda; Dolensek conducts an artificial insemination; George and Kay Schaller monitor the animals' activity, diet, and range; and, returning to the United States, National Zoo staff inseminate Ling-Ling. Each of *Save the Panda*'s primary segments represent the extent to which humans have intervened in their reproductive processes when their natural behaviors fall short of human goals for the species.

The opening segment uses archival photographs and newsreel footage of the panda's first encounters with Western hunters, naturalists, zookeepers, and zoo-goers. The narration contends that despite Western enthusiasm for the species, the Chinese government began to attend to wildlife conservation only in the post-Mao period, and then with little success.[40] Its early efforts regarding the panda were thwarted. A growing population continued to convert vast acreage of habitat within the first panda preserves to farmland, and a natural die-off of bamboo, the panda's main food source, took place in the early 1980s in the Wolong Nature Preserve in southwest Sichuan Province. An estimated 10 percent of its panda population starved to death during a similar die-off in northern Sichuan a decade earlier.[41] Hoping to avoid similar losses during the Wolong die-off, China accepted offers of help from the WWF and several researchers based at American zoos. With this background established, *Save the Panda* turns to the arrival of the American researchers at Wolong and their projects.

The National Zoo's Debra Kleiman is at Wolong to conduct research into panda vocalizations, which she believes are signs of different stages of the reproductive cycle and means by which males and females in the wild might locate one another when they want to mate. She visits a female panda at the Wolong center. Through the bars of the cage, with her back to the camera and microphone, she addresses the animal: "Good morning. How are you doing today? You've been bleating a lot in the past few days. Are you coming into heat, [name inaudible]? Are you bleating in response to Li-Li [referring to another nearby panda]?" Kleiman questions the animal as if the sound of her voice might coax it into additional vocalizations, examples of which are the evidence that she collects in her research. Just as other kinds of researchers, trained in "eliciting talk" from human subjects, might prompt an interviewee with questions, Kleiman theorizes aloud, hopefully, as if seeking confirmation of her theories from her animal subject, or at least more data to consider.[42]

Kleiman's project is intended to "facilitate natural breeding," that is, impregnation achieved through intercourse. When the female's behavior suggests, according to Kleiman's assessment, that she is at the most fertile stage of her estrous cycle, the male and female are put together in an outdoor enclosure. The camera that records the scene is indoors, so that bars of a cage come between viewer and the pandas. While the built environment is visible throughout the scenes of their encounter, the role of humans in the act is limited to choosing the moment; no humans are visible during these scenes. Even the voiceover is restrained, noting that at first the male was "unresponsive—then attempts to mate," then falling silent as he approaches the crouching female from behind. He begins to mount her, but she turns aggressively. They tussle briefly, and the male moves away from the female and out of the film frame. In the next scene, shot from a camera placed outdoors, the female settles down in the doorway that opens onto the yard, vocalizing the guttural moan that Kleiman calls a bleat as the narrator announces, "the mating attempt has ended in failure." The scene ends as the camera zooms out on the image of the solitary bear.

Kleiman's "natural breeding" fails, but Dolensek tries artificial insemination using frozen semen. The presence of metal tanks, liquid nitrogen, and the delicate blue straws that hold the semen indicate that the source of this breeding is at least as much advanced technology as it is nature. Once the American and Chinese researchers have reached consensus regarding the optimal moment to begin the procedure (one of the few moments in the film where their voices seem to count as much as those of the American researchers), six or seven people rush into her cage and hoist the sedated bear onto a plank table, belly down. Dolensek directs the insemination toward releasing the semen in the proper location. "Pull the tail up," he orders, and two pairs of hands grasp the panda's stump of a tail. As one of the Chinese veterinarians peers into the panda's vagina with the help of a flashlight, Dolensek asks, "Can you see the separation there? No,

Dr. Emil Dolensek oversees an artificial insemination in *Save the Panda*.

can you see the separation. See, we're still not at the cervix. See the separation across the top? Do you see it? Do you see it?" He takes the flashlight and takes a look himself.

Penetration of the female—by the male's penis in a natural mating— is in this procedure largely visual. Rather than an ejaculation caused by the muscle contractions of male orgasm, the release of semen is determined by a visual cue, the thin straw reaching the cervix, where sperm are most likely to enter the uterus. The success or failure of the insemination attempt depends on the visual acuity of the person who is looking into the panda's vagina, on his accuracy in claiming that the straw is as close as possible to the cervix. Dolensek's exhortations are insistent Lamaze-style coaching, but they are directed at his partner in the insemination rather than at the panda, and take place during insemination rather than birth. He cathects enormous energy onto the process, his urgency palpable in his repeated query, "Do you see it?" His displaced identification with the inseminator, even with the semen load itself, reveals itself as he claims, not "it's still not" or "you're still not" but rather "*we're* still not at the cervix."

Behind Dolensek, at the left-hand side of the frame, two Chinese men take photographs of the event. While the camera has been focusing on the faces of the men who crowd around the panda's rump, the scene ends with an image of the panda's head. This final shot crosses what is known in continuity editing as the center, or 180-degree line. The shot startles not only because it defies televisual convention, but also because it shows the sedated animal's face for the first time, in close-up. Suddenly she appears as an individual, sentient being, rather than an inert mass being worked on by a team of peering, photographing men. Her head is stroked by a pair of hands belonging to the only woman to have entered the panda's cage. The woman seems to be charged with the nurturing task of soothing the animal, signaling a gendered division of labor among the research team. Afterward, outdoors, the American researcher declares, "that was a good insemination!," shaking hands with his Chinese colleagues. As the whoops of their celebration fade out, the film cuts to a shot of the panda, waking and rubbing her eyes with her paws, and the narrator delivers the bad news: despite two more inseminations during her heat, this animal did not become pregnant.

The third intervention into panda sexuality and fertility depicted in *Save the Panda* occurs when, in March 1982, the National Zoo staff performs an artificial insemination on Ling-Ling, in a sequence that offers contrasts to the Wolong setting in parallel scenes. Ling-Ling is brought to an operating room on a stretcher rather than inseminated in her cage. Her roly-poly body is hoisted just as awkwardly onto the surgical table as the Wolong panda was plopped onto her plank. She is placed belly up, exposing perhaps a square foot of her belly, which has been shaved and treated (with, it appears, an antiseptic). A rapid sequence of shots indicates the hygienic practices of this team, as personnel tie on masks and pull on gloves, none of which were part of the Wolong team's process. A medium shot closes in on the panda, now covered with green sheets save for the bright orange square of her abdomen. The veterinary team huddles around her, all clad in green scrubs, and one of them shouts, "OK, we're in!" The next shot lingers on a video camera against a field of surgical equipment, and the narrator explains that a laparoscope is being "used to see when ovulation is occurring." As National Geographic's camera reframes the small video screen that exhibits the images sent from inside Ling-Ling, the narrator claims, "For the first time in history, a medical team is able to look inside the body of a female panda in heat." When the correct proximity to her cervix is reached, one of the team injects the semen.

While viewers of the Wolong insemination can only imagine what Dolensek and his team are seeing, the National Zoo's imaging technology give both medical team and TV audience access to scenes of the panda's bodily interior, the animal "bioscape." Here, the leap between unmediated

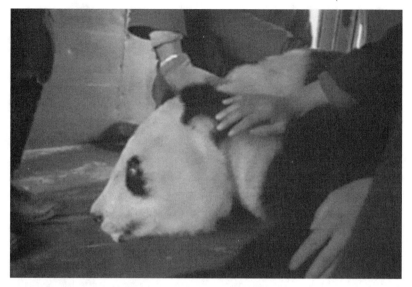

Soothing the panda, postinsemination, in *Save the Panda.*

and assisted vision re-marks the boundary between "inside" and "outside" the female body. As Judith Butler points out, "What constitutes through division the 'inner' and 'outer' worlds of the subject is a border and boundary tenuously maintained for the purpose of social regulation and control ... confounded by those excremental passages in which the inner effectively becomes the outer."[43] That border is, literally, a slippery slope. At Wolong, it is a boundary redrawn: only the gaze of Dolensek and his assistants penetrate the vagina. The view required no incision and left no mark, depending only on holding the orifice agape. As orifice, rather than true interior, the walls of the vagina are sufficiently accessible to physical and visual penetration that they constitute part of the female exterior, her surface. The laparoscope, in contrast, is inserted through an incision in the abdominal wall and used to observe internal organs and share images with TV audiences. Within the discourse of this program, it is cutting into the animal, and the visual assistance of the tiny video camera that captures images of her organs, where neither the male panda's penis nor the human's vision can reach unmediated by insemination and visual technologies, that constitute the true penetration.

After insemination, Ling-Ling continues to be observed on video when she is in her den. When, a few months later, her behaviors—nest-building, excessive grooming, and pelvic thrusting—suggest that she will soon give birth, scrutiny intensifies. Not only local researchers but also Dr. Kleiman, who is back in China, review daily videos sent from the National Zoo, but eventually the team must acknowledge to themselves and to the press and public that Ling-Ling is experiencing only a false pregnancy. Zoo director Dr. Theodore Reed promises at the press conference that "next year we'll try again."

Save the Panda was among the first of many wildlife films to feature the giant panda, but the wild panda is an elusive subject, and most films about pandas have focused on captive specimens. Cinematographer Norris Brock tried to film free-roaming pandas while working on *Save the Panda,* but managed to obtain only one very brief image; otherwise, all of the pandas shown are captive at the Wolong Research Center or contained and managed within the conservation park. An ABC film crew that visited other panda reserves in 1981 and 1982 had a little better luck, gathering footage of several wild pandas for an episode of the series *American Sportsman.* These scenes were actually the first of noncaptive specimens of the animal to reach U.S. television audiences, beating Brock's footage for National Geographic's *Save the Panda.* A Nippon TV crew that visited the Wolong reserve chose to focus *A Panda's Story* (1984) on a wild panda that lived near the Wuyipeng camp, scavenging and begging food.[44]

A decade later, National Geographic returned to panda territory. *Secrets of the Wild Panda* offers a condensed reprise of the historical background covered in *Save the Panda* (recycling some of the same archival footage), and presents new knowledge about panda behaviors such as dietary habits, communication, and maternal care. It also claims to provide both science and the popular audience with "an unprecedented opportunity": a research team has found an infant cub in a den, allowing for "the first comprehensive film record and first long-term study" of an individual panda's first year. But as much as *Secrets of the Wild Panda* takes the panda as its subject and offers her biography in the genre's classical form as a coming-of-age story, it is also, like *Save the Panda,* very much about the researchers and their quest to find and get to know animal life. This time, the human protagonists are not visiting Americans but rather Chinese biologists, led by Pan Wenshi of Beijing University. Like many wildlife films, *Secrets of the Wild Panda* opens with a series of establishing shots of the animals' habitat. It begins with a long shot of a mountain, two shots of a flowing stream, a close-up of bamboo leaves, another close-up that pans up the length of a bamboo stalk, and a first-person point-of-view shot in which a handheld camera shows the viewer what it would look like to wander through the dense forest. Viewers familiar with the genre's conventions might expect the next shot, the film's seventh, to reveal the title subject. Instead, it shows Professor Pan, clothed in camouflage, making his way through the foliage. In the eighth image, a panda appears in reverse shot, as though approaching or facing Pan, rather than being trailed by him.[45] The rest of the scene clarifies that the panda is simply seeking a spot in which to settle down to eat some bamboo and, later, to take a drink of water from the stream, in both instances followed and observed by Pan at some distance.

Pan Wenshi is presented as the panda's savior, its most important advocate within China, and a solitary warrior for its survival against tremendous odds, at great personal sacrifice. Like Jane Goodall in the *National Geographic Specials*, Pan is a heroic figure, as much an object of interest as his animal subjects, and a conduit through which knowledge of the animal flows to the viewer. The narrator, actor Peter Coyote, stresses Pan's personal sacrifice, noting that at the research station, he endures "primitive conditions, paying some research expenses out of his own pocket, working late hours to record and analyze data in a tiny cubicle that is both office and bedroom," as he is shown writing by candlelight on a desk pulled up to the foot of the bed on which he sits, then stretches and lies down in exhaustion. Moreover, Pan is described as willing to challenge dominant political, social, and economic forces, as well as the common sense of his colleagues and culture. Speaking through translators, he professes that he was inspired as a youth by Jack London's novels *Call of the Wild* (1903) and *White Fang* (1906), and dreamed of living in a "remote area like Western America or Alaska" and working with wild animals. As the narration attributes Pan's empathetic response to the negative effects of captivity on wild pandas to his own imprisonment during China's cultural revolution, Pan is shown peering through the bars of a panda's cage, clenching the bars with tight fists, as though he, not the panda, were caged. Over the next close-up, without the bars, the voiceover continues: "even some friends cannot understand why he leaves his home and family several times a year for the sake of a wild animal." National Geographic's film crew follows Pan to a Beijing classroom where he teaches small children, who are surprised to learn that pandas actually exist outside of zoos and about the animals' need for protection. Later, the crew accompanies Pan on the thirty-six-hour trip by train and bus to the Qinling mountains, where logging has rapidly consumed much of the panda's habitat. Despite "threats and harassment," the professor has won a lengthy struggle with government bureaucracies to protect a 125-square-mile region (and perhaps a few hundred pandas) from logging, despite what the narration describes as the "urgent human needs"—such as firewood and construction materials—of not only locals but China's entire population, then placed at 1.2 billion.[46]

Throughout *Secrets of the Wild Panda*, Pan Wenshi's work in panda conservation is set in competition with the needs of China's human populations, as if the needs of nature and the needs of humanity are inevitably at odds. Studies of environmental values suggest that protectionist attitudes toward nature can develop from various spiritual, moral, and utilitarian world views that understand conservation of the natural world and animals as desirable and compatible with human life.[47] However, the film's explanation for the panda's plight suggests that as a monolithic whole the Chinese have little regard for wildlife, a stereotype discounted by the existence of environmental advocacy in China.[48] The film offers Pan as an exception to this rule, but attributes his unusual views to Western influences; the professor himself claims to have culled his conservationist values from early twentieth-century American nature writing. Those who share his values are those he has influenced, as he has transmitted his dedication to saving the panda to his college students, and to the schoolchildren said to be "wildly receptive" to his conservationist message. In *Save the Panda*, scientific expertise, leadership, and funding arrived to elevate nascent conservationism with the American research teams; in *Secrets of the Wild Panda*, environmentalist values have reached China by means of ideology derived from American literature, adopted by a Chinese leader in his field, and disseminated to youth presented as both woefully ignorant of their own land's natural history and hungry for foreign ideas.

Secrets of the Wild Panda ends by revisiting both its subjects, Pan Wenshi and the young panda. While Pan is shown practicing the martial art of Qi Gong by a waterfall, the narration reiterates the ongoing theme that he persists in his sometimes controversial, possibly futile work against colleagues' common-sense disdain for such uncomfortable research conditions. In voiceover, through a translator, Pan explains their criticism and his response to it: " 'Why do you continue to work in the field? . . . Your work has been published, why don't you stop?' . . . My goal is to protect the panda. . . . Achieving this goal may take my entire lifetime and even that may not be enough." Heroicizing Pan's selflessness in a context of self-interested pragmatism, Coyote concludes: "One man perseveres, as solitary as his pandas . . . ," hyperbolically discounting the involvement of his students, the young schoolchildren in whom he inculcates environmentalist values, foreign NGOs, and even the sporadically supportive government agencies. Finally, a sequence of images of the young panda shows that, commensurate with the wildlife genre's coming-of-age narrative, she has left her mother. According to the narrative, she becomes, like all mature pandas and like the film claims Pan to be, a solitary creature who "represents for all her species the last fateful glimmer of hope."

Pan Wenshi and the pandas he studies appear again in *Giant Panda Sho-San and His First Year* (1995), produced by NHK Productions of Japan and aired on the Discovery Channel's *Wild Discovery* in 2000. Like National Geographic's *Secrets of the Wild Panda, Giant Panda Sho-San* documents events in the first year of a young male panda found by Pan Wenshi's research team in the Qinling mountains. Pan appears conducting his usual research tasks—tracking the collared animals by means of radio signals; observing, sedating, weighing and measuring them; and treating injured pandas—but the program forgoes biography and detailed explication of his research in favor of footage of the animals themselves. While the *Secrets* narrator noted the unusual fortune of its film crew in capturing footage of two pandas (the mother and cub) together, efforts of the NHK film crew, aided by a hidden camera set by a tree, produce four scenes totaling over six minutes of pandas interacting in mating behaviors. The first two scenes show a male (said to be Sho-San's older brother), scent-marking trees, first in a handstand position and then by rubbing his buttocks against a tree trunk. His efforts to attract a mate by means of these communicative scents are successful; a female arrives and is shown sniffing a marked tree. In the next scene, a female (Sho-San's older sister) shows curiosity about scent marks.

Staving off possible concern that Sho-San's siblings might find one another and mate incestuously, the narrator assures viewers that the female is far from sexual maturity, and that when she reaches about four years of age, she will leave the area in which she was born and establish her own territory among other pandas, where "she will begin having *children*" of her own (emphasis mine). Another female, described as "extremely particular," typical of her species of "curiously reluctant breeders," arrives in a male's scent-marked area. He is "eager"; she, "apparently not," climbs a tree and defecates as the male waits below. The narrator says that she lingers but continues to reject him for a week. The scene ends when she descends from the tree and tries to flee. He chases and wrestles with her, but she escapes, as the narrator laments that "failed couplings such as this one make it even more difficult for pandas to halt their declining numbers." Finally, an extreme long shot zooms toward a pair of pandas on a steep mountainside; he lounges on his back, and the female sits nearby. He sits up, approaches, and mounts her as she crouches in the receptive position. His mouth hangs open and he appears to pant as he grasps her hips and thrusts toward her. The scene ends with a long shot in which their intercourse continues but their bodies, rather than nearly filling the frame, appear as small swatches of black and white on the mountainside. The sequence cuts abruptly to the research station, where, concerned about possible inbreeding, Pan studies the impact of the Qinling pandas' isolation on their genetic diversity.

More panda documentaries appeared throughout the 1990s. Most focus on their reproductive difficulties and the efforts of Chinese conservationists and American zoo personnel to propagate the severely endangered species. For PBS's *Nature* series by Thirteen/WNET, actress Debra Winger and her son retrace the steps of Ruth Harkness, who brought the first live panda from China to the United States, in *In the Wild: Pandas with Debra Winger* (1995, Tigress Productions); they also meet Professor Pan. *Mutual of Omaha's Spirit of Adventure: Struggle to Survive—China's Giant Panda* (1987) is hosted by Jim Fowler, one of Marlin Perkins's former sidekicks. *Panda: A Giant Stirs* (1995, produced and directed by Jenny Walsh and Lesley Hammond for LJM Productions of Australia) and *Little Pandas* (1999, also by Walsh and Hammond for LJM) both revisit Wolong. The Discovery Channel aired *A Giant Stirs* as an episode of its *Wild Discovery* series; Animal Planet aired *Little Pandas* in the series *Animal Planet Safari*. In addition, two feature films dramatized aspects of the panda's story. *The Amazing Panda Adventure* (1995), filmed on location in Sichuan Province, used live and animatronic animals. Stephen Lang plays a panda researcher whose young son (Ryan Slater) visits him at the reserve, where he and a local girl (Yi Ding) save a cub from poachers. The IMAX Corporation, which usually specializes in large-format documentaries, produced the melodrama *China: The Great Panda Adventure* (2000) in collaboration with the World Wildlife Fund and the San Diego Zoological Society, based on Harkness's first expedition.[49]

These projects, from *Save the Panda* to *China: The Great Panda Adventure*, repeat much of the same information, sometimes the very same footage. They tread, literally, on much of the same ground to document a rare, elusive, minimally active animal with a small range of typical behaviors that take up most of its day (sleeping and eating). Their setting is a difficult-to-reach, often snowbound, disappearing habitat to which access and filming rights can be tightly restricted. The panda's story of reproductive malaise, poaching, and habitat loss lacks much of the buoyant resilience to adversity that resolves many wildlife narratives; there just isn't enough good news to alleviate the gloom-and-doom message. If the wildlife genre, like so many others, retains many of its viewers through a variety of means— among them, action and a promise to culminate in obligatory happy endings—one might predict that interest in the panda as a documentary subject would be short-lived. But in the late 1990s, changes in policies by China, the United States, and the international wildlife community, kept pandas in the media and in public—and political—attention.

"Panda Politics"

In the mid-1980s, while some panda experts contended that research and protection in the pandas' natural habitats floundered, China revised its policies governing the animal and began a brief spate of controversial short-term loans of the animals to eager zoos in North America.[50] Negotiations between the Chinese and U.S. governments, individual zoos, and other concerned wildlife organizations led to a temporary halt of the short-term loan program, which had become known pejoratively among activists and a sometimes-critical press as "rent-a-panda." In the 1990s the short-term loans were replaced by long-term arrangements incorporating research projects by panda-borrowing zoos. The on-again, off-again efforts to place pandas in zoos outside of China, negotiations over these efforts, and mostly celebratory media attention to the reappearance of the animals in American zoos alternated in the news with coverage of a series of confrontations involving U.S.-China trade agreements and military incidents. Economic and diplomatic relations tensed as the United States and China clashed over intelligence-gathering, an intelligence failure by U.S. forces in Belgrade with tragic consequences, trade, and human rights violations. Meanwhile, the panda cropped up in headlines and on TV screens, ever-warm and fuzzy, imbued as a sign of good will between nations, welcomed by adoring throngs. The animal and its image were deployed again and again in public rituals staged to diffuse suspicion and hostility in American popular opinion, as the Clinton administration sought more open trade relations and to smooth China's path to World Trade Organization membership—and as it navigated a series of deadly military missteps that heightened distrust between adversarial superpowers.

The China Wild Animal Protection Association sent two pandas to the Los Angeles Zoo in 1984, coinciding with the Los Angeles Olympic Games.

The Beijing Zoo loaned another pair to the Bronx Zoo for six months in 1987, then relocated them temporarily to Busch Gardens in Tampa, Florida. A pair of pandas loaned to the San Diego Zoo in 1987–88 for about six months increased attendance by 30 percent and netted $5.7 million in extra gate and souvenir receipts. While the Calgary (Alberta) Zoo obtained a pair of pandas when the city hosted the Winter Olympics in 1988, the WWF asked the United States to "stop accepting loans until China takes significant steps to assure the animal's long-term survival," arguing that the loans remove pandas from native breeding populations. In 1988 China agreed to stop short-term loans. In 1993 the American Association of Zoological Parks and Aquariums issued a new policy banning short-term loans of pandas among member zoos and providing guidelines for possible long-term loans that included personnel to monitor the use of funds sent to China intended for conservation.[51]

In 1993 the U.S. Fish and Wildlife Service denied the San Diego Zoo a permit to import two pandas on a long-term loan. Secretary of the Interior Bruce Babbitt, whose department oversees the service and is charged with enforcing the 1982 Endangered Species Act, had earlier warned the zoo in a letter that conservation efforts in China were inadequate and that the loan could set a precedent provoking "irresistible pressure for the capture and export of pandas." The zoo countered that bringing pandas to San Diego would enhance, not stifle, the species' reproduction, and that the government was obstructing both ecological good and U.S.-China relations. According to executive director Doug Myers, "The Chinese have asked for our help, and our Government has closed the door in their face."[52]

A year and a half later, Babbitt announced at a press conference at the San Diego Zoo that he would allow the permit, now convinced that the zoo's research on panda reproduction and communication would contribute to efforts to breed the animal in its native habitat. The zoo promised to "account for and return any increased revenue" generated by the pandas to China, where the money had to be earmarked for conservation, and to let the government audit its records. Babbitt's reversal was motivated at least as much by some behind-the-scenes administrative attention to the matter as by actual revisions in the conditions of the loan.[53] Reportedly, during President Bill Clinton's 1994 springtime holiday, which included "a VIP tour of the zoo's Wild Animal Park, Clinton asked his guide, 'Do you have your pandas yet?'" Babbitt told the *Los Angeles Times* that the president "took me aside at a Cabinet meeting and said, 'What are you doing to make this [panda application] work in San Diego?' Babbitt added jokingly, 'That, of course, had no impact on my decision to be here today.'"[54]

Still, distrust between China and the United States, and a contest for control over their conservation, stymied the plan. Chinese officials objected to provisions that would require them to use money from the deal—at least $1 million per year for twelve years—only for the preservation of panda habitat, and to open their books to international scrutiny. Babbitt and the San Diego Zoo had been negotiating with the China Wildlife Conservation Association, under the Ministry of Forestry, and thought that the two countries and various parties involved had reached an agreement. Zheng Schuling of the Ministry of Construction, which also oversees environmental matters, refused to approve the deal, and asserted that the United States had overstepped its appropriate role, arguing that China should be able to use funds earned from the loans for any "practical and urgent needs.... [The U.S.] should concentrate on the formulation of the U.S. policy instead of policies for the ministries of China."[55]

A year later, without apparent changes in the agreement, all necessary agencies decided to cooperate and proceed with the loan. Senator Diane Feinstein, who had taken up the zoo's cause and lobbied Chinese President Jiang Zemin, announced that "China's approval of the panda loan is a strong gesture by China that it is committed to building healthy relations between our two countries," thus strategically aligning panda diplomacy as a sign of China's good faith in ongoing trade negotiations.[56] Bai-Yun, a five-year-old female born in captivity at the Wolong Reserve, and Shi-Shi, a sixteen-year-old male injured in the wild and rescued by Wolong staff, arrived at the zoo in September 1996.[57] When they went on display in November 1996 after a quarantine and acclimatization period, an eager public flocked to the zoo, embracing both the commercial and reproductive imperatives of their visit. A *Los Angeles Times* reporter interviewed some of the most enthusiastic, including a woman who already owned 2,000 stuffed pandas (and presumably would be selecting at least one souvenir from the forty different stuffed panda designs offered by the zoo gift shop), to a retired Marine sergeant who said, "We're all here to cheer them on to do their duty: sex, sex, sex."[58]

Despite the largely warm reception for the pandas, their eventual reproduction would take place during a period of particularly strained relations between China and the United States. In April 1999 zoo staff impregnated the female panda through artificial insemination. In May 1999 faulty American intelligence led NATO planes to bomb the Chinese embassy in Belgrade, killing three people and injuring twenty-seven. As accusations were exchanged regarding responsibility for the bombing, and as anti-American demonstrations erupted in Beijing, San Diego zoo-goers and the American press eagerly awaited news of Bai-Yun's pregnancy. On August 21, 1999, Bai-Yun gave birth to a healthy female cub, the first panda born in the United States to survive more than just a few days. News outlets from local San Diego stations to NBC's *Today Show* and CNN covered the birth with enthusiasm. While the U.S. government negotiated monetary compensation for the unnecessary loss of human life and property in Belgrade, the San Diego Zoo planned to celebrate the success of its panda breeding program with a traditional Chinese naming ceremony, to be held November 8, 1999, exactly one hundred days after the cub's birth.[59]

The ceremony is depicted in the short video *Hello World: Hua-Mei's First Year* (2000), sold through San Diego Zoo gift shops. The cub's name was selected by the Chinese State Forestry Association and approved by the Ministry of Foreign Affairs. Following traditionally costumed Chinese dancers, two San Diego schoolchildren, a white boy and an Asian American girl, carried a scroll containing the name to Ambassador An Wenbin, Consul General of the People's Republic of China, who waited at a podium. Unrolling the scroll, the ambassador announced that the panda's name would be Hua Mei, which he translated literally as "China-USA," as a symbol of the two nations' "friendship and cooperation."

The timing of the November 8 naming ceremony was portentous. The ambassador's proclamation was cheerily, even ironically conciliatory despite persistently acrimonious relations between the two nations. In fact, yet another team of Chinese and American negotiators was forging a new commitment to "friendship and cooperation." The often-contentious nations were in the final stages of negotiating a trade agreement designed to lower tariffs and to open Chinese markets to U.S. firms; the agreement constituted an essential step toward China's eligibility for membership in the World Trade Organization (WTO). The agreement was signed on November 15, 1999, amid criticism from Human Rights Watch and other NGOs that lobbied, largely unsuccessfully, for new trade with China to be contingent on more rigorous international scrutiny of human rights abuses and judiciary reform. In 2000 Congress approved and President Clinton signed into law a bill that would establish permanent Normal Trade Relations with China once its WTO membership was finalized.[60] Meanwhile,

Split screen: on the left, closed-circuit surveillance of Bai-Yun's birthing den at the San Diego Zoo; on the right, local news covers the birth of Hua-Mei in *Hello World: Hua-Mei's First Year.*

China shipped more pandas stateside, to Atlanta in November 1999, Washington, D.C., in December 2000, and to Memphis, Tennessee's zoo in April 2003.[61]

These shifts in policy and the resulting panda loans sparked several new panda documentaries. Unlike most of the panda programming produced in the 1980s and through the mid-1990s, these new projects did not have to seek their subject in China: pandas, and panda stories, could be filmed in the United States (although domestic footage is often supplemented by scenes of panda habitat and research activities in China). Reusing news footage and limiting the length of film crews' assignments, these new documentaries appeared at a time when wildlife shows, long touted by television programmers as a relatively inexpensive genre with appeal to an attractive niche audience, flourished on an unprecedented number of broadcast and cable networks—PBS, the Discovery Channel, Animal Planet, the National Geographic Channel, most prominently— keeping demand for new product high.[62]

When a new panda pair arrived at the National Zoo on December 6, 2000, Animal Planet celebrated with *Meet the Pandas: Washington's New Power Couple* (2001).[63] Stockard Channing, concurrently playing the role of the First Lady in the NBC series *West Wing,* narrated. *Meet the Pandas* includes footage of President Clinton's visit to the zoo to see the pandas just before his term ended. PBS's *Nature* aired *The Panda Baby* (2001, a collaboration by WNET/Thirteen and the San Diego Zoological Society). *The Panda Baby* is a record of events in Hua Mei's first year (covered more thoroughly than in *Hello World*), and a history of attempts to breed pandas in American zoos narrated by actor Matthew Modine, who introduces the program as a story that "has it all...international intrigue, scientific breakthroughs, and a little bit of magic." In contrast to Washington's repeated failures, the program lauds the San Diego achievement as a heroic accomplishment.[64]

The fate of the giant panda as a living species remains subject to historical forces. The instances of their representation are reminders that our interpretations of animal behaviors—in science and in nonfiction, presumably "objective" media like news and documentary—are also historically situated. The panda, as a wildlife documentary subject, benefited from growth in the TV industry's appetite for nonfiction animal images in general after the cable boom of the 1980s and especially after the development of new niche channels for animal programming in the 1990s. Those representations, and their meanings, were shaped by cultural assumptions about nature and sex, by shifting geopolitical conditions, and by an intransigent Orientalism that has long constituted Western images of the East. The panda emerged as a topic of interest to the print media in the 1970s and as a documentary subject in the 1980s as a result of new diplomatic activity between East and West. Outside of the panda's shrinking habitat in China, few people had much knowledge of the animal until Mao Zedong's 1970s exports of the animals as diplomatic gifts, the post–Cultural Revolution opening of their habitat to Western researchers and film crews in the 1980s, and the embrace of the animal and its plight by conservationists. The panda was deployed as a strategic and inestimable symbol of thawing U.S.-China relations, both at the time of the Mao-Nixon talks and during Bill Clinton's presidency, when new rules regarding the importation of pandas coincided with new rules regarding U.S.-China trade relations generally. At times, the panda may have provided a distraction for Western media audiences, away from news of human-rights violations in China and toward its nascent conservation efforts, its unique and uniquely appealing wildlife, and the potential for ecotourism in a developing economy.[65]

A great deal of that distraction takes place in rapt attention to panda sex—sex roles, sexual behavior, failure to mate, failure to reproduce, and human interventions into reproduction. Some aspects of the panda story dovetail smoothly with the meanings constructed in other representations of wildlife, such as the assumption, which pervaded news coverage of the first pair to reside at the National Zoo, that reproduction would occur within the context of a fulfilling "relationship" between the male and female—more than a momentary sex act—despite pandas' natural solitariness and the absence of pair-bonding in the wild.[66] Other aspects of what is known and said about the panda contradicts convention. The sexual behavior of almost every other species is represented in both scientific literature and recent wildlife TV as the aggressive male pursuit of as many mating opportunities as possible, and female selectivity for fewer, higher quality mates, submissiveness to those chosen few, resistance to the rest, and sacrifice of the self for care of the young.[67]

If giant pandas simply haven't shown "proper" interest in reproduction, humans have interceded in the process to try to ensure the species' survival. In doing so, through science, they have attempted to remake the animal as more reproductive, more "natural," than it is naturally. The technologies of artificial insemination (shown in *Save the Panda* and *The Panda Baby*), in vitro fertilization (an experiment for "test-tube" pandas, described in *Little Pandas*), cloning, Viagra, and videos of panda mating shown to males in hopes of teaching technique, have all been utilized to improve on nature when it does not meet human goals for the species.[68]

While this chapter has focused on representations of panda mating, failure to mate, or human interventions into mating, many of the same preoccupations with panda motherhood, evaluations of its effectiveness, celebrations of its most self-sacrificing embodiments, occur throughout journalistic and documentary assessments of the chances of panda reproduction. Consider, for example, press coverage of the death of the first baby panda born outside of China, which was accidentally crushed by its mother in Mexico City's Chapultepec Zoo in 1980. A *New York Times* editorial mourned the loss, framing the death as a tragic accident, congratulating the zoo for its success in panda-keeping and breeding, and lauding the mother's skill: "by all accounts an exemplary mother, doing all that a giant panda ought to do."[69] Likewise, *Little Pandas* praises the "good mother," and laments the mother "frustrated" in pregnancy who rejects her infant; and mourns for the "depressed" female who year after year, despite "several good matings" and an apparently healthy reproductive system, fails to become pregnant. She was rescued from a poacher's trap as a juvenile and Wolong vets had to amputate one of her paws. The narration attributes her infertility to a "subconscious fear" of not being able to hold and care for a baby properly. These representations suggest yet again that the genre contains not only selected facts about selected animal species, and not only human goals for those animals, but also human goals for humans.

Conclusion

Learning from TV,
Learning from Animals

> The lioness has rejoined her cub and all is right in the jungle.
>
> —*Kill Bill Vol. 2*

On January 31, 2002, the Discovery Channel's series *Wild Discovery* aired two hour-long documentaries filmed in Iran, *Wild Jewels* (1999) and *Wild Treasures of the East* (1999). The broadcasts took place just two days after U.S. President George W. Bush's first State of the Union address, in which he declared that Iran, Iraq, and North Korea form an "axis of evil" that threatens national and international security. The administration accused Iran, specifically, of seeking to develop weapons of mass destruction, and supporting groups officially categorized by the U.S. government as terrorists. For days after Bush's speech, the American press contained a set of seemingly contradictory and confusing images. American politicians and pundits speculated about what measures would be taken against each of these states. Meanwhile, President Mohammed Khatami decried Bush's bellicose stance, declaring at a rally held on the anniversary of the 1979 Islamic Revolution, that his government seeks "ties and peaceful relations." News coverage depicted and described urban crowds holding signs bearing anti-American slogans and pictures of the late Ayatollah Ruhollah Khomeini.[1] While these representations accumulated in print and flowed across TV screens, the Discovery Channel, in all likelihood unintentionally, introduced another set of images into public discourse, familiarizing viewers with the previously unseen. Thanks to almost certain coincidence (Discovery was then announcing its schedule a month in advance), *Wild Discovery* offered images of Iran very different from those appearing in the daily newspapers and on television news.

Wild Jewels, quite conventionally, anthologizes footage depicting a wide array of animals in southern Iran: mudskipper fish, Indian pond herons,

Himalayan black bears, and many more. Produced by Nigel Marven and Mark Flowers for the BBC Natural History Unit of Bristol, the program demonstrates the spectacular cinematography typical of high-end wildlife production, rendering visible to the viewer scenes to which she would otherwise lack all access—if not from geographical distance, then from the limited capacity of the unassisted eye.[2] In slow motion, a group of brightly colored shelducks fly overhead of the cinematographer, exposing both their red-orange breasts and the motion of their wings flapping to scrutiny. In one of the few scenes to depict human subjects, young shepherd boys escape a hot day by joining the huge but sedate water buffalo they tend in a pond. "The peace of the buffalo's wallow is about to be shattered," the narrator notes, as the boys climb on the animals' backs, and dive off them as if they were springboards. Their play is captured with a sometimes-submerged camera, and replayed using slow motion, freeze-frame, and jump cuts.

Near the end of *Wild Jewels,* and immediately following the scene in which the boys swim alongside their buffalo, the filmmakers turn their attention to the Persian Gulf, where ancient rivers "run into the twentieth century, and a world where commerce dominates." However, industrial and shipping activity do not crowd out all wildlife. Abandoned ships become home to bird species including heron, osprey, ravens, Indian rollers, and kestrels. Against shots of tankers at sunset, the narrator says, "The Persian Gulf is rich in wildlife, but as everyone knows only too well, it's also rich in oil." Cutting to scenes of blazing fires, he continues, "The oil installations aren't dangerous in themselves, but an accident or war can have explosive and catastrophic results." An aerial camera pans a gray industrial zone, apparently oil refineries. When the narration resumes, the image changes, and thick oil, not seawater, laps the shore: "Mangroves, marshes and the sea itself can be covered by oil. When this happens, seabirds, fish, and all shore creatures are threatened by thick black oily death, a disaster for the wildlife of the Persian Gulf." In an underwater shot, fish swim under a layer of oil covering the water's surface and, ashore, a crab raises it pincers as if to scrape off the slick oil that coats its shell.

These scenes, replete with warnings of the ecological dangers caused by industrial accidents and by war, do not conclude *Wild Jewels.* As is conventional to the genre, bad news must be answered by good before the credits roll. As the picture cuts to an aerial view of a lush green forest, the narrator provides material for a more hopeful ending: "But all is certainly not gloomy. There are pockets of forest in the northern regions of the gulf where one of Iran's most beautiful and rare animals still survives—the Mesopotamian fallow deer." The deer first appears in an extreme close-up of the side of its body, so that its tawny and white-spotted hide fills the screen, an image replaced by a tangle of antlers, then a series of medium long shots of the full herd. The narrator likens them to animals that the audience (at least, some segments of its BBC audience) may be more familiar with: "Not very different from the herds of deer seen in an English country estate. But deer of Iran must be wary. These forests are patrolled by this country's most magnificent predator. It's one that would never be found in an English park. It's the Persian leopard."

The deer are likened to semi-domesticated British varieties, and portrayed as vulnerable prey—not to industry or war, to oil spills, fires, or bombs, but to an exotic, very Iranian animal. Like the deer, the leopard is introduced by an extreme close-up of its skin, tan with black spots. The camera tracks the leopard as it crosses and drinks from a stream, then the images begin to dissolve between animals and ancient bas relief and architectural monuments. Drawing *Wild Jewels* to a close, the narrator continues: "The elusive Persian leopard is one of the treasures of Iran, just as much as its ancient monuments. Iran has a great cultural history and a unique natural heritage. From birds to bears, crocodiles to deer, there is a remarkable variety of wildlife in this extraordinary country."

Wildlife films and television programs bring to our attention aspects of nature that might otherwise remain unknown. Its footage is endlessly recycled and rebroadcast regardless of the shifting context of world events. But to what end? On one hand, *Wild Jewels* and the companion program *Wild Treasures of the East* offered a visual experience of Iran's natural beauty, and a glimpse, however superficial, of the daily life of a few of the people who live there.[3] Depictions of unique and vital ecosystems suggest that this is an area to be protected from the destructiveness of warfare. Images of people going about their daily business—farmers gathering mangrove leaves to feed to livestock, fishermen harvesting sturgeon roe, boys swimming playfully in the same water in which their buffalo cool off, elites on skiing holidays—counter stereotypes that have pervaded America media for decades but that have gained additional currency since the terrorist attacks of September 11, 2001. I found something quite moving, and even a little bit subversive, in these admiring considerations of natural beauty, their fleetingly articulated antimilitarism, and their humane visions of a population then being vilified by much of the American press and by the U.S. administration.

Persian leopard, lapping water from a stream, in *Wild Jewels*.

On the other hand, *Wild Jewels* marginalizes the occasional Iranian citizen it depicts as happily, nostalgically out of step with time, as if they exist not in the present but in some premodern past. The narration acknowledges that the region exists in the twentieth century only when it briefly takes into account the potential impact of industry on nature. The impact of "accident or war" on people living in the region is not explored. While the flames of a refinery fire suggest what is meant by "accident," the regional and global contests that have in the past—and could again—bring war to the area go unmentioned. Raising the specter of ecological disaster, then deferring to images of Iran's "most beautiful and rare … most magnificent" wildlife, the *Wild Jewels* narrative insists that despite whatever adversity human culture produces, nature in its precious, aesthetic splendor remains resilient, even eternal, thus relieving humanity of any immediate obligation to restrain abuses of it.

The genre has done so in various ways since its origins. Very few Americans, Britons, or Europeans traveled to Africa or the Pacific Islands during the nineteenth and early twentieth centuries, but those who did—from photographer James Chapman in the 1860s to Cherry Kearton, Carl Akeley, and Paul J. Rainey in the 1910s, to Martin and Osa Johnson in the 1920s—provided images of previously undocumented species, scientific data, and doses of adventure-oriented entertainment to Victorian, Edwardian, and Roaring Twenties Westerners. The images they produced often made implicit claims about the expendability of nature, the glory of bloodsports, and the rights of imperial privilege. Beginning in 1948 Walt Disney's True-Life Adventures, and generations of wildlife films and TV programs that followed, began to acknowledge habitat loss, and to encourage conservationism, but tended to insist on the resilience of the natural world, the capacity of animals to survive adversity, to adapt to changed environmental circumstances, even when the evidence of habitat loss, or declining numbers of a given species, suggests otherwise. Since the 1970s conservationist messages have been articulated more explicitly, even if most wildlife films and television programs, dependent on commercial distribution or corporate sponsorship, evade discussion of specific causes and political solutions to environmental problems.

Typically, then, *Wild Jewels* sidesteps the controversies it raises. It provokes an emotional response by acknowledging potential threats to the wildlife it has rendered familiar to viewers over the previous fifty minutes, but neither names the economic and political interests that pose these threats nor explores possible solutions. The narrative seeks refuge in elements of the natural world at some distance from the Gulf tension, in the rare, remote, ancient, native deer and leopard species, hinting that these animals are so "elusive," so "wary," and so "magnificent" that they might resist or evade manmade disasters. As Todd Gitlin argues, "Again and again television acknowledges social and cultural conflicts, if only to tamp them down in the process of 'resolving' them."[4]

Even as the wildlife genre thrives to an unprecedented extent, commercial imperatives—network competition for audiences and advertisers—seem to thwart other possibilities. Televisual forms of nature have been made to fit a market that thrives on conflict that melts into happy endings, and drama that does not get mired in real-world political impasses but resolves in comfort. As discussed in chapter 2, a spate of network-produced public affairs documentaries was produced in the late 1950s and the early

1960s, many critical of establishment interests.[5] But by the mid-1960s, the networks began to abandon the form. Nature, science, and exploration documentaries replaced explicit political critique with ostensibly nonideological adventure- and knowledge-seeking quests, including *National Geographic Specials* and *Undersea World of Jacques Cousteau*. The commercial broadcast networks' commitment to documentary declined further over the 1960s and 1970s, and by the early 1980s the vast majority of television documentaries were found on public television, but corporate pressures on content remained largely in place. For example, Gulf Oil and then Chevron sponsored *National Geographic*'s run on PBS. As Alexander Wilson has observed, the series' dependence on corporate funding, and the oil industry in particular, contained the degree to which filmmakers could articulate sources of habitat destruction and wildlife endangerment, even as they sought to raise public awareness of environmental issues.[6]

By masking its political stakes, by diluting its environmentalist messages, the wildlife genre provides an illusory picture of a pleasurably ordered, harmonious, resilient natural world; that is, the comforting image of an eternal, "natural," depoliticized and heterotopically whole world. Such an image offers respite from real-world fears and hostilities. Another satisfying aspect of the genre derives from its knowledge-gathering, distinction-bestowing function: viewers can imagine themselves being educated while they are being entertained.[7] Both early film exhibitors and television programmers have exploited these qualities of the wildlife genre since its origins. Theater bookers used feature-length expedition films such as *Paul J. Rainey's African Hunt* (1912) to develop middle- and upper-middle-class audiences, attracting them to theaters seeking to differentiate from less reputable, lowbrow nickelodeons. This early version of the wildlife genre thrived through the 1920s, especially in the work of Martin and Osa Johnson, providing both education in the form of an introduction to the natural history of unfamiliar lands, and entertainment in the form of exotic spectacles of adventure and conquest.[8]

The appeal of genres that seem to educate while they entertain retains its hold on middle-class audiences and on programmers seeking the loyalty of the most profitable portions of an increasingly fragmented television audience. Commercial networks have looked to nature as a prestigious genre that appeals to niche audiences with demographic characteristics that appeal to advertisers.[9] For instance, in 1986, when cable systems including Cox and TCI began to acquire equity in the Discovery Channel, and to offer the network to their subscribers, cable executives (some of whom also served on Discovery's board of directors) boasted that the network would offer high-quality televisual education, benefiting a public undereducated in science.[10] In 1995, when NBC took over broadcasting the *National Geographic Specials* after two decades on PBS, it gained the attention of an audience believed to comprise mostly "male viewers aged 25 to 54, a typically tough crowd to reach with TV."[11]

Nature and wildlife continue to occupy a significant media niche in the United States, most prominently on the Discovery Channel, Animal Planet, the National Geographic Channel, PBS, but also on other networks and in syndication. Some of the work being done by and for these corporations is as astonishing as anything that wildlife filmmaking has ever had to offer: among them, the eight-part series *Blue Planet: Seas of Life* (2002, BBC/Discovery, previously aired by the BBC as *The Blue Planet: A Natural History of the Ocean*); *Pale Male* (2002, FL Productions with Devillier Donegan Enterprises for WNET/Thirteen's *Nature*), which made famous a pair of red-tailed hawks living on the facade of a luxury co-op building in New York City; and *Return to Gombe,* another installment in the story of Jane Goodall's deservedly legendary contributions to primate research and conservation (2004, Tigress Productions for Animal Planet). Wildlife, often stunningly rendered, also continues to abound among IMAX-format production in *Bears* (2001), *Jane Goodall's Wild Chimpanzees* (2002), *Bugs!* (2003), and *Roar: Lions of the Kalahari* (2003).

Meanwhile, some remarkable work in the genre, such as the serenely unnarrated Swedish film *Kestrel's Eye* (1999, directed by Mickael Kristersson), which wordlessly tracks the activities of a pair of birds of prey nested in a church tower, languishes in obscurity if it does not conform to the industry's current standards. Those standards require, according to Maureen Smith, who became the new general manager of Animal Planet in 2004, programming that is "very fast paced.... Today's audiences have very short attention spans. There has to be something incredibly exciting every few minutes." The global-positioning devices, cameras attached to animals in flight or on foot, infrared and thermal imaging, and other visual technologies used in the program Smith is hyping, *Spy on the Wild* (2004), a BBC/Animal Planet coproduction, certainly provided rapid-clip entertainment. The program is comprised of glimpses of a world unseeable by the unassisted human eye: for example, a pigeon's-eye view of the British countryside as the bird navigates its way home from an unfamiliar release point, and a slow-motion close-up of the unimaginably rapid beating of a bee's wings as it hovers near a flower in a smoky gust of artificial wind. It also provided for Animal Planet negative publicity from People for the Ethical Treatment of Animals, when a PETA spokesperson criticized the show for exploiting animals for entertainment purposes. In response, supervising producer Peter Bassett was quoted as defending neither the show's representations of animals nor the techniques used to gather them, but only the value of his response (and an assumed audience's response) to them: "The first time I saw the eagle's head, and the ground rushing underneath, I got a tingle in my spine. I don't know anyone who wouldn't be fascinated by that."[12]

While wildlife filmmaking continues to boom in new forms on traditional and specially niched TV channels, it has also been undertaken in less expected arenas. The Fox broadcast network continues to dabble occasionally in animal TV, following up its miniseries *When Animals Attack* (1996–97) and *When Good Pets Go Bad* (1998–99) with *Man vs. Beast* (2003), pitting humans against animals in athletic stunts, and *When Animals Attract* (2004), the latter survey of animal mating behaviors stocked with dating tips for humans by National Geographic Television, which partners with Fox and NBC in the global distribution of the National Geographic Channel. And *Wildboyz* (2003–, MTV) sets its stunts amid animals, borrowing wildlife (and sometimes ethnographic) filmmaking conventions while baiting attack and seeking out animal-inflicted injuries.

At the start of the twenty-first century, wildlife filmmaking, perhaps riding the coattails of the genre's TV boom, began to appear with more frequency in movie theaters, especially after the success of *Winged Migration* (2002). Most theatrical releases were modest in scope, such as Judy Irving's *The Wild Parrots of Telegraph Hill* (2005). The majority, like Jacques Perrin's *Microcosmos* (1996) and *Winged Migration*, originated from British or European sources. Andy Bryant and Alastair Fothergill's *Deep Blue* (2005), a follow-up to the BBC's made-for-TV *The Blue Planet* programs, was shelved for two years after Miramax purchased U.S. distribution rights, then slipped into a handful of theaters, almost unnoticed, not long before Bob and Harvey Weinstein's departure from the Disney-owned studio.

Animal films garnered more attention when filmmakers who usually work in other genres turned to wildlife. Leni Riefenstahl, whose career constituted an ideological racial project begun in Nazi propaganda and continued in photographic expeditions among the Nuba of Sudan and other African tribes, released a film based on footage gathered during her own scuba dives. The French-German television network Arte premiered *Impressionen unter Wasser* (Impressions of the deep) to celebrate Riefenstahl's hundredth birthday in August 2002 (she died in 2003).[13] Jean-Jacques Annaud, the French director with an eclectic resume (*Quest for Fire*, 1981; *The Bear*, 1988; *The Lover*, 1992; *Enemy at the Gates*, 2001), completed his second dramatic wildlife feature, *Two Brothers* (2004), an unlikely tale of twin tiger cubs separated at birth, abused in captivity, and eventually returned to the wild. James Cameron, director of the global blockbuster *Titanic* (1997), adapted 3D IMAX technology to document his visit to the site of the actual Titanic shipwreck, in *Ghosts of the Abyss* (2003). He continued to work in the large format on nature and wildlife subjects, producing *Volcanoes of the Deep Sea* (2003) and directing (with Steven Quale) *Aliens of the Deep* (2005).

The German filmmaker Werner Herzog, prolific in both narrative and documentary genres, also turned, if not precisely to wildlife, then to a human subject's life—and death—among wildlife. *Grizzly Man* (2005) interrogated, with alternating sympathy and skepticism, the relationship between self-made expert and vanguard advocate Timothy Treadwell and the brown bears he camped among for about a decade in Katmai National Park in Alaska. A bear unfamiliar with Treadwell and his companion, Amie Huguenard, killed and partially ate the couple in 2003. Herzog interviewed their acquaintances, and gathered clips from Treadwell's appearance on *Late Show with David Letterman* and video shot by Treadwell himself as if the former actor hoped to make his own documentary. Treadwell's footage, however, full of personal confessions and profanity-laden rants, says more about his desperate (and eventually fatal) alienation, his yearning to jump species, to become one with the bears, than about the bears themselves.

None of these projects, regardless of their associations with some of the most renown and, by different measures, most successful directors of the twentieth century, achieved the wide distribution of *March of the Penguins* (2005), by Luc Jacquet for Bonne Pioche, released in the United States by National Geographic Feature Films and Warner Independent Pictures. Almost irresistibly appealing in the beauty of its Antarctic setting and its easily anthropomorphized subjects, *March of the Penguins* returned classic wildlife filmmaking to the big screen in the form of a bona-fide hit. The film, which cost only $2 million to produce, earned $70 million domestically within three months of its U.S. release to become the all-time, second-highest grossing documentary, following only Michael Moore's *Fahrenheit 9/11* (2004). While Moore smashed documentary box-office records by engaging in controversial political critique, *March of the Penguins* appeared, upon release, to offer only a well-filmed, feel-good family picture that would entertain as it educated.

It is, after all, only the fact-based story of the emperor penguins' annual migration, from ocean to inland, where, each fall, males and females pair up and produce an egg. Throughout the severe winter, one partner tends the egg alone for weeks at a time while the other treks back to sea to feed. In spring, chicks hatch, and when they are mature enough to feed themselves, the entire group marches to sea. Overarchingly, *March of the Penguins* is a triumphant tale of the survival of a species adapted to its arduous environment. It also hits tragic notes, sometimes cloaked in euphemism: a penguin that dies during migration is said to "simply fall asleep and disappear." But the most provocative euphemism employed in narration prepared for the film's American release paved the way for its embrace by conservative and Christian groups already embroiled in debate over the teaching of creationism and intelligent design alongside or instead of the scientific theory of evolution in public schools.[14] The penguins' penchant for huddling close together during winter storms, for example, is explained in a claim that "this behavior is designed" to conserve body heat. While no deity or other agent is named as the "designer" of this behavior, words such as "evolve" and "adapt," known to offend fundamentalists, are avoided. Conservative talk radio and Christian publications championed the film as positively modeling monogamy (even if the penguins are said to bond with a new mate at the start of each breeding season).[15] Here, the penguin is understood (even if it was not so intended by the filmmaker) as not only a signpost for the "natural," but a sign of the holy, however removed from its own daily experience is the concept.

The Christian-fundamentalist sway in the movie marketplace is not confined to the promotion of a few favored themes and titles. Several IMAX films that explicitly mention evolutionary processes as accounting for various forms of life on Earth—*Cosmic Voyage* (1996), *Galápagos: The Enchanted Voyage* (1999), and Cameron's *Volcanoes*—have been passed over by theaters, mostly in the U.S. Bible Belt, where large segments of potential audiences are believed to ascribe to creationism. This trend calls into question the integrity of the scientific and educational missions of the institutions (such as the Fort Worth Museum of Science and Industry) where theaters have refused films because of market research showing that some sample audiences may be uncomfortable with scientific facts that conflict with their religious beliefs.[16] This isn't the representation of science subject to the distractions of its recontextualization within commercial entertainment; it is another ideological contest over the interpretation of natural facts and images of them.

March of the Penguins thrives—and other titles are rebuffed—in a particularly American discursive environment, defined by historically situated cultural and political discord, in which evangelical Christianity is staging an escalating attack on established science. TV's animal genres also continue to thrive outside the United States, in other cultural contexts, as shown in chapter 3's discussion of the global growth of Animal Planet and the National Geographic Channel. In the United Kingdom, in January 2002, the British Broadcasting Corporation's channel BBC1 outrated "its main commercial rival, ITV, for the first time since privately owned television was introduced here in 1954." BBC Director-General Greg Dyke attributed BBC1's slight edge in the January ratings (a tenth of a point) to three documentary series, two of them on nature: *History of Britain; Walking with Beasts*, a Discovery coproduction featuring computer-generated prehistoric life; and *The Blue Planet*.[17] Healthy ratings and critical acclaim for these series suggests that the wildlife genre, and perhaps an array of genres that are relatively inexpensive to produce, technologically or aesthetically spectacular, and educational as well as entertaining, will continue to be significant forces in the global media market.[18]

But what kind of education does the genre provide? In its film era, from the late 1890s to the 1930s, wildlife films often emphasized the differences between human and animal life. In expedition films, humans, specifically white British and American citizens, are controlling agents of their own actions; animals are replenishable natural resources to be expended by human will. Frequently, wildlife filmmakers, supported by the scientific discourse of eugenics that dominated thinking about racial difference of the era, suggested that the same kinds of differences distinguished whites of European descent from other racial groups. They assumed the "natural" superiority of the white colonial powers and "natural" animalistic inferiority of indigenous peoples encountered during expeditions, as in *Among the Cannibal Isles of the South Seas* (1918), *Simba* (1928), and *Congorilla* (1929), all by Martin and Osa Johnson, and the exploitation film *Ingagi* (1930), with its suggestion of sexual relations between African women and male gorillas. For reasons suggested in chapter 1—changing scientific knowledge, changing sociopolitical conditions, and changing generic conventions—when the wildlife genre emerged from a dormant period after World War II, its filmmakers shifted some attention away from overt racial representations and onto other themes. By and large, they seem to have sought to distance the genre from some of its troubling conventions by sidestepping, rather than engaging progressively with contemporary controversies and historical conditions. Since the 1960s wildlife television, from *Wild Kingdom* and *National Geographic Specials* to *Nature* and *The Crocodile Hunter,* has often continued to marginalize, patronize, or ignore indigenous people in the environments they explore while examining the state of animal life.

Foreshadowing the genre's postwar preoccupation with mating and reproduction was biologist Julian Huxley's *The Private Life of the Gannet* (1934), which foregrounded the birds' courtship rituals and how they care for their young, among other behaviors. In the 1950s Walt Disney's allegorical True-Life Adventures made parenting and growing up central themes of the wildlife film, and for decades the genre would pay close attention to the ways in which animals maintained daily "family" life in scenes of courtship, competition for mates, feeding and caring for young. In the 1980s brief scenes of animals in the act of mating began to appear on American TV and soon became stock-in-trade. The significance of these scenes is only in part found in their *showing.* Much of the ideological work takes place in their *telling,* in the narration, usually in authoritative, disembodied voiceover, that interprets the visual imagery to audiences. By the 1990s recent trends in behavioral and evolutionary genetics exerted tremendous influence on the wildlife genre's interpretive framework. Biologists themselves debate the extent to which genes script behavior, the occurrence of social learning among animals, the extent to which observations of animals can be extrapolated to humans, and even the language that should be used to describe animal behavior, or to differentiate it from human behavior. But as shown in chapters 4 and 5, many representations of wildlife draw on sociobiological theories of forcible copulation (animal "rape"), gendered division of labor, male dominance, and female submissiveness. When counterexamples found in nature simply don't fit prevailing master narratives—as in the case of same-sex sexual behaviors, and their politicization by both gay-rights advocates and antigay activists—they are simply set aside.

In many cases, the implications of these theories for humanity are only inferred. In others, narration meanders away from interpretation of the animal behaviors depicted on screen to explicit speculation about how humans exemplify the same findings. In fact, we have become so accustomed to seeking in animals models to explain our own behavior that we describe ourselves through animals in popular culture: when *Fear Factor* host Joe Rogan urges on a contestant who is excelling at some feat of physical strength or stamina, he is likely to shout, "You're an animal!," praising the contestant for overcoming the fetters of human phobias.[19] And when, in the final scenes of *Kill Bill Vol. 2* (2004), Quentin Tarantino seeks to celebrate the Bride's (Uma Thurman) disposal of Bill (David Carradine) and reunion with her small daughter, he inserts an intertitle that reads, "The lioness has rejoined her cub and all is right in the jungle." These words dismiss Bill's paternal care for the girl as unnatural and not right. In this jungle, only mother's care is natural and if it is natural, it must be right.

Or is it? The lessons of the wildlife genre are not the only possible lessons but are those chosen by some of the scientists engaged in the analysis of animal behavior and some of the film and television producers engaged in representing its historically situated expressions and contestations. The world and its inhabitants—including our human selves—are far more complex, and contain far more biological and behavioral diversity, than representations rendered in the form of oversimplified "pop sociobiology" have thus far suggested. It has been my concern throughout this project that the stories the genre tends to tell are ones reflecting particular, frequently conservative social values, with implications for our understanding not only of the environment, and of animal life, but also human racial, sexual, and cultural difference. What is projected onto nature reveals the most urgent struggles of human culture.

Notes

Introduction

1. This monologue is excerpted from *Magnolia,* written and directed by Paul Thomas Anderson. The character Frank T. J. Mackey leads a company called Seduce and Destroy that holds workshops for men seeking guidance in how to conduct sexual relationships with women. He first appears onstage in silhouette, striking body-builder poses to the notes of Richard Strauss's *Also sprach Zarathustra.* A banner unfurls behind him depicting a lascivious wolf chasing a diminutive fox. Leaping downstage and settling into a strutting pace, Cruise, as Frank, delivers these lines. What is important here is not whether Anderson or anyone else involved in the production embraces these views. That this view is articulated is sufficient evidence of its currency in the popular commonsense.

2. The term *sociobiology* has been to a great extent abandoned, and has been largely replaced by the broad label *evolutionary social science,* roughly divided between evolutionary psychology and human behavioral ecology. For a discussion of the disciplinary split, see Eric A. Smith, Monique Borgerhoff Mulder, and Kim Hill, "Controversies in the Evolutionary Social Sciences: A Guide for the Perplexed," *Trends in Ecology and Evolution* 16, no. 3 (March 2001): 128. The study of biological bases of behavior in animals takes place in scientific practices, including evolutionary biology, zoology, ethology, population and behavioral ecology, and molecular genetics. For another discussion of disciplinary categorization, see Patricia Adair Gowaty, "Introduction: Darwinian Feminists and Feminist Evolutionists," in *Feminism and Evolutionary Biology: Boundaries, Intersections, and Frontiers,* ed. Gowaty (New York: Chapman and Hall, 1997), 8.

3. On the sociobiological "zoomorphizing" of humans, see Eileen Crist, *Images of Animals: Anthropomorphism and the Animal Mind* (Philadelphia: Temple University Press, 1999), 161–63. Reconceptualization of the animal has also taken place in wildlife policy: Clark C. Gibson points out that policies regarding indigenous animal populations in many African nations, which during the still-largely colonial first half of the twentieth century accounted for wild animals primarily as *game* to be *controlled* (in part, to protect land used for livestock by European farmers), began in the postcolonial period to treat and refer to native species as *wildlife,* which were to be *conserved* as a renewable natural resource to be utilized in tourist industries and as sources of meat for local people; see Gibson, *Politics and Poachers: The Political Economy of Wildlife Policy in Africa* (Cambridge: University of Cambridge, 1999), esp. 33.

4. John Berger, "Why Look at Animals?," in Berger, *About Looking* (New York: Pantheon, 1980), 24.

5. I use the term *visual technology* in Nicholas Mirzoeff's broad sense, as "any form of apparatus designed either to be looked at or to enhance natural vision, from oil painting to television and the Internet," as Mirzoeff defined the term in *An Introduction to Visual Culture* (New York: Routledge, 1999), 3.

6. Fatimah Tobing Rony, *The Third Eye: Race, Cinema, and Ethnographic Spectacle* (Durham, N.C.: Duke University Press, 1996), 10.

7. Michel Foucault, "Of Other Spaces," trans. Jay Miskowiec, *Diacritics* 16, no. 1 (Spring 1986): 22–27. This essay is famously taken from notes for a lecture given in 1967. Foucault did not himself prepare the lecture for publication, but did allow its use by the Internationale Bauausstellung Berlin before his death in June 1984. It was first published posthumously in French as "Des Espaces Autres," *Architecture-Mouvement-Continuité* (October 1984).

8. Foucault, "Of Other Spaces," 24.

9. Ibid., 24–26. Alternatively, a heterotopia (or heterochrony) may be devoted to the "perpetual and indefinite accumulation of time in an immobile place," like the cemetery, library, or museum (26).

10. These shows represent only a fraction of the animal programming that could be found on TV on November 28, 2004: *Zambezi Shark* (1998, produced and directed by Peter Lamberti for Wild Side/Aqua Vision), on the Discovery Channel; *Polar Bear Invasion* (2001, by WNET/Thirteen and BBC) aired as part of the series *Nature* on PBS; "In Search of the Monster Rattler," an episode of *Steve Austin: Snakemaster,* and *The Crocodile Hunter Diaries'* "Celebrities and Practical Jokes #2," in which Steve Irwin hosts guests including the Dixie Chicks and model Joanna Krupa to Australia Zoo, both on Animal Planet; and the dramatic feature film *The Amazing Panda Adventure* (1995, directed by Christopher Cain), on the teen-oriented channel WAM!

11. Pierre Bourdieu, *Distinction: A Social Critique of the Judgement of Taste,* trans. Richard Nice (Cambridge: Harvard University Press, 1984), 6. Bourdieu compares taste in music, cinema, food, and other aesthetic and lifestyle-consumption practices against educational, economic, and inherited social capital. *Distinction* has little to say on television, except to measure in one instance not having a TV at all as a sign of cultural capital (118).

12. *Variety Film Reviews, 1907–1920,* vol. 1 (New York: Garland, 1983), reviews for the week of April 23, 1910, unpag.

13. Bourdieu, *Distinction,* 27.

14. Arjun Appadurai, "Disjuncture and Difference in the Global Cultural Economy," in *The Global Transformation Reader: An Introduction to the Globalization Debate,* ed. David Held and Anthony McGrew (Malden, Mass.: Blackwell, 2000), 232.

15. Chris Norris, "Ghetto Superstar," *Spin* 14, no. 12 (Dec. 1998): 146.

16. Grant Samuelson, "Are We the World? Internationalism at SAIC," *In the Loop* 1, no. 2 (Spring/Summer 1999): 5.

17. Mazur's comment also referred to an episode of the Fox sitcom *Malcolm in the Middle* in which the parents become sexually aroused while watching a wildlife program on the Discovery Channel. See Brendan A. Maher, "TV Mammals Set Sexy Example," *Pittsburgh Post-Gazette*, March 22, 2000, E4. A *Friends* episode ("The One with the Sharks," Oct. 17, 2002, on NBC) also situates nature filmmaking in erotic imaginary, when Monica (Courtney Cox Arquette) finds Chandler (Matthew Perry) masturbating with the television tuned to a documentary on shark attacks. She fears he's been hiding a disturbing fetish, when in fact he had only changed channels so that she would not see him watching pornography.

18. Edward O. Wilson, *Sociobiology: The New Synthesis* (Cambridge: The Belknap Press of Harvard University Press, 1975).

19. Peter Singer, *Animal Liberation: A New Ethics for Our Treatment of Animals* (New York: New York Review, 1975). Philosophical interrogations of animality and subjectivity continue in the work of Jacques Derrida, Alphonso Lingus, Judith Roof, and others, collected in *Zoontologies: The Question of the Animal*, ed. Cary Wolfe (Minneapolis: University of Minnesota Press, 2003). See also Akira Mizuta Lippit, *Electric Animal: Toward a Rhetoric of Wildlife* (Minneapolis: University of Minnesota Press, 2000); and Cary Wolfe, *Animal Rites: American Culture, the Discourse of Species, and Posthumanism* (Chicago: University of Chicago Press, 2002).

20. John Berger's "Why Look at Animals?" was first published in three parts: "Animals as Metaphor," *New Society* 39 (1977): 504–5; "Vanishing Animals," *New Society* 39 (1977): 664–65; and "Why Zoos Disappoint," *New Society* 40 (1977): 122–23. See also Keith Thomas, *Man and the Natural World: A History of the Modern Sensibility* (New York: Pantheon, 1983); Harriet Ritvo, *The Animal Estate: The English and Other Creatures in the Victorian Age* (Cambridge: Harvard University Press, 1987); Alexander Wilson, *The Culture of Nature: North American Landscape from Disney to the Exxon Valdez* (Cambridge, Mass.: Blackwell, 1992); and Harriet Ritvo, *The Platypus and the Mermaid and Other Figments of the Classifying Imagination* (Cambridge: Harvard University Press, 1997). On animals in popular culture and art, see Steve Baker, *Picturing the Beast: Animals, Identity and Representation* (Manchester, England: Manchester University Press, 1993); Jennifer Price, *Flight Maps: Adventures with Nature in Modern America* (New York: Basic Books, 1999); Steve Baker, *The Postmodern Animal* (London: Reaktion, 2000); and Nigel Rothfels, ed., *Representing Animals* (Bloomington: Indiana University Press, 2002). On zoos and animal performances, see Bob Mullan and Garry Marvin, *Zoo Culture* (London: Weidenfeld and Nicolson, 1987); Susan G. Davis, *Spectacular Nature: Corporate Culture and the Sea World Experience* (Berkeley: University of California Press, 1997); Jane C. Desmond, *Staging Tourism: Bodies on Display from Waikiki to Sea World* (Chicago: University of Chicago Press, 1999); Elizabeth Hanson, *Animal Attractions: Nature on Display in American Zoos* (Princeton, N.J.: Princeton University Press, 2002); and Nigel Rothfels, *Savages and Beasts: The Birth of the Modern Zoo* (Baltimore: Johns Hopkins University Press, 2002). On geography and

animals, see Jennifer Wolch and Jody Emel, eds., *Animal Geographies: Place, Politics, and Identity in the Nature-Culture Borderlands* (London: Verso, 1998); and Chris Philo and Chris Wilbert, eds., *Animal Spaces, Beastly Places: New Geographies of Human-Animal Relations* (New York: Routledge, 2000).

21. Animal bodies, alive and otherwise, would later appear in the works of artists Carolyn Chalmers, Mark Dion, Kathy High, Damien Hirst, and Eduardo Kac, among others.

22. For example, see Richard M. Barsam, *Nonfiction Film: A Critical History* (1972; Bloomington: Indiana University Press, 1992), esp. 42–55.

23. For example, see Erik Barnouw, *Documentary: A History of the Non-Fiction Film*, rev. ed. (1973; New York: Oxford University Press, 1983), 210.

24. See Donna Haraway, "Apes in Eden, Apes in Space: Mothering as a Scientist for National Geographic," in Haraway, *Primate Visions: Gender, Race, and Nature in the World of Modern Science* (New York: Routledge, 1989), 133–85.

25. Gregg Mitman, *Reel Nature: America's Romance with Wildlife on Film* (Cambridge: Harvard University Press, 1999).

26. Derek Bousé, *Wildlife Films* (Philadelphia: University of Pennsylvania Press, 2000).

27. Jonathan Burt, *Animals in Film* (London: Reaktion Books, 2002).

28. See Graeme Turner, "Nostalgia for the Primitive: Wildlife Documentaries on TV," *Australian Journal of Cultural Studies* 3, no. 1 (May 1985): 63–71; Stephen Papson, "'Cross the Fin Line of Terror': Shark Week on the Discovery Channel," *Journal of American Culture* 15, no. 4 (Winter 1992): 67–81; Gregg Mitman, "Cinematic Nature: Hollywood Technology, Popular Culture, and the American Museum of Natural History," *Isis* 84 (1993): 637–61; Barbara Crowther, "Towards a Feminist Critique of Television Natural History Programmes," in *Feminist Subjects, Multimedia: Cultural Methodologies*, ed. Penny Florence and Dee Reynolds (Manchester, England: Manchester University Press, 1995), 127–46; Derek Bousé, "Are Wildlife Films Really 'Nature Documentaries'?," *Critical Studies in Mass Communication* 15 (1998): 166–40; Meryl Aldridge and Robert Dingwall, "Teleology on Television? Implicit Models of Evolution in Broadcast Wildlife and Nature Programmes," *European Journal of Communication* 18, no. 4 (2003): 435–53; Derek Bousé, "False Intimacy: Close-ups and Viewer Involvement in Wildlife Films," *Visual Studies* 18, no. 2 (2003): 123–32; and Karen D. Scott, "Popularizing Science and Nature Programming: The Role of 'Spectacle' in Contemporary Wildlife Documentary," *Journal of Popular Film and Television* 31, no. 1 (Spring 2003): 29–35.

29. S. L. Harrison, "Prime Time Pablum: How Politics and Corporate Influence Keep Public TV Harmless," *The Washington Monthly* (Jan. 1986): 33.

30. Todd Gitlin, *Inside Prime Time* (1983; New York: Pantheon, 1985), 248. See also Stuart Hall, "Culture, the Media and the 'Ideological Effect,'" in *Mass Communication and Society*, ed. James Curran, Michael Gurevitch, and Janet Woollacott (1977; Beverly Hills, Calif.: Sage, 1979), 340–42; and Yuezhi Zhao, *Media, Market,*

and Democracy in China: Between the Party Line and the Bottom Line (Urbana: University of Illinois Press, 1998), 5.

31. Bill Nichols, *Ideology and Image: Social Representation in the Cinema and Other Media* (Bloomington: Indiana University Press, 1981), 5.

32. The ways in which wildlife filmmaking has incorporated the human as subject is of primary concern here, but I have, in the interest of drawing the line somewhere, not dealt in any depth in this text with ethnographic films (which often include footage of wild or domesticated animals) or documentaries about human behavior and the human body, such as *The Miracle of Life* (1990) and *Life's Greatest Miracle* (2001), both featuring medical photography by Lennart Nilsson and aired on PBS's *NOVA* series; *Desmond Morris' The Human Animal: A Personal View of the Human Species* (1997, BBC); *Humans: Who Are We?* (1999, by CineNova Production, the Discovery Channel, and Dogstar); and *The Human Body* (2001), an Imax film by Discovery Pictures/BBC.

33. Wildlife filmmakers have occasionally interrogated these terms. The narration for "Africa's Southern Deserts," which aired on the Discovery Channel's *Wild Discovery* series on August 26, 1999, defined "truly wild" as "not fenced in," noting that the black rhinoceros found in the Namib Desert are the last wild members of their species.

Richard West Sellars sheds light on the complexities that may be masked by casual use of the term *wild:* specifically, the ideological and material systems that determine and manage what counts as "wilderness." Sellars points out that the U.S. National Park Service decided in 1933 to preserve its lands as "original or primitive" wilderness, defined as the moment immediately preceding the arrival of white explorers and settlers. In disregarding the impact of hunting, grazing, and burning by Native Americans, their actions are likened to those of animals, part of the "wilderness"; see Sellars, *Preserving Nature in the National Parks: A History* (New Haven: Yale University Press, 1997), 97. Richard Slotkin also recognizes the racism that permeates this gesture in his analysis of frontier myths in which Indians are constructed as part of the "fatal environment itself"; see Slotkin, *The Fatal Environment: The Myth of the Frontier in the Age of Industrialization, 1800–1890* (1985; Norman: University of Oklahoma Press, 1998), 11, 79–80.

34. Stephen Mills, "Pocket Tigers: The Sad Unseen Reality Behind the Wildlife Film," *Times Literary Supplement,* no. 4899 (Feb. 21, 1997): 6.

1. The Wildlife Film Era

1. On the contributions of nature photographers to innovations in photographic equipment, see C. A. W. Guggisberg, *Early Wildlife Photographers* (New York: Taplinger, 1977), esp. 37–39. Among them was a flash kit invented by George Shiras III for photographing deer at night. Carl E. Akeley, frustrated by the difficulties he experienced while trying to film lion-spearing by paid Nandi hunters in

1910, later designed the Akeley Panoramic Camera; ibid., 75, 97. Akeley successfully filmed only two of six hunts; in most other cases the lions were killed long before he could get his equipment set up; see Akeley, *Special Zoology Leaflet No. 1: Lion Spearing* (Chicago: Field Museum of Natural History, 1920), 3–5. For further discussion of Akeley's modifications, which facilitated camera movement and access to an array of easily switched lenses, see Kevin Brownlow, *The War, the West, and the Wilderness* (New York: Knopf, 1979), 406–8, 469; and Pascal James Imperato and Eleanor M. Imperato, *They Married Adventure: The Wandering Lives of Martin and Osa Johnson* (New Brunswick, N.J.: Rutgers University Press, 1992), 260 n. 20.

2. Mark Orner, "Nature Documentary Explorations: A Survey History and Myth Typology of the Nature Documentary Film and Television Genre from the 1880s Through the 1990s," Ph.D. diss., University of Massachusetts, Amherst, 1996, 74; Mitman, *Reel Nature*, 8; and Bousé, *Wildlife Films*, 38–44.

3. See Rothfels, *Savages and Beasts*, 12–22.

4. Cited in Stephen Jay Gould, "The Hottentot Venus," in Gould, *The Flamingo's Smile* (New York: W. W. Norton, 1985), 192–305, esp. 293. See also Anne Fausto-Sterling, "Gender, Race, and Nation: Comparative Anatomy of 'Hottentot' Women in Europe, 1815–1817," in *Deviant Bodies: Critical Perspectives on Difference in Science and Popular Culture,* ed. Jennifer Terry and Jacqueline Urla (Bloomington: Indiana University Press, 1995), 19–48, esp. 36.

5. Tony Bennett, "The Exhibitionary Complex," in *Thinking about Exhibitions,* ed. Reesa Greenberg, Bruce W. Ferguson, and Sandy Nairne (New York: Routledge, 1996), 100.

6. Timothy Mitchell, *Colonising Egypt* (Berkeley: University of California Press, 1988), 7.

7. Ella Shohat and Robert Stam, *Unthinking Eurocentrism: Multiculturalism and the Media* (New York: Routledge, 1994), 104, 106.

8. Nwachukwu Frank Ukadike, *Black African Cinema* (Berkeley: University of California Press, 1994), 40. Ukadike elaborates this argument throughout chapter 1, "Africa and the Cinema," esp. 35–48. David Henry Slavin extends a similar argument to depictions of North Africa: "by disseminating colonial mythology, film helped Frenchmen . . . redefine themselves as bearers of civilization to the colonized"; see Slavin, *Colonial Cinema and Imperial France, 1919–39: White Blind Spots, Male Fantasies, Settler Myths* (Baltimore: Johns Hopkins University Press, 2001), 4.

9. Guggisberg, *Early Wildlife Photographers,* 13–14; and James R. Ryan, "'Hunting with the Camera': Photography, Wildlife and Colonialism in Africa," in *Animal Spaces, Beastly Places,* ed. Philo and Wilbert, 206–9.

10. Terry Ramsaye, *A Million and One Nights: A History of the Motion Picture* (1926; New York: Simon and Schuster, 1964), 21. In more recent examples, Marey's and Muybridge's "experiments . . . paved the way for the development of the motion picture camera," in James Monaco, *How to Read a Film: The World of Movies,*

Media, Multimedia: Art, Technology, Language, History, Theory, 3d ed. (New York: Oxford University Press, 2000), 53; "photographic images of movement set the stage for the development of cinema," in Marita Sturken and Lisa Cartwright, *Practices of Looking: An Introduction to Visual Culture* (New York: Oxford University Press, 2001), 136.

11. See Ramsaye, *A Million and One Nights,* 23; and Terry Barrett, *Criticizing Photographs: An Introduction to Understanding Images* (Mountain View, Calif.: Mayfield, 1990), 54. Erik Barnouw claims that Stanford hoped that Muybridge's findings would help trainers improve his horses' gaits; see his *Documentary,* 3. Muybridge's 1898 preface to one of many published version of the works says only that Stanford hired him to solve a "controversy" debated for several millennia; this preface is reprinted in an abridged monograph, *Animals in Motion,* ed. Lewis S. Brown (New York: Dover, 1957), 13.

12. For a discussion of the staged attack, see Wilson, *The Culture of Nature,* 124.

13. Linda Williams, *Hard Core: Power, Pleasure, and the "Frenzy of the Visible"* (Berkeley: University of California Press, 1989), 39–40. Williams cites John Berger, *Ways of Seeing* (1972; London: British Broadcasting Corporation and Penguin, 1977), 47.

14. Muybridge, *Animals in Motion,* plate 16.

15. Williams, *Hard Core,* 48–49.

16. Countless film histories textbooks discuss Muybridge et al. in relation to cinema. See Barnouw, *Documentary,* 4; Barrett, *Criticizing Photographs,* 54; Barsam, *Nonfiction Film,* 10–11; David Bordwell and Kristin Thompson, *Film Art: An Introduction,* 5th ed. (New York: McGraw-Hill, 1997), 442–43; Douglas Gomery, *Movie History: A Survey* (Belmont, Calif.: Wadsworth, 1991), 6; and Steve Neale, *Cinema and Technology: Image, Sound, Color* (Bloomington: Indiana University Press, 1985), 36–37.

17. Rony notes that Regnault rejected Darwin's concept of "arboreal" evolutionary change, literally branching out in various directions and shaped by "chance." Lamarckian evolutionists, including Regnault and fellow members of the Société d'anthropologie de Paris, insisted on linear, progressive "*transformisme,*" and the possibility that learned behaviors could be inherited. They sought to prove racial hierarchies of difference in which "sub-Saharan Africans and Australian Aborigines . . . were classified as 'missing links' between man and the animal kingdom"; see Rony, *The Third Eye,* 25–27, 33, 36.

18. On Broca and others in Regnault's circle, see ibid., 26–30. Boas's efforts to disprove the superiority of European intellect capacity date to a series of lectures begun in 1894, and collected for publication in *The Mind of Primitive Man* (New York: Macmillan, 1911); see also Franz Boas, *Race, Language and Culture* (New York: Macmillan, 1940).

19. Neale, *Cinema and Technology,* 40.

20. Ryan, "Hunting with the Camera," 206.

21. Guggisberg, *Early Wildlife Photographers*, 12–13, 14–15.

22. Ryan, "Hunting with the Camera," 211–15.

23. Michele H. Bogart, *Artists, Advertising, and the Borders of Art* (Chicago: University of Chicago Press, 1995), 358 n. 15.

24. Guggisberg, *Early Wildlife Photographers*, 21.

25. Catherine A. Lutz and Jane L. Collins, *Reading National Geographic* (Chicago: University of Chicago Press, 1993), 27.

26. Guggisberg, *Early Wildlife Photographers*, 15, 29, 64, 66–67; Mitman, "Cinematic Nature," 640.

27. For a discussion of these films, see Charles Musser and Carol Nelson, *High-Class Moving Pictures: Lyman H. Howe and the Forgotten Era of Traveling Exhibition, 1880–1920* (Princeton, N.J.: Princeton University Press, 1991), 53–55.

28. The Coney Island Museum continues to show the Edison film in a historical program; see Ed Boland Jr., "An Elephant's Demise," *New York Times*, July 8, 2001, http://www.nytimes.com/2001/07/08/nyregion/thecity/08FYI.html. Documentary director Errol Morris used *Electrocuting an Elephant* in *Mr. Death: The Rise and Fall of Fred A. Leuchter Jr.* (1999). Leuchter made a career building electric chairs, and later, lethal injection systems, until states terminated their contracts with Leuchter when he appeared as an expert witness in the trial of Ernst Zeundel, whose writings refuting the Holocaust violated Canadian law. Leuchter inspected the ruins at Auschwitz and testified in Zeundel's defense that no death camp existed there.

29. Musser and Nelson, *High-Class Moving Pictures*, 174–75, 177.

30. Ramsaye, *A Million and One Nights*, 519–22; Brownlow, *The War, the West and the Wilderness*, 405–6.

31. See Brownlow, *The War, the West, and the Wilderness*, 406. There are several competing explanations for how Kearton came to make his Roosevelt film. According to Guggisberg, Roosevelt did not take a cinematographer along (his son Kermit and naturalists in the entourage took photographs) but Cherry Kearton happened to meet the hunting party in Nairobi. Roosevelt, who admired Kearton's work, agreed to appear in some footage that became *Roosevelt in Africa*, and AMNH taxidermist James L. Clark assisted Kearton (*Early Wildlife Photographers*, 70–71). Mitman concurs with Guggisberg's account (*Reel Nature*, 6–7). Rony writes that the AMNH "funded several" expedition films, giving *Roosevelt in Africa* as an example (*The Third Eye*, 86). Imperato and Imperato assert that the filmmakers were working independently and Clark paid his own way (*They Married Adventure*, 93). Ramsaye claims that Roosevelt took along a British filmmaker (implying but not naming Kearton) funded by the Smithsonian Institution (*A Million and One Nights*, 521).

32. "Roosevelt in Africa," *Variety Film Reviews*, unpag., reviews for the week of April 23, 1910. A review in the same volume, for the week of April 16, 1910, gives

short shrift to a film that is likely Selig's *Hunting Big Game in Africa* but identified only as *In Africa,* a Laemmele release and a "willful deception."

33. *The Moving Picture World* also criticized the image as lifeless, "like a dead lion," but they were enthralled by Selig's captive lion. Assuring audiences that "there is no doubt about this lion," the reviewer mistook the realistic effects of artificial light and the studio set as the animal's "natural surroundings"; see Mitman, *Reel Nature,* 7, 10.

34. *Variety Film Reviews.*

35. Brownlow, *The War, the West, and the Wilderness,* 405–6.

36. Imperato and Imperato, *They Married Adventure,* 84, 97.

37. Musser and Nelson, *High-Class Moving Pictures,* 230–31.

38. London makes occasional references to Martin Johnson in *The Cruise of the Snark* (1911; Washington, D.C.: National Geographic Adventure Books, 2003), 33, and especially in regard to the illnesses Johnson suffered on the voyage; see 199, 201, 204–5.

39. Imperato and Imperato, *They Married Adventure,* 20–21, 52–55.

40. Musser and Nelson, *High-Class Moving Pictures,* 266.

41. Imperato and Imperato, *They Married Adventure,* 74–77.

42. Ibid., 74, 78–80, 83.

43. Ritvo, *The Platypus and the Mermaid,* 209.

44. See Michael Rogin, "Making America Home: Racial Masquerade and Ethnic Assimilation in the Transition to Talking Pictures," *Journal of American History* 79, no. 3 (Dec. 1992): 1050–51.

45. Imperato and Imperato, *They Married Adventure,* 83.

46. Osa Johnson, *I Married Adventure: The Lives and Adventures of Martin and Osa Johnson* (Philadelphia: J. B. Lippincott, 1940), 182.

47. Imperato and Imperato, *They Married Adventure,* 90–91, 97, 99, 110; see also Rony, *The Third Eye,* 87.

48. On the Snows' success, see Gomery, *Movie History,* 99; Imperato and Imperato, *They Married Adventure,* 110–11, 113. American distributors routinely handled such exploitive work in expedition and wildlife genres, but were sometimes more leery of ethnographic films. Accordingly, Flaherty was unable to secure distribution with any American company for *Nanook of the North* (1922), an ethnographic project with its own array of staged scenes (Rony, *The Third Eye,* 99–122). Pathé Frères, a French company, released the film both in the United States and abroad, with unexpected success (Barnouw, *Documentary,* 41–42).

49. Imperato and Imperato, *They Married Adventure,* 110–13, 114–16.

50. Terry Ramsaye, author of the history of early cinema cited above, coedited *Simba* with Martin Johnson, and wrote the text for its intertitles.

51. British colonial law prevented native Africans from using guns; African gun porters could carry but not fire weapons. Whites on safari provided fresh

meat for large entourages of porters through their own labor or by hiring a white hunter to do so. Osa Johnson's memoir—ghostwritten by radio scriptwriter Winifred Dunn—exaggerated her role as company markswoman (Johnson, *I Married Adventure*, 206, 230, 232–33). Both Johnsons had the habit of omitting from accounts of their adventures the presence of sharpshooters who accompanied them in the field (Imperato and Imperato, *They Married Adventure*, xii, 101–2, 261 n. 24).

52. Imperato and Imperato, *They Married Adventure*, 144.

53. See Rony, *The Third Eye*, 115, 137.

54. Imperato and Imperato, *They Married Adventure*, 143. See also Haraway, *Primate Visions*, 57. While Boas left the museum in 1905, he remained an ardent critic of Grant's work and the directions in which he led the museum. For a succinct account of the contests over the meaning of race in which these men competed, see Claudia Roth Pierpont, "The Measure of America: How a Rebel Anthropologist Waged War on Racism," *New Yorker* 80, no. 3 (March 8, 2004): 48–58, 60–63.

55. Haraway, *Primate Visions*, 45.

56. Madison Grant, *The Passing of the Great Race, or the Racial Basis of European History* (New York: Scribner's, 1916), 19.

57. Ibid., 14–16, 73.

58. See Nancy Ordover, *American Eugenics: Race, Queer Anatomy and the Science of Nationalism* (Minneapolis: University of Minnesota Press, 2003), esp. chap. 1, "National Hygiene: Twentieth-Century Immigration and the Eugenics Lobby," 1–56.

59. Julian Huxley, *Man in the Modern World: An Eminent Scientist Looks at Life Today* (New York: Mentor Books, 1948), 28, 31, 41. Perhaps Julian Huxley's most influential work was *Evolution: The Modern Synthesis* (1942; 3d ed., New York: Hafner Press, 1974), reviewing in one thick volume post-Darwinian work in evolutionary biology.

60. On the *Congorilla* controversies, see Barnouw, *Documentary*, 50–51; Johnson, *I Married Adventure*, 342; and Mitman, *Reel Nature*, 35.

61. André Bazin, "Cinema and Exploration," in *What Is Cinema?*, ed. and trans. Hugh Gray, foreword by Jean Renoir (1967; Berkeley: University of California Press, 1974), 154–55; first printed in two parts in *France-Observateur*, April 1953 and January 1956. Still, Bazin was not the only one to take jabs at *Africa Speaks;* it inspired parodies from MGM (*Africa Squeaks*, 1931, from Ub Iwerks' animated Flip the Frog series), Warner Bros. (another *Africa Squeaks*, 1940, a Porky Pig cartoon), and Abbott and Costello (*Africa Screams*, 1949).

62. Mitman, *Reel Nature*, 58.

63. The Ubangi River flows into the Congo River south of where Hoefler's party encounters these people; Hoefler uses "Ubangi" to refer vaguely to the region. In a memoir of the expedition, he identifies the tribal group as the Sara Kyabe, and their location, the village of Kiya Be, not far from the River Chari, a tributary of Lake Chad. In a foreword, Hoefler writes that the film "must, of necessity, in order to entertain, move swiftly to its climax"; the book, in contrast, is ploddingly detailed,

but more specific about the people, animals and places he encountered. See Paul L. Hoefler, *Africa Speaks* (Chicago: Winston, 1931), iv, and esp. 377–91.

64. Mitman, *Reel Nature*, 51–52. While president, Roosevelt granted an interview to the journalist Edward B. Clark, published as "Roosevelt on the Nature Fakirs" in *Everybody's Magazine* 16 (June 1907): 770–74. Roosevelt criticized the fanciful nature stories of writers such as William J. Long and Jack London as misrepresenting known facts about animals, and lamented that many schools used these books to teach natural history. For a discussion of the debates that the interview provoked, see Ralph H. Lutts, *The Nature Fakers: Wildlife, Science and Sentiment* (Golden, Colo.: Fulcrum, 1990), esp. chap. 4, "Roosevelt's War with the Nature Fakers," 101–38.

65. Thomas Cripps, *Slow Fade to Black: The Negro in American Film, 1900–1942* (Oxford: Oxford University Press, 1993), 41–42, 67, 119, 155.

66. The series, which mostly featured footage of animals in controlled conditions, adopted a more playful tone in the early sound era; inspired by Walt Disney cartoons with animal characters, they edited animals' movements to music in *Playtime at the Zoo* (1930), among other films. See Bousé, *Wildlife Films*, 59.

67. After *The Private Life of the Gannet*, Huxley tried to take up wildlife filmmaking again, in a failed plan to augment the Zoological Society of London's caged exhibits of live animals with films of the same species in the wild. See Mitman, *Reel Nature*, 75–78.

68. Huxley, *Man in the Modern World*, 90–91.

69. Mitman, *Reel Nature*, 60, 70, 72–74. A 1938 natural history resource book includes about sixty films on mammals, a hundred on birds, and dozens more on fish, reptiles, insects, and amphibians produced and distributed by Eastman Kodak, Bell and Howell, universities, museums, government agencies, national parks, and not-for-profit organizations such as the Audubon Society and the YMCA. See Richard James Hurley, *Key to the Out-of-Doors: A Bibliography of Nature Books and Materials* (New York: H. W. Wilson, 1938), 143–48, 160–63, 217–18.

70. See William Alexander, *Film on the Left: American Documentary Film from 1931 to 1942* (Princeton, N.J.: Princeton University Press, 1981), 7; and Barnouw, *Documentary*, 111–13.

71. See Robert L. Snyder, *Pare Lorentz and the Documentary Film* (Norman: University of Oklahoma Press, 1968), 37.

72. Painlevé continued to work with marine subjects, often working with captive sea creatures in aquariums, in *The Sea Urchins* (1954), *Dancers of the Sea* (1956), *How Jellyfishes Are Born* (1960), and *Lovelife of the Octopus* (1965). On Painlevé, see Andy Bellows and Marina McDougall, eds., *Science Is Fiction: The Films of Jean Painlevé* (Cambridge: MIT Press, 2000).

73. See Bousé, *Wildlife Films*, 61–62, 125. Sucksdorff went on to make the better-known short *A Divided World* (1948); see also David Davidson, "The Step Backwards: Arne Sucksdorff's Divided Worlds," *Scandinavica* 20, no. 1 (1981): 87–97.

74. Robert De Roos, "The Magic Worlds of Walt Disney," *National Geographic* 124, no. 2 (Aug. 1963): 178.

75. Leonard Maltin, *The Disney Films*, 3d ed. (New York: Hyperion, 1995), 18.

76. Richard Schickel, *The Disney Version: The Life, Times, Art and Commerce of Walt Disney*, rev. ed. (New York: Simon and Schuster, 1985), 284–85.

77. Despite unusually large shooting ratios (as high as 30 to 1) and lengthy field production commitments, wildlife films far undercut the expense of Disney's labor-intensive animated films; see ibid., 283, 286–87; also Barnouw, *Documentary*, 95, 97, 112, 235–36; Mitman, *Reel Nature*, 112; and Steven Watts, *The Magic Kingdom: Walt Disney and the American Way of Life* (Boston: Houghton Mifflin, 1997), 286.

78. Maltin, *The Disney Films*, 17–18.

79. Watts, *The Magic Kingdom*, 392. Disney's recapitulation of the racist imagery of colonialism should come as no surprise. In a pot-boiling biography, Marc Eliot sketches Disney's political alliances: he claims that in the late 1930s Disney attended meetings of the American Nazi Party, but speculates that he might not have been pursuing a political agenda as much as making contacts to reopen film markets in fascist countries that banned Disney films. Further, Disney was friendly with Aldous Huxley, author of *Brave New World* (1932) and brother of biologist Julian; Disney hired Aldous to write the script for *Alice in Wonderland* (1951) but severed the relationship when Huxley's son Matthew, an employee at Warner Bros., participated in a strike. See Marc Eliot, *Walt Disney: Hollywood's Dark Prince* (New York: HarperPaperbacks, 1994), 129–30, 200–201.

80. The Jungle Cruise was recreated at Walt Disney World Resort in Florida, which opened in 1971. While Disney cites footage from *The African Lion* as the inspiration for the Jungle Cruise, some sources suggest that memories of a boat trip into a Colombian rainforest, undertaken by Walt and some companions during his 1941 South American tour, also contributed (Bob Thomas, *Walt Disney: An American Original* [1976; New York: Hyperion, 1994], 173). The Office of Inter-American Affairs and its coordinator, Nelson A. Rockefeller, invited Disney to undertake the trip as a cultural ambassador while the U.S. government strove to strengthen ties with Latin America and deflect Communist influences. The office funded the journey and contributed to the costs of making Donald Duck vehicles *Saludos Amigos* (1943) and *The Three Caballeros* (1945) in collaboration with local animation studios in the countries where Disney traveled.

81. All unattributed quotes in this section are from the televised version of *Bear Country*, first broadcast May 1, 1957, along with *The Yellowstone Story*, a fifteen-minute piece directed by James Algar and written by Algar with Lee Chaney (for Disney's TV scheduling of its theatrical releases, see Maltin, *The Disney Films*, 358). Walt Disney's introduction to the program describes it as background filmed while on location for *Bear Country*. *The Yellowstone Story* dwells on tourists feeding and photographing bears, but Disney assures the viewer that *Bear Country* shows "how bears behave when no tourists are around."

82. The bird was a Clark's nutcracker and while the scene was staged under controlled conditions, it was an accurate depiction of the species' natural behaviors, according to ornithologist Robert Cushman Murphy, reviewing the film for the AMNH's magazine *Natural History,* March 1953, 139; discussed in Mitman, *Reel Nature,* 121.

83. For a provocative discussion of close integration of Disney's stories of animal families and child-rearing literature of the era, see Nicholas Sammond, *Babes in Tomorrowland: Walt Disney and the Making of the American Child, 1930–1960* (Durham, N.C.: Duke University Press, 2005), see esp. chap. 5, "Raising the Natural Child," 247–99.

84. The film does not delve into the secrets of avian, reptilian, amphibian, or mammalian life. On the stickleback sequence, see Bousé, *Wildlife Films,* 117.

85. *White Wilderness,* another Academy Award winner, has become notorious for a scene in which lemmings appear to plunge en masse off a cliff: they were pushed; see Lily Whiteman, "Violence, Lies and Videotape: Wildlife Filmmaking Takes a Few Liberties with the Truth," *E* 8, no. 3 (May–June, 1997): 24–25. See also Dennis Chitty, *Do Lemmings Commit Suicide?: Beautiful Hypotheses and Ugly Facts* (Oxford: Oxford University Press, 1996), for a debunking of the myth of lemming mass suicide, an unsubstantiated explanation for cyclical volatility in the rodents' population size.

86. The pups appear next to a caribou carcass on their own, not with adults, though they interact with adults in other scenes, in which the adults feed the litter regurgitated food, or, in a behavior described as a music lesson that comprises part of the litter's "schooling," they appear to coach the pups in howling. According to Mitman, the pups were hand-raised by the Crislers for use in the film; see *Reel Nature,* 117.

87. Carl R. Plantinga, *Rhetoric and Representation in Nonfiction Film* (Cambridge: Cambridge University Press, 1997), 153.

88. Schickel, *The Disney Version,* 288–89, and Bousé, *Wildlife Films,* 67, discuss reviews of *The Living Desert.* On *Seal Island,* see Mitman, *Reel Nature,* 110–11.

89. Thomas, *Walt Disney,* 238; and Schickel, *The Disney Version,* 308–9.

90. Gomery, *Movie History,* 239.

91. Schickel, *The Disney Version,* 309; see also Douglas Gomery, "Disney's Business History: A Reinterpretation," in *Disney Discourse, Producing the Magic Kingdom,* ed. Eric Smoodin (New York: Routledge, 1994), 73.

92. Maltin, *The Disney Films,* 117. *Vanishing Prairie* also won an Academy Award.

93. See Christopher Anderson, *Hollywood TV: The Studio System in the Fifties* (Austin: University of Texas Press, 1994), 149; Margaret J. King, "The Audience in the Wilderness: The Disney Nature Films," *Journal of Popular Film and Television* 24, no. 2 (Summer 1996): 63.

94. Maltin, *The Disney Films,* 188; Mitman, *Reel Nature,* 130.

95. King, "The Audience in the Wilderness," 64.

96. Bousé, *Wildlife Films*, 131, 144. The coming-of-age saga also pervades other media and literary genres, such as children's storybooks that feature animal characters.

97. Animal protagonists and allegories were largely new to film but they were common in turn-of-the-century magazines such as *McClure's* and *Harper's*. Nature stories in these magazines avoided hunting themes, and while their authors claimed to report unmodified observation of wildlife, they freely personified animals and fashioned allegories from their behaviors. A book in this genre, *Wild Animals I Have Known* (1898) by Ernest Seton Thompson, sold half a million copies; see Peter J. Schmitt, *Back to Nature: The Arcadian Myth in Urban America* (1969; Baltimore: Johns Hopkins University Press, 1990), 46–7.

98. Barnouw, *Documentary*, 210; see also Watts, *The Magic Kingdom*, 304.

99. David DeGrazia, *Taking Animals Seriously: Mental Life and Moral Status* (New York: Cambridge University Press, 1996), 128.

100. Crist, *Images of Animals*, 11, 166.

101. Randall Lockwood, "Anthropomorphism Is Not a Four-Letter Word," in *Perceptions of Animals in American Culture*, ed. R. J. Hoage (Washington, D.C.: Smithsonian Institution Press, 1989), 46–47. For a harsher critique of anthropomorphizing techniques in the animal-observing sciences, see John S. Kennedy, *The New Anthropomorphism* (Cambridge: Cambridge University Press, 1992), 158–62.

102. Watts, *The Magic Kingdom*, 305–6. The True-Life Adventures sometimes strayed into Canadian *(White Wilderness)* or Central American *(Jungle Cat*, 1960, the final entry in the series) locations; *African Lion* is the only other exception.

103. Wilson, *The Culture of Nature*, 118–20.

104. The Belgian Congo, for example, where *Congorilla* was made, secured its independence in 1960 as the Congo Free State (later, Zaire, and since 1997, the Democratic Republic of Congo); Rwanda achieved independence from Germany and Belgium in 1962; Zambia and Zimbabwe, former colonies of Great Britain, declared independence in 1963 and 1965, respectively.

105. Watts, *The Magic Kingdom*, 305.

106. Mills, "Pocket Tigers," 6.

107. Gregg Mitman describes several instances of Disney filmmakers working with animals under "controlled conditions" in *Reel Nature*, 121, 237.

108. William R. Koehler, *The Wonderful World of Disney Animals* (New York: Howell Book House, 1979), 11.

109. Peter Steinhart, "Wildlife Films: End of an Era?," *National Wildlife* 18, no. 1 (Dec.–Jan. 1980): 37.

110. David Payne, "Bambi," in *From Mouse to Mermaid: The Politics of Film, Gender, and Culture*, ed. Elizabeth Bell, Lynda Haas, and Laura Sells (Bloomington: Indiana University Press, 1995), 147.

111. Irwin Allen produced and directed *The Sea Around Us*. Later, he wrote

and directed the fiction film *Voyage to the Bottom of the Sea* (1961) and executive-produced a related TV series (1964–68, ABC), among other science-fiction, disaster, and fantasy film and television projects.

112. See Jean Rouch, *Ciné-Ethnography*, ed. and trans. Steven Feld (Minneapolis: University of Minnesota Press, 2003). On postwar ethnographic film and filmmakers, see David MacDougall, "Whose Story Is It?"; Paul Stoller, "Artaud, Rouch, and the Cinema of Cruelty"; and Eliot Weinberger, "The Camera People," all in *Visualizing Theory: Selected Essays from V.A.R., 1990–1994*, ed. Lucien Taylor (New York: Routledge, 1994), 27–36, 84–98, and 3–26 respectively.

113. Barnouw, *Documentary*, 213, 215–16.

2. The Quest for Nature on the Small Screen

1. On technological developments in wildlife filmmaking, see John Sparks, "Filming What Comes Naturally," *New Scientist* 24, no. 31 (Dec. 1988): 42, 44.

2. Lynn Spigel, "The Suburban Home Companion: Television and the Neighbourhood Ideal in Post-War America," in *Feminist Television Criticism: A Reader*, ed. Charlotte Brunsdon, Julie D'Acci and Lynn Spigel (Oxford: Oxford University Press, 1997), 211–34. See also Lynn Spigel, *Make Room for TV: Television and the Family Ideal in Postwar America* (Chicago: University of Chicago Press, 1992).

3. On the difficulty of studying early TV, see Mark Williams, "Issue Introduction: U.S. Regional and Non-Network Television History," *Quarterly Review of Film and Video* 16, nos. 3–4 (July 1999): 223. On the introduction of video-recording equipment, see William Lafferty, "'A New Era in TV Programming' Becomes 'Business as Usual': Videotape Technology, Local Stations, and Network Power, 1957–1961," *Quarterly Review of Film and Video* 16, nos. 3–4 (July 1999): 406.

4. Michael Ritchie, *Please Stand By: A Prehistory of Television* (Woodstock, N.Y.: Overlook Press, 1994), unpag. plates.

5. See John Ellis, *Visible Fictions: Cinema, Television, Video*, rev. ed. (New York: Routledge, 1992).

6. Bousé, *Wildlife Films*, 74.

7. Marlin Perkins, *My Wild Kingdom: An Autobiography* (New York: Dutton, 1982), 113–14.

8. Joel Sternberg, "Chicago Television: A History," *Quarterly Review of Film and Video* 16, nos. 3–4 (July 1999): 236. The show-and-tell format persists over six decades later, in visits by zoologists and other animal handlers to talk shows such as *Today* and *The Tonight Show*. Some sources name Julie Scardina, a leading animal trainer at SeaWorld of California, as the second most frequent guest appearing on *The Tonight Show with Jay Leno* since 1992; see Walter Scott, "Personality Parade," *Parade Magazine* (May 23, 2004), archive.parade.com/2004/0523/0523_personality.html (accessed July 28, 2004).

9. Sternberg, "Chicago Television," 236.

10. Perkins, *My Wild Kingdom*, 114–15.

11. Ibid., 115. In a previous volume, Perkins writes "*Zooparade*" as one word; see Marlin Perkins, *Marlin Perkins' Zooparade*, illus. Paul Bransom and Seymour Fleishman (Chicago: Rand McNally, 1954). Virtually every other source uses the two-word title *Zoo Parade*.

12. Sternberg, "Chicago Television," 243.

13. Perkins, *My Wild Kingdom*, 116.

14. Mitman, *Reel Nature*, 137–38.

15. Perkins also notes that the donkey's back and shoulders are marked with two intersecting lines, which have been accounted for in legend as a sign of the cross, given to the animal by Jesus in gratitude for helping him bear the load of the cross to his crucifixion. This is not the only time that Perkins references Christian iconography; in the 1956 Easter Show, he narrates an unabashedly secular story (illustrated with film footage) in which zoo animals are supposed to wonder about the origin of the church music they hear. An elephant explains that the service commemorates Christ's resurrection. Mitman also discusses the story in *Reel Nature*, 140–41. The episode, which also includes a lesson on the care of pet rabbits and a visit from the animal puppets of Burr Tillstrom's Kuklapolitan players, ends with an assurance to the audience (from the puppet "Ollie" Dragon) that next week's episode will feature "another of our thrilling African safari stories," surely a relief following this evening's awkward skits.

16. Tadamichi Koga had been director of the Ueno Zoological Gardens of Tokyo since 1937.

17. Foucault, "Of Other Spaces," 22–27.

18. Mitman, *Reel Nature*, 147.

19. Perkins, *My Wild Kingdom*, 122, 136, 154, 155.

20. Sternberg, "Chicago Television," 243.

21. David Stewart, *The PBS Companion: A History of Public Television* (New York: TV Books, 1999), 58.

22. Hal Erickson, *Syndicated Television: The First Forty Years, 1947–1987* (Jefferson, N.C.: McFarland and Co., 1989), 9.

23. See Imperato and Imperato, *They Married Adventure*, 223; also Kenhelm W. Stott Jr., *Exploring with Martin and Osa Johnson* (Chanute, Kan.: Martin and Osa Johnson Safari Museum Press, 1978), 113.

24. Bousé, *Wildlife Films*, 73–75.

25. Another British production company, Survival Anglia Ltd., reached the U.S. television market before the BBC, with Alan Root's Galapagos Islands special *Enchanted Isles* in 1968. Survival Anglia's *Survival* series, launched on the BBC-competitor Independent Television in 1961, aired in the United States a decade later as *The World of Survival* (1971–77, syndication); see Bousé, *Wildlife Films*, 76, 80.

26. See Anderson, *Hollywood TV*, 3–5.

27. Maltin, *The Disney Films*, 357.

28. Unlike ABC, NBC already boasted color-broadcasting technology, so the 1961 move prompted another name change, this time to *Walt Disney's Wonderful World of Color*. The series was renamed again as *The Wonderful World of Disney* for fall 1967, but remained on NBC until cancellation in 1981.

29. During the last two seasons that NBC produced *Wild Kingdom* (1969–71), the series aired on Sundays at 7:00 p.m., leading into *The Wonderful World of Disney* at 7:30.

30. Over forty years have passed since Disney's first live-action fictional animal films, but the company has never abandoned the form: for example, *The Incredible Journey* was remade some thirty years after the original's release as *Homeward Bound: The Incredible Journey* (1993), and spawned a sequel, *Homeward Bound 2: Lost in San Francisco* (1996). Disney continues to crank out pictures, many of them remakes and sequel-prone, in which animal actors (most frequently dogs) are augmented by animatronic and computer-generated special effects, such as *Jungle Book* (1994), *101 Dalmatians* (1996), *Air Bud* (1997), *Jungle Book 2: Mowgli and Baloo* (1997), *102 Dalmatians* (2000), and *Snow Dogs* (2002).

31. Uys is perhaps better known for the feature comedy *The Gods Must Be Crazy* (1984). *Animals Are Beautiful People* remains a durable home-video title, marketed as children's programming.

32. *Omnibus* (1952–56, CBS; 1956–57, ABC; 1957–61, NBC) was, due to Ford Foundation sponsorship, advertisement-free. It occasionally aired nonfiction films from the collections of the New York Zoological Society and the American Museum of Natural Historical, along with classical music, opera, and literary adaptations. *Omnibus* debuted not only Cousteau's first work for American television, but also National Geographic's first television productions; see William A. Jones and Andrew Walworth, "Saudele's *Omnibus:* Ambitious Forerunner of Public TV," *Current* (Dec. 13, 1999), www.current.org/coop/coopomni.html (accessed July 30, 2004).

33. Michael Curtin, *Redeeming the Wasteland: Television Documentary and Cold War Politics* (New Brunswick, N.J.: Rutgers University Press, 1995), 1–3, 18–19, 34, 39–41.

34. Ibid., 246–48, 252–53.

35. Wilson, *The Culture of Nature,* 137.

36. Chandra Mukerji, *A Fragile Power: Scientists and the State* (Princeton, N.J.: Princeton University Press, 1989), 150–51.

37. Wilson, *The Culture of Nature,* 137, 140.

38. Previous writers have pointed out the ironies and incoherencies of *Wild Kingdom*'s depictions of wildlife. Wilson notes how frequently the *Wild Kingdom* team captured animals only to pose as their saviors, with little impact on the conditions that threaten wildlife and their habitats (ibid., 133). Mitman, who describes the series' emphasis on the dangers of confronting wild animals, as when Perkins runs from a charging bull seal, or is nearly dragged underwater by an anaconda, also mentions the use of domesticated examples of species usually thought of as

wild for in-studio segments, offering a contradictory view of wildlife as docile and benign. Carol Perkins, Marlin's wife, also used "wild" animals that had been raised as pets in her environmental lobbying and fundraising work, which Mitman likens to other efforts in the 1960s by environmentalist and animal-rights' groups to gain support for their causes by making animals more familiar to potential constituents, and by appealing to the sentimental attachment of pet owners to nonhuman species; see *Reel Nature*, 151–54.

39. Around 1960, the networks retooled the relationship between sponsors and programming, adopting a magazine-style system of selling ads in discreet blocks without formally associating their brands with particular series. This was another strategy that might have helped shake off the medium's reputation as, in the words of FCC Chair Newton N. Minow, a "vast wasteland" under nonmedia corporate control and still haunted by the quiz-show scandals of the 1950s; see Curtin, *Redeeming the Wasteland*, 70; and Minow, "The 'Vast Wasteland,'" in Minow, *How Vast the Wasteland Now?* (New York: Gannett Foundation, 1991), 22. Mutual of Omaha's relationship to *Wild Kingdom* was a modified holdover from early television.

40. Mitman, *Reel Nature*, 152–55.

41. Perkins's wife, Carol, led American tourists on "photographic safaris" to many likely *Wild Kingdom* locations, and eventually tourism became a major source of income for the conservation parks that *Wild Kingdom* utilized; ibid., 155. According to Clark C. Gibson, tourism in Eastern and Central African countries—Zambia, for example—has sometimes benefited the government through taxation and wealthy owners of tour companies as much if not far more than rural residents have benefited from the creation of tourism-serving jobs and infrastructural development; see Gibson, *Politics and Poachers*, 128, 130, 132.

42. A television critic describing a CBS miniseries aired in 2002 as containing "several brief but clear scenes of female nudity—i.e., uncovered breasts—not seen before on American commercial broadcast television" might have more accurately qualified them as scenes of *white* female nudity not seen before on American commercial broadcast television; see Robert P. Laurence, "There Is a Top Secret That Is Exposed in Network's Revealing Look at 'Master Spy,'" *San Diego Union-Tribune TV Week* (Nov. 10, 2002): 6. Quasi-ethnographic filmmaking such as the *Wild Kingdom* episode and historical docudramas such as the landmark *Roots* miniseries (1977, ABC) televised numerous examples of the uncovered breasts of nonwhite women.

43. Lutz and Collins, *Reading National Geographic*, 16–17, 19, 27.

44. Melville Bell Grosvenor, "National Geographic's Newest Adventure: A Color Television Series" (reprint), *National Geographic* (Sept. 1965): unpag.

45. Herbert I. Schiller, *The Mind Managers* (Boston: Beacon Press, 1973), 89.

46. Lutz and Collins, *Reading National Geographic*, 37–38; Schiller, *The Mind Managers*, 90–92.

47. On what Barry Dornfeld calls "popular ethnography," see Dornfeld, *Pro-*

ducing Public Television, Producing Public Culture (Princeton, N.J.: Princeton University Press, 1998), 9–10. Dornfeld points out that some of these programs approach their subjects comparatively, investigating notions of identity and cultural difference from an American perspective. Similarly, he adds, the nature genre conducts similar comparative investigations between species—from an anthropocentric perspective, an idea he attributes to Toby Miller; see 10, 198 n. 10.

48. Grosvenor, "National Geographic's Newest Adventure," unpag. Wolper's prior productions credits included acclaimed documentaries such as *The Race for Space* (1958, syndicated) and *The Making of the President: 1960* (1963, ABC). His company went on to produce episodes of the *National Geographic Specials*, three hour-long specials aired by NBC as *The World of Animals* (1966–68), a season of *The Undersea World of Jacques Cousteau;* the landmark docudrama *Roots* (1997, ABC), and dozens of films, TV specials, series, and made-for-TV-movies.

49. Ibid.

50. Ratings by Arbitron: "Miss Goodall and the Wild Chimpanzee," internal memo on National Geographic Society letterhead from the office of Robert C. Doyle, Chief, Television Division, n.d. According to another undated internal document, labeled "National Geographic Specials: 1965–1966 Season," *Voyage of the Brigantine Yankee* (1966) attracted an even larger total audience (33.6 million viewers), and *The World of Jacques Cousteau* (1966) somewhat fewer (21.4 million viewers). Both documents viewed at the Records Library, National Geographic Society, Washington, D.C., Oct. 22, 2004.

51. Excerpts of received correspondence were typed and compiled for in-house circulation and recordkeeping. Transcripts from folder "Television Research: Miss Goodall and the Wild Chimpanzees" 86–1.2–13, Box 2 of 2, viewed at the Records Library, National Geographic Society, Washington, D.C., Oct. 22, 2004.

52. Schiller, *The Mind Managers*, 80.

53. Haraway, *Primate Visions*, 251.

54. Ibid., 154. Thus the *Specials*' racial representations are not so unlike those found in early twentieth-century expedition films by Martin and Osa Johnson, Paul L. Hoefler, and others.

55. Haraway, *Primate Visions*, 266.

56. Vedder and Webber recount their more than three decades in primate conservation in *In the Kingdom of the Gorillas: Fragile Species in a Dangerous Land* (New York: Simon and Schuster, 2001). See also Natalie Angier, "Joy in Rwanda: Signing on with the Gorillas," *New York Times*, Jan. 15, 2002, F1. Gorilla habitat spans the volcanic Virunga mountain range in the Democratic Republic of the Congo, Uganda, and Rwanda.

57. Haraway, *Primate Visions*, 245. A 1984 print advertisement run by Gulf Oil to promote the series featured a similar image, in which a white female hand, identified as Jane Goodall's, clasps an adult ape's hand; ibid., 133–34.

58. Ibid., 181–83.

59. Ibid., 179–84.

60. Harry M. Wegeforth and Neil Morgan, *It Began with a Roar! The Beginning of the World-Famous San Diego Zoo* (1953; San Diego: Zoological Society of San Diego, 1990), 171.

61. Ronald V. Bettig, "Who Owns Prime Time? Industrial and Institutional Conflict over Television Programming and Broadcast Rights," in *Framing Friction: Media and Social Conflict*, ed. Mary S. Mander (Urbana: University of Illinois Press, 1999), 138–39. See also Erickson, *Syndicated Television*, 12; and, on the rules vis-à-vis the wildlife genre, Steinhart, "Wildlife Films," 38.

62. Steinhart, "Wildlife Films," 38.

63. See Erickson, *Syndicated Television*, 91. Bill Burrud Productions, founded in the early 1950s to specialize in travel, adventure, and "lost-treasure" nonfiction, turned in the 1960s to half-hour nature programs, which Burrud produced and narrated himself, including *True Adventure* (1960–61); *Animal World* (which premiered as *Animal Kingdom;* 1968, NBC; 1969 and 1971, CBS; 1970, ABC; 1973–80, syndication); *The Challenging Seas* (1969, syndication); and *Safari to Adventure* (1969–75, syndication). Burrud also produced the special *Where Did All the Animals Go?* (1974), distributed free to TV stations to promote fundraising and antipoaching efforts by the Tsavo National Park, Kenya. At the time of Burrud's death in 1990, he was working on new series for the Discovery Channel; see Myrna Oliver, "Bill Burrud, Host of TV Animal Programs," *Los Angeles Times*, July 14, 1990, A30; Wolfgang Saxon, "William Burrud, 65, Television Producer of Nature Programs," *New York Times*, July 16, 1990, B10.

64. Steinhart, "Wildlife Films," 38, 41.

65. Susan Spillman, "One Program—One Sponsor: Four Programs Showcase Advertisers," *Advertising Age* (March 8, 1982): M21.

66. These series included *Untamed World* (1968–69, NBC; 1969–75, syndication), narrated by Phil Carey; *The World of Survival* (1971–77, syndication), narrated by John Forsythe and coproduced by Survival Anglia, Ltd., and the World Wildlife Fund; *Wild, Wild World of Animals* (1973–76, syndication), produced by Time-Life Films and narrated by William Conrad; *Friends of Man* (1974, syndication), narrated by Glenn Ford; *Inner Space* (1974, syndication), hosted by William Shatner and featuring underwater footage by Ron and Valerie Taylor; *Lorne Greene's Last of the Wild* (1974–79, syndication), by Ivan Tors Productions; *The Coral Jungle* (1976, syndication), filmed around Australia's Great Barrier Reef and narrated by Leonard Nimoy; *Animals, Animals, Animals* (1976–81, ABC), narrated by Hal Linden; and *Lorne Greene's New Wilderness* (1982–86, syndication).

67. While the FCC indicated its intention to reformulate these rules as early as 1982 and relaxed the FISRs in 1991, they were not fully repealed until 1993. Under the new rules, networks no longer had to air any non-network programming in primetime, and they regained the right to invest in independent production com-

panies and to reenter the syndication market; see Bettig, "Who Owns Prime Time?," 144, 149–50.

68. Steinhart, "Wildlife Films," 37.

69. William Hoynes, *Public Television for Sale: Media, the Market, and the Public Sphere* (Boulder, Colo.: Westview Press, 1994), 150; see also Curtin, *Redeeming the Wasteland*, 246.

70. Moving from commercial to public TV did not free the *Specials* from constraints similar to those imposed by advertiser-supported networks. While admitting that National Geographic forged "a more science-oriented tradition" than *Wild Kingdom*, Wilson's brief treatment of the *Specials* remains skeptical of their capacity to cultivate conservationist values in viewers (*The Culture of Nature*, 127). He cites a later film on the same subject, *The Grizzlies* (1987), to illustrate what he calls National Geographic's "cynical and accommodationist politics"; the film treats loss of the bears' Alaskan habitat as "inevitable," never remarking on interventions into these lands by the oil industry (ibid., 143). The omission is a possible by-product of the oil industry's sponsorship of National Geographic. First Gulf Oil and later Chevron underwrote the series during its PBS run. Further, the film discusses Alaska's tourist industry—represented by footage of "sport fishers and adventure photographers [crammed] onto the same narrow river delta where grizzlies are feeding on migrating salmon"—only as a source of risk to tourists who may wander too near a potentially dangerous bear, never as another industry endangering bears through habitat loss (ibid., 127, 143).

71. Daniel B. Wood, "National Geographic TV: 25 Years," *Christian Science Monitor* 82, no. 30 (Jan. 9, 1990): 14.

72. Derek Bousé writes that *Life on Earth,* made for the BBC in 1979, reached PBS in 1981 (*Wildlife Films,* 81). Another source gives the dates January 12 to April 6, 1982, for the series' PBS run; see Alex McNeil, *Total Television: The Comprehensive Guide to Programming from 1948 to the Present,* 4th ed. (New York: Penguin, 1996), 480.

73. See Stewart, *The PBS Companion,* 165. Stewart, a former Corporation for Public Broadcasting executive, bases his chapter, "Inventing NOVA," largely on an interview with Ambrosino (165–76). See also James Day, *The Vanishing Vision: The Inside Story of Public Television* (Berkeley: University of California Press, 1995), 397 n. 9.

74. Stewart, *The PBS Companion,* 166, 168, 169. On Oxford Scientific Films' history and methods, see Paul S. Crowther, *Animals in Focus: The Business Life of a Natural History Film Unit* (Exeter: A. Wheaton, 1981).

75. Lawrie Mifflin, "Getting Ready for a BBC Venture," *New York Times,* March 3, 1997, D7.

76. Walter Goodman, "Tracking a Nation's Wildlife from Desert to Tundra," *New York Times,* Oct. 5, 1992, C20. Another example of the praise heaped on *Nature*

can be found in the review "Nature's Greatest African Moments," *Christian Science Monitor* 86, no. 6 (Dec. 3, 1993): 17.

77. Price, *Flight Maps*, 246, 248–49.

78. Charles Siebert, "The Artifice of the Natural," *Harper's Magazine*, Feb. 1993, 45. See also Goodman, "Tracking a Nation's Wildlife from Desert to Tundra," C20.

79. Asked if the presence of observers altered the elephants' behavior, Moss was adamantly positivistic: "We're just flies on the wall. . . . It very rarely affects them"; see Alan Bunce, "PBS's Truthful Eye on Elephant Life," *Christian Science Monitor* 85, no. 64 (March 1, 1993): 13.

80. Mindy Sink, "The Call of the Wildlife Show: Aren't They Adorable? Viewers and Sponsors Certainly Think So," *New York Times*, April 15, 1996, C7.

81. Greg Spring, "Rysher's 'Wild America' Taking Off, Naturally," *Electronic Media* 17, no. 45 (Nov. 2, 1998): 2.

82. *Wild Dogs* first aired during the series' first season, and continued to be rerun after it went into commercial syndication in 1998.

3. Wildlife, Remade for TV

1. In 1980, 17.6 million television-owning homes, or 23 percent of the market, subscribed to cable; see Patrick R. Parsons and Robert M. Frieden, *The Cable and Satellite Television Industries* (Boston: Allyn and Bacon, 1998), 122. By the end of 1993, 60.3 million television-owning U.S. homes received some form of multichannel video programming distribution (MVPD, which at the time nearly always meant cable), with average channel capacity peaking around fifty (only about 5 percent subscribed to new means of delivering multichannel video signals, mostly satellite systems). By June 2003, cable systems increased channel capacity to an average of seventy analog channels, 120 digital channels, and additional on-demand and high-definition services; an estimated 94.1 million, or 85.25 percent, of television households subscribed to MVPDs: about 70 percent to cable, and the rest to growing noncable services. See Federal Communications Commission (FCC), *Tenth Annual Report: Annual Assessment of the Status of Competition in the Market for the Delivery of Video Programming* (Washington, D.C.: FCC, released Jan. 28, 2004), 4–5, 14, 20.

2. FCC, *Fourth Annual Report: Annual Assessment of the Status of Competition in Markets for the Delivery of Video Programming* (Washington, D.C.: FCC, released Jan. 13, 1998), 9; FCC, *Ninth Annual Report: Annual Assessment of the Status of Competition in the Market for the Delivery of Video Programming* (Washington, D.C.: FCC, released Dec. 31, 2002), 6, 14.

3. On practices of masculinity in the 1980s, see Susan Jeffords, *Hard Bodies: Hollywood Masculinity in the Reagan Era* (New Brunswick, N.J.: Rutgers University Press, 1994); also, Jeffords, *Remasculinization of America: Gender and the Vietnam War* (Bloomington: Indiana University Press, 1989). Her work provides a model

for understanding muscle-bound bodies and bellicosity that define popular culture and political policy during the George W. Bush administration.

4. Foucault, "Of Other Spaces," 25–26. On February 21, 2000, at 7:00 p.m., *Freshwater Crocs* on the Travel Channel was juxtaposed in simultaneous broadcast with *Brother Wolf* on the Discovery Channel's *Wild Discovery* series, and Animal Planet's *Emergency Vets* and *Wild Rescues*, which included a segment on manatees. Discovery Communications Inc. owns all three networks.

5. "Twenty Years of Discovery Quality" (interactive timeline), http://corporate.discovery.com/brands/discoverychannel.html (accessed Aug. 30, 2004).

6. Peter Steinhart, "Electronic Intimacies," *Audubon* 90, no. 6 (Nov. 1998): 10.

7. B. J. Bullert, *Public Television: Politics and the Battle over Documentary Film* (New Brunswick, N.J.: Rutgers University Press, 1997), 15.

8. Richard Tedesco, "Discovery Looks to Build a Programming Empire," *Cablevision* (June 18, 1990): 22.

9. Michael Wilkie, "'100 Cabooses, Two or Three Engines,'" *Advertising Age* 66, no. 13 (March 27, 1995): S4.

10. Mark Lewyn, "John Hendricks: The Conscience of Cable TV," *Business Week* (Aug. 31, 1992): 67.

11. "Discovery Channel Gets Four Backers," *Broadcasting* 110, no. 26 (June 30, 1986): 32–33.

12. Simon Applebaum, "Business Strategy Refinements Spur Prospects at The Discovery Channel," *Cablevision* 12, no. 1 (Sept. 29, 1986): 29; Lewyn, "John Hendricks," 68.

13. Laura Landro, "Four Companies to Buy Cable Learning, Gaining Control of Discovery Channel," *Wall Street Journal*, Feb. 27, 1989, B4.

14. "Discovery Buy," *Broadcasting* 111, no. 6 (Aug. 11, 1986): 14.

15. "Discovery Channel Gets Four Backers," 33; Applebaum, "Business Strategy Refinements Spur Prospects," 29.

16. Tedesco, "Discovery Looks to Build a Programming Empire," 22. TCI and Time Warner acquired about 17 and 15 percent, respectively, of Black Entertainment Network (BET) before its 1980 launch; see "A Walk on the Acquisition Side with TCI," *Broadcasting* 111, no. 5 (Aug. 4, 1986): 70–71.

17. In February 1989 United and most original investors sold their shares to TCI, Cox, and Newhouse; Simon Applebaum, "MSOs Consolidate Grip on Discovery Channel," *Cablevision* 13, no. 13 (March 13, 1989): 19–20. Discovery's ownership consortium remained stable for ten years, with TCI/Liberty Media holding a 49 percent share, Cox and Advance/Newhouse each holding not quite 25 percent, and Hendricks in control of an undisclosed figure just under 3 percent. In March 1999, three years after the Telecommunications Act of 1996 lifted the 1970 prohibition on cross-ownership of local telephony and cable systems, AT&T acquired TCI in a merger valued at nearly $60 billion; see Price Colman, "AT&T-TCI Merge Starts New Era," *Broadcasting and Cable* 129, no. 11 (March 15, 1999): 39.

18. See FCC, "First Report: Annual Assessment of the Status of Competition in the Market for the Delivery of Video Programming," *FCC Record* 9, no. 25 (1994), 7599. From 1994, when the FCC began to issue annual reports including these rankings, to 2003, these six networks have remained consistently at the top of the industry in numbers of subscribers. While Discovery equity is shared among major MSOs, CNN, TBS, and TNT are wholly owned by Time Warner. Of these top six, only Disney/ABC's ESPN and NBCU's USA Networks lack affiliation with an MSO. See FCC, *Tenth Annual Report*, 88, 142.

19. Michael Bürgi, "Cable's Promised Land," *Mediaweek* 5, no. 13 (March 27, 1995): 28.

20. By the 1995–96 season, Discovery produced or coproduced 400 hours of material, a figure more than doubled to 952 hours for 1996–7. See Jim McConville, "Discovery Boosts Originals," *Broadcasting and Cable* 126, no. 18 (April 22, 1996): 48.

21. Tedesco, "Discovery Looks to Build a Programming Empire," 22–26.

22. Penny Pagano, "Catch of the Day," *Cablevision* 16, no. 22 (May 4, 1992): 75.

23. The Discovery Channel first launched Shark Week in 1988. See Papson, "'Cross the Fin Line of Terror,'" 68.

24. Kate Fitzgerald, "At Discovery, It's Survival of the Fittest," *Advertising Age* 66, no. 48 (Nov. 27, 1995): 20, 22.

25. Robert La Franco, "Actors Without Agents," *Forbes* 157, no. 7 (April 8, 1996): 83.

26. Louise McElvogue, "Running Wild," *Los Angeles Times*, Feb. 13, 1996, D1.

27. Ibid.

28. La Franco, "Actors Without Agents," 82–83.

29. Ann Japenga, "It's a Jungle Out There," *Los Angeles Times*, April 11, 1991, F5; Patricia O'Connell, "Outlets Bloom for Features," *Variety* 86, no. 7 (Sept. 27, 1993): 76.

30. Matt Stump, "Cable Ready to Go Back to School," *Broadcasting* 119, no. 10 (Sept. 3, 1990): 38; and Nicholas Garnham, *Capitalism and Communication: Global Culture and the Economics of Information* (London: Sage, 1990), 43–44.

31. Dan Schiller, *Digital Capitalism: Networking the Global Market System* (Cambridge: MIT Press, 1999), 203.

32. Chris Barker, *Global Television: An Introduction* (Oxford: Blackwell, 1997), 29–31.

33. Discovery executives reported to the trade press that entering the global marketplace required trimming content that might violate local religious or dietary customs, finding translators for dubbing and subtitling adept in local dialects, and adapting market research techniques to local social and discursive practices, such as prohibitions against mixed-gender focus groups in Saudi Arabia, and habits of politeness that restrained participants in other countries. See Wayne Walley, "Programming Globally—With Care," *Advertising Age* 66, no. 37 (Sept. 18, 1995): I-14.

34. Alan B. Albarran and Sylvia M. Chan-Olmsted, "Global Patterns and Issues," in *Global Media Economics: Commercialization, Concentration and Integration of World Media Markets,* ed. Albarran and Chan-Olmsted (Ames: Iowa State University Press, 1998), 334.

35. Rich Brown, "New Frontiers for Discovery," *Broadcasting and Cable* 123, no. 40 (Oct. 4, 1993): 38.

36. John Sinclair, *Latin American Television: A Global View* (Oxford: Oxford University Press, 1999), 20, 43, 165, 167; Stephen D. McDowell, "The Unsovereign Century: Canada's Media Industries and Cultural Policies," in *Media and Globalization: Why the State Matters,* ed. Nancy Morris and Silvio Waisbord (Lanham, Md.: Rowman and Littlefield, 2001), 119.

37. Meredith Amdur, "Canada Names 10 New Cable Service Licensees," *Broadcasting and Cable* 124, no. 24 (June 13, 1994): 28.

38. Gerald Chuah, "Discovery Remains Asia's No. 1," *New Straits Times,* Malaysia (Dec. 17, 2002): 4; Samuel Lee, "Wright Way to Travel," *The Straits Times* (Singapore), Oct. 25, 2002, retrieved from http://www.lexisnexis.com (accessed Jan. 21, 2003). Discovery Networks Asia added Animal Planet in 2000, which quickly became one of the five most-watched networks in some Asian markets (Chuah, "Discovery Remains Asia's No. 1," 4). Discovery Travel and Adventure (DTA), also rapidly gained viewers' attention; for example, it was the third most-watched pay-TV network in Malaysia within a month after launch in January 2003; see Samuel Lee, "73% of S'pore Elite Watch Cable TV," *The Straits Times* (Singapore), Jan. 25, 2003, retrieved from http://www.lexisnexis.com (accessed Oct. 2, 2005).

39. Zhao, *Media, Market, and Democracy in China,* 168, 174, 177–78.

40. Michael Bürgi, "Through the Wall: Discovery Channel Places a Season's Emphasis on China," *Mediaweek* 5, no. 24 (June 12, 1995): 32.

41. Harsha Subramanian, "Discovery's Not Just Nature and Wildlife," The Hindu Business Line (Internet Edition, Aug. 29, 2004), http://www.blonnet.com/catalyst/2002/07/18/stories/2002071800010100.htm (accessed Aug. 29, 2004).

42. Helge Rønning and Tawana Kupe, "The Dual Legacy of Democracy and Authoritarianism," in *De-Westernizing Media Studies,* ed. James Curran and Myung-Jin Park (London: Routledge, 2000), 163. Most of the Discovery Channel Global Education Partnership activity has been centered in Africa, but Learning Centers have also been established in Mexico, Peru, and Romania; see Global Education Partnership, Projects in Action: Action Map, www.discoveryglobaled.org (accessed Dec. 8, 2004).

43. The digital channels Discovery Science, Discovery Kids, Discovery Home and Leisure, and Discovery Civilization (reorganized in 2002 as a joint venture with the *New York Times*) spun off familiar Discovery Channel content. Discovery Health, Discovery Wings, Discovery en Español, and BBC America, a joint venture with the BBC, followed in 1998. Meanwhile, DCI began to acquire equity in Paxson Communications' Travel Channel in 1997, a takeover completed in 1999. At the

start of the fall 2002 season, Discovery entered the broadcast market, taking over a two-and-a-half-hour Saturday morning day part from NBC, which it filled with *Walking with Dinosaurs, Croc Files,* and other shows from the Discovery Kids lineup; see Lisa de Moraes, "NBC Hands Discovery Keys to the Kid-dom," *Washington Post,* Dec. 7, 2001, C7; "NBC Rents Saturday Morning to Discovery," *Pittsburgh Post-Gazette,* May 9, 2002, C6.

44. Michael Bürgi, "Fox Offer Gets a Ten-Shun," *Mediaweek* 6, no. 20 (May 13, 1996): 6.

45. John M. Higgins, "Start-ups Burn DCI's Cash," *Broadcasting and Cable* 128, no. 13 (March 30, 1998): 53. The practice of launch support originated in 1995 when Rupert Murdoch's News Corporation offered cable systems $13.88 per subscriber to add the Fox News Channel to their lineups; see John M. Higgins, "Discovery's Big Stretch," *Broadcasting and Cable* 129, no. 4 (Jan. 25, 1999): 106. Now commonplace, the practice hiked the cost to launch—and therefore, barriers to entry—for new cable-programming services.

46. Carlos Grande, "Three's Company for Animal Planet," *New Media Markets* 16, no. 46 (Dec. 17, 1998): 1. The alliance signaled the BBC's increasing dependence on commercial activities. While the domestic BBC continues to rely on television-set license fees, BBC Worldwide operates as a separate for-profit division from which profits are returned to the parent company, compensating for its decreased access to public funds, cut during the Thatcher era, and increased exposure to competition; see "Come In, the Water's Lovely," *Economist* 346, no. 8049 (Jan. 3, 1998): 63; and Edward S. Herman and Robert W. McChesney, *The Global Media: The New Missionaries of Corporate Capitalism* (London: Cassell, 1997), 167–68.

47. Warren Berger, "A Family Channel That Even the Pets May Enjoy," *New York Times,* March 1, 1998, 36.

48. See Discovery Communications Inc., Businesses and Brands: U.S. Networks: Animal Planet, http://corporate.discovery.com/brands/animalplanet.html (accessed Aug. 29, 2004).

49. Jim Rutenberg, "Carnival of the Animals: On TV, It's Raining Cats and Dogs, Not to Mention Pot-Bellied Pigs," *New York Times,* June 29, 2000, E4.

50. "No Charges for Steve Irwin," *Cincinnati Post,* Jan. 23, 2004, C14; and "Croc Hunter Has Close Call with the Law," *Grand Rapids Press,* July 16, 2004, E10.

51. Richard Tedesco, "Basic's Home Video Hits," *Cablevision* 16, no. 6 (Sept. 9, 1991): 12; Terry Lefton, "Danger! Discovery's Animal Planet Stampedes into Universal's Parks," *Brandweek* 41, no. 28 (July 10, 2000): 4.

52. Kelly Barron, "Theme Players," *Forbes* 163, no. 6 (March 22, 1999): 53.

53. The leopard is not so elusive that it has not been filmed before. A decade earlier, *Nature*'s George Page introduced *Leopard: A Darkness in the Grass* (1986) as "what we believe is a first, a major film on the leopard," which he described as the big African cat "least often seen on film." Hugh Miles shot the film in Kenya's Maasai

Maura National Reserve for BBC Bristol. Page explains that Miles was able to film this leopard when the typically nocturnal animal resorted to daytime hunting because of competition from other carnivores at night. Van Lawick does not explain his subject's diurnal activity. Both films take up themes of good mothering, threats from lions, and cubs' growth toward independence. As well, both films end with images of leopards silhouetted against the sunset. Between *Leopard: A Darkness in the Grass* and *The Leopard Son*, leopards were featured in several films including *The Secret Leopard* (1986, Partridge Films/National Geographic), *The Silent Hunter* (1988, Londolozi Productions), and *Predators of the Wild: Cheetah and Leopard* (1992, Survival Anglia).

54. There is what seems to be an image of Goodall. The opening montage of photographs includes a picture of a vehicle with van Lawick in the driver's seat, his son in the front passenger's seat, and a woman who appears to be Goodall in the back seat. Goodall has described the difficulty of raising their son, Hugo, known as Grub, at the Gombe Stream Chimpanzee Reserve in Tanzania, where he had to be kept in a cage because apes may prey on human infants. See Jane Goodall–van Lawick, *In the Shadow of Man* (Boston: Houghton Mifflin, 1971), 258–59.

55. Larry Jaffee, "Plugged in Producers: A Guide to Working with Cable Networks," *The Independent* 14, no. 5 (June 1991): 26–28. Alexander Wilson observed such elisions in *National Geographic*'s treatment of grizzly habitat loss, which failed to name its causes or imagine its reversal, apparently for fear of offending sponsors; see his *The Culture of Nature*, 142–43.

56. Ray Richmond, "Critter TV Not Just for Cable Anymore," *Variety*, June 30–July 13, 1997, 27.

57. Mark Robichaux, "Hunger for Mayhem? TV's Nature Shows Offer You a Big Bite," *Wall Street Journal*, Aug. 7, 1995, A1.

58. *Trials of Life* was a lucrative home-video title for Time-Life Video, with almost 700,000 sales in its first six months on the market, some six times sales of other Time-Life nature videos and more than any other title in its "nontheatrical categories"; see Margot Slade, "Killers in the Mist: TV Nature Shows Grow Nastier," *New York Times*, June 14, 1992, E6; and "Wild at Heart," *New Yorker* 68, no. 38 (Nov. 9, 1992): 42. The series earned over $21 million in U.S. home-video sales and generated total revenue exceeding $100 million by 1996; see La Franco, "Actors Without Agents," 83, and McElvogue, "Running Wild," D1. Attenborough defended scenes of killer whales "toying with" sea-lion pups before killing and eating them as essential to representing "the truth of the subject" (Slade, "Killers in the Mist," E6). Other sources indicate "that he considered taking legal action" to halt the promotional campaign that emphasized violent content to the point of distorting viewers' understanding of the overall series; see Louise McElvogue, "Jaws, Claws, and Cash: Show Biz Jungle of Wildlife," *New York Times*, Sept. 29, 1997, B5; repeated in Mitman, *Reel Nature*, 206.

59. "Wild at Heart," 42.

60. Slade, "Killers in the Mist," E6.

61. "The Thought Behind the Image," *Christian Science Monitor* 85, no. 76 (March 17, 1993): 20.

62. Tom Kuntz, "Television's Most Violent: It's Payback Time," *New York Times*, Jan. 18, 1998, 7.

63. Mitman, referring to this title as *Dangerous Animals*, reports that Stouffer's early home-video efforts earned $20 million by 1996 (*Reel Nature*, 205–6).

64. Staci Lonati, "Animal Shows Charged with Fakery," *St. Louis Journalism Review* 26, no. 185 (April 1996): 7. Around the same time, Stouffer also incurred negative publicity generated by charges that he hunted elk in a Colorado national park illegally; he pled guilty and paid a $300,000 fine; see Whiteman, "Violence, Lies, and Videotape," 24.

65. Sink, "The Call of the Wildlife Show," C7.

66. Whiteman, "Violence, Lies, and Videotape," 24; McElvogue, "Jaws, Claws and Cash," B1.

67. Spring, "Rysher's 'Wild America' Taking Off, Naturally," 2. The rehabilitation of Stouffer's reputation may have gotten a boost from the release of the feature film *Wild America* (1997), a fictionalized account of Stouffer's boyhood and his early forays, with his brothers, into wildlife filmmaking. The film starred Jonathan Taylor Thomas.

68. McElvogue, "Jaws, Claws, and Cash," B5.

69. Whiteman, "Violence, Lies, and Videotape," 24.

70. Richmond, "Critter TV Not Just for Cable Anymore," 27.

71. Leo Braudy, "The Genre of Nature: Ceremonies of Innocence," in *Refiguring American Film Genres: History and Theory*, ed. Nick Browne (Berkeley: University of California Press, 1998), 280.

72. Louise McElvogue, "National Geographic, NBC Form Cable TV Partnership," *Los Angeles Times*, Dec. 5, 1996, D4.

73. Paul Farhi, "Mapping Out a Greater Society," *Washington Post*, Jan. 27, 1997, business sec., 13; David Ignatius, "Geographic: Exploring Renewal," *Washington Post*, May 17, 1999, A19.

74. McElvogue, "National Geographic, NBC Form Cable TV Partnership," D4; Paul Farhi, "Big-Game Hunting," *Washington Post*, Dec. 14, 1998, 13; Ignatius, "Geographic," A19.

75. "National Geographic to Shed TV Unit," *Los Angeles Times*, Aug. 1, 1995, D2.

76. Alan Bunce, "National Geographic Specials Migrate Back to Network TV," *Christian Science Monitor* 87, no. 38 (Jan. 20, 1995): 13.

77. National Geographic has also launched for-profit operations in multimedia publishing and retail. See Farhi, "Mapping Out a Greater Society," 12–14; Constance L. Hays, "Seeing Green in a Yellow Border," *New York Times*, Aug. 3, 1997, F12.

78. Hugo Davenport, "Does Late Launch Matter if Your Brand Is Strong?," *New Media Markets* 15, no. 42 (Nov. 20, 1997): 5–6; Michael Katz, "Geo, Carlton Sign Production Deal," *Broadcasting and Cable* 128, no. 17 (April 20, 1998): 66.

79. Lawrie Mifflin, "NBC Europe and Asia Channels to Carry National Geographic," *New York Times,* Aug. 21, 1998, D8.

80. Davenport, "Does Late Launch Matter if Your Brand Is Strong?," 5–6.

81. Mifflin, "NBC Europe and Asia Channels to Carry National Geographic," D8.

82. Steve Donahue, "It's a Jungle Out There: A Big Year for National Geographic," *Electronic Media* 17, no. 42 (Oct. 12, 1998): 1, 14.

83. Farhi, "Mapping Out a Greater Society," 12–14; Ignatius, "Geographic," A19.

84. National Geographic Channels International, http://www .nationalgeographic.com/channel/intl/index.html, accessed Sept. 3, 2004.

85. "Adding Local Flavour," *The Hindu* (Sept. 2, 2002), http://hindu.com/ thehindu/mp/2002/09/02/stories/2002090200200200.html (accessed Aug. 29, 2004).

86. Farhi, "Big-Game Hunting," 14.

87. See Ben Sisario, "What Animals Do When No One Is Looking," *New York Times,* Jan. 11, 2004, 55; and Wilson Rothman, "Reality TV Takes a Twist as a Kingdom Bares Its Secrets," *New York Times,* April 15, 2004, G7.

88. In 2002, the unit known as National Geographic Television was renamed National Geographic Television and Film (NGT&F) to reflect its diversification. *K-19,* a drama based on the true story of a 1961 nuclear accident that took place on a Soviet submarine, had a budget of $100 million, starred Harrison Ford and Liam Neeson, and made a disappointing $35 million in domestic box office, according to Variety.com. On National Geographic–licensed merchandise, see Martha McNeil Hamilton, "Mapping New Territory: National Geographic Society Adds to Revenue with Wider Licensing of Its Logo," *Washington Post,* June 25, 2001, E1.

89. "Are You Up for It?," *The Hindu* (June 24, 2001), retrieved from Lexis-Nexis' Academic Universe, http://web.lexis-nexis.com (accessed Jan. 23, 2002).

90. David Boey, "National Geographic, EDB Set Up Fund for Film-making," *The Business Times Singapore* (Dec. 19, 2001): 6.

91. "National Geographic Channels International & Singapore Economic Development Board renew commitment to develop Asian documentary production talent," press release, EDB Singapore (Aug. 28, 2003), http://www.sedb.com/ edbcorp/sg/en_uk/index/in_the_news/press_releases/2003/national_geographic .html (accessed Aug. 23, 2004). See also "NGC to Air Investigative Show 'Operation Hot Pursuit,'" Indiantelevision.com (Jan. 14, 2004), http://www.indiantelevision .com/tube/y2k4/jan/jantube11.htm (accessed Aug. 23, 2004).

92. National Geographic Channel Asia website, NGCI-EDB Documentary Fund 2004 Submission Guidelines, http://www.ngcasia.com/asiafilmmaker (accessed Aug. 29, 2004). While the themes sought from the Asian initiative seemed to

shift, National Geographic continued to obtain more traditional independent documentary fare through its All Roads Film Project, a festival launched in the fall of 2004 to feature the work of "indigenous and underrepresented minority-culture filmmakers" (including Maori, Native American, and Iranian projects), vying for TV sales and for seed grants for new projects; see "National Geographic All Roads Film Festival Premieres in Los Angeles and Washington, D.C., in October" (press release, Sept. 8, 2004), http://press.nationalgeographic.com/pressroom/index.jsp?pageID=pressReleases_detail&siteID=1&cid=1094737370911 (accessed Oct. 2, 2004).

93. Harry A. Jessel, "Fusing Fact and Fiction," *Broadcasting and Cable* 131, no. 10 (March 5, 2001): 15.

94. Joe Schlosser, "Just Call Him Judge Doolittle," *Broadcasting and Cable* 128, no. 32 (Aug. 3, 1998): 39.

95. Berger, "A Family Channel That Even the Pets May Enjoy," 36.

96. Network dramas with explicit religious themes include *Touched by an Angel* (1996–2003, CBS); *7th Heaven*, premiered in 1996 by The WB and entering its tenth season in 2005; and *Joan of Arcadia* (2003–5, CBS).

97. Neal Koch, "As Police Shows Thrive, Cable Grabs Its Share," *New York Times*, Dec. 25, 2002, E4.

98. See Scott, "Popularizing Science and Nature Programming," 29–35.

99. Berger, "Why Look at Animals," 24.

100. Chris Pontius's kinkajou kiss is not an isolated tactic; in the South Africa episode of *Wildboyz*, Steve-O, on stilts, coaxes a giraffe to lick and "kiss" him on the mouth while Chris photographs its genitals. Footage featuring a young gorilla sharing two long kisses with Steve Irwin appeared briefly on the Animal Planet website to promote the "British Gorillas" episode of *Croc Hunter Diaries* (http://animal.discovery.com/fansites/crocdiaries/crocdiaries.html, accessed Sept. 12, 2004).

4. Animal Sex

1. Elizabeth Grosz, "Animal Sex: Libido as Desire and Death," in *Sexy Bodies: The Strange Carnalities of Feminism*, ed. Elizabeth Grosz and Elspeth Probyn (London: Routledge, 1995), 278, emphasis in the original. While Grosz correctly points to a wide range of ways of looking at animals, and insightfully directs our attention toward that looking's yen for sexual knowledge, she may overenthuse in regard to the "immense popularity" of nature TV. Historically, the genre, at least in the United States, has attracted an audience that may be best described as modest.

2. No such scene appears in the book on which the film is based, but the character Bridget once writes in her diary that during an argument, she and Daniel "stared at each other transfixed like two African animals at the start of a fight on a David Attenborough program." See Helen Fielding, *Bridget Jones' Diary: A Novel* (New York: Viking, 1996), 67.

3. The narration for the wildlife film that Jane watches is condensed from a passage in the novel on which the film is based; the passage paraphrases a section from one of British zoologist Desmond Morris's many books. See Laura Zigman, *Animal Husbandry* (London: Hutchinson, 1998), 105; and, in turn, Desmond Morris, *Animal Watching* (London: Jonathan Cape, 1990), 27, 30.

4. The genre does not so often indulge other human behaviors—violence, for example—in explanations derived from animal observations. There are exceptions. Apparently murderous violence among chimpanzees is represented and discussed in several *National Geographic Specials* on primates, and documentaries on the elephant seal—or compilations using footage of this animal—regularly describe forcible copulation, which is discussed later in this chapter.

5. Bousé, *Wildlife Films*, 153, 154–55, 171–72.

6. Spigel, *Make Room for TV.*

7. Leonard Maltin provides a succinct review of the ban and its reversal in *The Disney Films*, 118.

8. According to Bousé, the BBC had allowed depictions of animals "in the act" since the late 1950s; see his *Wildlife Films*, 175.

9. Desmond, *Staging Tourism*, 191.

10. Slade, "Killers in the Mist," E6.

11. Ibid.

12. Williams, *Hard Core*, esp. 82–83.

13. The script forgets at this point that the offspring's health and strength are products of both parents' genetic material. Sperm is the father's only contribution to the reproductive process; he does not contribute to caring for young, while the mother and other female relatives do so for years.

14. In *The Trials of Life* episode "Continuing the Line," Attenborough explains that during wolf copulation, "his genitals have swollen so greatly inside her that they are locked together... no unfortunate accident" but an evolutionary adaptation that helps to ensure fertilization and therefore alpha paternity.

15. Craig Owens, "The Allegorical Impulse: Toward a Theory of Postmodernism," in *Beyond Recognition: Representation, Power, Culture*, ed. Scott Bryson, Barbara Kruger, Lynne Tillman, and Jane Weinstock (Berkeley: University of California Press, 1992), 54.

16. The mating-themed compilation has a precedent in the theatrical feature *Birds Do It, Bees Do It* (1974) by Nicolas Noxon. Unlike most (at least American) wildlife films and television programs of its time, this one included scenes of animals copulating, earning a PG rating. Promotional materials for the film touted its cinematographic achievements (in footage by some of the best known in the field, including Heinz Sielmann and Hugo van Lawick), its glimpses of rarely filmed and potentially provocative behaviors, and its educational value. An almost paradoxical tagline sought to draw viewers away from the too-safe television family hour and into theaters for a more authentic representation of nature than the domestic

medium could bear: "So real it will never be shown on TV. See it with your children." Noxon was a regular producer, director, and writer for the *National Geographic Specials*, but this film, not a National Geographic project, was coproduced by David L. Wolper and distributed by Columbia Pictures. *Birds Do It, Bees Do It* received a Golden Globes nomination as best documentary, and earned for composer Gerald Fried an Oscar nomination for Best Original Score.

17. Roger N. Lancaster, *The Trouble with Nature: Sex in Science and Popular Culture* (Berkeley: University of California Press, 2003), 10–13.

18. Most of the many syndicated nonfiction wildlife half-hours of the 1970s, even prolific TV producer Bill Burrud's long-running *Animal World* (1968–80), were off the market by 1980s; only *Mutual of Omaha's Wild Kingdom* (1963–88) and *Lorne Greene's New Wilderness* (1982–86) remained in active syndication well into the 1980s. ABC released the *National Geographic Specials* to PBS in 1975, where they remained until 1994; *Nature* and *Wild America* launched on PBS schedules in 1982. See chapter 2.

19. See Crist, *Images of Animals*, esp. "Darwin's Anthropomorphism," 11–51, and "Genes and Their Animals: The Language of Sociobiology," 123–65.

20. Charles Darwin, *The Variation of Animals and Plants Under Domestication* (London: John Murray, 1875); cited in Tim Birkhead, *Promiscuity: An Evolutionary History of Sperm Competition* (Cambridge: Harvard University Press, 2000), 15. In fairness to Darwin, Birkhead points out that this immeasurably influential thinker wrote under constraints both historical and familial: publishing at the height of Victorian prudishness, and, for later works such as the one cited here, allowing his squeamish daughter Henrietta a heavy hand in the preparation of final drafts; see Birkhead, *Promiscuity*, 16–17.

21. Konrad Lorenz, *On Aggression*, trans. Marjorie Kerr Wilson (New York: Harcourt, Brace and World, 1966), 221–22.

22. Desmond Morris, *The Naked Ape: A Zoologist's Study of the Human Animal* (New York: McGraw-Hill, 1967), 241.

23. Wilson, *Sociobiology*. Wilson's title evokes the multivolume *The Synthetic Philosophy* (1862–96), in which Herbert Spencer attempted to explicate and align biological, psychological, moral, and sociological principles; and Julian Huxley's *Evolution: The Modern Synthesis*. The third edition of Huxley's book was published a year before *Sociobiology*.

24. Wilson, *Sociobiology*, 4. This boundary around the discipline's range of interests poses a troubling question about where and why one might draw a line between "the more primitive contemporary human societies" and those that qualify as modern.

25. At the end of the book, Wilson clarifies his position on how modern "man" should be studied. Sociology in the 1970s, he wrote, remained in its "natural history stage," useful only as a means of describing and naming observed things

and events. It would mature as a science only when it, and psychology, become fully informed if not absorbed by neurobiology (ibid., 574–75). Over two decades later, scientists would still be writing that sociology and cultural anthropology "reject or ignore" behavioral genetics; David C. Rowe and Kristen C. Jacobson suggest that academic departments in these disciplines "[fail] to provide exposure" to biological sciences to their students. They also note that the social sciences has retained "dislike of eugenic policies," dating to the 1930s, longer than other disciplines; see Rowe and Jacobson, "In the Mainstream: Research in Behavioral Genetics," in *Behavioral Genetics: The Clash of Culture and Biology,* ed. Ronald A. Carson and Mark A. Rothstein (Baltimore: Johns Hopkins University Press, 1999), 14–15.

26. Wilson, *Sociobiology,* 564–75.

27. Richard Dawkins, *The Selfish Gene* (1976; New York: Oxford University Press, 1989), 11. See 19, 45–46, 62–63, 66, to name only a very few of the pages on which Dawkins uses these terms.

28. Ibid., 88. Other scientists have challenged the notion that a gene "tries," "helps," or engages in any purposive activity at all. Evelyn Fox Keller calls the tendency to ascribe causal properties to genes "the discourse of gene action," even the return of the homunculus to biology; she argues that these metaphors shape the direction of science: "the ways in which we talk about scientific objects are not simply determined by empirical evidence but rather actively influence the kind of evidence we seek (and hence are more likely to find)"; see Keller, *Refiguring Life: Metaphors of Twentieth-Century Biology* (New York: Columbia University Press, 1995), xvi, 10, 35. Richard Lewontin insists that many actions attributed to genetic material are actually actions performed on it: "DNA has no power to reproduce itself... in fact proteins (enzymes) produce DNA. The newly manufactured DNA is certainly a copy of the old... but we do not describe the Eastman Kodak factory as a place of self-reproduction" (cited in Keller, *Refiguring Life,* 22–23; see also Richard Lewontin, "The Dream of the Human Genome," *New York Review of Books,* May 28, 1992, 31–40).

29. For an alternative theoretical model of how gender differences are maintained, see the influential Judith Butler, *Gender Trouble: Feminism and the Subversion of Identity* (New York: Routledge, 1989), and, *Undoing Gender* (New York: Routledge, 2004).

30. See Richard Dawkins, *The Extended Phenotype* (Oxford: Oxford University Press, 1982), esp. chap. 2 "Genetic Determinism and Gene Selectionism," 9–29; Stephen Jay Gould, *The Mismeasure of Man* (New York: W. W. Norton, 1981), 325–27; Sandra Harding, *The Science Question in Feminism* (Ithaca, N.Y.: Cornell University Press, 1986), 92–105, 127; Ruth Hubbard, *The Politics of Women's Biology* (New Brunswick, N.J.: Rutgers University Press, 1993), 3; Ruth Hubbard and Elijah Ward, *Exploding the Gene Myth: How Genetic Information Is Produced and Manipulated*

by Scientists, Physicians, Employers, Insurance Companies, Educators, and Law Enforcers (Boston: Beacon, 1993); and Dorothy Nelkin and M. Susan Lindee, *The DNA Mystique: The Gene as a Cultural Icon* (New York: W. H. Freeman, 1995).

31. Jennifer Terry, "'Unnatural Acts' in Nature: The Scientific Fascination with Queer Animals," *GLQ: A Journal of Lesbian and Gay Studies* 6, no. 2 (2000): 152, 165. Terry makes these remarks in an essay examining discussions of homosexual behavior among nonhuman animals in primatology, in applied animal husbandry, and in Simon LeVay's correlation between human sexual orientation and the size of a portion of the hypothalamus known as INAH3. Among other speculative leaps she points to in LeVay's work on this subject was his use of comparative studies on rats, which measured a different area of the brain because rats have no INAH3, and "counted" as "homosexual" only male rats' willingness to be mounted by other males, not their selection of other males to mount (ibid., 163–64).

32. Marlene Zuk, *Sexual Selections: What We Can and Can't Learn about Sex from Animals* (Berkeley: University of California Press, 2002), 202. See also Gowaty, ed., *Feminism and Evolutionary Biology.*

33. Niles Eldredge, *Why We Do It: Rethinking Sex and the Selfish Gene* (New York: W. W. Norton, 2004), 25–32, 51–52, 111; see also chap. 9, "Up Close and Personal: Sex, Power, Money, and Babies," 142–68.

34. Evelyn Fox Keller, *The Century of the Gene* (Cambridge: Harvard University Press, 2000).

35. Interest in learned, or cultural, as well as genetic influences on behaviors persists. Primatologists report thirty-nine behavioral differences between geographically distinct chimpanzee groups, which could only be accounted for through socially learned behaviors, passed from generation to generation: Frans B. M. de Waal, "Cultural Primatology Comes of Age," *Nature* 399 (1999): 635–36; Andrew Whiten, Jane Goodall, William C. McGrew, Toshisada Nishida, V. Reynolds, Y. Sugiyama, C. E. G. Tutin, R. W. Wrangham, and C. Boesch, "Cultures in Chimpanzees," *Nature* 399 (1999): 682. Similarly, biological anthropologist Carel van Schaik and other researchers have identified behaviors involving particular ways of hunting, eating, and masturbating that vary so widely between distinct orangutan populations that they are attributed to cultural differences; see Carol Kaesuk Yoon, "Orangutans Exhibit Hallmarks of Culture, Researchers Say," *New York Times,* Jan. 3, 2003, A16.

36. Additional examples, alternative strategies could be added to this list. For example, *The Mating Game* (1998, Londolozi Productions), not to be confused with the *Triumph of Life* episode of the same name, treats the human largely as another species among many (if, it is acknowledged, one with extraordinary and often destructive impact on the planet). Most of the program, which aired on the Discovery Channel's *Wild Discovery* series, surveys reproductive behaviors of nonhuman animals at the Londolozi Game Reserve in South Africa and Maasai Mara, Kenya. In final scenes considering the evolution of "the most successful animal on earth . . .

modern man," Maasai youth engage in athletic contests and dance, each a ritual of sexual competition.

37. Dawkins gives the worker honeybee who stings intruders to the hive—and as a result dies—as an example of an animal that sacrifices itself for the good of its group, pointing out that the worker honeybee class is sterile, and preserves more of its DNA by protecting its hivemates than by surviving itself (*The Selfish Gene*, 171–72). Wilson suggests that among humans, genes determining homosexuality may survive despite their lesser chance of being passed on directly ("because of course homosexual men marry much less frequently and have far fewer children than their unambiguously heterosexual counterparts") due to favorable reproduction rates among kin, theorizing that "homosexual members of primitive societies may have functioned as helpers"; see *Sociobiology*, 555. Both Dawkins's discussion of honeybee self-sacrifice and Wilson's puzzling over how genes for homosexuality might manage to be passed on, show how determined they are to promote the idea that every individual (or gene) is only out for its own genetic material—and that every variation in behavior can be fully explained by genetics.

38. Contradictorily, the screen displayed the rating TV-G, which the FCC defines as "suitable for all ages . . . [containing] little or no sexual dialogue or situations"; see FCC, "FCC's Parents' Place: TV Ratings," http://www.fcc.gov/parents/tvratings.html (accessed Oct. 30, 2004).

39. The "sperm wars" described in "The Mating Game" is also detailed in *Desmond Morris' The Human Animal: A Personal View of the Human Species* (1997, BBC), complete with full-screen microscopic views of the battles. The concept derives from the work of Robin Baker and Mark Bellis of the School of Biological Sciences at the University of Manchester (both are thanked in *Human Animal* credits), postulating that only some sperm are "egg-getters," and the rest "killers" that actively seek and destroy "foreign" sperm from other males and "blockers" that prevent "invaders" from nearing the cervix. Tim Birkhead discusses methodological shortcomings of the study and the failure of other scientists to repeat its results; see Birkhead, *Promiscuity*. See also Lisa Jean Moore, "Extracting Men from Semen: Masculinity in Representations of Sperm," *Social Text* 73 (2002): 1–46.

40. A montage of mating scenes inserted midway through *Triumph of Life*'s "Mating Game" includes a few frames of computer-generated graphics that swirl double helixes (the shape of the coils of DNA that comprise genes) and tiny *X*s and *O*s across the screen. One might expect the letters *X* and *Y*, representing sex-determining chromosomes, rather than the colloquial symbol for "hugs and kisses" or markers in a game of tic-tac-toe.

41. If Fox premiered *When Animals Attract* as a pre–Valentine's Day mood-setter, the network offered grotesque consolation to anyone who found him- or herself without a date for Saturday, February 14, 2004: a special two-hour edition of *COPS*, disturbingly subtitled "Love Hurts," which compiled reality-footage of domestic violence calls answered by police officers in prior episodes.

42. Television represented a range of points of view on rape. CBS's sitcom *All in the Family* took the subject seriously, apparently influenced by the feminist movement. During the 1973–74 season, the character Gloria Stivic (Sally Struthers) was revictimized by the stereotypes held by police after a sexual assault; in a 1977–78 episode Edith Bunker (Jean Stapleton) grappled with the trauma of an attempted rape. In 1979, the same year that Barash's *The Whispering's Within: Evolution and the Origins of Human Nature* (New York: Harper and Row), was published, ABC's daytime soap opera *General Hospital* launched a storyline in which Luke (Anthony Geary) raped Laura (Genie Francis, then a minor). Months later, their characters were involved in a passionate romance and eventually married. See Sarah Projansky, *Watching Rape: Film and Television in Postfeminist Culture* (New York: New York University Press, 2001); and Sujata Moorti, *Color of Rape: Gender and Race in Television's Public Spheres* (Albany: State University of New York Press, 2002).

43. Susan Brownmiller, *Against Our Will: Men, Women and Rape* (New York: Simon and Schuster, 1975), 12–13. Brownmiller was correct that rape was not a *central* concern of scientists engaged in the study of animal behavior, but wrong that the behavior was unknown among animals. Since the 1930s ethologists Konrad Lorenz and Nikolaas Tinbergen had applied the term to behaviors they observed in birds, reptiles, and fish; see Suzanne Sunday, "Introduction," in *Violence Against Women: A Critique of the Sociobiology of Rape*, ed. Sunday and Ethel Tobach (New York: Gordian Press, 1985), 3.

44. Brownmiller, *Against Our Will*, 153–56, 391. In fact, Brownmiller suggests that the stigma born by raped women and their offspring further diminishes the efficacy of rape as a reproductive strategy, citing the prevalence of suicide, abortion, and infanticide among thousands of Bengali women raped by Pakistani soldiers in the war for Bangladesh's independence; ibid., 80–84.

45. David P. Barash, "Sociobiology of Rape in Mallards: Responses of the Mated Male," *Science* 197 (1977): 788.

46. Barash, *The Whisperings Within;* Randy Thornhill, "Rape in Panorpa Scorpionflies and a General Rape Hypothesis," *Animal Behavior* 28 (1980): 57; Randy Thornhill and Nancy Wilmsen Thornhill, "Human Rape: An Evolutionary Analysis," *Ethology and Sociobiology* 4, no. 3 (1983): 137–73; and Randy Thornhill and Nancy Wilmsen Thornhill, "The Evolutionary Psychology of Men's Coercive Sexuality," *Behavioral and Brain Sciences* 15 (1992): 363–421. Barash and the Thornhills were among the most prominent but not the only biologists to study forcible copulation among animals, and not all biologists studying these behaviors among animals moved into the study of human rape; see, for example, T. H. Clutton-Brock and G. A. Parker, "Sexual Coercion in Animal Societies," *Animal Behaviour* 19, no. 5 (1995): 1345–65.

47. Barash, *The Whisperings Within*, 54–55.

48. None of these authors believes that rape is a justifiable human act, regardless of its origins. Barash responded to criticism of *The Myth of Monogamy*, writ-

ing, "if we want to be ethical . . . rising above our human nature may be just what is needed"; David P. Barash, "The Tyranny of the Natural," *Chronicle of Higher Education* (Nov. 2, 2001): B16.

49. Daniel Q. Estep and Katherine E. M. Bruce, "The Concept of Rape in Nonhumans: A Critique," *Animal Behaviour* 29, no. 4 (1981): 1273. I have retained terms used in the original literature in order to convey the charged tone of these words. Primatologist Biruté M. F. Galdikas has used the terms *resisted mating* and *forced copulation,* using *rape* primarily when referencing papers by other researchers who use the term; see Galdikas, "Adult Male Sociality and Reproductive Tactics Among Orangutans at Tanjung Puting," *Folia Primatologica* 45 (1985): 9–24. Likewise, see Philip Clason Whitford, "Observations of Attempted Rape (Forced Copulation) in Canada Geese," *Passenger Pigeon* 55, no. 4 (Winter 1993): 359–61. Other researchers use the term *forced copulation:* see Lisa Guminski Sorenson, "Forced Extra-Pair Copulation and Mate-Guarding in the White-Cheeked Pintail," *Animal Behavior* 48, no. 3 (Sept. 1994): 519–33; Mats Olsson, "Forced Copulation and Costly Female Resistance Behavior in the Lake Eyre Dragon, *Ctenophorus maculosus,*" *Herpetologica* 51, no. 1 (March 1995): 19–24; and Adolfo Cordero, "Forced Copulations and Female Contact Guarding at a High Male Density in a Calopterygid Damselfly," *Journal of Insect Behavior* 12, no. 1 (Jan. 1999): 27–37. Clutton-Brock and Parker offer the broad category "sexual coercion" that encompasses forced copulation, harassment, and intimidation; Clutton-Brock and Parker, "Sexual Coercion in Animal Societies," 1345–65.

50. Patricia Adair Gowaty, "Sexual Terms in Sociobiology: Emotionally Evocative and Paradoxically, Jargon," *Animal Behaviour* 30, no. 2 (1981): 630, 631. Anne Fausto-Sterling also considers the early sociobiological theories of rape, and imagines their possible juridical consequences; see Fausto-Sterling, *Myths of Gender: Biological Theories About Women and Men* (New York: Basic Books, 1985), 156–57. While sociobiological theories of rape did not immediately alter rape law, they did enter other disciplines, which also produced critical responses. For instance, after Delbert Thiessen gave a talk titled "Rape as Reproductive Strategy: Our Evolutionary Legacy," at a meeting of the American Psychological Association (APA) in 1983, some members of the APA organized a symposium to discuss sociobiological theories of rape further. Their papers, which were collected for publication, examined the ways in which sociobiologists chose and redefined terminology, their use of data, and the possible implications of their theories; see Sunday and Tobach, eds., *Violence Against Women.*

51. See Richard A. Posner, *Sex and Reason* (Cambridge: Harvard University Press, 1992); and Kingley R. Browne, "An Evolutionary Perspective on Sexual Harassment: Seeking Roots in Biology Other than Ideology," *Journal of Contemporary Legal Issues* 8, no. 5 (1997): 5–77.

52. Randy Thornhill and Craig T. Palmer, *A Natural History of Rape: Biological Bases of Sexual Coercion* (Cambridge: MIT Press, 2000).

53. Randy Thornhill and Craig T. Palmer, "Why Men Rape," *The Sciences* 40, no. 1 (Jan. 2000): 30–36.

54. Ibid.

55. See Smith, Mulder, and Hill, "Controversies in the Evolutionary Social Sciences," 132–34.

56. A. Leah Vickers and Philip Kitcher, "Pop Sociobiology Reborn: The Evolutionary Psychology of Sex and Violence," in *Evolution, Gender, and Rape*, ed. Cheryl Brown Travis (Cambridge: MIT Press, 2003), 139–68; and Jerry A. Coyne, "Of Vice and Men: A Case Study in Evolutionary Psychology," in *Evolution, Gender and Rape*, ed. Travis, 171–89.

57. Barash, *The Whisperings Within*, 54–55.

58. Randy Thornhill is among those thanked in "Courting" credits.

59. Coyne, "Of Vice and Men," 179.

60. Bagemihl reminds the reader that animal homosexuality has been recognized, deplored, and associated with equally deplored same-sex human relations in eighteenth-century New England, under Nazism in Germany, in Anita Bryant's antigay crusade of the late 1970s, and in science writing. See Bruce Bagemihl, *Biological Exuberance: Animal Homosexuality and Natural Diversity* (New York: St. Martin's Press, 1999), 77, 82, 84–89.

61. In 2002 Channel Four brought the subject to British television audiences, with *The Truth about Gay Animals*, hosted by comedian Scott Capurro, as part of a trio of late-night programs on homosexuality that also included *The Truth about Lesbian Sex* and *The Truth about Gay Sex*. NBC Universal's cable channel Trio has aired the animal episode in the United States. On July 23, 2004, *Ultimate Explorer* (MSNBC), a science news series by National Geographic, aired a segment called "Girl Power" on same-sex sexual behaviors among female Japanese macaques.

62. See Dinitia Smith, "Love That Dare Not Squeak Its Name: Homosexuality Among Animals Is Common," *New York Times*, Feb. 7, 2004, A17, A19.

63. If the viewer is tempted to surmise that Cameron is a fictional foil, a character created by Stewart's writing team, on the contrary, he runs the nonprofit Family Research Institute and publishes an antigay tract that has included an attack on Bruce Bagemihl and the Central Park zookeepers; see "Homosexual Animals?," *Family Research Report: Journal of the Family Research Institute* 19, no. 4 (July 2004), http://www.familyresearchinst.org/FRR_04_07.html (accessed Oct. 22, 2004). On the barring of Cameron from the American Psychological Association for egregious flaunting of professional standards and practices, see Mark E. Pietrzyk, "Queer Science: Paul Cameron, Professional Sham," *New Republic*, Oct. 3, 1994, 10–12.

64. See Sara Diamond, "The Christian Right's Anti-gay Agenda," *Humanist* 54, no. 4 (July–Aug. 1994): 32–34. The catchphrase "gay agenda" is borrowed from the title of a videotape widely distributed in a twenty-minute version by Bob Horn's Springs of Life Church to a Christian home market, and aired in an hourlong version hosted by televangelist D. James Kennedy on March 13, 1993, on cable

TV's Family Channel, then still under the control of Pat Robertson's International Family. The religious right may have misappropriated some of its worst nightmares about the gay community from a (Jonathan) Swiftian satire published as an attack on homophobia; see Michael Swift, "The Gay Manifesto," *Gay Community News*, Feb. 15, 1987, http://rainbowallianceopenfaith.homestead.com/GayAgendaSwiftText.html (accessed Oct. 31, 2004). The catchphrase "gay agenda" continues to be used by rightwing antigay rights extremists such as Tom Coburn, Republican of Oklahoma elected to the U.S. Senate in November 2004, and Paul Burress, a Cincinnati-based activist whose Citizens for Community Values is affiliated with Dr. James Dobson's Focus on the Family. Coburn, a former member of the House of Representatives appointed by George W. Bush to serve as chair of the Presidential Advisory Council on HIV/AIDS, unsuccessfully introduced a bill in 1997 that would have outlawed anonymous HIV testing. He also campaigned in support of a constitutional amendment to ban same-sex marriage and has been quoted in a speech to fellow Republicans as follows: "The gay community has infiltrated the very centers of power in every area across this country....That agenda is the greatest threat to our freedom that we face today...abortion and multiple sex partners? That's a gay agenda"; see Robert Schlesinger, "Medicine Man," Salon.com (Sept. 13, 2004), http://archive.salon.com/news/feature/2004/09/13/coburn/ (accessed Nov. 4, 2004). Burress is a longtime organizer of campaigns against antidiscrimination bills that mention sexual orientation, protolerance education in public schools, same-sex marriage, and domestic partnership rights, all of which he calls "part of a homosexual agenda"; see Kevin Osborne, "'Discrimination' Key to Debate on Issue 3," *Cincinnati Post*, Oct. 29, 2004, A14; see also Citizens for Community Values, http://www.ccv.org (accessed Nov. 26, 2004).

65. Bagemihl navigates a dilemma over how to describe animals' homosexual behaviors. Claiming that "virtually no terminology for animal behavior—particularly sexual behavior—is entirely free of human (cultural, historical, etc.) associations," but admitting that some are more provocative than others, he advocates use of "the already available terms with careful qualification of their meanings"; see Bagemihl, *Biological Exuberance*, 4. In Bagemihl's text, "*gay* is never employed, while *lesbian* is used only sparingly...for cases of linguistic expedience" (emphasis original), noting that it appears more frequently in scientific articles on "lesbian" fruit flies, flamingos, chimpanzees, and other species; ibid., 3.

66. See Courtney Kane, "Only Real Surprise on 'Ellen' Was Lineup of Advertisers," *New York Times*, May 2, 1997, D2; and Dusty Saunders, "Somber 'Ellen' Goes Out with a Laugh," *Rocky Mountain News*, May 13, 1998, 2D.

67. The popular sitcom *Will and Grace* (1998–, NBC), reality-makeover series *Queer Eye for the Straight Guy* (2003–, Bravo), Showtime's *Queer as Folk* (2000–2005), and *The L Word* (2004–), and new gay-themed channels (the pay-per-view Here! and MTV Networks' Logo, launching on cable in 2005) are undeniable signs of more and more prominent representations of gay men and lesbians on TV, but

don't disprove long-term, spectrum-wide trends. *Will* and *Queer Eye* depend on stereotypes of gay men as helpmates; Showtime's serial melodramas are narrowcast to the fragment of premium cable audience's willing to "pay for gay" (thanks to Tony Freitas for this phrase). For extensive studies of the representation of gay men, lesbians, bisexuals, and transgender people on TV and in other media, see Suzanne Danita Walters, *All the Rage: The Story of Gay Visibility in America* (Chicago: University of Chicago Press, 2001); Larry P. Gross, *Up from Invisibility* (New York: Columbia University Press, 2002); and Stephen Tropiano, *The Prime Time Closet: A History of Gays and Lesbians on TV* (New York: Applause, 2002).

68. Experts on marine flatworms, which are also known as polyclads, refer to the encounter that takes place prior to mating as "penis fencing," a phrase that is not used in the narration for this segment; see Leslie Newman and Lester Cannon, *Marine Flatworms: The World of Polyclads* (Collingwood, Australia: CSIRO, 2003). Newman is mentioned in *Triumph of Life*'s "The Mating Game" credits.

69. The bonobo *(Pan paniscus)*, a distinct species but close relative of more commonly known chimpanzee *(Pan troglodytes)*, is also known as the pygmy chimpanzee or elia, the latter pluralized as "bilia" and derived from the word by which it is known in the local language; the research site is a protected area known as the Luo Scientific Reserve.

70. Excerpts of the same bonobo footage appears in the *World's Best* episode "Places to Find Sexy Beasts" (2001, produced by BBC Wildvision for the Travel Channel).

71. A range of bonobo characteristics, physiological and behavioral, are outlined in Frans B. M. de Waal, "Bonobo Sex and Society," *Scientific American* (March 1995): 82–88.

72. The percentage of shared genes is now usually put even higher. Niles Eldredge, for example, points to "near genetic identity (98.6 percent!)" between *Homo sapiens* and the chimpanzee *Pan troglodytes;* see Eldredge, *Why We Do It*, 110.

73. Zuk, *Sexual Selections*, 177.

5. The Giant Panda as Documentary Subject

1. The panda isn't the only species with these kinds of problems. Mating practices that are detrimental to a species also plague giant rock iguanas found at Guantánamo Bay, where the United States holds a military base on the island it shares with Cuba. The iguana isn't harmed by sexual ineptitude but rather the dominance rites of males. News coverage attributed the lizard's endangered status to the fact that only the most dominant males mate with females. Testosterone levels drop in subordinate males, who lose interest in even trying to mate. The resulting pool of mating males is too small to ensure the future of the species. The San Diego Zoological Society's Center for the Reproduction of Endangered Species intervened by removing dominant males temporarily from the colony, allowing other males

to mate (and boost their testosterone levels), diversifying the species' gene pool. See Valerie Hartouni, *Cultural Conceptions: On Reproductive Technologies and the Remaking of Life* (Minneapolis: University of Minnesota Press, 1997), 99–100.

2. Berger, "Why Look at Animals?," 24.

3. Bourdieu, *Distinction*, esp. 12.

4. Hartouni, *Cultural Conceptions*, 52.

5. Edward Said, *Orientalism: Western Conceptions of the Orient* (1978; London: Penguin, 1991), 202–3.

6. See Jay Mathews, "Wildlife Group, China Starts Drive to Save Pandas," *Washington Post*, May 14, 1980, A1; Marcus W. Brauchli, "Panda Habitat Gets New Hotel For Eco-Tourist," *Wall Street Journal*, March 8, 1994, B1; Douglas Wissing, "China's Panda Paradise," *Washington Post*, March 28, 2000, E4. Other reports place the panda population higher or lower. The Chinese Ministry of Forestry and the World Wildlife Fund once counted "fewer than 700" pandas, according to John Noble Wilford, "Intense Scientific Efforts Fail to Reverse the Panda's Decline," *New York Times*, March 17, 1987, C1. George B. Schaller suggests that censuses of the panda population have probably underestimated their numbers, and that "a minimum of thirteen hundred and fifty panda still existed in 1988, but numbers have no doubt declined since then, due mainly to poaching"; Schaller, *The Last Panda* (Chicago: University of Chicago Press, 1993), 230. In 2005 the Chinese State Forestry Administration reported counting 1,596 wild giant pandas, attributing their growing population to the protection of greater expanses of habitat; see "Giant Pandas Thriving in Wild," CNN.com (Jan. 20, 2005), http://www.cnn.com/2005/TECH/science/01/20/china.panda.reut/index.html (accessed Jan. 21, 2005).

7. Ramona and Desmond Morris compiled a twenty-point list in which they "dissect the species, not anatomically, but anthropomorphically," detailing its similarities to humans (flat face, minimal tail, thumblike digit) and other characteristics that seem to render the animal irresistible, especially to small children (softness, endomorphic form, lack of external sex organs, clumsiness), based on a survey they conducted on "animal favorites." See their *Men and Pandas* (New York: McGraw-Hill, 1966), 197–202. See also Stephen Jay Gould, "The Panda's Thumb," in Gould, *The Panda's Thumb: More Reflections on Natural History* (New York: W. W. Norton, 1980), 19–26. For more on panda habitat, physiognomy and behavior, see Byron Preiss and Gao Xueyu, eds., *The Secret World of Pandas* (New York: Harry N. Abrams, 1990), which was produced in cooperation with New China Pictures Company.

8. Douglas Martin, "Year of the Panda Is Lengthened by a Few Days," *New York Times*, Nov. 4, 1987, B1.

9. Morris and Morris, *Men and Pandas*, esp. 22–23, 36, 41–42, 52–54.

10. Ibid., 81–84. See also a memoir by Ruth Harkness, *The Lady and the Panda: An Adventure* (New York: Carrick and Evans, 1938); and a biography, Vicki Constantine Croke, *The Lady and the Panda: The True Adventures of the First American Explorer to Bring Back China's Most Exotic Animal* (New York: Random House, 2005).

11. George B. Schaller, Hu Jinch, Pan Wenshi, and Zhu Jing, *The Giant Pandas of Wolong* (Chicago: University of Chicago Press, 1985), 265.

12. In 1939, influenced by the panda craze, Universal Studios animator Walter Lantz (better known for Woody Woodpecker) developed the character Andy Panda, who appeared in cartoons until 1949, and in comic books from 1941 to 1962.

13. The panda's image appeared on postcards, dolls, jewelry, wallpaper, and bathing suits sold in London in 1938; see Morris and Morris, *Men and Pandas*, 104–9, 194–95.

14. According to Morris and Morris, "Bombs fell on the zoo. . . . Her hair was thinning un-naturally and in the summer of 1943 she started walking backwards"; ibid., 110–14.

15. Ryan, "Hunting with the Camera," 206.

16. See Morris and Morris, *Men and Pandas*, 84–85, 87, 109; and Schaller et al., *The Giant Pandas of Wolong*, 231. Currently, most scientists classify the giant panda *(Ailuropoda melanoleuca)* as most closely related to bears *(Ursidae)*. Alternatively, the giant panda has sometimes been grouped with the red (or lesser) panda *(Ailurus fulgens)* among the raccoon family *(Procynonidae)*, or the two species have been classed as a distinct family of their own.

17. Morris and Morris, *Men and Pandas*, 166–70, 187. See Schaller et al., *The Giant Pandas of Wolong*, 180, on the brevity of panda fertility. It should also be noted that human ignorance of animal behavior can also thwart captive breeding. Common knowledge once held that pandas are entirely solitary save for brief mating encounters, but zoos that introduced males and females only when the females reached heat usually found that the animals responded to one another with indifference or hostility. Realizing that each wild panda's territory would border others, and that they would at least come upon scent markings throughout the year, the Chapultepec Zoo in Mexico City allowed its pandas to get to know each other throughout the year; their cub was the first born outside of China to survive. See "Panda Debut," *New York Times*, Jan. 18, 1982, A18. Similarly, attempts to breed the even-rarer Sumatran rhinoceros failed until researchers realized that the female does not ovulate until *after* a mating encounter. The discovery, and new ideas about when to put the male and female together, resulted in the birth of a calf at the Cincinnati Zoo on September 13, 2001. See Claudia Dreifus, "A Conversation with: Terri Roth; Birth of Rare Rhino Is a Bright Spot for Species' Future," *New York Times*, Dec. 25, 2001, F3.

18. Morris and Morris, *Men and Pandas*, 265.

19. An unsigned *Wall Street Journal* editorial notes that in its relationship with China, "the U.S. often makes important concessions, [but] it too often receives only pandas in return"; see "Panda Bear Diplomacy," *Wall Street Journal*, April 16, 1984, E32.

20. China also sent pandas as diplomatic gifts to Tokyo in October 1972 (with more to follow in 1980 and 1982), Paris in 1973, London in 1974, Mexico City in

1975, Madrid in 1978, Pyongyang in 1979, and West Berlin in 1980; see Schaller et al., *The Giant Pandas of Wolong,* 265–66. Inspired by the Tokyo pandas, the Japanese animé master Hayao Miyazaki created a two-part series, *Panda koPanda* (Panda, little panda, 1972–73), in which pandas become members of a little girl's family.

Larry Collins, who became head panda-keeper when Ling-Ling and Hsing-Hsing arrived at the National Zoo, points out that diplomatic gifting of animals is not unusual, and that animals received under these circumstances constitute a portion of the National Zoo's holdings. Collins, with James K. Page Jr., recounts the pandas' first months in Washington in *Ling-Ling and Hsing-Hsing: Year of the Panda* (Garden City, N.Y.: Anchor, 1973), esp. 7.

21. John M. Broder, "Hsing-Hsing the Panda, A Gift from Mao, Dies," *New York Times,* Nov. 29, 1999, A14.

22. Estep and Bruce, "The Concept of Rape in Non-humans," 1272–73; Gowaty, "Sexual Terms in Sociobiology," 630–31.

23. See Sammond, *Babes in Tomorrowland,* esp. chap. 5 "Raising the Natural Child," 247–99.

24. "Panda Keeps Experts Baffled on Pregnancy," *New York Times,* July 10, 1982, A45.

25. Mike Sager, "As Cameras Roll and Tourists Wait, Panda Shows No Signs of Pregnancy; Ling-Ling the Panda Gives No Hint of Birth," *Washington Post,* Sept. 10, 1980, C1. Despite Hsing-Hsing's renowned example of reproductive failure, not all male giant pandas are so disinterested. Males in the wild have been observed fighting in brief skirmishes over females; see Chris Catton, *Pandas* (New York: Facts on File, 1990), 84–85.

26. Ed Bruske, "National Zoo's Ling-Ling: A Case of Fruitless Love," *Washington Post,* Oct. 6, 1980, B5.

27. Dale Jamieson, "Against Zoos," in *Reflecting on Nature: Readings in Environmental Philosophy,* ed. Lori Gruen and Dale Jamieson (New York: Oxford University Press, 1994), 292; and Singer, *Animal Liberation,* 22.

28. Bruske, "National Zoo's Ling-Ling," B5.

29. Joann Stevens, "Zoo Hopes Male Rival Will Spur Panda On," *Washington Post,* Feb. 20, 1981, B3.

30. For more on the panda's reproductive behaviors, see Morris and Morris, *Men and Pandas,* 163; Schaller et al., *The Giant Pandas of Wolong,* 180, 187; and Schaller, *The Last Panda,* 67–69.

31. Al Kamen, "New Beau Found for Ling-Ling the Lovelorn Panda," *Washington Post,* Feb. 16, 1981, C1; Stevens, "Zoo Hopes Male Rival Will Spur Panda On," B3.

32. United Press International, "2 Pandas Unlikely to Get Second Mating Chance," *New York Times,* May 4, 1981, A19.

33. "Panda Romance Blooms in Capital," *New York Times,* March 19, 1983, 6; "A Very Discreet Panda," *New York Times,* March 26, 1983, 22; "Private Lives," *New York Times,* Dec. 4, 1983, E20; Henry Mitchell, "Panda Watch VI; In Which the English

Suitor Is Sent Packing," *Washington Post,* April 18, 1981, D1; Henry Mitchell, "The Brute Gets the Boot," *Washington Post,* June 9, 1981, B1; "The Panda: A Brief Sojourn," *Washington Post,* July 23, 1983, A22.

34. Ken Ringle, "Love Finds a Way for Ling-Ling, Hsing-Hsing," *Washington Post,* March 19, 1983, A1; Ken Ringle, "Panda Debate: Should Ling-Ling Again Be Encouraged to Mate?," *Washington Post,* Feb. 24, 1984, C1, C6.

35. Berger, "Why Look at Animals?," 24. Not only wildlife filmmakers, and manufacturers of stuffed animals and other souvenirs contribute to the animals' representation: as in previous flurries of attention to pandas, animators used its image in children's media. In 1982–83, as panda fans watched the National Zoo's attempts to breed Hsing-Hsing and Ling-Ling, CBS produced a Saturday morning cartoon called *Pandamonium* featuring a group of teenagers and three talking pandas.

36. Schaller, *The Last Panda,* 11–15. Around the same time, the Smithsonian Institution also made an agreement with the Chinese government to undertake a panda research project on another reserve, but the deal dissolved over China's condition that the Smithsonian would be financially liable if a panda suffered injury or death during the course of the research; ibid., 87–89.

37. "*Save the Panda:* Project Panda Works to Help Threatened Species Survive," press release, National Geographic Society, n.d.

38. See Tom Shales, "Save the Panda," *Washington Post,* March 9, 1983, B1; Melvin Maddocks, "Setting the Panda Watch," *Christian Science Monitor,* Feb. 22, 1983, 22; Randall Rothenberg, "Home Video: Documentary," *New York Times,* April 19, 1987, sec. 2, 22H. Despite the panda's photogenic appearance, its typical activities would seem to be ill suited to lengthy cinematic forms that depend on action-oriented drama. The quite solitary animal spends some 40 percent of each day at rest, and most of its waking time eating bamboo; see Schaller et al., *The Giant Pandas of Wolong,* 152–54. For a critical discussion of Schaller's analysis of the panda's nutrient-poor diet, see Stephen Jay Gould, "How Does a Panda Fit?," in Gould, *An Urchin in the Storm: Essays about Books and Ideas* (New York: W. W. Norton, 1987), 22–25. Pandas don't engage in many of the behaviors which are the stock-in-trade of the wildlife genre: they do not migrate, hunt, build elaborate nests, or socialize with other animals except in brief annual mating encounters and while raising young.

39. Schaller, *The Last Panda,* 113–15.

40. Other sources date China's modern conservation efforts to 1956, when the nation established its first nature reserves, but acknowledge that state-sponsored hunting and trade in animal skins did not consistently avoid protected areas and endangered species. Effective conservation legislation and enforcement emerged in 1983, with the founding of the China Wildlife Protection Association, and in 1988, with the China Wildlife Protection Law; see Li Yi-Ming, Gao Zenxiang, Li Xinhai, Wang Sung, and Jari Miemela, "Illegal Wildlife Trade in the Himalayan Region of China," *Biodiversity and Conservation* 9 (2000): 903–4.

41. Bamboo trees produce flowers and then wither at intervals of 60 to 120 years; each forest takes several years to regenerate. See Michael Parks, "Giant Panda Population Faces Starvation as Bamboo Dies Off," *Los Angeles Times*, Aug. 6, 1983, A1.

42. For discussion of ethnographers' and audience researchers' techniques for gathering data from subjects through conversation, see Ellen Seiter, *Television and New Media Audiences* (Oxford: Oxford University Press, 1999), esp. 52, 60.

43. Hartouni, *Cultural Conceptions*, 52; Butler, *Gender Trouble*, 133–34.

44. Schaller writes that President Gerald Ford, before he left office, secured permission for the ABC film crew through Deng Xiaoping; that Ford's son was involved with the production; and that ABC paid a fee of $200,000 for the right to gather footage of the pandas. See Schaller, *The Last Panda*, 37, 115; Bousé, *Wildlife Films*, 148.

45. This contradictory visual cue may not be so much a "mistake" as per the rules of continuity editing as it is likely a result of the conditions in which footage of free-roaming animals is obtained; the editors have to work with whatever coverage the cinematographers manage to capture. In either case, it is prescient of ways in which the pandas in Pan's purview often allow the researchers close physical proximity, even hands-on contact, and occasionally seem to seek out humans, as in cases of sick or hungry pandas that enter homes or barns and accept food and care. *Secrets of the Wild Panda* depicts such an incident; several were reported during the bamboo die-off of the early 1980s. See also Zhiyen Zhang, "Pandas Get a Little Help from Their Friends," *Los Angeles Times*, May 1, 1985, sec. II-5.

46. Pan's appeal resulted in a plan to provide early retirement compensation to older workers, and retrain younger loggers to work in other local industries. In 1993 the central Chinese government provided 25 million yuan (then valued at about US$3 million), the Shaanxi provincial government 30 million yuan (over US$3.5 million), and the World Bank US$4.7 million, to the project; see Fiona Holland, "The Man Who Spells Hope for the Panda," *South China Morning Post*, Oct. 16, 1997, 21.

47. Willett Kempton, James S. Boster, and Jennifer A. Hartley, *Environmental Values in American Culture* (Cambridge: MIT Press, 1996), 87.

48. In 2003 the Sichuan government solicited suggestions on panda conservation from the public, and received 411 proposals. See Xinhua News Agency, "Sichuan to Look at Citizen's Proposals on Panda Protection," Jan. 6, 2003, retrieved from http://web.lexis-nexis.com, Jan. 23, 2003. The Environmental Education Television Project for China, founded in Beijing in 1994, lists over forty nongovernmental environmentalist groups on its English-language website, http://www.eetpc.org (accessed Dec. 8, 2004).

49. Also, with new pandas having arrived in Tokyo, animé artist Isao Takahata remade *Panda koPanda* as *Panda! Go, Panda!* (2000), also released on home video in the United States.

50. This section shares its title with chapter 3 of Schaller's *The Last Panda*, 36–43. Responding to criticism, in particular from the WWF, the Chinese Association

of Zoological Gardens began to coordinate breeding pools of captive pandas dispersed throughout the nation's zoos, reinvited the WWF's involvement in training and habitat protection, and instituted harsher penalties for poaching and trade in panda pelts. Late in 1987, the sentence for panda poaching or pelt smuggling increased from a two-year prison term to "ten or more years, life imprisonment, or even death." By 1991 three people had been condemned to death and sixteen given life sentences for acts against pandas; ibid., 220–28. Capital punishment persists for these crimes (and many others) into the early twenty-first century, as China enacted "Strike Hard" campaigns against crime, regularly executing over a thousand people each year and leading the world in executions, despite protests by the European Union, Amnesty International, and the Hong Kong–based group Human Rights in China. See "A World Shift from Execution," *Christian Science Monitor,* June 8, 2001, 1.

51. Jack Jones, "Russians May Not Be Coming, but Pandas Are," *Los Angeles Times,* June 2, 1984, II-4; Martin, "Year of the Panda Is Lengthened by a Few Days," B1; Roy J. Harris Jr., "Panda Loans to Zoos Cause Ruckus," *Wall Street Journal,* June 8, 1993, B1, B9; "S. Diego Zoo Seeks Panda Extension," *Los Angeles Times,* Oct. 31, 1987, I-31; Timothy Aeppel, "Groups Try to Stem Panda Diplomacy," *Christian Science Monitor,* Feb. 23, 1988, 3; John Schwartz, "American Zoos Unveil Panda Conservation Plan," *Washington Post,* April 23, 1993, A14; Jon R. Luoma, "Saving the Popular Giant Panda from Being Loved to Death," *New York Times,* April 27, 1993, C4.

52. "U.S. Leaves a Zoo with a Vacant Panda Home," *New York Times,* Sept. 26, 1993, 36.

53. Tony Perry, "Panda-monium," *Los Angeles Times,* Jan. 15, 1995, A3, A18; Jon R. Luoma, "2 Pandas Bound for U.S. May Be Just First Wave," *New York Times,* Jan. 17, 1995, C7. The WWF also reversed its opposition to the exportation of pandas from China, and now collaborates with the San Diego Zoo on its captive breeding program and on research that zoo staff conduct at Wolong. Still, some environmental activists continued to voice opposition to loans that removed panda from the breeding pools centered in protected reserves in China. In 1998 a group called the Panda Release Fund passed out handbills outside the zoo that urged boycotts of zoos that "imprison" pandas ("Emergency Action: Is This the Point of No Return?," handbill, collection of the author).

54. Perry, "Panda-monium," A3, A18.

55. Tony Perry and Rone Tempest, "Panda Deal May Be in Jeopardy," *Los Angeles Times,* June 16, 1995, A3, A33.

56. Ken Ellingwood, "Panda Pair," *Los Angeles Times,* June 28, 1996, A3, A17. Around the same time, Hong Kong officials refused (for the second time) pandas offered to commemorate its reincorporation into China, on the grounds that such loans may deplete breeding stock in natural panda habitat. See Holland, "The Man Who Spells Hope for the Panda," 3.

57. Tony Perry, "Panda Express Hits San Diego at Last," *Los Angeles Times,* Sept. 11, 1996, A3, A14.

58. Tony Perry, "Pandering to Fans," *Los Angeles Times,* Nov. 3, 1996, A3.

59. In late August 1999, the United States announced restitution of $4.5 million was being paid to the survivors and to families of victims; in December, the United States agreed to provide $28 million to the Chinese government in compensation for damage to the embassy; in turn, China promised $2.87 million for damages to the American embassy in Beijing, which resulted from anti-American demonstrations that erupted following the bombing. See Oliver August, "U.S. Pays $4.5M for Bombing Chinese Embassy," *Ottawa Citizen,* Sept. 1, 1999, A8; Elisabeth Rosenthal, "U.S. Agrees to Pay China $28 Million for Bombing," *New York Times,* Dec. 1999, A6.

60. Human Rights Watch, "Use WTO Process to Push China on Rights," press release, Nov. 24, 1999; http://www/hrw.org/press/1999/nov/china1025.htm. China's entry into the WTO was made official in December 2001, after a year's delay. Trade provisions in the bill signed by President Clinton were written to assume membership in the year 2000. President George W. Bush asked Congress to renew the temporary provision for Normal Trade Relations with China only on May 30, 2001, a day after China agreed to return an American spy plane that had collided with a Chinese fighter jet on April 1, killing the pilot and landing without permission on the island of Hainan. The twenty-four-person crew had been detained eleven days. See Erik Eckholm, "China Agrees to Return Partly Dismantled Spy Plane as Cargo," *New York Times,* May 29, 2001, A8.

61. Pandas went to Ocean Park in Hong Kong in 1999, to a zoo in Kobe, Japan, in 2000 and 2002, and to the Chiang Mai Zoo in Northern Thailand in October 2003. In 2005 China offered pandas to Taiwan in the midst of trade and travel negotiations. Mandalay Bay Resort and Casino in Las Vegas, which runs a for-profit aquarium called Shark Reef, also applied for panda permits, so far without success. Mandalay Bay lacked accreditation from the American Zoo and Aquarium Association—and a clear research program—but estimated that proceeds from the panda exhibit might return five times the standard $1-million-per-year fee to China; see James Steinberg, "Hotel May Ante Up for Pandas," *San Diego Union-Tribune,* July 27, 2002, A1.

In 2004 the Hong Kong Society for Panda Conservation offered special access to the animals to a group of children whose parents were lost during the SARS epidemic of the previous year. Just as Ming provided war-weary Londoners of the early 1940s with amusement, the Hong Kong pandas, An An and Jia Jia, seem to have been expected to provide some distraction to these still-grieving young "honorary panda keepers" in this former British colony. See Stella Lee, "Breakfast with Pandas Helps Youngsters Forget SARS Grief," *South China Morning Post,* April 6, 2004, 3.

62. Slade, "Killers in the Mist," E6; La Franco, "Actors Without Agents," 82–3.

63. In February 2001, not long after Washington welcomed its second pair of pandas, the new Bush administration declared that the United States would condemn China's human rights record at the April 2001 United Nations Commission on Human Rights meeting in Geneva. The resolution was the eleventh such proposal submitted by either the United States or the European Union since 1990. Beijing countered with a plan to issue its own report on human rights abuses by the United States. See John Schauble, "China and US Clash Over Human Rights," *Sydney Morning Herald,* Feb. 28, 2001, 10; and "US Motion Against Beijing Falls," *Australian Financial Review,* April 20, 2001, 24.

64. The San Diego Zoo's monthly magazine, *Zoonooz,* also regularly features the giant pandas as a central zoo attraction, placing photographs of Bai Yun, Shi Shi, Hua Mei, and Mei Sheng, born at the zoo in August 2003, on at least five covers since their arrival. Shi Shi sired only the first San Diego–born cub; when he reached an advanced age, he was returned to China and replaced by Gao Gao (Mei Shing's father) in 2002.

65. Brauchli, "Panda Habitat Gets New Hotel For Eco-Tourist," B1; Wissing, "China's Panda Paradise," E4.

66. Ringle, "Love Finds a Way for Ling-Ling, Hsing-Hsing," A1, A12.

67. For example, see Thornhill and Palmer, *A Natural History of Rape,* esp. chap. 4, 53–84.

68. On the use of sexually explicit videos shown to pandas being trained for mating, see Jack Boulware, "Bear-naked Video!," http://www.salon.com/health/sex/urge/world/2000/04/21/panda (accessed April 21, 2000). On the use of Viagra among pandas, see "Panda's a Hero Mother," *The Australian,* Sept. 22, 2000, 28. On the Chinese Academy of Science's attempt to clone a giant panda, see Associated Press, "Chinese Scientists Try to Clone Giant Panda," *New York Times,* June 22, 1999, F5.

69. "Aztec Obstetrics," *New York Times,* Aug. 23, 1980, 22.

Conclusion

1. Leigh Strope, "Lieberman Calls Hussein 'Time Bomb,' " *San Diego Union-Tribune,* Feb. 11, 2002, A3; Neil MacFarquhar, "Millions in Iran Rally Against U.S.," *New York Times,* Feb. 12, 2002, A1; Ali Akbar Dareini, "Iranians Chant: Death to America," *San Diego Union-Tribune,* Feb. 12, 2002, A3.

2. Closing credits for *Wild Jewels* and *Wild Treasures of the East* indicate, as do many recent wildlife coproductions, that they are international joint ventures of the BBC/CIMA Film and I.R. Iran Co., in association with the Discovery Channel and Merlin International Television Ltd. Queries about the production, scheduling and future availability of these programs went unanswered by Discovery and Nigel Marven's management. A representative of the BBC reported that her office "cannot find any information" on them; e-mail correspondence, Heidi Bjorklund, BBC Information, Sept. 21, 2004.

3. *Wild Treasures of the East* covers much of the same literal territory and depicts many of the same animal species, sometimes repeating footage. It does, however, place more emphasis on human life and activities—rice cultivation, the trade in sturgeon roe, elite ski resorts outside of Tehran. It opens by explicitly addressing its presumed audience's ignorance. Moving from images of men smoking water pipes to children studying, the narrator opens the program: "Most of us know very little about Iran except that oil has made it rich and that there was an Islamic revolution under the Ayatollah Khomeini. And religion is very important here. School children learn to recite the holy Koran." (That oil has made this nation *universally* rich is contradicted within both programs by the depictions of small-scale farmers.) The filmmakers posit the city of Esfahan as evidence of Iran's "highly evolved and ancient culture," showing mosques, ornate tilework, and town squares, "the glories of Esfahan [that] date back nearly 400 years," then immediately contextualize human cultural achievements within eternal nature: "But infinitely older than any human culture here is the country's astounding natural heritage," its variety of ecosystems and the wildlife living in them.

4. Gitlin, *Inside Prime Time,* 248.

5. Curtin, *Redeeming the Wasteland,* 246.

6. Wilson, *The Culture of Nature,* 143.

7. The wildlife genre is not unique in this respect. Surely, viewers experience most genres and especially nonfiction forms—cooking shows (such as *From Martha's Kitchen*), home-repair series *(This Old House),* quiz shows *(Jeopardy!),* and talk shows *(The Oprah Winfrey Show)* as sources of both information and pleasure.

8. See Imperato and Imperato, *They Married Adventure,* 84, 97; and Musser and Nelson, *High-Class Moving Pictures,* 31.

9. Slade, "Killers in the Mist," E6.

10. Tedesco, "Discovery Looks to Build a Programming Empire," 22.

11. La Franco, "Actors Without Agents," 83.

12. Charles Duhigg, "Sighting Tooth and Claw; Technology and the Exciting Visuals It Makes Possible Take a Lead Role in Animal Planet's 'Spy on the Wild,'" *Los Angeles Times,* Dec. 10, 2004, E42.

13. Steven Erlanger, "Still Making Films, Still Explaining the Hitler Connection," *New York Times,* Jan. 8, 2002, B1.

14. In the original French version *(La Marche de l'empereur),* actors voiced the parts of mother, father and baby penguins. The American version used a more conventional "voice of God" voiceover; actor Morgan Freeman read Jordan Roberts's script. Joe Leydon, "March of the Penguins" (review), *Variety,* June 21, 2005, http://www.variety.com/review/VE1117927432?categoryid=31&cs=1&query=march+of+the+penguins&display=march+of+the+penguins (accessed Sept. 23, 2005).

15. See Jonathan Miller, "March of the Conservatives: Penguin Film as Political Fodder," *New York Times,* Sept. 13, 2005, F2.

16. Cornelia Dean, "A New Test for Imax: The Bible vs. the Volcano," *New York Times*, March 19, 2005, A11.

17. Alan Riding, "What Price Success for a Newly Popular BBC?," *New York Times*, Feb. 3, 2002, AR1.

18. Even high-end nature programming like *The Blue Planet*, which utilized thirty-five cinematographers in making an eight-hour series, costs less per hour than dramatic or comedy series, in large part due to well-known actors' salaries; see Julie Salamon, "A Sense of Wonder Under the Sea," *New York Times*, Jan. 27, 2002, sec. 2, 10.

19. In this episode (April 8, 2002), Tom Trundle won the $50,000 prize money by holding his breath underwater for over two minutes (no other contestant in this final face-off broke the half-minute mark), earning host Joe Rogan's "You're an animal!" exclamation. Rogan congratulated the winner, as he does in other episodes, with the phrase, "Fear is not a factor for you."

Index

Cynthia Chris is assistant professor of media culture at the College of Staten Island/City University of New York.